The Struggle for Canadian Copyright

A companion website to this book is available at
http://thestruggleforcanadiancopyright.ca.
On this site you will find many of the original archival documents
cited in the endnotes and bibliography of this book.

The Struggle for Canadian Copyright

Imperialism to Internationalism, 1842-1971

Sara Bannerman

UBCPress · Vancouver · Toronto

21 20 19 18 17 16 15 14 13   5 4 3 2 1

Printed in Canada on FSC-certified ancient-forest-free paper
(100% post-consumer recycled) that is processed chlorine- and acid-free.

Library and Archives Canada Cataloguing in Publication

Bannerman, Sara, 1975-
The struggle for Canadian copyright :
imperialism to internationalism, 1842-1971 / Sara Bannerman.

Includes bibliographical references and index.
Also issued in electronic format.
ISBN 978-0-7748-2404-0 (bound); ISBN 978-0-7748-2405-7 (pbk.)

1. Copyright – Canada – History. I. Title.

KE2799.B35 2013   346.7104'8209   C2012-906708-3   KF2995.B35 2013

Canadä

UBC Press gratefully acknowledges the financial support for our publishing program
of the Government of Canada (through the Canada Book Fund),
the Canada Council for the Arts, and the British Columbia Arts Council.

This book has been published with the help of a grant from the Canadian Federation for
the Humanities and Social Sciences, through the Awards to Scholarly Publications Program,
using funds provided by the Social Sciences and Humanities Research Council of Canada.

Printed and bound in Canada by Friesens
Set in Garamond Condensed and Minion by Artegraphica Design Co. Ltd.
Copy editor and proofreader: Francis Chow
Indexer: Patricia Buchanan

UBC Press
The University of British Columbia
2029 West Mall
Vancouver, BC V6T 1Z2
www.ubcpress.ca

Contents

Acknowledgments

MANY THANKS TO ALL those who have given of their time to read and discuss this book at various stages: Michèle Martin, Norman Hillmer, Myra Tawfik, Michael Geist, Paul Keen, Ross Eaman, Sheryl Hamilton, Peter Yu, Robin Mansell, Howard Knopf, Bruce Couchman, Loris Mirella, Peter Drahos, Heiko Baumgärtner, Susan Sell, Frank Keyes, Gina Grosenick, Maureen Smith, Andrew Wolgemuth, and the anonymous peer reviewers whose careful work has improved this book immensely. Tim Robertson provided invaluable assistance in sifting through and photographing hundreds of files at Library and Archives Canada; thanks to him for sharing so much of the work and many cafeteria lunches. My thanks as well to the staff at Library and Archives Canada, the staff at the World Intellectual Property Organization, and the staff at the Carleton University Library. I would also like to thank the Social Sciences and Humanities Research Council, Fulbright Canada, the Institute for Global and International Studies at George Washington University, the Regulatory Institutions Network at the Australian National University, the Canadian Federation for the Humanities and Social Sciences, and McMaster University; without these, this work would have been impossible. Special thanks to Melissa Pitts, Ann Macklem, Francis Chow, and the rest of the team at UBC Press.

Many friends and colleagues have borne with me through the years that I have worked on this project, and I deeply appreciate their support. Most of all, I would like to thank my family – Mom, Dad, Molly, Dennis, Grandma, Grandpa, Aunt Cheryl, Uncle Barry, Katie, and Mary Caldbick, my wonderful love – for all their support.

All errors are my own.

The Struggle for Canadian Copyright

CHAPTER ONE

Introduction

MOST HISTORIES OF COPYRIGHT focus on major powers such as Britain, France, and the United States. This focus on more powerful countries has effectively effaced some of the most important issues and conflicts in the history of international copyright. By examining a less powerful country and a former British dominion's historical experience with international copyright, this book reveals the roots of today's international copyright system in an imperial copyright system that preceded it. It highlights not only the struggle between various Canadian interest groups vying to shape Canadian copyright but also the struggle for a Canadian copyright system that responds to the interests of Canadians while conforming to imperial and international copyright systems broadly shaped by more powerful states. This book shows that conflicts in international copyright between net copyright exporters like the United States and the so-called developing countries are not, as some suggest, relatively recent problems.[1]

Copyright is one type of intellectual property law. Intellectual property law includes copyright law, patent law, and trademark law, among others. Whereas trademark law grants rights in words or symbols such as "Nike" or the Nike swoosh, and whereas patent law grants rights in inventions, copyright law grants rights in literary and artistic works such as books, movies, plays, and music. "International copyright" refers to those sets of arrangements under which domestic copyright is granted to foreign nationals, making it possible for a copyright holder from one country to claim copyright in another.

The *Berne Convention for the Protection of Literary and Artistic Works* was the world's first broadly multilateral treaty on international copyright, and still acts as the cornerstone of international copyright today.[2] First signed in 1886, the agreement established a set of minimum standards for recognition of the rights of foreign copyright holders that was revised approximately every twenty years until 1971.[3] It was originally administered by the Swiss government and an international office in Berne, but is now administered by the World

Intellectual Property Organization (WIPO), a special agency of the United Nations in Geneva. The history of the *Berne Convention* continues to be relevant today; its main provisions have been incorporated into the intellectual property provisions of the multilateral trade agreements made under the World Trade Organization (WTO) in 1994, and into the 1996 multilateral copyright treaties under WIPO. Conflicts over international copyright today have roots that extend deep into the history of the *Berne Convention*. This book shows that conflicts between the major copyright exporters and the less powerful net copyright importers threatened the *Berne Convention* in its earliest days.

This book deals primarily with Canada's experience with the *Berne Convention* between 1886 and 1971. It also provides some necessary background about the years prior to this period, when Canada was subject to the British imperial copyright system, and a brief summary of events since 1971. That year 1971 was when the last revision of the *Berne Convention* took place and marks the end of an era in which international copyright negotiations were focused on revision of the *Berne Convention*. By 1994, the *Berne Convention*, in its settled 1971 format, had become the unrivalled foundation stone of international copyright, upon which all other major international copyright agreements would be built. This book deals with the period prior to this settlement – the period during which this foundation was still being contested. A variety of other works deal more fully with the period since 1971.[4]

This book focuses almost exclusively on the *Berne Convention* and, to a lesser extent, the *Universal Copyright Convention*, its major rival between 1952 and 1994. In the interest of focus, it does not deal with other related treaties, such as the *International Convention for the Protection of Performers, Producers of Phonograms and Broadcasting Organizations (Rome Convention)* of 1961 or the *Convention for the Protection of Producers of Phonograms Against Unauthorized Duplication of Their Phonograms (Phonograms Convention)* of 1971, or in detail with post-1971 treaties such as the 1994 *Agreement on Trade-Related Aspects of Intellectual Property Rights*, the 1996 WIPO Internet Treaties, or other trade-based agreements.

While some argue that the Berne system of international copyright encourages economic growth in developing countries by providing incentives for the creation and dissemination of works, critics assert that the main beneficiaries of the Berne system are those in rich countries, that the system impedes access to knowledge around the world, and that it raises the input costs of economic growth in poorer countries.[5] In the course of history, Canadians themselves have raised many of these same arguments.

The struggle for Canadian copyright is more than a struggle for formal sovereignty over Canadian copyright law. Even after such sovereignty was achieved in the 1920s, Canadian policy makers struggled to identify and implement a copyright law that reflected Canadian interests while also taking into account imperial and international copyright norms and pressures. Outside interests have had a tremendous influence on Canadian copyright lawmaking up to the present day, when American pressure seems able to trump widespread Canadian opposition to some copyright provisions.[6] Treaty-making remains an important vehicle of influence over domestic copyright policy.

Canada's experience with the *Berne Convention* can be viewed as the struggle of a former British colony to move from imperialism to internationalism – to find a place within the international system and to project an image of a country engaged in a community of the most powerful nations while also reflecting the reality of Canada as a net copyright importer with a relatively small but growing creative industry. In a sense, Canada's international copyright policy has been used as a vehicle for portraying Canada to the international community – as a sovereign country, a good international citizen, a developed and developing country, and a middle power. Canadian international copyright has been used as an exercise in image building, to win prestige and respect for Canada and to dispel the image of Canada as a hewer of wood and drawer of water. Copyright policy has been communication policy: not only has it regulated the reproduction and use of works but it has also been influenced by larger concerns about guarding and shaping Canada's international image.

Canada quietly joined the *Berne Convention* in 1886 as a British colony before attempting to denounce (exit) the treaty in 1889.[7] Canada would have been the first country to withdraw from the Berne Union,[8] and fears that such an act would destroy the nascent union led the British government to use its imperial control to prevent Canada's withdrawal.[9] For many years, Canadian governments maintained that the treaty should be denounced by the British government on Canada's behalf, but Canada eventually joined the union as a full-fledged signatory in the 1920s. Canada's relationship to the *Berne Convention* continued to be conflicted, however: it refused to ratify the 1948 revision of the treaty, did not sign the 1967 or 1971 revisions, and was largely disengaged from the Berne Union up to the late 1960s. Debates in the late 1960s and early 1970s regarding the place of developing countries within the Berne Union led to Canada's re-engagement, but the country did not accede to the most recent (1971) revision of the convention until 1998. Canada's path from imperialism to internationalism has been marked by resistance to elements of an international copyright system that did not at the time reflect the interests and economic objectives of significant Canadian groups.

On the matter of international copyright, Canada is currently aligned with the coalition of industrialized countries that includes the United Kingdom, the

United States, and European countries. This book shows how such an alignment developed as a result of the historical structures of the norms and institutions of Canadian international relations. Although Canada has never been
considered a "developing" country under the UN system – a term that came
into prominent use only after Canada's development from a British dominion
into an independent state – common interests between Canada and today's
developing countries have long been acknowledged. Canada's nineteenth-
century copyright history highlights these commonalities. The major concerns
of the Canadian government during that period were similar to those of many
developing countries today: encouraging a diverse domestic industry, which
included a printing and publishing sector, and the need to ensure affordable
access to imported works. From the 1920s onward, there was greater concern
for encouraging domestic creators by ensuring that Canadians had robust
international copyright provisions, but a focus on Canada's status as a net copyright importer re-emerged in the 1960s and 1970s. It was during the latter decade
that Canada's representatives at international copyright negotiations proclaimed,
"We are all developing countries."[10] However, the historical structures of the
norms and institutions of Canadian international relations, and moves to align
Canada with more powerful nations, took precedence, to some extent, over the
realization of the alternative copyright norms once advocated in Canada, norms
that have more recently been advocated by India, Brazil, and numerous African
countries.

Today the international copyright system has as its foundation the *Berne
Convention*, but this convention represents only one model of international
copyright. Competing models of international copyright have also existed,
including copyright nationalism or protectionism, whereby copyright is primarily granted to nationals rather than to foreign nationals as a protectionist strategy
for encouraging domestic access to and production of foreign works; copyright
bilateralism, whereby international copyright is negotiated on a bilateral rather
than multilateral basis; and other multilateral copyright treaties, such as the 1952
Universal Copyright Convention, which offered an alternative set of norms governing international copyright. Competing norms and alternative conceptualizations of copyright have also existed within domestic laws. The American approach
to copyright, for example, differed significantly from the norms of the *Berne
Convention* up to the 1980s. To comment on the international copyright system
today, therefore, is to comment on the *particular* set of copyright norms that
now stand unrivalled as the foundation of international copyright.

A number of specific norms are at the core of the *Berne Convention*. First,
under this convention, countries agree to the principle of national treatment;

nationals of countries of the Berne Union, as well as other nationals who first or simultaneously publish their works in a country of the Berne Union, are to be treated the same as nationals of the country in which protection is claimed. Second, the convention sets out a number of minimum standards that each country of the Berne Union must conform to in its own copyright system. These minimum standards set out the types of works in which copyright must subsist, certain minimum rights that must be granted to the creators[11] and copyright holders of such works, and the minimum term for which these rights should subsist.

Several of these norms have been historically controversial. Provisions requiring that countries grant copyright for a minimum period of the life of the creator plus fifty years have been considered by some to be inordinately long. It has also been argued that different terms of protection would be appropriate for different types of works. Provisions that prohibit member states from requiring domestic registration or manufacture of works as a condition for the grant of copyright have also been controversial; the *Berne Convention* requires copyright to be granted automatically without such formalities, although such registration requirements would facilitate the location of rights holders for royalty payment and licensing negotiations. Also controversial has been the right of translation, which under the convention is deemed generally to rest with the copyright owner for the full term of copyright. Since foreign copyright owners have often declined to license their works to local printers, publishers, manufacturers, and translators, these provisions have been especially problematic to developing countries wishing to develop domestic printing, publishing, or manufacturing industries, and to countries wishing to encourage more strongly the local availability of foreign works in translation. Such countries have therefore sought to limit translation rights in foreign works.

These contested norms have been challenged by alternative norms in domestic legislation and in other international treaties. For example, the 1952 *Universal Copyright Convention* required a minimum period of protection of just twenty-five years after the death of the creator, was more flexible in allowing countries to require domestic manufacture or registration (although these requirements were waived among countries party to the agreement), and allowed compulsory licensing mechanisms that would permit the unauthorized translation of a work after seven years from the date of first publication. The more relaxed provisions of the *Universal Copyright Convention* catered more fully to developing countries and to contemporary American policy preferences.

The 1957 Ilsley Commission concluded that the Canadian government was "not too well advised" in joining the *Berne Convention,* arguing that a course of action more closely following the realist copyright policies of the United States would have better served Canadians.[12] This book explores why Canada did adhere to the *Berne Convention,* what policies and actors played into that decision, and some of the problems and benefits that have resulted from Canada's adhesion to the convention.

The path of Canadian international copyright has been, in part, a product of the norms, institutions, and policies of Canadian foreign relations. These, in turn, reflect Canada's real and envisioned place in a world framework in the process of transitioning from imperialism to internationalism. Canadian international copyright has been used to project an image of Canada to the world and to connect Canada to a community of powerful nations.

CHAPTER TWO

Canada and the International Copyright System

CANADIAN COPYRIGHT IS SITUATED, like Canada, between powerful cultures and traditions. Canadian and international copyright can be seen as having been influenced primarily by two competing legal traditions: the "copyright" tradition and the tradition of *droit d'auteur*. These two traditions emerged from a single event: the invention of movable type printing.

The copyright tradition arose in England, which, in the midst of the Industrial Revolution, took a pragmatic view of copyright as a product of legislation rather than a natural right. This legislation was seen as balancing competing interests, including those of creators, publishers, and the public.[1]

The term "copyright" has come to be associated with economic rights granted in common law jurisdictions, whereas the term *droit d'auteur* embodies the French approach and encompasses both economic and moral rights.[2] While the copyright tradition emphasizes economic rights, including the right to authorize the reproduction of a work, moral rights include the right to claim attribution in a work or to protect its integrity and were originally associated with *droit d'auteur.* Under the tradition of *droit d'auteur,* more emphasis was placed on the protection of creators than on the interests of users or the public, with creators' or authors' rights being viewed as a natural right to the fruits of their labour, integral to their personhood. *Droit d'auteur* recognized creators as a group seen as contributing uniquely to the advancement of civilization.[3]

Despite the two systems' identifiable differences, they have, to a certain extent, been combined in the laws of many countries, Canada in particular. The *Berne Convention* was one vehicle for the interweaving of the two traditions.[4] The British tradition from which Canadian legislation was copied was in turn influenced, through the internationalization of copyright law that took place under the Berne Union, by the French tradition. The United States, on the other hand, stood aloof from the Berne Union until 1989.[5] Thus, the French tradition and the British-influenced American tradition came to be seen as two poles between which the British and Canadian laws were pulled.

The first Canadian copyright law, established in Lower Canada in 1832, followed the British-influenced American tradition rather than the French tradition in copyright; the American law was rooted in English legislation but with unique characteristics of its own.[6] The 1839 statute of Nova Scotia was also influenced by American legislation.[7] Lower Canada's legislation formed the basis of Canadian copyright when Upper and Lower Canada were united as the Province of Canada in 1841, and was again the basis of the statute passed by the new Dominion of Canada in 1868. The copyright law of 1875 maintained, until its replacement in 1921, the basic American copyright model.[8] Canada's 1921 legislation was largely copied from the British act of 1911, thus ending the reliance on American statutory models.[9] Up to 1931, when moral rights were introduced into Canadian copyright law, Canadian legislation was very much based on the British tradition (via the United States or, from the 1920s, via direct modelling on British legislation) rather than the French, despite the French influence in Quebec. Reliance on either British or American legislation as models for Canadian copyright legislation has since been abandoned.[10]

Even in Quebec, the more strongly British or utilitarian view of copyright was often preferred, especially in the earlier part of Canadian copyright history. During this time, Canadian publishers, both in Quebec and the rest of Canada, were not publishers in the modern sense of one who initiates, organizes, and finances an edition; rather, they were largely reprinters or distributors of works first published outside Canada.[11] The Quebec printing and (re)publishing industry was generally in accord with printers and (re)publishers in the rest of Canada. They were, with some exceptions, less influenced by the French tradition of *droit d'auteur* but had a more utilitarian view of copyright that would permit the reprinting of foreign works, on compulsory licence if necessary. This view was very different from those of the authors and publishers of France, whose literary and artistic traditions were strong and drove the interest in stronger rights that was reflected in the tradition of *droit d'auteur*.

The promotion of Canadian and particularly Québécois culture was also an important concern to some in the nineteenth and early twentieth century. Joseph-Charles Taché and Louvigny de Montigny (the latter working on behalf of copyright holders in France) promoted the recognition of imperial and international copyright while promoting stronger copyright as being in the long-term interests of Canadian and Québécois cultural producers. These voices often conflicted with Quebec industry groups in printing and publishing or in theatre, which had an interest in the unauthorized reprinting and performance of foreign, especially French, works. Towards the middle of the twentieth century, as Quebec cultural exports grew, a greater number of Quebec interest groups highlighted the importance of international copyright as a means of encouraging cultural production and cultural exports. In 1971, the gap between the views of Quebec interest groups and the official views of the federal government had grown so wide that a public controversy ensued. By the mid-1980s, however, the federal government had fallen more consistently in line with Quebec interest groups in emphasizing the importance of cultural exports and strong international copyright.

Canada as a Middle Power

Canada has been portrayed as a middle power in the writings of many scholars and diplomats. This portrayal often takes on somewhat mythical qualities. For example, Arthur Andrew, a Canadian diplomat from 1947 to 1979 who served as the head of the Canadian delegation to the diplomatic conference to revise the *Berne Convention* in 1967, wrote in *The Rise and Fall of a Middle Power: Canadian Diplomacy from King to Mulroney*:

> Looking back over the years during which the Department [of External Affairs] reached the peak of its influence, it seems as if Canada had a destiny to be in all things a Middle Power, an agent of influence for moderation in the geopolitical middle; a crossroads and entrepôt, politically, ideologically, culturally, commercially and spiritually.[12]

Although the image of Canada as a middle power in international affairs is a popular one, many dispute the notion, arguing that Canadian foreign policy is best viewed in light of Canada's relationship to American power. Adam Chapnick, for example, has argued that Canada acted more like a satellite than a middle power in the founding of the United Nations, and that Canada's actual international contributions at the UN have been more practical than visionary.[13] Others, such as Andrew Cohen, argue that whatever leadership Canadian governments might once have demonstrated in international diplomacy and foreign aid has since declined.[14] Roy Rempel has argued that Canadian foreign affairs should focus not on Canadian middle power ideals but, in a realist manner, on Canada's relationship with its powerful neighbour, the United States.[15] Similarly, Allan Gotlieb has argued that idealistic conceptions of Canada as a middle power that acts as a visionary force for world peace "risk ignoring the central reality of where power resides in the contemporary world."[16] Further, he argues that the idea of a middle power, as a product of Cold War geopolitics, is no longer relevant.[17]

Mark Neufeld argues that the middle-power language that portrays Canada as an honest broker is used by dominant groups to advance and legitimize Canadian foreign policy and the existing international order. He argues that the language of "middlepowermanship" has come to be used by some activist groups who, beginning in the late 1960s and early 1970s, recast the idea of a middle power "to signify the influence enjoyed by a country like Canada, and the potential such influence offers to effect radical progressive change in terms of disarmament, economic development and wealth re-distribution, environmental policy and democratization of the foreign policy-making process."[18]

In this examination of Canada's role in international copyright, we see that Canadians have exerted little influence in the Berne Union, falling short of the middle-power ideal for much of Canada's international copyright history. Canada was very much a satellite of Britain into the 1920s, during the period when the fundamental norms of the *Berne Convention* were established, and the Canadian government declined various opportunities to take an independent path, opting instead to remain under the imperial copyright system. Canada did not appear as a middle power in international copyright until 1971, when the last revision of the *Berne Convention* took place. At that point, the Canadian government considered more radical proposals that would have seen Canada break with the positions of the larger cultural exporters, but these proposals were set aside in favour of a rhetorical middle ground that portrayed Canada as being in solidarity with developing countries while also associating the country with more powerful nations. Canadian participation has always been much desired by the Berne Union's more powerful members, not only to protect their copyright exports but also to lend legitimacy to the system.

Progress, Civilization, Development

Progress has, as Shanin points out, gone by various names: "modernization," "development," "growth," or "civilization."[19] Martti Koskenniemi argues that international law in the nineteenth and early twentieth century was driven by a group of international lawyers whose sensibility and motivation were based on an idea of law as the guardian of civilization. Those who founded the international copyright system at Berne shared the sensibility he discusses.[20] Despite the inequalities upon which it was founded – the status of much of its membership as colonies with no voice in its negotiation, and the inequality with which the types of literary and artistic creations that it recognized were distributed – the *Berne Convention* was portrayed as a system founded "on principles which commend themselves to the civilized world," as bringing a "population of four or five hundred millions"[21] under its "civilized" umbrella. Blind to its underlying inequalities, its founders saw international law as a way of exporting rational law and administrative structures, thereby disseminating the benefits of "civilization" around the world.[22] The Berne Union invited members of the "civilized world" as members[23] and set out a powerful vision of progress in the governance of literary and artistic works, an ideology of progress that made it difficult to take an alternative path.

As international institutions transformed in the mid-twentieth century, so did this vision of progress. In the 1950s, '60s, and '70s, the Berne Union, like other international organizations, took on the agenda of development. As Escobar shows, beginning in the 1950s, the discourse of development came to be universally accepted and omnipresent.[24] The mission of international organizations, now engaged in the agenda of development, was similar to that of the early lawyers and diplomats who saw themselves as exporting the structures of civilization to the world:

> Officials in [international organizations] often insist that part of their mission is to spread, inculcate, and enforce global values and norms. They are the "missionaries" of our time. Armed with a notion of progress, an idea of how to create the better life, and some understanding of the conversion process, many [international organization] elites have as their stated purpose a desire to shape state practices by establishing, articulating, and transmitting norms that define what constitutes acceptable and legitimate state behavior.[25]

The discourse of development divided the world into categories, classifying societies and peoples according to particular systems and ideas of progress – some societies and peoples as "developed," others as "underdeveloped."[26] These categories fit only partially, however. They divided the developing from the "developed," obscuring commonalities, buttressing divisions, and dividing and reinforcing existing political communities along given lines.

Canadian politicians struggled to identify not only the copyright policies most appropriate to the nation's economic interests but also policies appropriate to the type of country Canada was discursively framed as being. Government officials had struggled in the nineteenth century over the question of what copyright policies were appropriate for Canada, as a developing country that was viewed as the leading British colony. In the mid-twentieth century, they asked, what policies encompassed Canada's position as a net copyright importer, similar in that sense to developing countries, and an industrialized country aligned with some of the biggest copyright exporters? This book shows that the weight of categorization, of common-sense notions of the type of country Canada was, played a significant role in determining the copyright policies that Canadian governments adopted. The discourse and categories of development and progress have been powerful in setting impressions of the copyright policies and positions acceptable for "developed" countries to take.

The categories of development had power alongside material realities because of their ability to organize, mobilize, and legitimize the actions of powerful interests and states. Those who have used and defined particular ideas of civilization, progress, modernity, development, and growth have done so, as Shanin notes, with some arrogance – projecting the future shape of all societies in their own image, portraying themselves as a natural leader of all.[27] According to Shanin, this vision of progress portrays

> all societies ... advancing naturally and consistently "up," on a route from poverty, barbarism, despotism and ignorance to riches, civilization, democracy and rationality, the highest expression of which is science. This is also an irreversible movement from an endless diversity of particularities, wasteful of human energies and economic resources, to a world unified and simplified into the most rational arrangement. It is therefore a movement from badness to goodness and from mindlessness to knowledge, which gave this message its ethical promise, its optimism and its reformist "punch."[28]

The system of copyright established at Berne became hegemonic; it became the foundation stone of international copyright, and the universal foundation upon which all countries considered to be part of the international community must build. All countries that are members of the World Trade Organization must conform to the basic tenets of the *Berne Convention*.[29]

"The rhetoric of 'progress,'" says Shanin, "will not disappear so long as it serves powerful interest groups."[30] Despite its roots in imperialism, and despite its often unsuccessful attempts to meet the interests of developing countries, the international copyright system founded at Berne in 1886 remains hegemonic. Its vision of universal community has been largely achieved, and the treaties built on its foundation define "progress."

The need to question what appear as common-sense notions of progress and to formulate alternative conceptualizations of progress and order is reflected in critical theory. Critical theory, or "the critical attitude," as Horkheimer terms it, "is wholly distrustful of the rules of conduct with which society as presently constituted provides each of its members."[31] In critical theory, the frameworks of progress and order are recognized as being socially constituted and therefore open to re-examination and reordering. Although open to re-examination, such frameworks are also material, sticky, and difficult to change. The efforts of Canadian officials in the late 1960s and early 1970s to set forth a new vision of the international copyright system failed due to inadequate resources and support.

International law, according to Koskenniemi, has lost the sense of purpose and morality that early lawyers associated with it: "Today, it has become much harder to believe that there is a rationality embedded in international law that is independent from the political perspectives from which it is seen."[32] Similarly, many now view international copyright as a political field of conflicting interests.[33] It has been called "an ideology exported to the South" – a set of rules so familiar that they seem natural, so natural that their justice is rarely questioned. Alan Story, for example, argues that copyright is a system of property constructed to maintain and extend the power of the ruling class – to benefit copyright producers located largely in "developed" rather than developing countries. Story and others argue that any justification of the international intellectual property system is an "ideology exported to the South," an "ideological fairy tale" designed to hide the systemic exploitation and inequality that it underwrites.[34]

Although attempts to meet the interests of developing countries have often been half-hearted and unsuccessful, Koskenniemi maintains a hope that international law might be transformed, might overcome the exclusions of its past, and might embed this overcoming at the core of its ongoing practices. International law, he argues, is based on "a formal ideal that seeks community by understanding that very community is based on an exclusion and that therefore it must be a part of an acceptable community's self-definition that it constantly negotiates that exclusion, widens its horizon."[35] It is only by forming an awareness of the material and discursive structures of international copyright – an awareness that is formed by examining the historical experiences of weaker countries and groups as well as the views of the stronger ones – that such a transformative commitment can be made.

CHAPTER THREE

Imperialism: Canadian Copyright under the Colonial System, 1842-78

UNDER THE SEVENTEENTH-CENTURY mercantile system, British colonies had been discouraged from developing domestic industries that might compete with British imports.[1] Copyright law in the British imperial system was intended, up to the end of the nineteenth century, to encourage British book publishing rather than book publishing in the colonies. Although there was some local book publishing in Canada – where printing offices employed 3,500 people in 1871 – its relatively small and poor population meant that Canada remained greatly dependent on British and American book imports.[2]

Beginning in 1842, British imperial copyright law explicitly granted to British copyright holders rights that applied throughout the British colonies.[3] This imperial copyright system can be seen as a predecessor of the multilateral copyright system; much like international copyright, imperial copyright was intended to expand the recognition of copyright in British works beyond England's borders. Under the imperial system, however, Canadian authors publishing first in Canada did not qualify for protection. Imperial copyright required publication in London and did not extend to works first published in Canada or the other colonies.[4] Canadian legislation, in place alongside British copyright law, protected works first published in Canada,[5] but whereas British copyright provided protection throughout the Empire, Canadian copyright protected works only in Canada.

Many Canadian parliamentarians valued their connection to Britain, viewing it as a defence against American dominance.[6] Most accepted Canada's role as a British colony and the secondary position given to Canadian interests as a result. For example, an 1843 legislative committee examining copyright argued that copyright policy ought to uphold British morality and institutions by encouraging Canadian reprinting of British books as a way of defending Canadians against American values.[7]

Canada was a British colony or dominion until 1931. Its first prime minister, John A. Macdonald, envisioned Canada as subordinate and loyal to Britain, but also as having its own identity and nationhood.[8] The relationship with Britain was not always harmonious; there were pockets of strong objection to British governance – or, as some saw it, governance by British privileged classes and their Canadian hangers-on – that had led to uprisings as recently as 1837. However, British Loyalist elites dominated both public life and the press in Canada.[9]

Tensions with the United States led to a Canadian nationalist movement. The 1871 *Treaty of Washington* settled a number of Canada-US disputes and paved the way for peaceful coexistence between the two countries.[10] However, the perceived unfairness of the settlement towards Canada contributed in part to an anti-American nationalist movement in English Canada called Canada First. Canada Firsters called for the cultivation of a common culture within Canada: "Unless we intend to be mere hewers of wood and drawers of water until the end, we should in right earnest set about strengthening the foundations of our identity."[11]

In 1879, the Macdonald government put in place what was referred to as the National Policy, a system of tariffs designed to protect key Canadian industries, doing so primarily in response to concerns about emigration of workers to the United States. This policy was intended to build a diverse economy with varied occupations and opportunities in order to keep Canadians in Canada. It promised jobs and was intended to foster Canadian competition – simultaneously an attempt to safeguard what was distinctive about Canada by encouraging a diverse economy at home, and to imitate the great industrial country to the south.[12] Canadian copyright policies were related to this philosophy, in that they were intended to encourage a domestic printing and publishing industry and domestic cultural production. Furthermore, a domestic industry that published reprints of British and American books would reduce Canadians' reliance on American imports, thus acting as a bulwark against American influence.

Until 1891, the United States did not provide for copyright in foreign works. This enabled American printers and publishers to reprint British books without being obligated to pay British copyright holders or obtain permission from them. American printers and publishers were therefore able to produce very cheap editions of British books. Canadian printers and publishers, on the other hand, were bound by the imperial copyright system and the restrictions it placed on reprints of British works.[13] The American Revolution had done away with British law and imperial copyright in the United States, leading to an explosion in reprinting that gave rise to a strong American publishing industry that enabled American publishers to build capital. Canadian printers were blocked by imperial copyright from following the same path.[14] Unlike their American counterparts, they were prevented from acquiring sufficient capital through republication of British works, or of French works covered by British copyright, in order to become true publishers (in the sense of initiating, organizing, and financing the publication of books). As a result, despite occasional instances of publishing in Canada, including the publication of magazines, there were no true publishers, in the modern sense of the word, in Canada before the First World War. This was largely due to the copyright policies of the day.[15]

By 1900, after the completion of the Canadian Pacific Railway in 1885, domestically owned printing industries spread across the country. Some Canadian publishing enterprises were profitable, but they were still not publishers in the modern sense; their business primarily involved republishing British, French, and American works.[16] They could not afford the risks associated with new Canadian authors, and none had the capacity to publish on a national scale.

The fact that there was little in the way of a domestic literary movement in Canada in the mid to late nineteenth century can also be attributed largely to the copyright policy of the day, which encouraged emigration of writers who sought out publishers in other countries who could afford to invest in new authors.[17] The Canadian census of 1871 counted a total of 590 "artists and litterateurs," the bulk of whom were in Ontario and Quebec.[18] Successful Canadian authors such as Susanna Moodie and Catharine Parr Traill generally found publishers in London, the United States, or Europe.[19] As many as half of Canadian writers emigrated from Canada at the end of the nineteenth century, many attracted by the flourishing American magazine business in New York.[20]

The main areas of conflict that emerged in nineteenth-century Canadian copyright were between British authors and publishers on the one hand, and Canadian printers and (re)publishers on the other. Whereas authors and publishers in Britain were relatively united in promoting international copyright protection for British works, their counterparts in Canada were divided: many authors favoured strong international copyright recognition, while Canadian (re)publishers wanted more flexible copyright provisions. Canadian preferences differed also from those of the smaller British colonies, who, while concerned about access to foreign works, did not have a large enough economy to support a domestic reprinting industry.[21]

A weak Canadian literary movement meant that the concerns highlighted most prominently in Canada were those of Canadian printers, who were more numerous and highly organized. In light of this, the issue of access to works, rather than protection of works, was the dominant concern in nineteenth-century Canadian copyright policy making.

In 1842, the British imperial government passed the imperial *Copyright Act,* which dealt with copyright in books, magazines, periodicals, dramatic representations, and music.[22] The act was written explicitly to apply throughout the

British dominions, and made Britain the sole legal supplier of British books, pamphlets, sheet music, maps, charts, and plans to British colonies by prohibiting the import of these into British dominions by anyone other than the copyright owners. In particular, this prohibited the import of cheap, unauthorized American reprints of British works that Canadians had enjoyed until then. British publishers favoured expensive library editions of their books, versions that most Canadians, especially those in remote and rural areas, could not afford.[23] This raised concerns about access to information and literature among Canadians, who were accustomed to having newspapers and affordable American editions of books in their homes.[24]

The line between the anglophone tradition of copyright and the civil law tradition of *droit d'auteur* was not clearly drawn in nineteenth-century Canada. Many printers and (re)publishers were from Montreal and, like their counterparts in other parts of Canada, they often supported a utilitarian approach to copyright rather than an approach focused on creators' or authors' rights. Those who supported utilitarian provisions that would allow the reprinting and republishing of foreign works could be found among Members of Parliament from both Quebec and the rest of Canada. At the same time, at least one powerful Quebec policy maker would prioritize authors' rights over the interests of printers and would-be publishers, and this left an impression on Canadian copyright that has lasted to the present day.[25]

Some Canadians were concerned that the 1842 imperial law would corrupt the minds and morals of a generation of Canadians by forcing them to turn to American rather than British works, thereby discouraging their allegiance to British institutions and opening cultural ties to the neighbouring country. They argued that

the exclusion of American Reprints of English Literature, if possible, would have a most pernicious tendency on the minds of the rising generation, in morals, politics, and religion; that American Reprints of English Works are openly sold, and are on the tables or in the houses of persons of all classes in the Province; that a law so repugnant to public opinion cannot and will not be enforced; that were that exclusion possible, the Colonists would be confined to American literary, religious and political Works, the effect of which could not be expected to strengthen their attachment to British Institutions, but, on the contrary, is well calculated to warp the minds of the rising generation to a decided preference for the Institutions of the neighboring States, and a hatred deep rooted and lasting of all we have been taught to venerate, whether British, Constitutional, or Monarchical, or to cling to, in our connection with the Parent State.[26]

As a result of the concerns being raised about the effects of the imperial *Copyright Act* on Canada, the British government considered granting copyright independence to Canada. It initially advised that it would bend to the wishes of the colonies, granting colonial legislative independence on copyright law.[27] British copyright interests ultimately thwarted this plan, however, and the promise of copyright sovereignty was broken. British colonies would not be given legislative independence on copyright for more than sixty years.

The discontent resulting from the imperial *Copyright Act* eventually led in 1847 not to colonial copyright independence but to a British *Foreign Reprints Act,* which loosened somewhat the stranglehold of British publishers on colonial markets. It lifted the prohibition on importation of foreign reprints in cases where colonial legislation adequately protected British publications. The prohibition was accordingly lifted in Nova Scotia, New Brunswick, Prince Edward Island, Newfoundland, and Canada when duties were imposed on the importation of foreign reprints in 1850. The duties, set at 12.5 percent, were intended to be collected as compensation to British copyright holders and were seen as providing "adequate protection" to British works. Imperial copyright law continued to be active in Canada.[28]

Because of the 1847 *Foreign Reprints Act,* American printers, operating under American laws that did not recognize international copyright, were able to reprint British works without permission and export them to Canada upon payment of the 12.5 percent duty, but Canadian printers, who were subject to British copyright law, were not able to legally reprint British works, or French works covered by British copyright, in Canada without authorization from the copyright holder. It was illegal for Canadian (re)publishers to compete in the Canadian market by selling unauthorized British reprints.

1867: Confederation

Britain's powers, first, to impose British legislation alongside Canadian legislation within Canada and, second, to invalidate Canadian legislation, shaped the early evolution of Canadian copyright. The founding document of today's Canada, the *British North America Act* of 1867 (now the *Constitution Act, 1867*), conferred on the Canadian federal parliament the authority to make laws on copyright as well as on patents:

> The exclusive Legislative Authority of the Parliament of Canada extends to all Matters coming within the Classes of Subjects next hereinafter enumerated; that is to say [...]
> 22. Patents of Invention and Discovery.
> 23. Copyrights.[29]

Canadian Confederation should not be confused with Canadian independence, however.[30] The newly formed Canada was a British dominion, and Britain retained the powers to reserve Canadian legislation for approval in Britain, to disallow Canadian legislation, or to declare Canadian legislation invalid.[31]

Although Canadian legislation operated independently in many areas, some areas, including merchant shipping, extradition, naturalization, the preservation of neutrality, and copyright, were subject to legislation from both the imperial and Canadian parliaments.[32] Canada operated under two sets of copyright laws: imperial law, which was in force in Canada as a British colony, and Canadian law. Britain held legislative control over Canadian copyright, first through its ability to reserve Canadian legislation, and second through the imposition of British copyright law on Canada.

1868: *Routledge v. Low*

A few years before Confederation, American novelist Maria Susanna Cumins published a book titled *Haunted Hearts*. Just prior to its American publication, she arranged to publish the book in England in order to obtain British copyright in the work. Under British copyright law, foreigners residing temporarily in the United Kingdom were eligible for British copyright; an 1854 decision of the Judicial Committee of the Privy Council, *Jefferys v. Boosey*, had held that British copyright was available to foreign nationals temporarily residing in the United Kingdom:

> The object of 8 Anne c 19 was to encourage literature among British subjects, which description includes such foreigners as, by residence here, owe the Crown a temporary allegiance; and any such foreigner, first publishing his work here, is an "author" within the meaning of the statute, no matter where his work was composed, or whether he came here solely with a view to its publication.[33]

Cumins arranged to take advantage of this by sending her manuscript to Sampson Low and Company and temporarily residing in Montreal during its publication. The book was registered and assigned to Sampson Low at Stationers' Hall in London, in accordance with the 1842 imperial *Copyright Act,* and was published by Sampson Low in London in May 1864. No copyright was registered under Canadian legislation. That same month, London booksellers Routledge and Company printed a cheaper edition of the work, and Sampson Low sought an injunction.

The question in the case was whether an American residing temporarily in Canada was entitled to copyright under the imperial *Copyright Act* of 1842. The House of Lords decided in 1868 that the 1842 act did apply in all the British dominions, including those with their own copyright legislation, and that a foreign national temporarily resident in a British dominion was not prevented from acquiring copyright under the imperial *Copyright Act*.[34]

The Law Lords differed among themselves on whether residence in the British dominions was, in fact, even required for a foreign national publishing in the United Kingdom to be eligible for copyright. Although *Jefferys v. Boosey* had suggested that "copyright commences by publication; if at that time the foreign author is not in this country, he is not a person whom the statute meant to protect,"[35] some of the Law Lords disagreed with this view. The Lord Chancellor and Lord Westbury argued that anyone publishing in the United Kingdom, wherever resident, and whatever state he or she was subject of, was eligible to obtain copyright in the United Kingdom. Lords Cranworth and Chelmsford, on the other hand, argued that residence of some sort was required. Lord Colonsay, while reserving his decision, commented that there was nothing "more shadowy than a distinction depending upon the circumstance of a few hours' or a few days' residence within some part of the widely-extended dominions of Her Majesty."[36] The question of the necessity of residence in the British dominions would be resolved in 1906, when the Ontario Divisional Court ultimately held that residence was not required.[37]

The case of *Routledge v. Low* was important because it affirmed that imperial copyright law continued to apply in Canada, and because it opened a "back door" to Americans through which they could gain British copyright through a short stay in Canada while their work was published in the United Kingdom.

1868: The Canadian *Copyright Act* and a Proposal regarding Colonial Reprints

Beginning in 1868, a campaign was initiated to enact compulsory licensing under Canadian copyright law. The Canadian government wanted to encourage a domestic printing and publishing industry that could compete viably with American printers and publishers in serving the Canadian market. The imperial government, on the other hand, wanted to hold the Canadian market, if not for British publishing houses, then as a trading card in Anglo-American copyright negotiations.

The Canadian Parliament passed its first post-Confederation copyright act in 1868, as well as an act to reimpose the 12.5 percent duty on foreign reprints of British works that had been in place in the Province of Canada.[38] Upon the passage of *An Act to Impose a Duty on Foreign Reprints of British Copyright Works,* the Canadian government requested of the imperial government that Canadian printers be put on the same footing as American printers reprinting British works.[39] There were suggestions that Canadian printers be allowed to pay a compulsory licensing fee – perhaps at a rate of 12.5 percent, similar to the amount paid by Americans importing reprints of British works under the provisions of the 1847 *Foreign Reprints Act* – and thereby obtain the legal right to republish the work in Canada without permission from the British copyright holder.[40] This plan was framed as a win/win opportunity, whereby "British authors will be more effectually protected in their rights, and a material benefit will be conferred on the printing industry of this Dominion."[41] It would simultaneously help to supply the Canadian market with affordable books and put Canadian printers and would-be publishers on a more equitable footing vis-à-vis their American counterparts.

The British government refused to sanction such a licensing system, for a number of reasons. Besides concerns about the practicality of the proposal and its fairness to British copyright holders, the British wanted to prevent the circulation of Canadian reprints that would be cheaper than those sold in the United Kingdom.[42] They were also apprehensive that the Canadian proposal might affect British international copyright interests. British officials were interested in establishing a bilateral copyright agreement with the United States and were worried that the United States would not be willing to establish a treaty recognizing British copyright "whilst every publisher in Montreal can reprint [British works] on payment of a moderate per-centage without the author's leave, and can smuggle them into the United States."[43] There were also anxieties that other countries might be upset over such an arrangement and that additional British bilateral copyright treaties might be threatened as a result.[44] Finally, there were concerns that such a system would threaten the principles of international copyright preferred by British authors and publishers, by enshrining compulsory licensing at its core.[45] In the end, the potential benefits of the proposal for Canadian interests and British copyright holders were outweighed by larger British interests in the international copyright system. Nothing changed.

Canada's 1868 *Copyright Act* was modelled on earlier legislation of the Province of Canada and Lower Canada, which, in turn, were based on American legislation, itself based on British copyright norms.[46] Like British copyright, the new Canadian law required those wishing to register a copyright to comply with several formalities. First, the work had to be registered in the "Register of Copyrights," a book kept at the Department of Agriculture,[47] with the payment of a fee of one dollar.[48] This was similar to the British system, which also provided for registration, with one important difference: under the imperial *Copyright Act*, registration was a requirement only for an action to sue or claim copyright infringement and was not a condition of copyright, whereas the 1868 Canadian act required registration as a condition of copyright.[49] Mandatory registration made it easy to identify copyright works and the owner of a copyright. Second, two copies of the work were to be deposited with the department, one to be kept by the department and the other to be deposited in the Library of Parliament.[50] This followed the British system, which required the deposit of works with the British Museum and various libraries.[51]

The Canadian *Copyright Act* also differed from the British model in several ways that mirrored the American approach. First, unlike in the British case, a copyright notice was required to appear on most types of works ("Entered according to Act of Parliament of Canada, in the year __ by A. B., in the Office of the Minister of Agriculture").[52] Second, the term of protection for copyrighted works followed that of the United States: twenty-eight years with a possible extension of fourteen years, whereas Britain had recently switched to a term of the life of the creator plus seven years, or forty-two years from the date of first publication, whichever was longer.[53] Third, the Canadian act extended only to works "printed and published in Canada" by residents of Canada or British subjects resident in Great Britain or Ireland.[54] Whereas British copyright extended to any creator resident (even temporarily) in the British dominions at the time of publication in the United Kingdom, American copyright extended only to citizens and bona fide residents of the United States.[55] American law would, by 1891, also add domestic manufacture provisions.[56]

Along with the rights of printing, reprinting, publishing, reproducing, and vending the work, the 1868 law granted to copyright holders a right of translation that lasted the full twenty-eight-year term of the copyright. This would, *inter alia*, prohibit Quebec printers and publishers from producing unauthorized translations of English-language works.[57]

The institutional foundations of Canadian copyright were not well equipped to take on issues of imperial copyright. Those institutions charged with responsibility for copyright were domestically focused, and Canadian policy makers had few resources with which to challenge imperial law.

Following Confederation, many of the departments that would become deeply involved in the administration of Canada's international copyright relations were formally constituted. These included the Department of Agriculture (with a staff of twenty-six at its headquarters),[58] the Department of Justice (taking over from the Crown Law Office with a staff of nine in Ottawa),[59] and the Secretary of State (with a staff of seventeen in Ottawa).[60]

The Department of Agriculture had initial responsibility for copyright. Many of the most important inventions of the mid-nineteenth century were agricultural equipment and products. It made sense, therefore, to administer patents in the same department as other matters related to agriculture, and copyrights went along with patents.[61]

From its establishment in 1853 until the early twentieth century, the Department of Agriculture tended to house the miscellany of odd jobs that did not belong in any other government department. It also acted as a sort of greenhouse in which young but growing departments were nurtured.[62] Along with agricultural matters, it was responsible for collecting statistics from census data, immigration, patents, and copyright.[63] The institutional locus of Canadian copyright was therefore very much occupied with domestic concerns. Although the Department of Agriculture had an international component, being tasked with organizing Canadian representation at international fairs and exhibitions, its concerns were primarily domestic.[64]

The department was small, and the section charged with copyright was somewhat under-resourced. When the department was established in 1853, it housed a headquarters staff of about thirteen.[65] The department and its growing intellectual property section had difficulties due to a shortage of space, first at its original offices in Quebec and later in the Ottawa offices.[66] Fees were collected upon registration of copyrights, trademarks, and patents.[67] By 1886, these fees would make the Patent Office and the copyright and industrial design branch the only branches of any government department where revenue exceeded expenses.[68]

1872: An Attempt at a Canadian Solution

Following the passage of the 1868 *Copyright Act* and the accompanying request that Canadian printers be put on the same footing as American printers reprinting British works, the Canadian government continued to press for compulsory licensing provisions that would allow Canadian printers to print British works. In 1872, its 1868 request unfulfilled, the Canadian Parliament took matters into its own hands and unanimously passed a copyright act that contained provisions allowing Canadian printers to reprint British works in Canada upon licence from the Governor General for a fee of 12.5 percent. The importation of foreign reprints of works published under such a licence was banned.[69] The act, however, was refused British royal assent.[70]

In response to the 1872 bill, the British government proposed a compromise in 1873. The compromise would have replaced the 1847 British *Foreign Reprints Act* with a new act allowing any person to apply through the courts for a compulsory licence to reprint British books "not published in such a British possession in such a number and manner as are suitable for general circulation therein" within a reasonable period (to be specified in colonial legislation) from original publication in Britain. It would also have allowed the importation of foreign reprints upon payment of a duty, only if the book was "not published in such a British possession in such a number and manner as are suitable for general circulation therein" within a period of not less than six months.

The Canadian government refused this solution because of its intricacy and because it was seen as likely to lead to litigation.[71] Soon after taking office as the second prime minister of Canada, Liberal Alexander Mackenzie expressed the view that the proposed solution was inadequate and, in any case, the licensing issue was "not urgent." According to him, only Canadian (re)publishers were advocating the change – authors objected to compulsory licensing because compulsory licences could be granted without their consent, the public seemed "satisfied with the supply of books which it now gets," and those in the book trade were satisfied with the situation as it stood. He therefore felt that "a postponement of the final solution of this complicated question would not be likely to cause detriment to the public interest."[72]

1875: Canadian *Copyright Act*

Two key individuals were important in shaping Mackenzie's views on copyright. One was a proponent of authors' rights; the other was a British copyright expert. Joseph-Charles Taché, Canada's Deputy Minister of Agriculture, and Frederick Daldy, secretary of the Copyright Association representing British publishers, worked with Mackenzie to formulate the 1875 *Copyright Act*, which ultimately received royal assent from Britain.[73] Taché was a Quebec author who had dedicated himself to furthering Canadian national literature and promoting Canadian folklore.[74] In an 1888 letter, he made his perspective on copyright clear: "Copyright laws are not made to protect the printer, but the author who is sole proprietor of the thing he has produced."[75]

By 1875, the proposal for a system of compulsory licensing for colonial reprints had lost steam. Canadian publishing interests backed down on their demand for a licensing clause, in part because they believed, incorrectly, that an Anglo-American copyright agreement would soon be concluded. Were such an agreement to be put in place, it would no longer be legal for Americans to reprint British books without authorization, the 12.5 percent tariff on American reprints would no longer be necessary, and both American and Canadian publishing interests would be on an equal copyright footing. The compulsory licensing system would therefore not be necessary.[76]

The *Copyright Act*, passed in 1875 by the Mackenzie government and sanctioned by the British Parliament, did not include the long-requested licensing system.[77] It granted Canadian copyright to works first or simultaneously printed or published in Canada (or reprinted or republished in Canada), subject to the same set of formalities (domestic printing, registration, and deposit) that had been in place under the 1868 act, and banned the importation of foreign copies of such works (except for British copies). In prohibiting the importation of foreign copies of works copyrighted in Canada, the act put in place a compromise solution that did not go as far as the compulsory licensing provisions of the 1872 act in encouraging domestic printing, or the British-proposed compulsory licensing provisions suggested in 1873, but that did provide some incentive for foreign and British publishers to republish their work in Canada. Under British law, unauthorized American reprints could be imported under the Canadian 12.5 percent duty. Under the 1875 act, only by obtaining Canadian copyright protection via printing and publishing (or reprinting and republishing) in Canada could British and foreign publishers gain exclusive access to the Canadian market by excluding American reprints.[78]

Under the 1875 act, a Canadian copyright holder of a foreign work in translation (an English translation of a French book, for example) had rights over the work in all languages. This meant, for example, that if a (re)publisher in Ontario had rights over a French work in English translation, Quebec publishers could be prevented from importing the work in the original French.[79]

Like the 1868 act, the *Copyright Act* of 1875 was modelled on American legislation in that it adopted the term of protection of twenty-eight years plus a possible renewal of fourteen years, required registration, required a copyright notice in the front of the book, and required domestic printing and publishing or reprinting and republishing.[80] As before, it differed from the British model in the imperial *Copyright Act* of 1842, which gave a term of the life of the creator plus seven years, or forty-two years from publication, whichever was greater; required registration not as a requirement for the grant of copyright but only for the right to sue or claim copyright infringement; and required no copyright notice.[81]

Neither the 1868 nor the 1875 act required first or simultaneous publication in Canada. However, in the interests of foreign publishers who might undertake to publish simultaneously in Canada, the 1875 act provided for interim copyright protection – a short term of protection *before* publication in Canada to last for no more than one month from the date of original publication elsewhere. The advantage of interim copyright was that foreign publishers would have a month to achieve publication in Canada without worrying about competition from American foreign reprints.[82]

Whereas the 1868 *Copyright Act* had made "any person *resident* in Canada or any person being a British subject, and resident in Great Britain or Ireland" eligible for copyright, the 1875 act required copyright owners to be "*domiciled* in Canada or in any part of the British Possessions, or being a citizen of any country having an international copyright treaty with the United Kingdom."[83] As Roper explains: "In the original draft of the act, the word 'resident' had been crossed out and the word 'domiciled' written in – for the purpose of making the law precisely correspond to the law of the United States, where 'resident' meant 'permanent resident.'"[84]

Questions arose as to whether the 1875 *Copyright Act* might be repugnant to, or conflict with, the order-in-council passed in accordance with the British *Foreign Reprints Act* of 1847, so the 1875 act was reserved by Canada's Governor General for signification of Her Majesty's pleasure. This meant that the act would require special approval by the imperial parliament via the passage of enabling legislation.[85] This enabling legislation, when passed, provided that Canadian reprints of British works were banned from importation into the United Kingdom.[86]

Frederick Daldy, the representative of British publishers who had helped formulate Canada's 1875 *Copyright Act,* had placed himself as a key gateway not only in British but also in Canadian copyright policy processes. Prime Minister Mackenzie and Deputy Minister Taché felt that Daldy's approval was needed if the act was to receive imperial assent. As Taché later recounted: "Mr. Daldy is an authority on copyright, and no changes are made in the English law affecting copyright without first consulting him. Mr. Mackenzie consented to do this, and we got a reply to the cable that Mr. Daldy would leave for Canada by the next steamer."[87] Asked by a newspaper reporter whether Daldy approved of the bill, Taché replied: "He approved of it entirely. It passed both Houses of Parliament here, was approved by the British Parliament without the slightest difficulty or hitch of any kind."[88] Mackenzie and Taché appear to have considered Daldy as an unproblematic, even neutral, source of experience, authority, and expertise on copyright law. Expertise, knowledge, and authority thus played a role in reproducing the imperial copyright relationship.

Daldy may also be a seen as a tool used by Taché to advance a more author-centric view of copyright – an approach more closely in line with the French tradition of *droit d'auteur* and perhaps Taché's own view of copyright from a Quebec civil law–inspired perspective. MacLaren writes that his views on copyright "flowed from a particular form of conservative French Canadian politics ... He saw the shoring up of British North America as the best means to preserve the distinct culture of Quebec from assimilation by the United States ... [he took the] view that a strong, united empire offered the best protection for a developing Canadian culture."[89]

For a time, the new Canadian copyright law led some Canadian publishing interests to assume that British copyright no longer had effect in Canada – that foreign works not registered under the Canadian act were not protected by copyright in Canada – and that British works were, as such, fair game for reprinting in Canada. Under this belief, the Belford Brothers of Toronto reprinted Mark Twain's *Tom Sawyer* in 1876 following its initial London publication in

June. Due to delays in the American publication of the work, the Belfords profited enormously by selling the edition in the American market. Mark Twain protested loudly, threatening to stop writing books.[90]

1877: *Smiles v. Belford*

The argument that imperial copyright no longer had effect in Canada was ended by an Ontario Court of Appeal decision that the imperial *Copyright Act* remained in force in Canada and continued to protect British works.[91] Samuel Smiles had published his book *Thrift* and had acquired imperial copyright by registering the book at Stationers' Hall in London. He did not register the book in Canada. Claiming that the work was not copyrighted in Canada, the Belford Brothers of Toronto reprinted the book at great profit. When Smiles took legal action, the Ontario Court of Appeal decided in his favour, holding that, following *Routledge v. Low,* the imperial *Copyright Act* remained in force in Canada and was not displaced by the Canadian act.[92] In Quebec, the idea that the 1875 act alone applied in Canada was more persistent, lasting until a 1906 decision of the Quebec Superior Court denied that such was the case.[93]

Canadian publishing interests continued to be required to recognize imperial copyright in British works, which placed anglophone publishers at a disadvantage vis-à-vis American publishers, who did not recognize copyright in foreign works.[94] The resulting diversion of profits to British and American publishers hindered the accumulation of capital by Canadian firms serving anglophone Canada, rendering them less able to compete or to take on Canadian authors.[95] For the next four decades, aspiring Canadian publishers serving the anglophone market would work primarily in distributing American and British books.[96]

1878: Report of the British Royal Commission on Copyright

In 1875, the British government appointed a Royal Commission on Copyright, "to make inquiry with regard to the laws and regulations relating to home, colonial, and international copyright, which reported in 1878."[97] Although the members of the commission were mainly British politicians, officials, and publishing interests, they were convinced by arguments in favour of a compulsory licensing system in the colonies. The commission's report suggested a shift away from strategies of economic imperialism within the imperial copyright policy. If anything, the commission showed that imperial copyright policies that attempted to reserve the Canadian market for British publishers and the modified policies of 1847 had been "a complete failure."[98] The Royal Commission did not have any immediate effect on British imperial copyright policies but did provide a foothold for later arguments, made in the late 1880s, for Canadian copyright sovereignty.

Three of the commissioners had links to Canada. John Rose, Canadian Minister of Finance and the Canadian government's unofficial representative in Britain, sat as one of the fifteen commissioners, as did Frederick Daldy and Edward Jenkins, the latter an ardent imperialist, having acted as Canada's first British agent-general in London.[99] Jenkins had spent much of his youth in Canada before returning to London, where he was called to the bar and where he became a satirist and politician.[100] In 1870, he had published a satire called *Ginx's Baby;* the work had been republished in Canada but he had not received the 12.5 percent duty owed to him. He chose not to pursue his rights, explaining tongue-in-cheek that he feared, were he to raise the issue, that "the Dominion militia would be immediately called out to vindicate the right of Canada to legislate for herself, and to rob an Englishman."[101] Despite, or perhaps because of, his experience with Canadian reprinting, Jenkins, along with Daldy and Rose, generally concurred in the recommendations of the Royal Commission.[102]

These recommendations were especially important from a Canadian perspective, but would not be implemented in the years immediately following. The first recommendation was that works first published in Canada should be granted British copyright throughout the British Empire. Second, a compulsory licensing system, similar to the one advocated by Canadian (re)publishers, was recommended. Under the suggested system, Canadian publishers, upon payment of a royalty set by the colonial government, would have been permitted to publish British works that had not been published in the colony by copyright holders within a reasonable period of time.[103] Along with this, the commission recommended that more stringent measures be taken to collect royalties on imported reprints.[104] Third, the commission recommended that British colonies be granted a legislative sovereignty on copyright that could be reversed if colonies deviated too far from the norms established under the imperial copyright law. The commissioners suggested that once imperial copyright was granted to works first published in the colonies, the colonies might voluntarily give up their own legislation, confining it only to matters of detail.[105] Alternatively, the grant of colonial copyright sovereignty could be made conditional on the enactment of colonial copyright laws that met certain standards of conformity to the imperial norms.[106] The latter was the path eventually taken in Canada's case.

The Royal Commission's report stressed that it was "highly desirable that the literature of this country should be placed within easy reach of the colonies."[107] This position was advocated not only for English-speaking colonies like English Canada but also for India: Sir Charles Trevelyan, the first witness to give evidence, believed that the dissemination of cheap British literature in India was a necessary part of Indian education that would benefit the people of India. He advocated a policy that would allow colonial reprints to circulate freely among the colonies, such that Canadian reprints of British works, done under a system of compulsory licensing, would supply the market in India.[108]

The Canadian question interrupted a grand narrative that saw international intellectual property protection as the gradually increasing recognition of creators' rights. This narrative of expanding protection was accompanied by a counter-hegemonic vision: the provision of affordable access to information, products, and works.

Compulsory licensing of intellectual property has been proposed as a solution to many public access problems both today and throughout the history of copyright and patenting in Canada.[109] A solution much disliked in the nineteenth century by the international literary class, it continues to be viewed with disdain by many rights holders today. As copyright became a subject of international policy, many rights holders would continue their efforts to stamp out compulsory licensing as a legitimate policy option, fearing that it would spread through the international copyright system. They would do so with considerable success, but that success should not be portrayed as an inevitable path of historical development. Critical theory emphasizes the importance of highlighting counter-hegemonic efforts that produce alternative models. In Canada, such models were intended not only to encourage a stronger publishing industry domestically but also to ensure affordable access to copyright works in a country operating under materially different conditions from those in which the dominant copyright norms originated.

Imperial copyright norms in the 1870s represented an uneasy settlement between the British publishing industry and the colonial government. Canadian counter-hegemonic ideas about copyright were not supported by a material capacity to promote Canadian models, to flesh them out in convincing detail, to engage the necessary players, to influence decision making, or to inscribe them in law. Legislative, institutional, and cultural dependency meant that the conditions that would enable those ideas to prevail were lacking. This would change, but not right away.

CHAPTER FOUR

United Empire:
Canada and the Formation of the
Berne Convention, 1839-86

THE CANADIAN GOVERNMENT'S MOVE to join the *Berne Convention* in 1886 was part of a policy of copyright unity throughout the British Empire. Canada had emerged from Confederation in 1867 as a self-governing British colony. Between 1867 and 1887, anti-colonial sentiment grew in both the metropole and the colonies, but in Canada colonial protests against the imperial government did not gain sufficient political momentum to be successful; many supported the unity of the British Empire. Even in Quebec, protests against imperial unity were supplanted by ambivalence.[1] Gradually preservation of the unity of the Empire became part of both British and Canadian policy. This policy was driven to some extent by what was perceived as general satisfaction with the current relationship among the colonies, and unwillingness to see the relationship with the mother country altered or reduced.[2] It was also driven by general unease about economic conditions and the relationship between Canada and the United States.

The policy of the Canadian government to cement British ties instead of raising the issue of copyright sovereignty during a time of political and economic uncertainty may be interpreted as an effort by the government to shore up and to use for its own purposes the power and prestige resulting from its association with the British Empire. It also reflected the influence of key bureaucrats who promoted, against popular sentiment, an author-centric approach to copyright.

Canada still lacked the diplomatic machinery to chart its own international affairs. There was no Canadian foreign affairs department, and the new Canadian government would only gradually assume responsibility for foreign affairs. For the time being, the British government was in charge of international affairs for all the dominions.[3] A Canadian representative to London had not yet been officially established, and the legislative and executive branches of government generally communicated with the imperial government in writing through the Canadian Governor General. In 1868, John Rose was "accredited ... as a gentleman ... with whom Her Majesty's Government may properly communicate on Canadian affairs,"[4] and he acted as the Canadian government's unofficial representative in London. The links through which Canadian interests were communicated to the British government were thin.

Out of a population of 4 million, about 600 Canadians were classified as "artists and literatures" in Canada's 1881 census, along with 479 musicians, 765 photographers, and 356 engravers and lithographers.[5] These numbers had risen only slightly from 1871.[6] Books published in Canada were largely British, French, and American.[7] As noted in Chapter 3, Canadian authors who were successful during this period generally took their business to London or Europe.[8] In 1886, just 574 copyrights were registered at the Department of Agriculture, compared with 178 ten years earlier.[9] Relatively few Canadians would benefit from the internationally expanded copyright protection that would result from participation in the *Berne Convention*.

By 1881, there were 488 printing firms in Canada employing 6,831 people, and the industry was expanding. The number of people employed had almost doubled since 1771, and by 1891 it would reach 9,000.[10] At the same time, the industry was suffering and authors were also affected. Novelist and journalist William Kirby argued, in an 1885 letter to Prime Minister John A. Macdonald, that his concern was "not primarily to secure copyright to Canadian Authors – they have plenty of that," but to "give our publishing industries such fair play and protections as they might obtain or the trade will become extinct in Canada." According to Kirby, the Canadian publishing trade was being "slaughtered" by imperial copyright, and along with it a "fair prospect for Canadian writers."[11]

Although the government received correspondence about copyright from interested parties, including printers and authors in Canada, there was not yet a full spectrum of organized copyright interest groups. Local printers' unions had formed across the country, and some had forged links with the International Typographical Union in the United States.[12] The Wholesale Booksellers' Section of the Toronto Board of Trade was formed in mid-century, and the Toronto Booksellers' Association in 1876.[13] However, major copyright lobby groups such as the Canadian Copyright Association, the Canadian Society of Authors, and the Canadian Authors' Association had yet to form.

Anglo-American Copyright Negotiations

Prior to the 1886 establishment of the multilateral *Berne Convention*, British international copyright policy makers focused on bilateral copyright relations between Britain and the United States, a relationship in which Canada was heavily invested. Decisions made with regard to the Anglo-American agreement would set precedents that would be drawn upon when Canada joined the *Berne*

Convention. As in the case of the 1871 *Treaty of Washington,* Canada was caught in the middle of the Anglo-American relationship. Ultimately, the Canadian government took the path of British unity, paving the way for entry into the Berne Union.

The British government had been attempting since 1837 to negotiate a bilateral copyright treaty with the United States.[14] These negotiations continued into the late nineteenth century. Under certain circumstances (including temporary residence in the British dominions during publication) the British recognized the copyright of Americans from 1868 and, to a greater extent, beginning in 1886 (when the requirement of temporary residence during publication was dropped). The United States granted copyright protection to British subjects beginning in 1891, also under limited conditions.[15] Although this mutual recognition did not, in the end, lead to a treaty, the Anglo-American negotiations were nevertheless important for the precedent they set. Although the exact terms of an Anglo-American treaty were never finalized, it was generally envisioned that British copyright holders would be allowed to obtain copyright recognition in the United States, perhaps on condition of their printing or reprinting their work in that country; similarly, American copyright holders would have been able to obtain copyright recognition in the British territories covered by the treaty, likely without a domestic printing or reprinting requirement.[16]

The British negotiators were in a somewhat weaker negotiating position than the Americans for two reasons. First, whereas the United States granted copyright protection only to American citizens, Americans were *already* able to gain copyright recognition in Britain by having their work published in London while vacationing in a British colony.[17] Second, the British market was smaller than the American market, meaning that copyright recognition for British authors in the United States was more valuable than copyright recognition for Americans in Britain. An important variable, therefore, was whether the British were able to offer the Americans copyright recognition in the Canadian market as well, which would have made the agreement more attractive to the Americans. Thus, Canada was implicated in the Anglo-American copyright negotiations.

By the 1880s, the British government was aware that copyright was a sensitive issue that could upset colonial relations. Canadian policy makers were therefore actively consulted with regard to the Anglo-American copyright agreement, and were invited to send an expert consultant to assist the British negotiator.[18] Minister of Finance Leonard Tilley was sent as a delegate to advise Britain's negotiator, Lionel Sackville West, on the Canadian perspective. Samuel E. Dawson of the Canadian publishing industry, who acted as an expert adviser, accompanied Tilley.[19]

The treaty was objectionable to Canadian publishing and printing interests because, in effect, it would have granted to Americans a British copyright that was enforceable in Canada without requiring printing or publishing in Canada, whereas the Americans would, in all likelihood, require that Canadians (and the British) print or reprint in the United States in order to receive American copyright protection.[20] Dawson advised that Canadians were much better served by the existing system, under which Canadians could purchase cheap reprints of British authors from the Americans and cheap reprints of American authors from the British, all while a "publishing industry was steadily developing in Canada ... in proportion to the wants of the country, without infringing any legal or moral rights."[21] In November 1881, Tilley informed West during negotiations in Washington that the Canadian government wished Canada to be excluded from the Anglo-American copyright treaty.[22]

Britain expressed an initial willingness to allow Canada to be excluded from the treaty until the concern arose that such exclusion might precipitate the end of the Anglo-American negotiations. The Earl of Kimberly then wrote to Canada's Governor General, the Marquis of Lorne, suggesting a bargain: if the Canadian government would go along with the Anglo-American treaty, Britain would exempt Canada from the 1842 imperial copyright law.[23] This would have meant virtual copyright sovereignty for Canada. The Canadian government agreed to continue the negotiations, but subsequently softened its demands, retreating from its request for copyright sovereignty.[24]

A number of individuals played key roles in this decision: John Henry Pope, the Minister of Agriculture; Joseph-Charles Taché, the Deputy Minister of Agriculture; John Mortimer Courtney, the Deputy Minister of Finance; and Frederick Daldy, secretary of the British Copyright Association. The decisions made are highlighted in two sets of minutes of the Canadian Privy Council and a letter from Daldy to Robert Herbert, British Under-Secretary of State for the Colonies.

John Henry Pope gave the key advice that was adopted by the Canadian government in its initial decision not to stand in the way of the Anglo-American copyright treaty, on certain conditions. His advice was incorporated into a decision of the Privy Council on 3 November 1882, in which it was suggested that the Canadian government would be willing to allow the Anglo-American treaty to go forward on two conditions. First, the government asked to be exempted from the British 1842 imperial *Copyright Act,* leaving the Canadian Parliament free to pass its own copyright legislation without a second layer of imperial legislation. Second, the government requested that the principles embodied in Canada's 1875 *Copyright Act* be incorporated into the agreement. Those principles prohibited the importation of foreign (including American) reprints of British books if the same books were printed or reprinted in Canada and registered under Canadian copyright.[25] These principles were important to the Canadian printing and publishing industry because they offered British copyright holders a monopoly in the Canadian market, thereby encouraging them to republish their books in Canada and bolstering the Canadian industry. While setting these conditions, the Canadian government also made it clear that it did not want to appear to be standing in the way of the Anglo-American negotiations.[26] The British appeared ready to accept these two demands. The Board of Trade, responsible for copyright, saw "no ground for objecting to the proposals of the Canadian government," and the Foreign Office felt that "the main difficulty in regard to Canada has been removed."[27]

Notwithstanding these demands, Pope was very much in favour of the Anglo-American treaty and stronger copyright protection. He advised that the treaty would be beneficial to Canadian creators; he drew an analogy to patents, noting that the extension of Canadian patent law to allow foreigners to hold Canadian patents had fostered, improved, and increased manufacturing in Canada. He further advised that any difficulties that the recognition of American copyright might pose, such as higher prices for American books, would be mitigated by market forces and offset by advantages to Canadian creators.[28]

Pope was influenced in his position by Joseph-Charles Taché, who had also worked with Prime Minister Alexander Mackenzie to formulate Canada's *Copyright Act* of 1875.[29] As explained in Chapter 3, Taché was an author himself, and from Quebec; he viewed copyright as a law intended to serve the interests of authors, not the interests of publishers or printers.[30]

Independence from the imperial *Copyright Act* had been promoted by Tilley, who had been sent to Washington to advise the British on the Canadian government's position.[31] He had formulated Canada's National Policy and was sympathetic to the interests of Canadian industry.[32] He was also influenced by Dawson, the Canadian publisher who accompanied him as an expert adviser in Washington.

Taché, on the other hand, was not in favour of legislative independence for Canada in the matter of copyright. He objected to the idea of compulsory licensing advocated by Canadian publishing and printing interests, and did not wish to see compulsory licensing incorporated into Canadian copyright law. He therefore advised Pope that "absolute independence from the United Kingdom as regards copyright ... might turn out, if it were conceded, to the future detriment of Canadian authors."[33] Taché's ideas about what was good for Canadian authors differed from the views of William Kirby described earlier.

Kirby saw provisions that would help the Canadian publishing industry compete with the Americans as being favourable to Canadian authors.[34]

In January 1883, two months after the first decision of the Privy Council was issued, Daldy consulted with Pope, Taché, John Lowe (Pope's secretary), and Courtney. These consultations took place in the absence of the Governor General, Prime Minister Macdonald, and Finance Minister Tilley. Their absence is significant because it allowed officials from the Department of Agriculture to effectively revise the demands that had been made in the first decision of the Privy Council and to circumvent the position advocated by Tilley.[35]

From Courtney, Daldy learned that Pope had been "a little jealous" of the involvement of Tilley in the copyright agreement. Finance, he said, had therefore transferred the matter back to Pope. Pope and Taché told Daldy that the November 1882 minutes of the Privy Council had been condensed by a clerk, and that it did not contain the meaning they had wished to convey. In fact, they did not expect to be released from the imperial *Copyright Act* of 1842; they merely wanted a change to that act such that works first published in Canada would receive protection throughout the British Empire and, as before, to preserve the principles of the Canadian 1875 *Copyright Act*.[36]

Daldy expressed the view that neither of these demands would pose any problem. Thus, an informal understanding was reached between the Agriculture officials and Daldy, who conveyed it to the British Colonial Office.[37] The new position was incorporated into a second decision of the Privy Council, of 24 July 1883, which requested simply that a clause be added to the draft Anglo-American treaty to ensure the preservation of the principles of the Canadian 1875 *Copyright Act*. It also anticipated that new British legislation would ensure that works first published in a British colony would receive protection throughout the Empire.[38]

The significance of this shift, orchestrated by officials from the Department of Agriculture with Frederick Daldy, may not have been fully realized at the time. As a result, the struggle for copyright independence would continue until 1911, and Canadian printing and publishing interests would continue for some time to be on an unequal footing vis-à-vis their American counterparts.

The American market was larger and more important to British publishers than the Canadian one – so important that Britain initially maintained imperial authority over the Canadian market more to be able to trade the Canadian market for access to the American market than for the benefit of British publishers, who had failed to fully exploit the Canadian market in any case. By May 1882, however, in response to the Canadians' desire to withdraw from negotiations, the British government appeared willing to grant Canadian copyright sovereignty in the interests of concluding a successful Anglo-American treaty with Canadians on board. However, key Canadian policy makers who viewed their government's protectionist copyright policies as being potentially detrimental to future Canadian authors, alongside British lobbyist Daldy, embarked upon a path that delayed Canadian copyright sovereignty and established instead the policy of copyright unity with the British Empire. Daldy was also influential in bringing the British to the negotiating table in Berne,[39] and Canada's policy of copyright unity was then used as a precedent that led to Canadian participation in the *Berne Convention*.

Besides the bureaucratic politics involving the Departments of Agriculture and Finance, institutional factors played a role in decisions regarding the Anglo-American copyright treaty. At the time of the Anglo-American copyright discussions, Canadian officials were not yet able to conduct independent international negotiations. Although the Canadian government had the power to regulate commercial policy, this power only slowly evolved to include the power of treaty making. In the early 1880s, it was not yet the norm for the government to have a seat at the negotiating table. Canadian participants would be granted independent diplomatic status eventually, but the Anglo-American copyright negotiations took place just before this shift and the Canadian representative's role was purely advisory.[40]

One of the reasons that the British government had been opposed to direct colonial participation in negotiations in the 1870s was a concern that a colonial representative could prejudice the British position in cases where the interests of Great Britain differed from those of the colony.[41] Copyright is one case where this concern was justified: the Canadian government's interests in protecting the Canadian market for Canadian publishers and printers were opposed to those of the British government, and the Canadian market was one of the key drawing cards that the British wished to offer to the Americans as part of the negotiations. The Canadian government's unwillingness to be a part of the treaty at one point threatened to derail the process and what the British were trying to achieve.

The initial Canadian request to be excluded from the Anglo-American copyright agreement was not extraordinary. Although the Canadian government did not have full capacity to negotiate international treaties, the dominion was at this time recognized as being fully able to request exclusion from British-negotiated treaties, and did arrange for exclusion from various treaties in the early 1880s.[42] Had Daldy and Taché not intervened, another outcome would have been entirely possible.

Canada's lack of full independent representation in the Anglo-American copyright negotiations placed it in the disadvantageous position of being unable to bring its position directly to the negotiations. Further, Canada's status as a part of the British Empire meant that the Canadian government had to balance the interests of the imperial government with its own domestic interests.

In summary, various factors were important in determining the course of the Anglo-American treaty negotiations. These included British economic interests in gaining copyright protection in the American market, and the Canadian market's potential as a deal sweetener to be offered to the Americans; the influence of key government departments and individuals; the bureaucratic politics that resulted in control over copyright policy being wrested from Finance Minister Tilley back to the Department of Agriculture; and institutional and normative factors related to Canada's status as a British dominion. A few top officials at the Department of Agriculture, including Taché, played an important role in setting the precedent of Canadian support for international copyright treaties despite the concerns of domestic printing and publishing interests. As a result of all of these factors, a precedent was set that would influence the country's position on international copyright for years to come.

The *Berne Convention*

Although support for the idea of a universal copyright law can be traced to 1839, work towards such a law first reached an internationally organized scale in 1858, when an international Congress on Literary and Artistic Property held in Brussels was attended by artists, journalists, lawyers, economists, publishers, and printers, as well as representatives of learned societies and universities, and unofficial delegates from all of the major European countries and the United States.[43] The congress resolved that copyright should be recognized in all "civilized" countries and that the principle of national treatment should be applied to copyright – namely, that countries should recognize the copyright of foreign nationals in the same way that they recognize the copyright of their own citizens, even in cases where those foreign countries did not provide reciprocal protection.[44] This principle, conceived in 1858, would be of particular importance in the Canadian case. Once incorporated into the *Berne Convention* in 1896, it would act as a stumbling block for Canadian compliance with the convention for almost twenty years.[45]

The next international meeting on copyright took place in Antwerp in 1877, with resolutions similar to those of the 1858 congress. The Institute of International Law was delegated to prepare a draft universal law of copyright, but nothing came of it.[46]

The project of an international law on copyright did not take flight until 1878, when a literary congress of the *Société des gens de lettres,* chaired by Victor Hugo, took place at the Universal Exhibition in Paris. A second congress in the same year proposed that the French government summon governments to an international conference on copyright.[47] Initially open to writers and literary societies, the *Société des gens de lettres* expanded to include artists five years later, when it became the *Association littéraire et artistique internationale* (ALAI). Membership in ALAI was open to literary societies and writers from all countries, but no Canadians were represented initially,[48] although there were numerous British, American, and French members.[49] ALAI still exists today, with chapters throughout the world, including in Canada.[50]

ALAI proposed to initiate discussion in the press of each country about the formation of an international copyright union, modelled somewhat on the recently established international postal union and encompassing all interested parties, including publishers, booksellers, composers, and music houses.[51] If any effort was made through the press to generate public support in Canada for an international copyright union, it met with little success. Despite reporting on Canadian copyright law and the progress of Anglo-American copyright negotiations in the 1870s and 1880s, Canadian newspapers took no note of ALAI and little note of the idea of a multinational copyright union until after the *Berne Convention* was finalized in 1886.[52]

The French government never followed up on the request that it initiate a meeting of governments on international copyright. Berne, Switzerland, where a number of international meetings had recently been held, was now suggested as the meeting place for the proposed union,[53] with the support of the Swiss government.

ALAI appointed a drafting commission. A draft convention consisting of ten articles was produced at an 1883 meeting of academics, artists, writers, editors, and delegates from literary societies, and formed the basis for government-level discussions and for what eventually became the *Berne Convention*.[54] The draft convention was circulated to the "governments of civilized countries," along with an invitation to a conference in 1884 to discuss its contents.[55] Canadian officials were not invited, as was usual for a British colony at the time. Many governments, including those of Britain and France, responded positively, but Greece, Denmark, the Dominican Republic,[56] Nicaragua, and Mexico declined to attend, citing conflicts between the proposed international convention and their domestic laws, as well as the lack of literary development in their respective countries. The United States, noting that the interests of printers, paper manufacturers, typesetters, and bookbinders might stand in the way of their participation in the convention, did not attend either.[57]

Conferences were held in 1884 and 1885 to discuss the draft convention and negotiate the provisions that would be carried forward. Although the French

and German delegates hoped to encode a universal law of copyright, fundamental and universal principles could not be agreed upon due to wide divergence among the delegates regarding the form that copyright protection should
take. How long should it last? What sorts of rights should it entail? As a result,
the *Berne Convention* took the form of a set of minimum standards, the interpretation and implementation of which would, to a large degree, rest at the
national level rather than in a codified universal law.[58]

Initially, the British were hesitant to take part in the negotiations, for two
important reasons. First, they feared that the *Berne Convention* might require
the adoption of copyright norms that were objectionable to the United States,
thus endangering the possibility of an Anglo-American copyright treaty. This
concern was somewhat alleviated when the Americans sent a delegate to the
1885 meeting. Second, the British were concerned that the agreement might stir
up, once again, calls for copyright sovereignty on the part of the colonies, and
that the Candian government in particular might desire to opt out of the *Berne
Convention*. At the conference in 1885, however, the British negotiators successfully argued for a clause that would allow countries to accede to the *Berne
Convention* on behalf of their colonies, either in whole or in part. This made it
possible to exclude colonies from the terms of the agreement.[59] The 1885 meeting
resulted in a final agreement on a text to be signed. The Canadian press took
only cursory note of this progress, and the text was sent to the Canadian
government.

In preparation for the 1886 conference at which the *Berne Convention* would
be signed, the British government passed a bill that would implement the
convention.[60] Britain's colonies were consulted in the drafting of the bill, which
was designed to consolidate British copyright law, to conform to the *Berne
Convention*, and to maintain the principle of imperial copyright. The new law
was intended to allow colonial copyright legislation insofar as it did not conflict
with imperial law or the *Berne Convention*.[61]

In consulting with the colonies on the proposed act and the accession of the
British Empire to the *Berne Convention*, the Colonial Office did not frame the
possibility of colonies remaining outside the *Berne Convention* as a viable option; imperial copyright was portrayed as advantageous to the colonies, and the
convention as removing problems between "civilized states":

> As regards to ... British Imperial copyright, it seems obviously unnecessary to
> dwell on the advantages of making the Empire one for the purposes of copyright.
> Indeed, any other system seems to lead to what may be termed inter-colonial
> piracy, and would tend to create as between the Colonies the same difficulties

which the Berne Conference has sought to remove as between all civilized States
... The Bill, as introduced, deals ... with copyright as an Imperial question ... The
effect of this provision will be not only to give colonial authors full rights throughout the whole British Empire, but also to make the Law of Copyright uniform
throughout the Empire, as the Berne Conference desired to do for all civilized
States.[62]

In a concession to the colonies, the new law, once passed, corrected the long-
standing inequity under the former imperial copyright law that saw works
published in Britain protected throughout the Empire but works published in
a colony protected only in that colony; under the 1886 act, works published in
a colony were be protected throughout the Empire as well.[63] It was also made
clear that any colony's wish to stand aside from the *Berne Convention* would be
respected:

> It is therefore hoped that the various Colonies and India will cordially accept the
> provisions of the present Bill, which have been drafted with the utmost desire to
> meet what we believe to be their requirements and wishes, and to secure their
> co-operation. But in case India or any Colony should wish to stand aloof and be
> excepted either from joining the International Copyright Union, or from the
> provisions for giving colonial authors copyright in the United Kingdom and in
> the Colonies, its wishes will be duly complied with.[64]

Colonies would not be permitted to remain outside of imperial copyright,
however. According to the Colonial Office, this would oppose "the tendency,
which has happily grown stronger of late years, for every part of the English-
speaking race to draw closer to every other part."[65] Furthermore, "both Parliament and public opinion would refuse to extinguish the existing copyright rights
of British authors."[66] The colonial governments, including Canada's, assented
to these proposals.[67]

On 6-9 September 1886, a diplomatic conference was held for the signing of
the *Berne Convention*. On 9 September, Germany, Belgium, Spain, France, Haiti,
Italy, Liberia, Switzerland, the United Kingdom, and Tunisia signed the agreement.[68] In signing, the British delegates declared that the British accession
comprised "the United Kingdom of Great Britain and Ireland, and all the
Colonies and Foreign possessions of Her Britannic Majesty." They reserved "to
the Government of Her Britannic Majesty" the power to denounce the convention separately on behalf of one or several of its colonies and possessions, namely,
"India, the Dominion of Canada, Newfoundland, the Cape, Natal, New South

Wales, Victoria, Queensland, Tasmania, South Australia, Western Australia, and New Zealand."[69] The French made a similar declaration, and the Spanish declared that they would announce their intent with regard to their colonies at the time of exchange of ratifications of the agreement.[70]

Only the United States and Japan, both of whom were present as observers, did not sign the agreement, but the United States signified that it might soon do so.[71] Although the United States would not in fact to join the convention until over a century later, the British delegates felt that this statement was significant. In their report to the Earl of Iddesleigh, they called particular attention to it "as giving promise that the important literary and artistic interests of Great Britain in the United States may before long be afforded adequate protection."[72]

In summing up the outcome of the conference, the British delegates expressed the view that the convention would bring substantial benefits to British copyright holders and their hope that the Berne Union would be expanded to encompass all the major states of the world:

> We believe that the International Copyright Union, which may now be said to be founded, will not only efficiently replace the existing Conventions, but will confer upon British owners of literary and artistic property far more extensive and satisfactory protection than is now enjoyed by them abroad; and we entertain strong hopes that, before the expiration of many years, the Union will comprise all the principal States of the world which have any practical interest in the matter.[73]

A tremendous sense of pride and achievement accompanied the agreements. Henry Bergne, one of the British delegates, would later make note of the "great difficulty" that was surmounted in coming to an agreement, and the great benefits it would confer on British authors.[74] It is clear that the delegates viewed their work as advancing the progress of international law for the benefit of authors and publishers. Some might have seen themselves as playing a role in a larger process of expanding international law and civilization.

Commentary in international legal periodicals about the formation of the Berne Union was mostly positive. Some American and British law journals ran short articles on the progress of the international copyright convention, but Canadian law journals did not.[75] A few Canadian newspapers mentioned the signing, but coverage was restricted to one or two lines reporting that the conference had taken place.[76] In a short article, Toronto's *Globe* lauded the benefits that British implementation of the agreement would bring to Canadian authors, noting that Canadians would now have copyrights recognized "in all the other colonies and dependencies as well as in the Motherland, and in all the countries of the International Copyright Union as well."[77]

A number of institutional and normative factors explain why Canadian officials were not directly involved in the *Berne Convention* negotiations. First, the government was small and therefore had to prioritize its use of limited resources. In 1886, Canada had no foreign affairs office. Communication on international aspects of copyright continued to pass through the offices of the Secretary of State and the Governor General. The Canadian High Commissioner in London would gradually take over from the British-appointed Governor General responsibility for representing Canada's interests in international treaties.

The first international conference to which Canadian delegates had been invited to attend in their own right had taken place in 1881.[78] At the time of the negotiations leading to the *Berne Convention,* however, it was not yet the norm for Canadian delegates to be invited to international conferences, although Canadians were regularly attending international negotiations with British delegations in an advisory capacity.[79] In the case of the *Berne Convention* negotiations, no Canadian advisor was invited or sent.[80]

Canadian officials do not appear to have been consulted on the negotiations as they were taking place, nor were there any communications between the British and Canadian governments on the subject of the *Berne Convention* before March 1886, after the text of the convention had been finalized but before it had been signed.[81] Canadian policy makers were informed after the fact about the results of the 1885 and 1886 conferences, and were asked, rather hurriedly, whether they wished Britain to sign the convention on Canada's behalf. Reports of the 1885 conference were sent to Canada, with apologies for their tardiness, in April and May 1886, just one or two months before the government had to decide whether to join the *Berne Convention* and six months before the convention's September signing.[82] Copies of correspondence relating to the position of the colonies under the convention, as well as the final reports of the British delegates to the 1886 conference, were sent after the convention was signed.[83]

It does not appear that Canadian government officials, in the years leading up to the agreement or the months immediately following, expressed objections to the *Berne Convention* or its implementation by Britain. Rather, the Canadian government expressly consented to join the convention.

On the whole, the move to join the *Berne Convention* cannot be attributed to the norms of imperialism at the time. Mechanisms and norms were in place for greater consultation with Canada than actually occurred, for Canadian attendance in an advisory capacity at international negotiations, and for colonies to stand aside from British international treaties. The major institutional factor that may have contributed to the Canadian government's decision to join Berne may have been a combination of time constraints and restricted channels of communication, which limited the imperial government's ability to consult with the colonies on the matter.[84]

One of the main reasons that the *Berne Convention* was not debated in Canada was that members of the Canadian government actively discouraged such a debate. Liberal Member of Parliament James Edgar attempted to have a committee formed to examine copyright issues on 29 March 1886, several months before the *Berne Convention* was due to be signed and before the details of the British proclamation regarding Canada and the colonies had been fully determined.[85] This idea was firmly blocked, however, by Conservative MP Hector Louis Langevin, the Minister of Public Works. At the time that he requested the committee, Edgar may not have been aware of the *Berne Convention* or the progress of its negotiation, as he did not raise it as a particular matter for the proposed committee to discuss; he was primarily concerned with Canadian legislative independence on copyright generally and with the state of the Canadian printing and publishing industry. Several members of the House were aware of the *Berne Convention,* however, despite being somewhat vague on its details and whether negotiations had been concluded. Once the issue of international copyright was raised, several members argued that it was all the more reason to appoint a committee on copyright. The government expressed concern, however, that such a committee might focus too much on the interests of printers as opposed to authors and other groups, such that the interests of printers "would acquire a prominence which it did not deserve."[86] It became apparent that a prominent debate showcasing the interests of Canadian publishing and printing interests would be inconvenient for the government, as it might interfere with the international processes already under way. In particular, a protest from Canadian printers hoping to adopt what Conservative politicians referred to as the shameful piratical ways of American publishers might embarrass the government. Liberal Robert Newton Hall encouraged Edgar to ask for copies of government correspondence on the subject of the *Berne Convention,*[87] but in the face of strong government opposition, Edgar withdrew his motion to form a committee to examine the issue of copyright.[88] Hall suggested that the opposition "should wait another year, and see what will be the consequences of that convention."[89] By the time that year was up, the 1886 agreement would be signed and consented to by the Canadian government.

Whereas the Conservatives in power now favoured joining the *Berne Convention,* the Liberals continued to call for copyright independence and provisions to assist Canadian printers and publishers. The debate over whether to form a committee on copyright also split somewhat along linguistic lines. Edgar and John Charlton, both Liberal anglophones from Ontario ridings, along with Peter Mitchell, an independent anglophone from New Brunswick, supported the call for a committee and copyright debate. Liberal Hall and Conservative Langevin, both of whom were from Quebec, did not.[90] Reports of the debate ran in *La Presse*, the *Montreal Gazette*, and the *Ottawa Citizen*.[91]

Ten days before the debate initiated by Edgar took place in the House of Commons, Prime Minister John A. Macdonald received a telegram in code from Charles Tupper, Canada's High Commissioner in London. On 16 March, Tupper had attended a meeting at the Foreign Office to discuss the copyright situation.[92] The telegram explained that a bill was about to be introduced in the British Parliament to enact the *Berne Convention* on behalf of Britain and the colonies. Tupper asked whether Macdonald concurred with this action.[93] Following this, the British government inquired through various channels about the Canadian government's willingness to enter the *Berne Convention*.[94] Macdonald referred the matter to Minister of Agriculture John Carling (of London, Ontario), whose reply expressed the government's willingness to join the convention.[95] Macdonald also replied personally by telegram from the library at his home at Earnscliffe Manor on 10 June 1886: "Canada consents to enter Copyright Convention."[96] This telegram, passed from the British Colonial Office to the British Foreign Office, was taken as "an Act" of the Canadian government.[97] The Privy Council also confirmed the decision to assent to the *Berne Convention* on 22 June 1886, and a memorandum to this effect was accordingly forwarded to the British government.[98] The Canadian government's assent to join the *Berne Convention* went unannounced in the press.[99] The matter passed as a common-sense step under a policy of acting in accord with the mother country.

Two reasons for the government's willingness to join the *Berne Convention* were cited in the Privy Council's decision. First, Privy Council members had before them a bill that had been introduced in the US Senate providing for international copyright. Many, including not only members of the Privy Council and the British delegates to the Berne meetings but also legal commentators and members of the press, reported that the United States was on the verge of recognizing international copyright.[100] Second, the Privy Council was acting in accordance with the advice of John Carling, now the Minister of Agriculture, that such a treaty would greatly expand the scope of protection for Canadian authors so as "to give copyright taken in Canada protection throughout the civilized world." The interests of Canadian printers were not mentioned in the decision.[101]

As it turned out, the Senate bill did not pass and the United States would not join the *Berne Convention* until over a century later.[102] For years to come, Canada, as a party to the *Berne Convention*, was used as an access point by American authors, who would publish their works in Britain or a British dominion (usually Canada), and thereby gain the benefits of the Berne Union as well as copyright protection throughout all the countries of the union without itself complying with the agreement. On the other hand, since Canada had no copyright treaty with the United States, Canadian authors would receive no reciprocal protection for many years, until the United States joined the *Berne Convention* in 1989.

DOMESTIC ATTEMPTS TO GENERATE discussion of copyright issues had come too late. It is possible that by the time the idea of a committee to examine copyright issues was raised, the government had already indicated its willingness to join the *Berne Convention*. In any case, the government's response would have been required before any such committee could have reported, and the committee's conclusions would have led to controversy over a decision that was a fait accompli.

Several individuals at the Department of Agriculture played key roles in shaping the government's decision to join the *Berne Convention*. Prime Minister Macdonald's telegram indicating his government's consent was premised on a series of documents shown to him by John Lowe, secretary to the Department of Agriculture. As Lowe later explained, these documents laid down "the principle that the author's interest should be primarily considered in all Copyright arrangements, the publisher's interest being a matter for Tariff legislation, and that Canada should be in accord with the mother country in the matter of Copyright."[103] According to Lowe, the impression left with Macdonald was that Canadian adhesion to the *Berne Convention* was based on an established principle dating back to 1872: "The whole of the Departmental action since 1872, as shown by me to Sir John Macdonald, established a principle, of which the Berne Convention was a logical extension."[104]

One of the most important documents shown to Macdonald was the 1882 Privy Council decision not to stand in the way of the Anglo-American copyright treaty.[105] This decision, which cited the benefits that international copyright recognition could provide to Canadian authors and opined that the disadvantages it might create for Canadian consumers would be mitigated by market forces, had also been signed by Macdonald.[106] Lowe was acting under Deputy Minister of Agriculture Joseph-Charles Taché, whose sympathies rested primarily with the interests of authors. Later, when Lowe succeeded Taché as deputy minister, the department's copyright policies would change, but in the meantime, Taché, who was deputy minister from 1868 to 1888, through both the Anglo-American negotiations and the birth of the *Berne Convention,* played a powerful role in ensuring that Canada, in staying under British legislative control and joining the *Berne Convention,* did not depart from the copyright norms established by British and other powerful copyright interests.

Although Canadian newspapers did not follow in any detail the progress of the *Berne Convention,* they greeted it with approval in September 1886, while noting that its implications for Canada were still far from being fully understood:

> The importance, as touching themselves, of the International Copyright Convention recently held at Berne, is no doubt imperfectly understood by many British colonists ... Before the [1886 British implementation] Act was passed all the Colonial Governments had expressed a desire to enter the Copyright Union, and signified approval of the provisions mentioned above. They were also unanimous in deciding against any colony being exempted from the provisions of the Act and allowed to remain outside the Union.[107]

Before long, this perceived approval would be interrupted by increasingly organized dissenting domestic voices.

CHAPTER FIVE

Berne Buster: The Struggle for Canadian Copyright Sovereignty, 1887-1908

We make our own tariff; we raise our own troops; we regulate our own Patent laws, but our Copyright law is dominated by an Imperial statute passed in 1842, which still binds us.

– ATTRIBUTED TO JOHN ROSS ROBERTSON[1]

CANADA BECAME A PARTY to the *Berne Convention* under Britain's signature in 1886, but implementation of its provisions awaited action by the Dominion legislature.[2] Finally, in May 1888, Minister of Justice John Thompson announced that the Canadian government would put in place laws giving effect to the convention.[3] Two aspects of this bill are important. First, it would have abandoned the requirement that works be printed and published or reprinted and republished in Canada.[4] Second, compulsory licensing provisions, which had long been sought by printing and publishing interests, were not included.[5]

A draft memo explained the reasoning behind the implementation legislation, focusing on the benefits it would provide "in the event that" a Canadian author should become internationally successful: "By the act of joining the Berne Convention, Canadian copyright also runs throughout all the countries parties to it, as above recited. This privilege would be of the highest importance both to the Canadian author and publisher *in the event* of the production of a work for which there should be an Imperial and an international demand."[6] Further, it was still believed that the United States would soon pass an international copyright bill. Officials argued that the sort of licensing clause that printing and publishing interests wanted would be inappropriate: "The present would seem to be an inopportune time to ask for the creation of a right of literary piracy in Canada, when the neighboring States, which have so long practiced it, are about to give it up."[7]

The passage of the *Berne Convention* and its adoption into British law – even before it was implemented in Canada – dramatically extended the range of protection afforded to Canadian copyright owners. Under British law, works first published in Canada would now receive copyright recognition in Britain, the colonies, and all countries of the Berne Union, which also included Germany, Belgium, Spain, France, Haiti, Italy, Switzerland, and Tunisia.[8]

For many, the *Berne Convention* symbolized the forward march of international law, civilization, and progress. In some countries, however, this idea collided with national sentiment and nationalistic trade policies. This was particularly true in Canada, where a National Policy had been implemented by the federal government in the 1870s in order to create and reinforce national economic boundaries through a system of tariffs designed to protect key Canadian industries. This system had expanded and matured into the foundational strategy of the Macdonald government,[9] and its protectionist approach came to be reflected in other areas of government policy, including copyright. The decision to join the Berne Union was soon called an act of "profound ... almost criminal – negligence" on the part of Canadian politicians, because the principles of the international agreement were out of step with what the majority of Canadian interest groups at the time were calling for.[10] Views within Quebec were similar to those in the rest of Canada: reprinting and republishing were important in both Quebec and Ontario, the Americans were important competitors in the reprinting of works both in English and in French,[11] and the *Berne Convention* would require copyright recognition in Canada for both British and French works.

The announcement that the Canadian government would implement the *Berne Convention* in this manner provoked protests. Printers, (re)publishers, booksellers, and papermakers objected that they would be "ruinously affected."[12] Printers in both Quebec and the rest of Canada would be affected; the *Berne Convention* would mean that the works of French as well as British authors would be granted copyright in Canada. Opposition to the agreement from printers, (re)publishers, and related industries grew and mobilized, especially in Toronto. The Canadian Copyright Association was formed following the announcement in 1888 to lobby on behalf of these different interests, and other organizations followed.[13] As well, the Canadian Manufacturers' Association, founded in 1871 and incorporated by an act of Parliament in 1902 "to promote Canadian industries and to further the interests of Canadian manufacturers and exporters," became active in lobbying the government on copyright at the turn of the century.[14] Other organizations, such as the Employing Printers' Association of Toronto, the Canadian Press Association, the Toronto Conservatory of Music, and even the Young Men's Christian Association (YMCA), became concerned with copyright issues.[15] The most important group to appear around the time of the introduction of the 1888 bill was the Canadian Copyright Association; its efforts to enlist the Canadian government in the interests of the Canadian printing and aspiring publishing industry would lead to a dramatic shift in policy. National organizations for creators were formed about a decade later (the Ontario Society of Artists was founded in 1872,[16] but it was not until 1899 that the Canadian Society of Authors was formed by Goldwin Smith to lobby on copyright issues[17]).

Much of the opposition to the *Berne Convention* was centred in Toronto rather than Montreal. Although Montreal printing and publishing interests faced many of the same problems as those in the rest of Canada, they were less organized and operated longer under the impression that the *Berne Convention* did not apply in Canada.[18] Quebec-based organizing became more prominent after the turn of the century.[19]

Outcry over the proposed implementation grew especially sharp when it became apparent that the Americans, even if they did pass an international copyright act, intended to require domestic printing; the copyright bill then before the US Congress contained such a requirement.[20] The Canadian Copyright Association sent a delegation to Ottawa with a petition signed by over two thousand members of the printing and (re)publishing industry. The petition received prompt attention: the government withdrew the implementation bill almost immediately on their arrival shortly after a large protest meeting in Toronto on 17 May.[21]

Minister of Justice Thompson came to see the *Berne Convention* as disadvantageous to Canadian interests. He summarized the main reasons for opposition to its implementation in 1892. The convention, he felt, would allow foreign copyright holders to gain a monopoly on publishing their works in the Canadian market, causing Canadian printers and aspiring publishers to lose out. In his view, the benefits that Canadian copyright holders would receive under the convention did not offset the harm caused to the Canadian printing and publishing industry:

> The condition of the publishing interest in Canada was made worse by the Berne Convention ... The monopoly which was, in former years, complained of in regard to British copyright holders is now to be complained of, not only as regards British copyright holders, but as to the same class in all countries included in the Berne Copyright Union. Canada is made a close market for their benefit, and the single compensation given by the convention for a market of five millions of reading people is the possible benefit to the Canadian author ... [who has been described as] "belonging rather to the future than to the present."[22]

Thompson argued that the terms of the convention largely favoured densely populated and highly urbanized countries such as those in Europe, but were unsuited to relatively less developed countries like Canada:

> The Berne Convention had in view considerations of society which are widely different from those prevailing in Canada. In Europe the reading population in the various countries is comparatively dense; – in Canada, a population considerably less than that of London is dispersed over an area nearly as large as that of Europe. In the cities of Europe, especially in Great Britain, the reading public is largely supplied from the libraries, while, in Canada, as a general rule, he who reads must buy. In European countries the reading class forms but a fraction of the whole population, while in Canada it comprises nearly the whole population.[23]

Howard Hunter, educator, civil servant, and author, had similar views.[24] He called the *Berne Convention* a step towards reinstating an exploitative colonial system. For him, the agreement represented the imposition of the interests and values of a few countries on others for whom its strictures were entirely inappropriate: "The Berne Convention had in view conditions of society happily very different from those prevailing in Canada. England and the other European Countries that formed this convention for their own convenience took no account of any other continent than Europe."[25] Canada's population distribution and class structure was very different, he argued, from those in the countries that negotiated the convention. Canada did not have public libraries where rural or less wealthy people could borrow books. Books, therefore, were accessible only to Canadians who could purchase them. Hunter thought that a more equitable class structure, wherein all Canadians could afford books, should be preserved:

> It is not the policy of any Canadian Legislature to reproduce here the social conditions of European Countries, with their dangerous antagonisms of classes and masses, of vast wealth and appalling destitution, of privileged intellect and brutish ignorance. It is the bound duty of the Parliament of Canada to see that under color of any international convention our social and economic conditions are not interfered with.[26]

He argued further that the convention would limit Canada's right to self-government, reimposing the strictures of the previous colonial system:

> Self-governing powers of Canada would be cut down to narrower jurisdiction than any of the Provinces of Canada had continuously enjoyed since 1847. The

present pretension really involves an attempt to re-impose upon Canada in respect of copyright ... such a monopoly or exclusive privilege as was characteristic of the old colonial system ... long since abandoned in respect of all other commodities other than books.[27]

There were economic and political incentives for the government to reverse policy: the printing and (re)publishing industry was growing strongly and was becoming more politically organized, whereas those working as authors, artists, or other creators were not as highly organized and their numbers were not increasing as dramatically.

Alongside these incentives was a set of ideas about the role of the state in the development of the country. As Owram has suggested, the Canadian government had traditionally taken a hand in guiding the development of the nation, and was generally recognized as the only body with the resources to shape society in the face of dramatic change taking place worldwide.[28] In 1889, the government began actively attempting to influence industrial development through copyright law.

1889: Copyright Challenge

In 1889, the Canadian Parliament passed a new copyright act that was radically different from the implementation bill proposed in 1888. This new bill did not simply include the domestic printing and publishing requirements that had been part of previous Canadian acts;[29] it went further to require *first or simultaneous* printing and publishing in Canada – that is, printing and publishing in Canada within one month of publication or production elsewhere.[30] Works that were not first printed and published in Canada or printed and published in Canada within a month of their publication or production elsewhere would not be eligible for the protections provided by Canadian copyright. One such protection was the right to exclude foreign reprints from importation into Canada. Furthermore, failure to meet these requirements would open the door to the granting of compulsory licences to reprint the work in Canada without permission of the copyright owner.

Because it was anticipated that this act might conflict with imperial law, provision was made for its proclamation into force by the Governor General.[31] The act received royal assent on 2 May 1889 but awaited proclamation.[32] In August that year, the Canadian government, acknowledging that the 1889 act did not conform to the requirements of the *Berne Convention,* informed the British government that the passage of the new copyright law would require the denunciation of (announcement of exit from) the *Berne Convention* on Canada's behalf.[33]

The British government was loath to allow Canada to abandon the convention, as denunciation "would involve abandonment of the policy of international and Imperial copyright which Her Majesty's Government adopted, and to which Canada assented only six years ago."[34] Denunciation, British Secretary of State for the Colonies Lord Knutsford informed Canada's Governor General in 1890, would be unnecessary since the 1889 act contravening the *Berne Convention* would not receive the necessary approval from Britain.[35]

The Canadian government continued to press for confirmation of the 1889 act in the Imperial Parliament and for denunciation of the *Berne Convention*. By 1891, with the imperial government having made no move to proclaim the act into force, a resolution was passed in the Canadian Parliament asking that the International Office of the Berne Union be notified of Canada's denunciation of the convention.[36] The imperial government responded by commissioning a report on the matter and forwarding it to Canada for consideration.[37] The Canadian government replied to the report in 1894, noting that it did not change the government's position in requesting denunciation of the *Berne Convention*:

> The Minister [of Justice] deems it unnecessary to remind your Excellency that Canada has been repeatedly assured that her continuance in any treaty arrangement of this kind would be subject to her desire to withdraw at any time on giving the prescribed notice, and, now that the policy of Canada has been so firmly established and repeatedly pressed upon Her Majesty's Government, both by Parliament and by your Excellency's advisers, he (the Minister) recommends that your Excellency be requested to remove [sic] Her Majesty's Secretary of State for the Colonies to cause such notice to be given without further delay.[38]

In the summer of 1894, Frederick Daldy came once again to North America and asked to meet with Thompson, who, however, declined the visit:

> I have nothing further to say about Copyright at present ... I regard the subject as quite past the stage of negotiation. The treatment which Canada has received on this subject is too bad to be spoken of with patience ... the policy of our Parliament was so clear, and so firmly established, that we could not make it a matter for argument.[39]

The influence of British lobbyists, and in particular the influence, stretching back to the 1870s, of Daldy, in Canadian policy making was thus curtailed. Individuals such as the president of the Canadian Copyright Association, John Ross Robertson, newspaperman, publisher, and later Member of Parliament, were heavily involved in lobbying the government on copyright questions and in helping to draft the 1889 *Copyright Act*.[40]

In an effort to force the imperial hand, the Canadian government moved in March 1894 to formally stop collecting the 12.5 percent tariff on foreign reprints, which had never been effectively collected in any case. As a result, the 1847 *Foreign Reprints Act* automatically ceased to have effect, and the provisions of the 1842 imperial *Copyright Act* preventing the importation of foreign reprints of British copyright works into Canada returned into force.[41] The *Foreign Reprints Act* had lifted the 1842 prohibition on importation of such reprints only in cases where colonial legislation adequately protected British publications. In Canada, this condition had been considered to be met by the 12.5 percent duty on foreign reprints, intended to be collected as compensation to British copyright holders.[42]

1900: *George N. Morang & Co. v. The Publishers' Syndicate Ltd.*

The 1842 provisions were deemed to have come back into effect in a 1900 judgment of the Ontario High Court of Justice.[43] The case arose when the book *A Half Century of Conflict* by Francis Parkman was imported into Canada from the United States for sale by the Publishers' Syndicate without the permission of George N. Morang and Company, who claimed to have been assigned the British copyright in the work. The Ontario High Court of Justice determined, however, that since the 12.5 percent duty had ceased to be collected (the provisions for such collection having been repealed and collection under the 1894 *Dominion Tariff of Customs Act*[44] abandoned),[45] the prohibition on the importation of foreign reprints had come back into effect and Morang would have been entitled, if its copyright had been validly registered at Stationers' Hall, to prohibit the importation of American foreign reprints of the work by a third party. It was found, however, that Morang's copyright had not been properly registered in London.[46]

THE EFFORT TO FORCE the imperial government's hand by ending the 12.5 percent duty failed. Although the 1889 *Copyright Act* had passed unanimously in the Canadian Parliament, it was never proclaimed into force by Britain.[47]

There were several problems with the act from a British perspective. The first problem was the requirement that works first published elsewhere be reprinted and republished or reproduced in Canada within one month in order to qualify for Canadian copyright.[48] British publishers saw this window as being too short, and some felt that this requirement would amount to the abolition altogether of Canadian copyright recognition of British works.[49]

Second, the act allowed the Canadian Minister of Agriculture to grant to "any person or persons domiciled in Canada" a licence to reprint copyright works in cases where foreign copyright holders had not published their works in Canada, and to prohibit the importation of other unauthorized reprints (from the United States, for example).[50] This compulsory licensing scheme would have allowed the reproduction of British books without authorization.

Further, and perhaps most important, the 1889 act was a threat to the ongoing negotiations towards an Anglo-American copyright agreement. It was still felt that such an agreement might be reached in the near future. Were the 1889 act to come into effect, American authors would be required to publish in Canada in order to obtain Canadian copyright, and the act made American authors not domiciled in Canada or British possessions ineligible for Canadian copyright.[51] The Canadian market would therefore not be freely opened to American printers and publishers under any Anglo-American agreement, making any such agreement much less palatable to the Americans. This threat to an Anglo-American treaty was the primary reason given by the British government in 1891 for its refusal to proclaim the 1889 act into force.[52] It was a concern that had coloured the British perspective on the issue for over twenty years, ever since it was cited as a reason for refusing a compulsory licensing system in 1868.[53]

For these reasons, according to some, the 1889 act was doomed from the start. Canadian publisher Samuel E. Dawson saw it as no ordinary act; it was "nothing more nor less than a Declaration of Independence." Writing to John Lowe, now Deputy Minister of Agriculture, Dawson expressed his belief that Britain could not concede Canadian independence on an act such as this one "and maintain any self-respect" because it not only asserted Canada's legislative independence but also challenged British copyright laws, imperial uniformity, and British interests.[54] According to him, the act would bring down the wrath of the powerful English literary class or, as he put it, "every man in England who holds a pen."[55] If the 1889 act were to be allowed, similar acts would follow in other colonies, breaking up imperial uniformity and the markets for British copyright works: "They know that this Bill of yours means shutting them up to their own little islands."[56] According to him, the act would thus surely be struck down by England as soon as someone tried to use its licensing provisions.[57]

Dawson's assessment of the importance of the act was accurate. The International Office of the Berne Union also highlighted the importance of the situation; a lengthy multi-part examination of the Canadian controversy was front-page news in the office's monthly publication, *Le droit d'auteur,* through the winter of 1890.[58] Continuing concern about the situation led the office to inquire with the Canadian government about the status of the act.[59]

It infuriated some members of the British government that a colony such as Canada might threaten to break up the Berne Union. Henry Bergne, who had been a British delegate to the early meetings creating the *Berne Convention,* wrote:

> An International Union has only just been accomplished, with great difficulty, and on principles which commend themselves to the civilized world. To this, Great Britain and all her Colonies are parties, with the express and unanimous consent of the latter. Is a British colony, like Canada, for the sake of their infinitesimal interest in the publishing business, or for the supposed benefit of Canadian readers, to be the first to withdraw, and so to raise a hand to destroy the Union, which comprises a population of four or five hundred millions?[60]

Bergne and others feared that if Canada were to withdraw from the *Berne Convention,* other countries would follow. A British committee studying the matter wrote that if "the interests of publishers or printers were allowed to prevail over those of authors, the lead given to Canada would not improbably be followed by other colonies, and thus the whole system of Imperial copyright would be broken up."[61]

British efforts to hold together the Berne Union were successful. There have been, in its entire history, been only six actual denunciations of the *Berne Convention:* Montenegro in 1900, Liberia in 1930, Haiti in 1943, Indonesia in 1960, Syria in 1962, and Upper Volta in 1970.[62] Each of these countries has since rejoined.[63] Mauritius also left the union, although through a declaration of non-application rather than formal denunciation.[64]

Some questioned whether Canada was truly a party to the *Berne Convention.* Howard Hunter argued that Canada was not actually a party to the convention: the 1888 bill that had originally been proposed to implement the convention had been dropped, and the 1889 act was unlikely to conform to the convention. Therefore, he observed, the Canadian Parliament had never sanctioned the treaty. Furthermore, he noted that "when any international convention affecting the Dominion is enacted into by England it is the practice for the Government of Canada to promulgate the convention by prefixing it to the next published volume of the Statutes of Canada." This, he noted, had never been done.[65] At the same time, as discussed in Chapter 4, Prime Minister Macdonald had personally assented to the convention on 10 June 1886, sending the message by telegram: "Canada consents to enter Copyright Convention."[66] The Canadian Privy Council had also confirmed the decision to assent to the *Berne Convention* on 22 June 1886. A minute of the Privy Council stating that decision was accordingly forwarded to the British government.[67]

According to the principle of responsible government, well established by the late 1880s, Canada should have been able to gain enactment of the 1889 *Copyright Act*. It was a long-established practice that British authorities did not stand in the way of Canadian bills – even those with which they disagreed.[68]

Provisions had also been made for British colonies to denounce the *Berne Convention* separately; the British government had reserved "the power of announcing at any time the separate denunciation of the Convention by one or several ... Colonies or possessions."[69] A denunciation would take effect one year from the date it was declared.[70] Although in principle this would normally have meant that Canada could be withdrawn from the agreement at any time, the power was in fact reserved to the *British* government to denounce the treaty *on behalf of* the British possessions, which, in the case of the *Berne Convention*, the British government was unwilling to do.[71] The Canadian government did not have the authority to autonomously denounce the treaty. The norms of late nineteenth-century imperialism, which would normally have given Canada more autonomy, were set aside based on British perceptions and fears related to British economic and political interests.

A number of key battles waged over competing interpretations of the new international copyright norms enshrined in the *Berne Convention* were important in determining the place of countries like Canada in the international regime. These battles took place first of all at home in Canada, but would later also be waged at the international conferences to revise the *Berne Convention*.

Domestic lobby groups that had formed following the introduction of the 1888 bill to implement the *Berne Convention* challenged what had been the dominant opinion at the time: that the convention was a good thing for Canada. As well, the critical view of the convention was advanced by several powerful politicians, foremost among whom was Justice Minister and later Prime Minister John Thompson, who lobbied Britain fiercely for the 1889 *Copyright Act*. In the House of Commons, bipartisan opposition to the *Berne Convention* included not only Thompson but also James Edgar, a key Liberal organizer in Ontario.

Views within the government bureaucracy had also shifted. Prior to Thompson's involvement in copyright, the Department of Agriculture, with Deputy Minister Joseph-Charles Taché of Quebec at the helm, had had primary control of the copyright issue. Thompson's involvement brought the more substantial legal resources and expertise of the Department of Justice into play on the issue. Views at Agriculture also shifted around the time that John Lowe became Deputy Minister of Agriculture in 1888. When Canada joined the *Berne Convention* in 1886, Lowe had been secretary of the Department of Agriculture under Taché, and had provided advice to Prime Minister Macdonald that focused on the interests of authors, who favoured joining the *Berne Convention* because of the level of international protection it would bring, to the exclusion of the printing and publishing industries, which did not favour the convention because it disallowed domestic printing and publishing requirements. After Taché's retirement in July 1888, Lowe took over as Deputy Minister of Agriculture. With the departure of this key Quebec bureaucrat, the author-centric approach lost its most important supporter within the bureaucracy. Some of the changing views at the department might have been related to Lowe's own interests; Lowe's parents had emigrated from England to Montreal, where he had owned various ultimately unsuccessful printing operations before entering the civil service.[72]

The growing intellectual engagement on copyright issues, and growing sympathy for printers and publishers within the Canadian government, led to fruitful and important debates over key issues in international copyright. On one singularly important issue, John Thompson and John Lowe disagreed. A question arose over a key interpretation of the *Berne Convention* and whether it allowed countries to require domestic printing and publishing in their copyright laws, as the 1889 act did. The issue hinged on competing interpretations of Article 2 of the convention, which stated:

> Authors who are subjects or citizens of any of the countries of the Union, or their lawful representatives, shall enjoy in the other countries for their works, whether published in one of those countries or unpublished, the rights which the respective laws do now or may hereafter grant to natives.
>
> The enjoyment of these rights shall be subject to the accomplishment of the conditions and formalities prescribed by law in the country of origin of the work.

According to one interpretation of this clause, a country could require foreign authors to submit to domestic printing requirements in order to obtain copyright in that country. According to the other interpretation, the article specifically states that a country *could not* require foreign authors to submit to domestic printing requirements.

Criticism arising from the suggestion of abandoning Canada's domestic printing requirements in its plan to implement the *Berne Convention* in May 1888 led Lowe to investigate whether it might be possible to adhere to the convention while retaining domestic printing requirements. As he prepared to take over as Deputy Minister of Agriculture, he wrote to Frederick Daldy to ask whether it would be possible to retain such requirements and still conform to the *Berne Convention*.[73] Lowe hoped to obtain Daldy's support for the 1889 bill, just as Daldy had supported and eased the passage of the 1875 *Copyright Act*. Daldy's opinion was that Article 2 was specifically drawn to *allow* countries like Canada and the United States to maintain their domestic printing and registration clauses, rather than to forbid them.[74]

Lowe therefore interpreted Article 2 to mean that it was possible to adhere to the convention while retaining the domestic printing requirements, a position that was supported by some experts. He wrote Thompson on numerous occasions, insisting on his more liberal interpretation of the convention. Thompson held that the printing requirements would have to be abandoned if Canada was to adhere to *Berne*.[75] Lowe's position was to be the one officially maintained by Britain, because to admit otherwise would be to admit that Canada, though party to the convention, was not in conformity with the treaty.[76] Although this issue was not resolved until 1896, the dominant position taken in 1889 was that, under the *Berne Convention,* accomplishment of the formalities prescribed by the country of origin alone was sufficient to guarantee protection in other countries.[77] The eventual position taken by the Canadian government was that the 1889 act did not conform to the *Berne Convention* and that denunciation was required.[78]

This battle among politicians and legal experts was crucial to settling key interpretations of international copyright norms that would be maintained for years to come. The dominance of certain interpretations was crucial not only to whether Canadian domestic printing requirements were compatible with the *Berne Convention* but also to whether American domestic manufacture provisions were. This battle would not be settled for several years, when it would be taken to the international level.

American International Copyright

In 1891, the United States passed a new copyright act, providing another front on which the Canadian government would attempt to assert copyright independence. The *Chace Act,* named for Senator Jonathan Chace, who introduced the bill, extended copyright protection, under specific conditions, to citizens of certain other countries, which were to be declared by presidential proclamation. Eligible countries included those that granted copyright to American citizens on substantially the same basis as their own citizens, and countries "party to an international agreement which provides for reciprocity in the grant of copyright, by the terms of which agreement the United States of America may at its pleasure become a party to such agreement."[79] The law further specified, in what is known as the "manufacturing clause," that, to be recognized under American copyright law, a work had to be "printed from type set within the limits of the United States, or from plates made therefrom, or from negatives, or drawings on stone made within the limits of the United States, or from transfers made therefrom," and that publication in the United States had to be simultaneous with its original publication elsewhere.[80] This meant, in effect, that works had to be printed in the United States, since it was not economically feasible to have works typeset in the United States, shipped abroad for printing and binding, and returned to the United States for sale.[81]

There was some question as to whether the United States would, under the 1891 act, be eligible to join the *Berne Convention*. As in Canada, there was uncertainty about whether the domestic manufacture requirements of the act were permissible under the international agreement.[82] The eventual conclusion was that they were not, and the United States did not become party to the convention.

Between 1891 and 1908, presidential proclamations granted copyright recognition to citizens of Belgium, France, Great Britain and its possessions (including Canada), Switzerland, Germany, Italy, Denmark, Portugal, Spain, Mexico, Chile, Costa Rica, the Netherlands and its possessions, Cuba, Norway, and Austria.[83] Great Britain and British possessions were first proclaimed to be eligible for recognition on 1 July 1891.[84] This followed assurances from British Prime Minister Lord Salisbury that "the law of copyright in force in all British possessions permits the citizens of the United States of America the benefit of copyright on substantially the same basis as to British subjects."[85]

While it was true that British copyright law protected citizens of the United States and was in force in Canada, the Canadian Department of Agriculture was not consulted on Salisbury's declaration. In a policy move that was embarrassing to the British Prime Minister because it appeared to directly contradict his declaration to the United States, the Canadian government refused to grant domestic Canadian copyright to American citizens when American copyright applications began to be received in 1891.[86] The Canadian position was that, under the Canadian 1875 *Copyright Act,* copyright was available to "any person domiciled in Canada or in any part of the British possessions or any citizen of any country which has an International copyright treaty with the United Kingdom."[87] Prior to the American act of 1891, Americans had not been eligible for Canadian copyright unless they were legitimately domiciled in Canada. For example, Mark Twain was famously denied the Canadian copyright he attempted to obtain by temporarily domiciling in Canada. The Department of Agriculture deemed his temporary visit to Canada insufficient to meet the requirement of domicile in Canadian law.[88] Americans had hoped that the 1891 arrangement might make them eligible under the second provision, made for citizens of a country party to an international copyright treaty with Britain. However, because the new American recognition of international copyright was not the result of a treaty with Britain, since no actual treaty had ever been concluded, Americans were considered ineligible for Canadian copyright under that provision.[89] In August 1891, the Department of Justice advised the Department of Agriculture: "In view of the provisions of the United States Copyright Act of March last and its proclamation by the President, I am to say that the enactment referred to does not constitute an International Copyright Treaty: and that, therefore, citizens of the United States cannot register under our Act."[90] Thus, the Department of Agriculture arrived at the policy of rejecting American copyright applications completely unaware of Salisbury's declaration to the Americans, which it received only in January 1892.[91]

By November 1891, the Canadian position had been noted by policy makers and newspapers, and in January the International Office of the Berne Union published its first summary of the situation in *Le droit d'auteur.*[92] Americans were indignant. The *Philadelphia Telegraph* declared: "As Canada has no literature, no authors to protect, no writers who could profit by copyright privileges in America, the Government has everything to gain and nothing to lose by continuing the old state of affairs under which Canadians can steal from Americans as much as they please."[93] In fact, Canadians remained bound by British copyright, which protected American works in Canada without requiring domestic printing,[94] and American publishers were actually well aware of this.[95] Nevertheless, in December the US State Department demanded explanations and threatened that the Anglo-American arrangement might have to be abandoned: "The Declaration of Lord Salisbury and its acceptance by the United States Government constitutes an international arrangement which this Government desires to observe and maintain in its entirety, and I should much regret if any untoward circumstance should constrain its abandonment or essential qualification."[96] Over the next several years the Canadian government was pressed to respond to this situation but held to its position, maintaining that American citizens were ineligible for Canadian copyright under the *Copyright Act* of 1875.[97]

British control over Canadian copyright continued. Although it could refuse to grant copyright to Americans under domestic legislation, the Canadian government had no control over whether Americans were entitled to *British* copyright protection in Canada. British copyright continued to have effect in Canada, and would for another thirty years, so the Canadian refusal to grant copyright protection to Americans had little effect. British law granted copyright to Americans publishing works in Canada.[98]

A period of turmoil within the Conservative Party raised the profile of the copyright issue once again after 1891. In 1892, after Prime Minister Macdonald's death and the resignation of his successor, John Abbott, due to ill health, John Thompson became prime minister.[99] Despite also being plagued by ill health and encumbered by the duties of his new office, Thompson continued to press the British government on copyright issues, arguing extensively for Canadian copyright sovereignty and recounting Canada's long and tumultuous history with the issue. The question of copyright sovereignty became a high priority. Whereas the Canadian government under Macdonald had kept a low profile on copyright, Thompson placed copyright sovereignty on the agenda when he visited the Colonial Office in London in November 1894, calling it a matter that had "now reached what I consider a critical stage."[100] A meeting between Thompson and other interested parties was arranged in London; as a result of the meeting and the discussions that were to follow, Toronto's *Globe* reported, "a decided step is likely to be taken in the settlement of this vexed question."[101]

Shortly after, however, the 1889 Canadian copyright act lost its most important supporter. With the copyright issue still on the agenda and his trip to London not yet complete, Thompson suffered a fatal heart attack at Windsor Castle on 12 December, after being sworn in to the Queen's Privy Council.[102] His body was brought back to Canada on the HMS *Blenheim,* its sides painted black, and a state funeral was held at Halifax.[103] The *Globe* noted the particular loss that would be felt by Canadian copyright interests.[104] No other Canadian prime minister would give the issue as much thought and salience as Thompson had.

Britain's policy of imperial copyright continued in force. The American copyright policies of 1891 had finally enabled British subjects to obtain copyright protection in the United States, although only on the condition that British works be manufactured in that country. The economic necessity of holding Canada to the Berne Union as a part of the Anglo-American negotiations had diminished, but the policy had firm roots.

In Canada, *economic* nationalism and a copyright policy that echoed the National Policy pushed *cultural* nationalism, associated with the primacy of authors' rights, to the perimeter of copyright policy making. This shift depended in part on the level of organization displayed by printing and publishing groups, as well as the depth and passion of Thompson's and Lowe's positions on the issue. Thompson, a lawyer and judge by profession, had abandoned the ideal of British unity and reframed the copyright issue as one of Canadian sovereignty.

The Conservative Party had followed the lead of the Department of Agriculture under Deputy Minister Lowe and Agriculture Minister John Carling, establishing a position critical of strict adhesion to the *Berne Convention* that would last until the late 1920s.[105] In contrast, the Liberals would adopt a different position after coming to power in 1896, and by 1910 would begin to advocate conformity with the *Berne Convention*.

Diplomatic Conference in Paris: 15 April to 4 May 1896
In succeeding years, Canada's copyright rebellion advanced to the international
stage. Although the first revision of the *Berne Convention* had been expected
to take place between 1890 and 1892, the conference was in fact held in 1896.
By this time, Luxembourg, Monaco, Montenegro, and Norway had joined Great
Britain, Germany, Belgium, Spain, France, Haiti, Italy, Switzerland, and Tunisia
as a part of the Berne Union, and an International Office had been established
in Berne.[106] The 1896 conference saw broad international representation, with
fourteen non-member countries present for the meetings.[107]

Canada and other British colonies were represented by British delegates. No
Canadian adviser was sent in 1896 nor to the next revision conference in 1908.
This was somewhat unusual for the time; Canada had a High Commissioner
posted in London who was tasked with representing Canadian interests in international commercial negotiations. By 1884, the High Commissioner had gained
the status of full plenipotentiary in some international negotiations, and the
first treaty concluded by independent Canadian negotiation had been signed
in 1893.[108] In fact, a Canadian adviser had, as early as 1881, accompanied British
negotiators at the Anglo-American copyright negotiations.[109] It is likely, however,
that the Canadian government's insistence on denunciation of the *Berne Convention* would have made it difficult for a Canadian representative to attend the
conference; it would have placed both Canadian and British delegates in awk-
ward and conflicting positions in relation to the Berne Union and to each other.

Most of the changes made to the *Berne Convention* at the 1896 conference
were relatively minor. They included an alteration to the definition of "publishing" (it was made explicit that "published" meant "published for the first time");
the addition of a right of translation, expiring if not put to use within ten years,
to the list of creators' rights; and a prohibition on the unauthorized reproduction of serial stories published in newspapers or periodicals (the 1886 text had
allowed the reproduction of articles in newspapers and periodicals unless it was
expressly forbidden).[110]

Two issues arose at the 1896 convention that would be of great significance
to the Canadian situation: the rights granted to non–Berne Union creators, and
the formalities required in the country where protection is claimed. First, the
1896 text enabled creators from outside the union who first or simultaneously
published their works in a *Berne Convention* country to have their copyrights
recognized in the same way as citizens of the member states.[111] Although the
1886 text had granted a similar right, it was worded in such a way that the right
was actually granted to the publisher resident in a member country, rather than
to the author.[112] This article was rewritten in 1896 based on widespread agreement that copyright should be granted not to the publisher but to the author.[113]

This revision caused great controversy in many countries, and although it was little noted in Canadian newspapers, no country was more affected than Canada.[114] The revised text confirmed that American authors could, without actually signing on to the *Berne Convention*, secure their copyrights throughout all *Berne Convention* countries by first or simultaneously publishing their works in Canada or another member state. The fact that Canada had no representative at the 1896 conference meant that key Canadian interests were overlooked. The importance of this change to Canada does not appear to have been foreseen by the British government or by the British delegates. It was a point not fully covered in the instructions to the British delegates, who felt it unobjectionable at the time.[115]

Second, the interpretation of Article 2 of the *Berne Convention* – on whether countries could require foreign creators to submit to domestic formalities and printing requirements – had to be clarified.[116] This article was felt by most to be clearly worded to mean that submission to formalities in the country of origin would be sufficient for protection throughout the countries of the Berne Union.[117] The fact that the convention had made it possible to gain international copyright through a single process in the country of origin was, in fact, considered to be one of the greatest accomplishments of the Berne Union.[118] Britain, however, was unable to accept this interpretation of Article 2, as it would have been tantamount to admitting that Canada, a British dominion, did not comply with the tenets of the *Berne Convention*.[119] Britain declared that it would not be able to sign if the dominant interpretation of Article 2 was incorporated into the new text of the agreement.[120] Its signature, however, was highly desired by the rest of the conference delegates, who expressed their willingness to "meet in a conciliatory spirit" the concerns of the British delegation. A compromise was reached: the dominant interpretation of Article 2 was included not in the actual text of the 1896 revision but in a separate additional declaration of interpretation that Britain did not sign.[121] As a result, Britain did sign the convention, and exchanged ratifications on behalf of itself and all its colonies and possessions on 9 September 1897.[122]

Canadian Member of Parliament James Edgar, who in 1886 had unsuccessfully pressed the government for further discussion of the *Berne Convention* before it agreed to join the convention, was now speaker of the House under the Liberals and Prime Minister Wilfrid Laurier, who had come to power in 1896. By 1910, the Liberals would support Canadian adhesion to the *Berne Convention,* but at this stage they did not. Edgar argued that the government should oppose the Paris revision, advising Laurier as follows:

> It cannot be denied that for the Canadian Government to give its sanction to an important amendment to the Berne Convention, such as is contained in the Act

of Paris last summer, would properly be held to be a withdrawal of the request so emphatically made for the denunciation of the original Treaty.

It would seem reasonable to explain this position to any of the countries interested, and to express the hope confidently entertained by the Canadian government, that at an early date legislation may be had in Ottawa which will remove the friction existing with reference to the delay in the approval of the Act of 1889, and which may render it unnecessary for Canada to persist in her request for the denunciation of the Berne Convention.[123]

Canada's opposition to the new text of the agreement had little effect, however: Britain signed and ratified the convention on its behalf.

Pressure continued on the Laurier government to reverse its position on the 1889 act, and eventually it did begin to recognize that the act and accompanying denunciation were unlikely to receive the necessary approval of the British government. In 1900, therefore, the Liberals proceeded to pass a new *Copyright Act*.[124] Although this new act was not intended to indicate that the Canadian arguments regarding copyright sovereignty raised by the 1889 act were in any way being dropped, it did not provide a compulsory licensing system for Canadian publishers and was therefore in some ways a retreat from the earlier position on the 1889 act.[125] The 1900 act left in place the domestic printing requirements of the 1875 act.[126]

Diplomatic Conference in Berlin: 14 October to 14 November 1908

The next diplomatic conference to revise the *Berne Convention* took place in Berlin in 1908. By then, Denmark, Sweden, and Japan had acceded to the convention.[127] Twenty-one non-member states were represented at the conference, including the United States and Russia.[128] The United States again expressed its sympathies with the efforts of the Berne Union but its continuing unwillingness to join the convention.[129]

The Berlin conference resulted in a number of substantive changes to the text of the *Berne Convention*. Mandatory copyright protection was extended to architectural works, choreographic works, and pantomimes; translations, adaptations, and arrangements of music were deemed to be the subject of a copyright independent of the original works, with translation rights now being granted in full to creators;[130] and a limited form of protection was extended to photographs.[131]

The term of copyright protection was also extended. A term of protection of the life of the creator plus fifty years was accepted in principle, although it was not made mandatory. Nationals of countries with shorter terms would not be able to claim the full term of protection in other countries.[132]

In addition, several new rights were created as a result of growing industries based on new technologies, including a non-mandatory right in the reproduction of musical works onto phonograph records and piano rolls. The wording of the agreement was broad enough to allow it to be met by systems of compulsory licensing. Copyright protection was also extended to films.[133]

The most significant change from a Canadian perspective was the adoption of the principle of absence of formalities: it was deemed that member countries should not make copyright protection dependent on compliance with certain formalities, such as domestic manufacture or printing, or registration of a work in a central registrar.[134] This principle meant that Canada's domestic printing and registration requirements would contravene the 1908 version of the *Berne Convention*.

Ricketson and Ginsburg have observed that the 1908 conference sowed the seeds of a number of future challenges that would be faced by the *Berne Convention:*

> The most notable was the threat posed to authors' rights by the emergence of new technological means of reproducing and disseminating their works, and the growth of powerful interest groups engaged in the exploitation of these new technologies. In this regard, the gramophone recording and the cinematographic film were the harbingers of other more startling developments which were already in train, such as sound and visual broadcasting. A second problem for the future was that of developing countries which were in the position of "users" rather than "producers" of copyright material. Although their time was still to come, their concerns had been clearly anticipated, even at this early stage, in the Japanese proposal [rejected at the conference, that translations into the Japanese language should be allowed].[135]

Britain signed the revised convention on 13 November 1908 on behalf of all its colonies and possessions.[136] Two days later, the lead British delegate, Henry Bergne, who had fallen ill during the proceedings, passed away at his hotel in Berlin.[137] Bergne was one of the few delegates who had been present since the inception of the *Berne Convention;* he had been an active British delegate at all the conferences since 1885, the year the convention was drafted. Despite retiring in 1902, he had remained a part of the British delegation and, as a member of the British Society of Authors, had served as chairman of the general committee and a member of the management and copyright committees.[138] He had been one of the strongest voices opposing the Canadian bid to denounce the convention, and his death heralded a new approach to imperial copyright that, several years later, finally resulted in a greater degree of independence in copyright for Canada and the other British colonies.

Although Canada was considered a party to the 1886, 1896, and 1908 texts of the *Berne Convention* as a colony of Britain, the Canadian government refused to allow Britain to ratify the 1908 text on Canada's behalf.[139] The primary difficulty lay with the convention's requirement, beginning with the 1896 revision, that countries grant national treatment to citizens of non–Berne Union countries. This problem would be resolved only through an additional protocol to the convention in 1914 that permitted union countries to restrict the protection offered to non-union countries in cases where the latter did not offer adequate protection to the former.[140]

Colonial Influence on the Revisions

Britain's control over Canada's international copyright commitments remained firm throughout the 1896 and 1908 diplomatic conferences. Canada, without its own voice at the meetings, without control over all of the copyright laws that were in effect domestically, without the autonomous ability to denounce the *Berne Convention*, and without the ability to refuse its signature or (in 1896) ratification, was dragged along in international copyright affairs.

Canada, however, did exert some influence over the positions that could be taken by the British at the 1896 and 1908 meetings. Although Canadian legislation was regulated by imperial control, the British government was, for its part, influenced by colonial pressures.[141] British negotiators were caught, due to the imperatives of imperial copyright, in a multi-level game that required the negotiation of solutions acceptable not just to the other parties to the convention and to the public at home but also to colonial governments.[142]

In his instructions to the British delegates to the 1896 conference, Lord Salisbury noted that many of the proposed changes to the convention that had been presented for discussion by various countries prior to the 1896 conference were acceptable to Britain but would not be acceptable to the colonies. Salisbury was greatly concerned that, if too many changes were made, Canada or other colonies might leave the convention altogether. This limited the types of proposals and changes that the British delegates could support. Proposed changes on which Britain and the colonies had opposing positions in 1896 included changes to Article 2 regarding formalities, but also other items, such as the inclusion of photographs as protected works (Britain protected photographs under its copyright law but was uncertain whether this protection applied in the colonies) and the seizure of counterfeit works.[143]

In his instructions to the British delegates to the 1896 conference, Lord Salisbury therefore wrote that they should not sign the revised convention:

Whilst Her Majesty's Government find themselves in agreement in principle, either partially or wholly, with many of the proposals formulated by the French Administration and the International Bureau, they do not consider the amendments of the original Convention which are suggested to be of any very great or pressing necessity. For the purpose of procuring any amendments in the existing Convention in this direction, it would not be worth while to run any risk of rendering the secession of any Party to the Union more probable ...

The Berne Convention was only obtained after great and protracted labour. Her Majesty's Government attach great value to its provisions, and anything tending to a break up of the Union would be regarded by them as a misfortune.

It is, therefore, especially desirable that nothing should be done which would tend to induce any of the British Colonies to retire from the Union.[144]

A declaration to this effect was made at the conference by British delegates: "Great Britain attaches the greatest value to the Convention of Berne, and does not wish to run the risk of any of her Colonies withdrawing from the Union, as might happen if she were at the present moment to accept definitively any material changes in the text of the Convention."[145]

Only because the other delegates were willing to sequester controversial changes in a separate protocol, allowing Britain to sign the main agreement while remaining aloof from the protocol, could Britain sign the revised text of 1896.

The situation was similar in 1908, when Britain once again took the position that, in light of colonial copyright issues, it would be unable to implement any changes to its own copyright law that might be necessary to implement the new 1908 text of the *Berne Convention*. British delegates were sent to the conference with the following declaration:

It is needful, however, to state clearly that there exist for Great Britain very serious difficulties in connection with the subject of copyright, especially as regards harmonizing the interests of the mother country with those of the great self-governing Colonies.

Unless it should be found possible to remove these difficulties, His Majesty's Government would not probably find themselves in a position to propose to Parliament the legislation which would be necessary in order to give effect to any considerable alterations in the Convention of Berne.[146]

Thus, although Britain retained a rather firm grasp on Canadian copyright, Canadian and colonial issues restricted Britain's ability to negotiate. This made certain major alterations to the *Berne Convention* impossible, constraining the movement of international copyright norms.

Key interpretations of the international copyright norms remained some-what in flux, and this flexibility ensured both that imperial copyright unity was maintained and that the Canadian government, and those of other countries, did not abandon the Berne Union. The British interpretation of Article 2 during the 1896 meeting served the primary purpose of holding together international and imperial copyright. By refusing to concede that Canadian domestic printing requirements were disallowed under the new international norms, and that Canadian law and those of other countries fell outside the union, Britain pre-vented the recognition of a direct conflict. It would eventually be accepted that domestic printing requirements were not compatible with the convention, and Canadian law would be brought in line with this understanding in the end. In the meantime, British knowledge and expertise in interpreting the *Berne Convention* preserved a veneer of international and imperial unity.

CHAPTER SIX

The New Imperial Copyright, 1895-1914

FOLLOWING PRIME MINISTER John Thompson's death in 1894, the government's position on copyright moderated, leading to a number of attempts at compromise. The Canadian government was invited to send a representative to London to continue copyright discussions. Deputy Minister of Justice Edmund Newcombe was sent in August 1895 and prepared a report on his findings, with input from imperial parliamentary counsel.[1] He suggested to the imperial government that Canadian officials were prepared to be more flexible than previously, and he proposed a compromise solution that would involve some modifications to the 1889 *Copyright Act* that, Newcombe felt, would not alter its basic principles.[2] Nothing came of the draft bill that he prepared, however.[3]

Representatives also came to Canada. Hall Caine, a representative of British authors, spoke to publishers as well as to Prime Minister Mackenzie Bowell, Justice Minister Charles Tupper, and a subcommittee of the Privy Council. They reached a compromise solution that involved more limited licensing provisions.[4] This plan was dropped, however, in part because of concerns that it did not conform to the *Berne Convention*.[5] The secretary of the British Society of Authors, G.H. Thring, also visited Canada to consult with government officials. Various solutions were discussed but were also not adopted.[6]

Other efforts to find an acceptable compromise were made. James Mavor, the president of the Canadian Society of Authors, testified before the British government and suggested a compromise that would have allowed, under imperial legislation, colonial legislators to pass acts preventing the importation of British and other colonial editions where a Canadian had a licence to reproduce the work. This solution was not adopted, although several attempts at modifying imperial legislation were made.[7]

The Liberal Party, in power since 1896 under Prime Minister Wilfrid Laurier, eventually moved away from its insistence on denunciation of the *Berne Convention*, recognizing that the imperial government was unlikely to concede.[8] The party's most vocal supporter of the 1889 *Copyright Act* and denunciation of the *Berne Convention,* James Edgar, died in 1899,[9] and in 1900 the party passed a short series of amendments to the 1875 *Copyright Act.* Whereas the 1875 act had allowed a publisher who had obtained a licence from the copyright owner to publish a British work in Canada to exclude the importation of foreign copies from foreign countries *except* British originals, the 1900 act would also allow the licensee to apply to the Minister of Agriculture for an order that would prohibit *all* imports of the same work, thus reserving the Canadian market entirely for the licensee.[10]

A licence could be applied for only in the case of works first published in any part of the British dominions other than Canada, and therefore could not be used to prohibit originals first published in France, for example. The 1900 act was therefore much less useful to Quebec publishers, who continued an un-authorized trade in reprints of French books until 1906, when a Quebec Superior Court decision (see below) confirmed the illegality of unauthorized reprints following a campaign in the press, initiated by a Canadian representative of French authors, decrying such practices.[11]

The amendments of 1900 instituted the agency system of publishing in Canada, allowing an English-Canadian firm to acquire and enforce a monopoly on the importation of a British work. This system encouraged the establishment of branch plants of foreign publishers in Canada, where Canadian publishers, often operating as subsidiaries of foreign publishers, imported works for sale in Canada or printed them locally. This system would dominate Canadian publishing up to the 1960s.[12]

The Conservatives feared that the new legislation would be seen as a conces-sion of Canada's position on copyright sovereignty that had been so strenuously maintained since 1889.[13] The Liberals argued that the bill did not touch on the constitutional issues, and the fight for Canadian copyright sovereignty con-tinued, albeit quietly.[14] When Justice Minister David Mills visited London in 1901, imperial authorities argued that Canadians would have great difficulty achieving copyright reciprocity with the United States if they abandoned im-perial copyright and the *Berne Convention.* In response, Mills declared that, to his government, "legislative independence ranked higher than the profits of Canadian authors."[15]

1900: *Carte v. Dennis*

As the battle for legislative independence continued, imperial copyright re-mained in force in Canada. The D'Oyly Carte Opera Company was the English owner of the copyright in the musical *The Pirates of Penzance,* the copyright having been registered under imperial copyright law at Stationers' Hall in

London. D'Oyly Carte took legal action after the Regina Musical Society sold tickets and performed *The Pirates* at the Regina Town Hall. The defendants, members of the Regina Musical Society, argued that, since the *British North America Act* of 1867 had conferred on the Canadian Parliament the power to legislate on copyright, imperial copyright no longer applied in Canada. However, the precedent set in *Smiles v. Belford* and *Routledge v. Low*[16] was followed in determining that imperial copyright law was still in force in Canada, and the Northwest Territories Supreme Court ruled in favour of the D'Oyly Carte Opera Company in *Carte v. Dennis*.[17]

1902-03: *Graves v. Gorrie*

Although imperial copyright applied in Canada to literary and dramatico-musical works, the same was not true of pictures, drawings, and photographs. Henry Graves and Company held the copyright in a picture of a bulldog on a Union Jack, titled "What We Have We'll Hold," published in London in 1896 and registered at Stationers' Hall under the *Fine Arts Copyright Act* of 1862.[18] This act conferred copyright in pictures, drawings, and photographs, these not having been covered previously under British copyright. Whereas other British copyright acts explicitly extended to the British dominions, the *Fine Arts Copyright Act* conferred copyright on British subjects or residents within all the dominions but did not include the colonies in its area of protection.

Graves filed for an injunction in the Ontario Court of Justice Common Pleas Division against George T. Gorrie, a Toronto printer and publisher, to restrain Gorrie from making, printing, publishing, selling, or exposing to view any copies, prints, reproductions, or representations of "What We Have We'll Hold." The case was ultimately appealed to the Judicial Committee of the Privy Council in London, which found that Gorrie had not infringed the rights of the copyright holder. They concluded that to obtain copyright in a painting, drawing, or photograph in Canada, it was necessary to comply with Canadian law. This gave rise to questions regarding conformity of Canadian copyright legislation with the *Berne Convention*, since some works that were agreed, under the *Berne Convention*, to receive copyright protection were not covered by Canadian copyright.[19]

1904: *Black v. Imperial Book*

Around the same time, the question arose as to whether the 1877 Ontario Court of Appeal's decision in *Smiles v. Belford* had not been in effect overruled by subsequent decisions of the Judicial Committee of the Privy Council relating to the *British North America Act* of 1867. This question was tested when a

Canadian defendant, the *Imperial Book Company*, imported copies of the *Encyclopaedia Britannica* from the United States to sell in Canada. The owners and licensees of the copyright, Adam and Charles Black and the Clark Company, respectively, sought to restrain such importation and sale. Ultimately, the Supreme Court of Canada affirmed the Ontario Court of Appeal's decision, which followed *Smiles v. Belford*, finding that *Smiles v. Belford* had not been overruled and that imperial copyright law continued to have effect in Canada. The Supreme Court, however, not being bound by the precedent of *Smiles v. Belford*, refused to rule on whether that case had been correctly decided on the question of whether the Canadian Parliament, "having been given exclusive jurisdiction to legislate upon the subject of copyright, may not, by virtue of that jurisdiction, be able to override Imperial legislation antecedent to the British North America Act, 1867."[20]

1906: *Hubert v. Mary*

The continued force of the imperial *Copyright Act* with regard to books, as well as the applicability of the *Berne Convention* in Canada, was affirmed again in 1906. Unauthorized reprinting ("piracy") had receded to some extent in English Canada following the various decisions that affirmed the continuing effect of imperial law and following the US *Chace Act* in 1891, but it was slower to ebb in Quebec.[21] In 1893, Jules Mary, a French citizen, published in France his novel titled *Tante Berceuse*, conforming to French law. Montreal publisher Barthelemy Hubert then published the book in Canada without authorization. This was brought to light in 1903 in a bulletin of the Montreal chapter of the Paris-based Chamber of Commerce.[22] Louvigny de Montigny, a Quebec lawyer, author, and publisher – and later in life journalist as well as the principal translator for the Canadian Senate – took an interest in the case and helped to found the *Association des journalistes canadiens-français* (AJCF) that year, heading its committee on authors' rights.[23] The AJCF, with the support of the French *Société des gens de lettres* and the Canadian-French organization *La Canadienne* of Paris, mounted a campaign in the press, arguing that the *Berne Convention* was indeed in effect in Canada and that stemming the piracy of French works would help create opportunities for Quebec authors.[24]

Not everyone in Quebec agreed with the AJCF campaign. The *Théâtre national* of Montreal challenged the idea that French works were protected by copyright in Canada, arguing that under the *Copyright Act* of 1875, the presentation of French plays without permission was lawfully permitted.[25] The Montreal daily *Le Journal* argued that ideas could not be owned in the same way that one might own a piece of land, and that newspapers should be permitted to reprint freely, in the interest of the public good. If Canadian theatres were forced to pay for French "masterpieces," the theatre argued, theatres would be forced to present second-rate Canadian works. Canadian literature, it argued, was still in its infancy.[26]

In the legal proceedings, Mary argued that *Tante Berceuse* was protected in Canada under the *Berne Convention*, whereas Hubert argued that the work was not registered in Canada under Canadian law, that the *Berne Convention* was not in force in Canada, and that, in any case, the *Berne Convention* granted rights in Canada only under the same conditions available to the citizens of Canada – on condition of printing or publishing or reprinting or republishing and depositing the work in Canada. The Quebec Superior Court, however, affirmed by the Court of King's Bench of Quebec, concluded that the *Berne Convention* was indeed in force in Canada, that under the convention the completion of formalities in France was sufficient to confer Canadian copyright without printing or publishing or reprinting or republishing the work in Canada, and that imperial copyright law continued to have effect in Canada.[27]

1906: *Life v. Rose Publishing*

Also in 1906, the Ontario Divisional Court ruled in a case involving the re-printing as postcards, by Toronto's Rose Publishing, of photographs published in *Life* magazine. The court noted that, since the 1868 decision of the House of Lords in *Routledge v. Low*, foreign authors seeking to obtain copyright through-out the British dominions had vacationed for a few days in one of the dominions while their work was published. The court noted that the requirement of tem-porary residence was open to question, as the 1854 case *Jefferys v. Boosey*[28] no longer had binding authority. It was also noted that since 1891, it was no longer necessary to be an American citizen or resident in the United States in order to obtain copyright in that country. Noting "the tendency of modern judicial deci-sions to extend the operation of Imperial statutes to aliens," it was deemed unnecessary to reside, even temporarily, in the British dominions in order to obtain copyright under the imperial *Copyright Act* of 1842, so long as the work was first or simultaneously published in the United Kingdom.[29] The court held that Charles Dana Gibson, the photographer, had a valid copyright in the photographs despite being an American citizen and not (even temporarily as a visitor) a British subject.

BY 1911, THE CANADIAN population, now including the burgeoning new prov-inces of Alberta and Saskatchewan, had grown to about 7 million, an enormous expansion of 70 percent.[30] Printing, publishing, and the arts had expanded even more quickly. The number of people employed in the printing and publishing industry had expanded by 200 percent, from about 5,800 to about 18,000, and the number of authors and artists by 150 percent, from 600 "artists and literatures" in 1881 to about 1,500 in 1911.[31] New technologies also brought new copyright interest groups. Emile Berliner and his sons Herbert and Edgar had established a gramophone industry, setting up their first retail outlet on Catherine Street in Montreal at the turn of the century; they had acquired exclusive rights to gramophones and discs under a Canadian patent in 1897.[32] Berliner, who has been called the father of the Canadian recording industry, began pressing records in Montreal in January 1900.[33] The company prospered, adding a recording studio and a factory in 1906, and was joined by competitors Columbia and Edison.[34] In film, Andrew and George Holland of Ottawa had become Eastern agents for Edison's Kinetoscope, and in 1894 had built a Kinetoscope parlour, hosting the first commercial screening of moving pictures in North America.[35] Canadians imported equipment and films, and film distributors rented to travelling exhibitors before the first permanent film theatres were established around the turn of the century. The first permanent theatre in Canada was established in Montreal in 1906.[36] The Allen theatre circuit was established in 1907 and by the 1920s had become the largest theatre chain in Canada.[37] These would prove to be important interest groups in debates over Canadian copyright.

In 1909, the Liberal government of Prime Minister Laurier created a new Department of External Affairs. The department, which reported directly to the Prime Minister after 1912, had little policy-making responsibility initially, remaining more of a "filing and post office" until the mid-1920s.[38] Nevertheless, the office was kept in the loop on matters of international copyright by the Governor General's office, and eventually became involved in Canadian international copyright affairs.

In 1910, the British government wished to proceed with ratification of the 1908 text of the *Berne Convention,* following the 1909 report of Britain's Law of Copyright Committee, which recommended ratification and advised the government on the necessary legislative revisions.[39] Aware of Canada's difficulties with the *Berne Convention,* however, the imperial government felt it necessary to consult the colonies before proceeding with the legislation.[40] The date set for the exchange of ratifications was 9 June 1910, and Britain hoped to have the dominions on board by that date.[41] In January, Laurier instructed Joseph Pope, head of the new department as Under-Secretary of State for External Affairs, to consult with Agriculture Minister Sydney Fisher regarding the upcoming conference on copyright.[42] A suggested date in April was not acceptable to Fisher, whom Canada hoped to send, so the conference was postponed until the middle of May, when he would be available.[43] Fisher's presence at the conference was very important, as Canada was the greatest obstacle to Britain's ratification of the 1908 revision. The challenges of Canadian copyright were foremost among those that the British hoped to solve through the 1910 conference.

The Imperial Copyright Conference was convened on 18 May 1910 and met several times in May and June. Because its recommendations were not finalized until the last meeting, on 30 June, Britain missed the 9 June deadline. Exchange of ratifications among other countries proceeded without Britain.[44]

Representatives from Newfoundland, Australia, New Zealand, India, and the South African colonies (Cape of Good Hope, Natal, and the Orange River Colony) attended the Imperial Copyright Conference. Sydney Buxton, the president of the British Board of Trade, presided. The impetus for the conference, he said, came from Britain's desire to ratify the 1908 revision of the *Berne Convention*. He stressed two points: (1) that Britain wished to maintain uniformity of copyright throughout the Empire, and (2) that Britain wished to promote uniformity of copyright throughout the "principal nations of the world."[45] He said that Britain was working on a draft copyright bill that would ratify the 1908 revision, and the British government wished to know what might be required by the dominions for this project to go ahead.

From the start, Canadian concerns were pre-eminent. After his introductory speech, Buxton referred immediately to Fisher, asking for his opinion on how matters might proceed.[46] Fisher, a man of elegant manners who had also represented Canada at other international conferences, was quick to express his country's desire for independence to legislate on copyright.[47] He pointed to Canada's geographical proximity to the United States, which made the Canadian situation different from that of the other colonies, and cast doubt on the idea that uniform legislation might be acceptable throughout all the British dominions: "Our position there is so peculiar that it may be that our difficulties are not shared by either the Mother Country or the other self-governing Dominions, but there are very great difficulties in the way of uniform legislation."[48]

Australia and New Zealand took an opposing view. Australia was represented by former Governor General Hallam Tennyson, son of the famous British poet Alfred, Lord Tennyson. Hallam Tennyson, a strong imperialist, advocated uniform British legislation that would apply to all the colonies. "A great opportunity is now before our Empire to stand in union before the world," he said.[49] He disputed any claim of Canadian independence to legislate over copyright, and disagreed with an approach that would see the colonies legislate independently on the matter, fearing that this would make uniform legislation impossible. Instead, he proposed that the dominions should have the power to repeal British legislation, but that repeal should come with a strong penalty, namely, that international recognition would cease to be granted to authors in a dominion that stood outside the imperial copyright system.[50] The delegate for New Zealand, Hall Jones, generally agreed with the Australian proposals.[51]

The South African colonies, India, and Newfoundland stood closer to the Canadian position. The delegate for the South African colonies, Richard Solomon, agreed with Fisher in expressing his government's wish that the colonies should pass their own acts.[52] India, represented by Thomas Raleigh, expressed a general willingness to go along with the imperial copyright project, but also wanted to see space given for independent colonial copyright provisions. Raleigh noted that India had many special interests of its own, and drew particular attention to its cultural differences from England and its "indigenous forms of literature and drama which have never come within the purview of our laws at all, and to which it would probably not be expedient to apply the elaborate code of your European law."[53] When asked whether India had had any difficulty in the past under imperial copyright and the *Berne Convention,* he replied that there had been no great difficulties.[54] The delegate for Newfoundland expressed few specific views regarding what that colony wished the future direction of imperial copyright to be. At the same time, he contributed generally to the discussion, especially as it related to Canada.

After Fisher explained at some length the Canadian predicament with regard to its copyright relations with the United States, it was agreed that an acceptable solution would be for Britain to somehow abstain from Article 6 of the revised *Berne Convention* (the article extending protection to authors of non–Berne Union countries).[55] It was recognized, however, that Article 6 had been included in the *Berne Convention* as a mandatory item, from which reservations were not allowed. Special permission from the other countries of the union would be required.[56]

Many delegates wished to discuss the details of the proposed imperial copyright bill that would implement the *Berne Convention* revisions, and were dismayed to find that no draft bill had been prepared as a basis for discussion.[57] On 14 June, a month after the first meeting, a draft was presented, and it was discussed in detail during the remaining days of the conference. Several points proved to be contentious: the length of the term of copyright protection, formalities, and the protection of various types of works, including architecture, "music-hall turns," pantomimes, gramophones, works in periodicals, and photographs. Of particular interest from the Canadian perspective was a discussion of what protection would be given to foreign authors who were resident in a country of the Berne Union.

In 1910, many countries were operating on a term of protection fixed at a certain number of years from the date of copyright registration. Canada's term of copyright protection, for example, was set at twenty-eight years from the date of copyright registration, with a possible extension of fourteen years.[58] The 1908 revision of the *Berne Convention* set the term as the lifetime of the author plus fifty years, although this provision was not mandatory.[59] Life plus fifty years was considered too long a term by a number of delegates. The president of the British Board of Trade confessed to being "rather shocked" when he saw this proposed term,[60] and doubted that the British House of Commons would accept it.[61] Fisher also found the term long but was prepared to go along with it, as was India.[62] Tennyson, the Australian delegate, argued, however, that "authors and artists feel very properly that their own creations are more real property than anything else, and the longer you can give them freedom from legalised plunder the fairer."[63] It was Hall Jones, the delegate for New Zealand, who took the strongest stance. He strongly objected to a term of life plus fifty years and blocked the adoption of a unanimous resolution on the point.[64] As a result, the resolutions of the conference were said to be "generally agreed" rather than unanimous; they included a resolution that a term of life plus fifty years should be adopted, but that this recommendation was conditional on the enactment of a public interest clause to ensure that "the reasonable requirements of the public be met as regards the supply and the terms of publication of the work, and permission to perform it in public."[65]

The need for a new method of measuring the term of copyright protection was linked to the principle, also mandated by the 1908 revision of the *Berne Convention,* that no formalities, such as copyright registration, should be required as a condition of copyright protection.[66] Canadian law still required copyright registration and measured the term of protection from the date of registration. Fisher predicted that the Canadian government would choose to continue with the registration requirement insofar as it applied to domestic copyright holders, but was willing to abandon it in the case of foreign copyright holders.[67] This concession was enough to enable the conference to resolve that formalities such as registration should be abandoned as a condition of copyright, although optional registration, to be used only in cases of copyright infringement, might be retained.[68]

The conference also passed a number of resolutions that set standards for protection of architecture and gramophones.[69] As well, delegates discussed the extent to which the new imperial copyright act would apply to other new types of works, including copyright coverage of music-hall turns (performances at a variety theatre, popular through the nineteenth and early twentieth centuries[70]), pantomimes,[71] works in periodicals, and photographs.

The conference produced a number of resolutions and agreements. It resolved to ratify the 1908 revision of the *Berne Convention* with as few reservations as possible, but that "no ratification should [...] be made on behalf of a self-governing Dominion until its assent to ratification has been received; and provision should be made for the separate withdrawal of each self-governing Dominion."[72]

It was also agreed that the new imperial *Copyright Act* would extend to a British dominion only "if declared by the Legislature of that Dominion to be in force therein, either without modifications or additions, or with such modifications and additions relating exclusively to procedure and remedies as may be enacted by such Legislature."[73] Any modifications or additions would be valid only insofar as they related to authors resident in the British possession and works published therein.[74] At the same time, it was agreed that self-governing dominions should be allowed, if they signed on to the new act, to withdraw and repeal it later on.[75]

Flexibility was adopted such that the self-governing dominions would, as an alternative, be allowed to pass their own copyright acts, as long as these were "substantially identical" to the imperial act.[76] In cases where a self-governing dominion failed to do so, it could expect to lose copyright recognition throughout the British Empire;[77] however, the imperial copyright acts would continue in force in any such dominion until they were repealed by the dominion.[78]

It was further agreed that Britain would endeavour to ratify the 1908 revision of the *Berne Convention* in such a way as to enable the Canadian government to limit the extent to which Canadian copyright was extended to Americans:

> The Conference is of opinion that, if possible, it should be made clear on ratification that the obligations imposed by the Convention on the British Empire should relate solely to works the authors of which are subjects or citizens of a country of the Union, or *bonâ fide* resident therein; and that in any case it is essential that the above reservation should be made in regard to any self-governing Dominion which so desires.[79]

It was agreed that the self-governing dominions would be at liberty to recognize or not, through orders of the Governor-in-Council, foreign copyrights; copyright in the dominions would no longer be extended to foreign countries by the British government. This would leave the Canadian government at liberty to extend recognition to American copyright holders or to refuse it.[80]

The British government had feared that the conference might open the difficult constitutional questions surrounding colonial legislative independence, and that the uniformity of copyright laws throughout the Empire might be lost as a result.[81] The British were pleased with the outcome of the conference, however. Secretary of State for the Colonies Lord Crewe felt not only that important questions had been usefully discussed but also that the unity of imperial and international copyright might, as a result of the conference's recommendations, be preserved:

> His Majesty's Government desire to place on record their very great appreciation of the care with which this important subject has been discussed by the representatives of the self-governing Dominions. It is their confident hope that in removing the restrictions on the powers of Dominion Legislatures which have hitherto existed with regard to Copyright they will in no way have affected the unity of Imperial and International Copyright, but will have secured that it shall owe its continuance to the concerted action of the Dominion Parliaments.[82]

Newspapers made general note of the conference as it was taking place, but few details were released to the public.[83] A simple eight-page summary of the meeting and its recommendations was all that was released.[84]

As Buxton had outlined at the beginning of the 1910 Imperial Copyright Conference, the new set of arrangements was not intended to mark the end of the imperial copyright system; rather, its purpose was to maintain two things: uniformity in imperial copyright and uniformity among "principal nations of the world." Thus, it can be said that at this conference the Canadian government traded its bid to denounce the *Berne Convention* for a form of copyright sovereignty. According to the new deal, this sovereignty was linked to (1) compliance with certain copyright norms agreed upon at the conference and thereafter written into the 1911 British copyright law that granted Canada that sovereignty; and (2) an expectation that the Canadian government would implement the *Berne Convention*.

In October, Toronto's *Globe* proclaimed in a front-page article: "Canada to Control Its Copyright Law." Fisher had announced the forthcoming introduction in the House of Commons of a bill that would repeal British copyright legislation in Canada and take hold of Canada's newfound copyright sovereignty. He told the *Globe* that the Imperial Copyright Conference had given Canada "complete emancipation" on matters of copyright.[85] Regarding ratification of the 1908 Berlin revision of the *Berne Convention,* he said that he would do so "in a modified way," likely adopting the term of life plus fifty years but not going so far as to do away with the requirements of registration and domestic printing: "The Berlin convention does away with formalities, that is to say, what would be in Canada registration and printing in Canada. I am not prepared to say that I will agree with that part of the convention, and in adhering to the Berlin convention I would do so in a modified form."[86]

A similar article ran in *The Times* of London. The article noted that British copyright would be recognized upon registration in Ottawa, and that Canadian printing and binding would be required.[87] This led to a flurry of action on the part of British interests, the British Board of Trade, and the Colonial Office, expressing concern that British publishers would now be required to manufacture their works in Canada in order to obtain copyright there.[88] These concerns would be addressed after the Liberal government's Speech from the Throne.

Following Fisher's comments to the *Globe,* copyright was included in the government's agenda when the parliamentary session began, in November 1910, with the Speech from the Throne, which stated: "In view of the Imperial Conference on Copyright, at which unanimous conclusions were reached in favour of harmonious legislation on this subject throughout the empire, a Bill to revise and consolidate the law on copyright will be submitted to you."[89] The Liberal position, favouring imperial copyright uniformity and conformity with the *Berne Convention,* lasted into the mid-1920s and can be contrasted with the more skeptical position of the Conservatives. In April 1911, the new office for External Affairs replied to British concerns through the Governor General, with copies of the proposed bill, and the Governor General gave assurances that the Canadian bill would give complete reciprocity to British subjects and residents, via order-in-council, without condition.[90] The bill was introduced on 26 April.[91]

The government had intended to pass the Canadian act concurrently with the new imperial *Copyright Act.*[92] This was especially important given that international copyright recognition for Canada would depend on Canada's act being "substantially similar" to the British act. The latter was amended substantially, however, and its passage was delayed, which in turn delayed and ultimately halted the progress of the Canadian act.[93]

The British *Act to Amend and Consolidate the Law Relating to Copyright* was passed on 16 December 1911, not long after the Canadian election of September 1911 brought the Conservatives, under Prime Minister Robert Borden, to power. It was set to come into force on 1 July 1912.[94] Several days after its passage, the Colonial Office forwarded to the dominions a letter from the British Board of Trade with the act enclosed. The letter stated:

> The Copyright Act has been framed in accordance with the Resolutions of the Imperial Conference, so as to enable legislation to be enacted by the Dominions in such a manner as not to impair, but to extend, the existing uniformity of copyright law throughout the Empire. This object will be attained in the case of any Dominion which declares the Act to be in force, or which passes legislation granting substantially identical rights to British authors. In any other case, however, there will be considerable danger that the mutual interchange of the benefits of copyright not only with the United Kingdom but also with other parts of the Empire and with foreign countries may be seriously impaired, and the Board

express their earnest hope that each Self-Governing Dominion may find it possible to adopt one or another of the two alternative courses indicated above which will ensure uniformity of Copyright Law throughout the Empire, enable the Empire as a whole to accede to the Berlin Convention, and give effect to the unanimous resolutions of the recent Imperial Copyright Conference.[95]

It was hoped that the legislation could be enacted by the dominions on the same day it came into force in Britain.[96]

The Conservatives were in no rush to implement the imperial copyright policies agreed to by the former Liberal government. The government's reply to Britain simply noted that it was too late in the Canadian parliamentary session to introduce legislation.[97] When the idea of reintroducing the bill from the previous session had been raised in the House of Commons in early December, the British act had not yet passed.[98] The session ended in late January 1912.

Although both the Authors' and Composers' Association of Canada and the (British) Incorporated Society of Authors would urge the adoption of the new imperial *Copyright Act* in succeeding years, up to 1919,[99] and although Prime Minister Borden drew the attention of both his Ministers of Justice and Agriculture to the petition of the Incorporated Society of Authors in this regard,[100] this was not the path that they would follow.

Elements of the British act were objectionable to Canadian officials. First, it appeared that Britain would renege on some of the resolutions made at the Imperial Copyright Conference, including its commitment to a reservation with regard to Article 6 of the revised *Berne Convention*. Canadian officials feared that if Britain did not make such a reservation, there was little chance that a reservation made by the Canadian government alone would be accepted by the Berne Union countries.[101] The Governor General telegraphed the British Secretary of State for the Colonies, warning that if Britain reneged on its commitments, Canadian denunciation of the *Berne Convention* would necessarily follow.[102]

Britain's response to the Canadian concerns seemed to be negative initially, from both the government and the press; *The Times* mocked the idea that "all the countries of Europe may somehow modify the International Union for the sake of Canada."[103] Nevertheless, within eleven days of Canada's protest, a confidential dispatch was sent by the British Foreign Office to Paris, Berlin, Rome, and Berne, asking whether their governments would accept a reservation by Britain limiting the rights guaranteed by British dominions only to works where authors belonged to a country of the Berne Union. The dispatch noted that it was unusual to grant rights to countries that stood outside of a treaty. It asked that inquiries on the matter be made in a semi-private way so that Britain might be able to proceed with legislation. Britain threatened to withdraw from the *Berne Convention* altogether if the reservation was not allowed:

> If the answer is unfavourable, it may be necessary for His Majesty's Representative at Berne to give notice of withdrawal from the Copyright Union of Berne. As His Majesty's Government are extremely anxious to avoid this step, and to ratify the revised Convention, they earnestly hope that the principal signatory states will accept a reserve on the lines indicated.[104]

As a result of this consultation, Britain acknowledged that it would be impossible to carry out its promise to ratify the revised *Berne Convention* with a reservation on Article 6 regarding copyright recognition to countries outside the Berne Union. Instead, an additional protocol to the convention would have to be adopted. A draft protocol was circulated to the countries of the Berne Union, and Britain proposed that it would go ahead with its own ratification of the revised convention, while indicating again to the other governments of the Berne Union that if the additional protocol were not accepted, Britain might find it necessary to withdraw from the convention.[105]

After a number of additional minor modifications, the text of the protocol was agreed to.[106] By November 1912, Britain was writing anxiously to ask for Canada's urgent response concerning acceptance of the protocol.[107] Borden, who as Canada's prime minister also acted as Secretary of State for External Affairs from 1912 to 1920, recommended that the Privy Council accept the protocol with the minor revisions suggested by the British Board of Trade, which was done.[108] The Governor General sent notice of Canada's acceptance in December 1912; the draft protocol was circulated by the International Office of the Berne Union on 26 December 1912[109] and was unanimously accepted by the countries of the union. In January 1914, the International Office invited members of the union to a meeting in March in order to sign the protocol. The protocol was signed at the Federal Palace of Switzerland in Berne on 20 May 1914.[110]

In the meantime, Britain had gone ahead and ratified the revised *Berne Convention* on 14 June 1912 without a reservation regarding Article 6, and had extended British copyright protection to the countries of the Berne Union and to the British dominions except for Canada, Australia, New Zealand, South Africa, and Newfoundland, which had neither adopted the 1911 act nor passed substantially similar legislation.[111] This meant that works copyrighted in Canada would not be recognized in Britain under the 1911 act, a view that was confirmed in 1914 by British Law Officers who considered the question (see Chapter 7).[112]

Canada's international relations were regulated by the fundamental question of imperial unity and how it would or would not be maintained. The Canadian government's willingness to submit to the new arrangement of imperial copy-right unity may have been influenced in particular by views within the new Canadian Department of External Affairs. With a total staff of fourteen, the department was led by Joseph Pope, who, as Hillmer and Granatstein note, "had a limited view of its responsibilities and of the country's possibilities."[113] Pope had no aspirations for Canada to achieve independence. Rather, he commented that "Canada by herself is not a nation, and I hope I may never live to see her one."[114] The departmental legal adviser, Loring E. Christie, was also an imperialist who favoured a foreign affairs policy centralized in London with tangible input from Canadians.[115] Moreover, Canadian relationships and networking ties with other countries were not yet established. Although Canadians had common copyright interests and concerns with the other British colonies involved in the 1910 Imperial Copyright Conference, no known networking or policy dis-cussions had taken place with them ahead of that conference. The ability to hold such discussions would have depended on the capacity of the other colonies to conduct international or intercolonial relations, and most did not have as great a capacity as Canada in this regard. Thus, Britain acted as a hub, with each colony isolated from the others and communicating primarily with Britain.

The configuration of interest groups within Canada had changed, with grow-ing numbers of authors and other creators, as well as growing numbers of people employed in the printing and publishing trade. Canadian interest groups were in the dark about the 1910 Imperial Copyright Conference, however. The secrecy surrounding the conference enabled the state to reformulate Canadian inter-national copyright policy without public input.

International meetings and international organizations can have a socializing effect on diplomats, "educating" or influencing them to adopt the policy prefer-ences of the hegemonic core.[116] In 1910, Agriculture Minister Fisher built upon, but also altered, the vision of copyright sovereignty held by John Thompson and his contemporaries. Fisher's actions and the 1910 Imperial Copyright Conference contributed to a new common sense of how Canada would act as an independ-ent state – as a "civilized" rather than rebellious one – a state associated with the power and prestige of the British Empire.

CHAPTER SEVEN

Copyright "Sovereignty," 1914-24

FOLLOWING THE SIGNING OF the protocol to the *Berne Convention* on 20 May 1914, the British government was anxious for Canada to enact copyright legislation conforming to the imperial copyright framework and the 1908 revision of the *Berne Convention*. British officials drew the Canadian government's attention to the fact that the protocol was now in place, asking whether it could now see its way clear to legislate. They also, perhaps in an attempt to put additional pressure on the Canadian government, drew attention to the opinion of British Law Officers who had been asked to assess Canada's eligibility for copyright recognition in Britain and the rest of the Empire under Britain's new copyright act of 1911. In the Law Officers' opinion, Canadian copyright could not be recognized under this act; since neither it nor substantially similar legislation been adopted in Canada, protection under the act had not been extended to Canada. Britain nevertheless offered, if Canada accepted the opinion of the Law Officers, to extend temporary protection to Canada in the interim, until Canada was able to pass the requisite legislation. This offer was made especially in view of the fact that, as the 1842 and 1886 British copyright acts were still in force in Canada, British works continued to be protected in Canada.[1] The Canadian government delayed its response to this offer, taking the position that the matter was under continuing consideration.[2] The outbreak of the First World War in August 1914, several months after the signing of the additional protocol to the *Berne Convention,* meant that it would be some time before further legislative action was undertaken in Canada.[3]

Canadian ties to Britain remained strong; Prime Minister Borden and opposition leader Wilfrid Laurier immediately declared Canada's readiness to stand alongside Britain in the war, and anglophones and Quebecers both were enthusiastic about joining Britain and France overseas.[4] Some saw the war as a way to forge closer imperial ties and to highlight the importance of broader international goals over and above parochial nationalisms.[5] At the outset, Borden subscribed to the vision of an autonomous Canada working in full partnership with the Commonwealth of Nations. A coordinated partnership between British dominions, he felt, would offer the best of both worlds: nationhood and empire.[6]

Unified policies would prove difficult to maintain, however.[7] Imperial unity in copyright policy would decline over the coming years. The war paved the way for Canadian independence in foreign policy and independent statehood; a greater measure of independence was expected in exchange for Canada's enormous war effort.[8]

When the war ended, the dominion premiers were granted the right of direct communication with the British Prime Minister and representation at the 1919 Paris Peace Conference, with a signature alongside that of the British Empire. Canadians fought successfully to send a separate representative to the Paris Peace Conference, to sign the *Treaty of Versailles* that ended the war, and to have membership in the League of Nations.[9] Borden began to think that, "in the end, and perhaps sooner than later, Canada must assume full sovereignty."[10] Canada was far from an independent actor on the international stage, however. Its signature at Versailles came after that of the British Prime Minister, who signed for the entire British Empire, including Canada.[11]

Copyright was not entirely forgotten during the war. In February 1915, the Canadian House of Commons passed a motion that "stricter measures should be taken for the carrying out of the Berne convention relative to copyright."[12] As well, the question of suspension or cancellation of enemy-owned copyrights was raised, but does not appear ever to have become a major issue in Canada, where none or few enemy copyrights were registered or transferred during the war. No special provisions with regard to enemy copyright were put in place.[13]

During the last months of the war, the Canadian government underwent restructuring. The Department of Agriculture was streamlined in 1918 and many of its odd jobs were transferred to other departments. Responsibility for patents, trademark, and copyright was transferred to the Department of Trade and Commerce. The staff of the Patents, Trade Marks, and Designs office was transferred as well, and George O'Halloran, Deputy Minister of Agriculture and Commissioner of Patents, became Solicitor of Patents and Copyright in the Department of Trade and Commerce.[14]

Between 1914 and 1922, partly to meet the demands of a new Canadian nationalism, and partly in response to the feeling that American films did not adequately portray Canadian military heroism during the war, more than thirty Canadian film production companies were established. Most produced a couple of films; Ernest Shipman's *Back to God's Country* (1919) was a great success, others less so.[15] In 1924, the Motion Picture Distributors and Exhibitors of Canada, funded and directed by the Motion Picture Producers and Distributors

Association of America in New York (otherwise known as the Cooper Organization) and by American film distributors, was formed to defend the American motion picture industry's interests.[16] Canadian broadcasting industries also began to take root during this time. In 1919, radio station CFCF in Montreal received the first broadcasting licence in Canada, and other stations were licensed throughout the 1920s.[17] Radio stations were not required to pay royalties for the use of copyright works until the new broadcast right was added to Canadian copyright law in 1931.

Canada's burgeoning creative industries faced American competition in a number of areas. By the 1920s, imported American magazines such as *Ladies' Home Journal* and *Saturday Evening Post* had swamped the market. For every $100 spent on American magazines, only $1 was spent on Canadian ones. Canadian magazine publishers demanded protection in the form of higher tariffs on imported American magazines.[18] American radio stations broadcast across the border, reaching all the populated areas of Canada, while smaller Canadian radio stations reached only part of the Canadian audience. The Canadian National Railway's cross-country radio network provided only three hours of national programming per week by 1929. Production of Canadian films, which had experienced a boom after the First World War, declined, and the Canadian Allen theatre chain was bought by Famous Players of Hollywood.[19] Concerns in these areas would lead to Canadian cultural nationalism and a variety of projects to support Canadian communication systems and the arts. Copyright policy at this time reflected both the loosening connection to Britain and the more general drive to protect the Canadian publishing industry and Canadian creators.

A few domestic, as well as foreign, interest groups lobbied the Canadian government on copyright concerns in the years between 1910 and 1918.[20] First among these was the (British) Incorporated Society of Authors, which pressed for retention of Canada's imperial ties.[21] In Quebec, the primary group lobbying on copyright issues was the *Association des journalistes canadiens-français* (AJCF), which was formed in Montreal in late 1903. It was joined by the French authors' association, the *Société des gens de lettres de France,* France's *Chambre de commerce française,* and the French Canadian organization *La Canadienne* of Paris in calling for recognition of the *Berne Convention* in Canada.[22]

With the end of the war in November 1918, Britain returned to the task of prompting the Canadian government to legislate on copyright. Alfred Milner, the new British Secretary of State for the Colonies, wrote to Canada's Governor General in April 1919, noting that Canadian creators were no longer eligible for protection in other British dominions, and that British creators were deprived in Canada of the additional rights that had been conferred by the British

Copyright Act of 1911.[23] The British were anxious that the Canadian government should re-establish reciprocal copyright relations with the rest of the dominions, and wished to take steps to ratify the 1908 revision of the *Berne Convention* on behalf of Canada.[24] In response, Canadian officials sent copies of a copyright bill that had been introduced in the Senate in March, referred to as "Bill E."

Bill E was intended to bring Canadian law into conformity with the *Berne Convention* and was, to a large extent, modelled on the imperial *Copyright Act* of 1911 and on the copyright acts of other nations that adhered to the *Berne Convention*.[25] The British Board of Trade thought that the bill offered sufficient protection to British subjects to justify the issuance of a British order-in-council giving reciprocal protection to Canadian copyright holders, but felt that it would not meet the requirements of the revised *Berne Convention,* primarily because of its provisions on formalities: Bill E required a copyright holder to meet any formality requirements in the country of origin, something disallowed under the revised *Berne Convention.*[26] The Board of Trade further noted that Canada was the only dominion that had not yet ratified the revised convention; by this time, Newfoundland, Australia, and South Africa had declared the imperial *Copyright Act* of 1911 to be in force.[27] New Zealand had enacted a separate *Copyright Act* in 1913.

The Canadian government responded attentively to the British concerns regarding Bill E. Although the Department of Trade and Commerce was anxious to pass the bill – the Deputy Minister wrote to a colleague that without a new bill Canada was "an outlaw among the copyright nations of the world"[28] – the bill was postponed to the next parliamentary session, and the government sent word to Britain that, "before again introducing a Bill respecting Copyright, the various points set forth in this memorandum of the Board of Trade will receive most careful consideration."[29]

Other considerations were also cited when the bill was postponed. Senator James Lougheed, who had introduced the bill, explained that it had come up against a great deal of opposition from interest groups that wanted to add domestic printing requirements, and from Canadian authors who were concerned that the bill would not pave the way for adequate copyright protection of their works in the American market.[30]

By 1921 Canada was still growing fast. Whereas population growth around the world had slowed as a result of famine, pestilence, and the First World War, Canada's population had grown another 22 percent, to about 8.8 million.[31] In 1921, those employed in the printing and publishing industry totalled about 26,000, an increase of 40 percent from 1911, and the number of authors and artists had increased by 30 percent, to 2,000.[32] The gramophone company set up by Emile Berliner and his sons at the turn of the century had prospered, and beginning in 1916 Berliner introduced a series of Canadian recordings in English and French on the His Master's Voice (HMV) label in an effort to reduce its expenditure on royalties for American recordings. It also established the Compo Company in Lachine, Quebec, in 1917, to manufacture records.[33] By 1920, most of the Berliner Gram-o-phone Company's records were recorded and pressed in Canada.[34] This caused tension with the American Victor Talking Machine Company, whose royalties from Berliner were reduced as a result. By 1921, Herbert Berliner had resigned from the Berliner Gramo-o-phone Company to concentrate on Compo's manufacture of records for other labels – advertising especially to American companies that they could reduce customs costs by pressing their discs in Canada – and the HMV series was replaced with Victor recordings.[35] Compo produced, along with foreign recordings and records for radio broadcast (advertisements, religious or political messages, sound effects, and station identifications), a number of anglophone Canadian records through-out the 1920s, and was prolific in its francophone productions up to 1959.[36] In 1924, Victor acquired controlling interest in the Berliner Gram-o-phone Company, which became the Victor Talking Machine Company of Canada.[37] Royalties for the reproduction of songs and music in gramophone recordings were not yet required under Canadian copyright, an issue that would be addressed in years to come.

The Canadian Authors' Association was formed in 1921 and met for the first time in March, just after the introduction of the next copyright bill in February (see below). The association was formed in a large part because of concerns expressed by Canadian author Stephen Leacock that Canadian authors did not understand the complexities of copyright or their rights. Future Prime Minister William Lyon Mackenzie King, also an author, was among those invited to the meeting, from which those present "came away with a thorough knowledge of the situation, after Louvigny de Montigny took them through the background of copyright in Canada up to the present time. It was a long after-noon session."[38]

De Montigny had helped found the *Association des journalistes canadiens-français* in Montreal in 1903, and had led its Committee on Authors' Rights, campaigning for recognition of the *Berne Convention* on behalf of France's authors in Canada. Many members of the *Association des journalistes canadiens-français* formed a French-language section of the Canadian Authors' Association, the *Société des écrivains canadiens,* in 1921.[39] In 1922, de Montigny also became the Canadian representative for France's *Société des gens des lettres,* a position he would hold for over thirty years.

Canadian songwriters in particular lobbied the government for new legisla-tion. They had found a niche writing patriotic songs during the war. Many complained because, under the old Canadian *Copyright Act,* they were not entitled to royalties when their songs were reproduced on phonograph records and piano rolls at home, in England, or in the United States.[40]

Other organizations representing copyright interest groups were also formed. The Canadian Copyright Association continued to be active into the 1920s,[41] and was joined by the Magazine Publishers Association of Canada, formed out of the Magazine Section of the Canadian National Newspapers and Periodicals Association in 1922 and representing publishers of ten or fifteen general-interest commercial magazines, including *Maclean's* and the *Canadian Magazine.*[42] The Publishers' Section of the Toronto Board of Trade (renamed from the Wholesale Booksellers' Section of the Toronto Board of Trade in 1911) became active in copyright issues.[43] The Authors' and Composers' Association was established in 1919 to represent songwriters' rights, with songwriter and music publisher Gordon V. Thompson as its first president.[44] The Canadian Manufacturers' Association and the Toronto YMCA continued to be involved in copyright lobbying, and even the Kiwanis Club took a position.[45] A few noted individuals became involved in the copyright debates, including Canadian author Arthur Stringer.[46] All of these groups would be important in the upcoming debates over a new Canadian copyright law.

Views on copyright would not divide clearly along provincial lines. The Members of Parliament who were most vocal in supporting strict adhesion to the *Berne Convention* were Quebec and francophone MPs, but other Quebec politicians, as well as politicians from the rest of Canada, wished to see compulsory licensing provisions incorporated into Canadian law and a less strict interpretation of authors' rights under the convention.

1921: *An Act to Amend and Consolidate the Law Relating to Copyright*

In February 1921, the National Liberal and Conservative Party government under Prime Minister Arthur Meighen introduced a new copyright bill.[47] Justice Minister Charles Doherty argued in the House of Commons that Canada was, due to the present state of its copyright laws, "a sort of outsider in the general community of nations which have interested themselves in the subject of copyright."[48] The bill's first stated purpose, according to Doherty, was "to make our law conform to the provisions of the Berne Convention and similar laws in other countries."[49] A significant portion of the bill reproduced the wording of the imperial *Copyright Act* of 1911.[50] Similar concerns that Canada was "lagging behind all up-to-date nations" were expressed in the Senate.[51]

Doherty noted that international pressure was being brought to bear on Canada to change its copyright laws – from Britain and the other parties to the *Berne Convention,* and particularly from the authors of France.[52] Britain's Society of British Authors, Playwrights, and Composers, the British Book Publishers' Association, the Music Publishers' Association of Great Britain, and France's *Syndicat français pour la protection de la propriété intellectuelle* had become quite active in calling for new legislation.[53]

The Canadian government wished to make a distinction in the way it treated nationals from countries of the Berne Union and nationals of the United States. Under the new bill, therefore, copyright was granted only to British subjects, residents in British dominions, and citizens or subjects of countries adhering to the *Berne Convention*.[54] None of these categories included the United States. Doherty argued: "It is not possible to treat in the same way [as authors of the Berne Union] authors of the United States, because that country does not form part of the Copyright Union."[55] The bill also provided, however, that should conditions change, or should the United States join the Berne Union (something that Doherty did not expect to happen soon[56]), the Canadian law could be easily extended by order-in-council to the United States[57] – that is, the law could be extended, through a certificate granted by the minister administering the act, to countries granting rights "substantially the same basis as to its own citizens or copyright protection substantially equal to that conferred by this Act."[58] Under this provision, the United States would, in 1924, be granted copyright protection under the Canadian act.

Even when extended to American authors through a certificate, there would still be differences in the way it applied to countries outside the Berne Union, including the United States. Compulsory licensing in serial works would apply to all such countries. As of 1924, the compulsory licensing provisions for books would also apply only to countries outside the Berne Union, including the United States.

There had been a great deal of controversy over Canadian attempts to include domestic printing requirements in Canadian legislation and whether such requirements were permissible under the *Berne Convention*. It was now acknowledged throughout the union that such provisions were not permitted under the convention. The National Liberal and Conservative Party government nevertheless felt compelled to include such requirements so that Canadian printers and publishers could remain competitive with the Americans.

The Meighen government continued to favour protectionist policies reminiscent of the National Policy, and even the Liberals, who returned to power in December 1921, would campaign on a policy of "less protection if necessary but not necessarily less protection."[59] Canadian manufacturers, including book manufacturers, were in favour of protectionism.[60] Unionist MP John Allister Currie argued: "The United States by their legislation have attracted a great deal of the world's book printing, and we must do something to keep the printing of the works of our own authors in Canada. That is what we are legislating for."[61]

The 1921 bill contained a somewhat novel compulsory licensing provision. On occasions where a copyright owner did not print a work in Canada, a licence to print the work in Canada could be granted by the Minister to anyone who applied.[62] The licensee, who was required to pay a royalty to the copyright holder at a fixed rate set by the Minister, would then have the sole right to print and publish the book in Canada for five years. These provisions were a compromise that fell short of the full domestic printing and publishing requirements that had long been in place.[63]

Many argued that these provisions contravened the *Berne Convention*. Conservative Fernand Rinfret of Quebec, who sat on the Special Committee of the House of Commons that considered the bill and who was also a member of a writers' association in Canada, argued, along with other MPs, that the compulsory licensing clauses contravened the *Berne Convention* by taking away a creator's ownership and control of the work, and that, were those clauses passed into law, they would have to be removed later anyway in order to conform to the convention.[64] It was argued that protection of the creator was the whole purpose of copyright law and the *Berne Convention,* and that the interests of creators should therefore take precedence over other interests in the legislation.[65]

Many, including future Liberal Prime Minister Mackenzie King, supported giving the creator full control over the product of his or her work.[66] Some feared that if compulsory licensing clauses were enacted, Canada would become "one of the most important countries in the world that will be beyond the pale of that law – the pale of the Union."[67] Senator Charles-Philippe Beaubien asked: "Are we willing to be in that position? For my part I would be very sorry. Is Canada going to be a piffling country, able to steal from any author in the whole world who may have a work of value?"[68]

Further criticism of the bill appeared in the official publication of the International Office of the Berne Union itself, *Le droit d'auteur.*[69] This article, brought before the Senate, warned about the inclusion of formalities in the bill, and seemed to take the view that the compulsory licensing provisions could be reconciled with the *Berne Convention* only "by straining a point."[70] Some senators warned that *Le droit d'auteur* should not be taken as authoritative in its statements, arguing that the publication served merely as a newspaper.[71]

Despite such criticism, officials with the Department of Justice felt that the licensing provisions would meet the requirements of the *Berne Convention.*[72] They argued that, under the proposed provisions, copyright was not *denied* to those copyright holders who did not print in Canada. Rather, copyright holders would still own their copyrights; they would simply be required by the government to allow their works to be printed in Canada by an applicant who would pay a fee set by the Minister. The officials argued that all property was subject to restrictions in the public interest:

> Is it an unfair thing to say to the author: Now that we are extending to you this special protection, we think that we ought at the same time to have present to our minds the interests of the Canadian people in connection with that publication. In the work there is the author's intellectual effort; there is also the printer's and publisher's material work. Now what we think we have achieved [in this bill] is to have done something to enable a Canadian to take part in that material work, at the same time giving full compensation to the author for the use of the intellectual work.[73]

Further, Doherty argued that "the public" contributed greatly to the profits available for a work. Printers and publishers contributed by printing and publishing it, the public purchased it, and, according to Doherty, authors ought not say, "You must think of nobody else but me in regard to that work and to all the copies of it, although other people contribute to produce the copies; nobody is to have any consideration from Parliament except me, the author." This, he argued, was not an attitude that would "preserve sympathy or gain it for the authors."[74]

Canadians were no longer dealing with simply British opinion on Canadian copyright; the International Office of the Berne Union disseminated opinions around the world not only through its official publication, *Le droit d'auteur,* but also through general correspondence. Doherty, in his belief that the licensing clauses would comply with the *Berne Convention,* relied on a letter of opinion from the International Office, in which it was argued that the licensing clauses did not contravene the convention.[75] This view conflicted with the earlier opinion published in *Le droit d'auteur.*[76]

Doherty argued that it would be impossible to pass a bill at all without these concessions to Canadian printers.[77] His plan was to pass the provisions, and, if they were found to contravene the *Berne Convention,* he would come back to the House to make any changes necessary.[78]

Compulsory licensing clauses were also included for serial publications – such as stories published in several parts in the daily or weekly editions of newspapers and magazines – where the foreign copyright holder had refused Canadian publishers a licence to publish the stories. Because the *Berne Convention* explicitly prohibited the reproduction of serials without the consent of the copyright holder, these provisions applied only to copyright holders from countries outside the Berne Union, particularly American copyright holders. They were a response to the problem of American magazine publishers who, because they sold copies of their magazines in Canada, would refuse to allow Canadian magazines to publish the same content, even in the case of Canadian authors who first published their work in American magazines. According to one MP, "one magazine after another in Canada has gone into bankruptcy simply because the publishers could not get past this impediment put in their way."[79] The value of these licensing clauses would be evidenced not in the issuance of compulsory licences but in the fact that foreign publishers would negotiate with Canadian publishers for simultaneous printing and publishing of short stories and serial fiction in Canadian publications; without the licensing clauses, the Canadian market was thrown in with the American market when authors sold their rights to American publications.[80]

The second major change introduced in the 1921 bill involved compulsory licensing for gramophone recordings. Because Canada's earlier laws had not provided rights over gramophone recordings, gramophone companies were free to record and produce recordings without payment to the copyright holder. The 1921 bill required a royalty of two cents per disc (and four cents if the disc was printed on both sides) to be paid by gramophone companies to the copyright holder.

The rate to be paid to copyright holders was very much influenced by the rate being used in the United States. Doherty reminded members of the House who argued for the lower rate preferred by gramophone companies that Canadian creators should not be deprived of benefits equivalent to those available in the United States, since the recognition of Canadian creators under US copyright rested on assurances that American creators had as great a protection in Canada as they had in their country.[81] The two-cent rate was therefore retained, despite concerns that it might put Canadian gramophone companies out of business, and despite concerns that most of the royalties from such a system would be paid to American copyright holders.[82]

Canadian copyright had long had registration requirements, and the bill continued to provide for registration, making it, however, optional. Registration was no longer a necessary step to obtaining copyright; rather, it would now act more narrowly to provide evidence of copyright that could be used in court, and it was necessary in certain cases for claiming damages for copyright infringement. Registration was made non-compulsory in order to be compatible with the British system and to comply with the *Berne Convention*.[83] This provision reflected the arrangement struck at the Imperial Copyright Conference of 1910, where it was agreed that formalities such as registration would be abandoned as a condition of copyright, although optional registration, to be used only in cases of copyright infringement, might be retained.[84] In reply to some who were concerned that the bill's registration requirements might contravene the *Berne Convention,* James Lougheed suggested that the registration system included in the bill was "a great improvement on the Berne Convention. They will probably copy this at the next convention."[85]

The option of operating outside the *Berne Convention,* and thereby maintaining domestic printing requirements as the Americans did, was not seriously entertained by Parliament. In fact, this idea was raised only once, in the middle of the Senate debates on the copyright bill. Conservative Senator Wellington Bartley Willoughby mused: "There is another aspect which has occurred to me ... which I have never heard discussed publicly. What advantage is Canada actually going to derive from adherence to the Berne Convention?"[86] Willoughby went on to point out that the Canadian government, now able to legislate independently on copyright, was absolutely free, as was the United States, to make individual agreements with any country of the world on copyright, "even if we went absolutely outside the terms of the Berne Convention."[87] "There may be," he continued, "in adherence to the Berne Convention some advantage which is not apparent to me; but I rather think that we in Canada, a country that has not a great many authors or a large reading public, overrate the advantages to ourselves of adherence to the Berne Convention."[88] He further noted that Canadian authors did not have a large international audience, and what audience they did have was concentrated in Great Britain, the United States, and Canada.[89] He did not pursue this point, however, and in his closing comments joined the others in calling for measures to ensure that Canada's copyright act would conform to the *Berne Convention.* His question was neither answered nor raised again.

A final unusual feature of the bill was that it was set to come into force upon proclamation of the Governor-in-Council rather than immediately upon receiving royal assent. The purpose of this was to allow time after its passage for negotiations to be entered into with Britain and the United States. This would allow officials to confirm that the new act gave both countries sufficient copyright recognition to receive reciprocal protection from them, and to confirm that Britain deemed the act sufficiently in conformity with the revised *Berne Convention* to certify Canadian ratification of the treaty.[90]

Liberal MP Rudolphe Lemieux, who had served as Canada's postmaster general from 1906 to 1911, raised a point during the debates that would become very important in the next chapter of Canada's relationship to the *Berne Convention.* He asked whether a Canadian representative would be sent to the International Office at Berne or whether Canada would continue to be represented by British representatives. He noted that, under the international postal convention, Canada had its own representative.[91] This was a matter that, Justice Minister Doherty admitted, had not yet been addressed. He suggested, however, that the 1908 convention, which provided that Britain would adhere to the convention on behalf of Canada, could probably be given an updated interpretation such that Britain's adhesion would involve Canada's being directly represented as "one of the countries members [sic] of the union."[92] This may have been the first point at which independent representation at the Berne Union was contemplated, an idea that grew out of experience with the Universal Postal Union.

1923: Legislation Amended

By 1923 the copyright issue was still not settled; parliamentarians now called it "the most contentious, the most controversial subject that has ever been before the Parliament of Canada," a subject that had "probably occasioned more friction in the parliament of Canada, both in colonial days and afterwards under self-government, than any other subject with which we have been confronted."[93] Copyright was a subject fraught not only with conflict but also with confusion and misinformation. The most basic questions, such as whether or not Canada was a party to the *Berne Convention,* had no clear answers; some legislators contended that Canada was currently part of the *Berne Convention,* but there was widespread opinion to the contrary.[94]

It is perhaps not surprising, therefore, that in 1923 the 1921 *Copyright Act* had still not been proclaimed into force by the Governor-in-Council. In December 1921, the Liberal Party came to power under Prime Minister Mackenzie King, taking all of the seats in Quebec, and the government's stance on the compulsory licensing clauses changed.[95] The new government did not take the position that the licensing clauses that were part of the 1921 act were in conformity with the *Berne Convention.* The Liberal Minister of Trade and Commerce, who now led the drive for copyright revision, pointed to an article published on 15 July 1921 in *Le droit d'auteur* that examined the new Canadian law in depth, lauded the valiant fight of Canadian authors and certain parliamentarians for Canadian adhesion to the *Berne Convention* and against the compulsory licensing provisions, condemned the pernicious American influence on Canadian copyright, and argued that the new act's compulsory licensing provisions were not in conformity with the *Berne Convention.*[96]

As in 1921, there was some question in 1923 regarding the status of *Le droit d'auteur* and the opinions expressed therein. It was even suggested that the article that the Minister had cited had been written not by the International Office itself but by a Canadian civil servant, and therefore represented simply one view, not an authoritative legal opinion of the International Office.[97] It was later discovered that the article, which was published anonymously, had in fact been written by the International Office with information provided by an Ottawa civil servant.[98]

The opinion published in *Le droit d'auteur,* although it appears to have been the main opinion drawn upon by the government, was not the only basis for the government's desire to amend the 1921 legislation. The Minister of Trade and Commerce was also concerned about suggestions made by the British government that they would not, given the Canadian act as it stood, be able to recognize copyright in works published in Canada under the 1911 imperial *Copyright Act.*[99]

Some were also reluctant, however, to accept the opinion of the British government as an impediment to Canadian retention of the compulsory licensing clauses as they stood. Conservative MP Hugh Guthrie argued that the British had long objected to various aspects of Canadian copyright legislation but that the government could not act on this opinion alone; what was required was an independent Canadian legal opinion on the matter.[100]

By 1921, Canadian policy makers were feeling less bound by the strictures of British uniformity. Despite the fact that the British "had a horror that the British Empire might appear disunited,"[101] Conservative Prime Minister Meighen had "implicitly rejected the notion of consensual empire policies reached in the interests of the whole" by refusing to bend on Canadian demands at the Imperial Conference in 1921.[102] Hillmer and Granatstein conclude that the idea of a British Empire with unified policies was doomed from the start by its sprawling geography and rising Canadian nationalism. Canadians believed more and more strongly that they would control their own future.[103] The British, however, were not entirely without influence in matters of Canadian copyright.

Given the objections published by the International Office and those of the British government, the compulsory licensing clauses of the 1921 act were narrowed to apply only to works by Canadians and by the creators of non–Berne Union countries. These amendments received royal assent on 13 June 1923 and negotiations with the United States and Britain for mutual copyright recognition were therefore able to proceed as a prelude to proclamation by the Governor-in-Council.[104]

In July, Canada's Privy Council approved the ratification of the revised *Berne Convention* and the 1914 additional protocol. British involvement was still required; the Privy Council requested that Britain undertake "such action as may be necessary to declare the adhesion of the Dominion of Canada to the Revised Convention of Berne ... and the Additional Protocol thereto."[105] It was also requested that Britain publish a notice in the *London Gazette* declaring that Canadian copyright was "substantially identical" to that provided under the imperial *Copyright Act* of 1911.[106] Under the 1911 act, publication of such a notice would confer on Canada reciprocal copyright recognition with Britain.[107]

By the end of December, both Britain and the United States had declared the Canadian act to be acceptable. The British government published a notice in the *London Gazette* declaring the act to be "substantially similar" to the imperial act of 1911, thus extending to Canada protection under that act.[108] Canada's Minister of Trade and Commerce issued a certificate granting protection to the United States on 26 December 1923, effective 1 January 1924.[109] President Calvin Coolidge then issued a proclamation the next day enabling Canadians to receive copyright recognition in the United States, effective that same date.[110] Thomas Allen, chairman of the Book Publishers' Section of the Toronto Board of Trade, claimed in his address to the section's annual meeting that the American proclamation had not been made. This information formed the basis of an erroneous article in the *Globe,* which was corrected the following day.[111]

On 7 January 1924, British delegates notified the Swiss government of Canada's adhesion to the revised *Berne Convention* and the 1914 additional protocol, effective 1 January 1924.[112] As required under the 1914 protocol, notice was also served that copyright granted to American creators would be somewhat restricted in the sense that Canada's compulsory licensing clauses could be applied against their works.[113]

Canadian newspapers trumpeted the country's entry into the Berne Union; the *Globe* headline read: "Copyright Troubles Finally Adjusted: Canada at Last Adheres with Other Nations to the Berne Convention."[114] Canadian authors, however, were still unhappy with the compulsory licensing clauses of the act, which no longer applied to authors from countries that were members of the Berne Union while still applying to Canadian authors and authors of non-Berne countries. Lawrence J. Burpee, past president of the Canadian Authors' Association, objected to the clauses, saying that "these compulsory licensing clauses are humiliating to the Canadian-born artists. After all, the poor devil of a Canadian writer is made a victim, while the mantle of justice is thrown over the authors of France and England, Italy and Spain."[115] He further commented in 1928: "[The *Berne Convention*] is designed to protect the interests of an author in countries other than his own. It was naturally assumed that no Parliament would inflict upon its own nationals burdens that it did not impose upon citizens of other countries. Our Canadian Parliament demonstrated that this was impossible."[116] Some authors left Canada, possibly at least partly as a result of these provisions. Author/illustrator Arthur Heming left for England, commenting that "the only way a Canadian author can protect his work in Canada is to swear allegiance to a foreign country and then that privilege is at once granted to him."[117]

Canada's adhesion to the *Berne Convention* did not go off entirely without a hitch. A group of lawyers representing Canadian newspapers and theatres claimed that steps required under the British *Copyright Act* of 1911 in order to ratify the *Berne Convention* had been missed, and that Canada's ratification of the revised convention was therefore not valid. The lawyers claimed that British law required notice of Canada's ratification to be published in the *Canada Gazette,* whereas notice had been published instead in the *London Gazette.*[118] They also claimed that, since the *Copyright Act* of 1921 repealed all previous copyright acts, including the British *International Copyright Act* of 1886, which enacted the *Berne Convention* and which had been in force in Canada, Canada had effectively exited the *Berne Convention* when the 1921 act came into force.[119] This, of course, was exactly the opposite of what the Canadian government intended to do, the opposite of what the British government understood the Canadian government to have done, and the opposite of what the International Office recognized the Canadian government as having done.

This matter was of great concern to the French government, since the Canadian newspapers and theatres represented by the group of lawyers making this claim had stopped paying royalties to French authors based on the idea that international copyright obligations no longer applied in Canada. Although the lawyers maintained their view for some time, the Canadian and British governments, along with the International Office took the position that the Canadian ratification was valid and that any suggestion that a step required by the British act had been missed was based on a misinformed understanding of the law; in particular, it was emphasized that Canadian international copyright was now governed by Canadian law rather than the 1911 British *Copyright Act.*[120] This position eventually calmed the fears of the French authors.[121] From that point onward, Canada's relationship to the *Berne Convention* stood beyond any doubt.

THE CHANGING SHAPE OF Canadian copyright interests – particularly the organization and mobilization of authors and other creators – played a significant role in shifting the debate over copyright policy and the *Berne Convention.* Just as important, the Canadian government was beginning to shape an image as an international player and wished to avoid any sense that it was an "outsider in the general community of nations."[122] The desire to continue to be associated with the powerful British Empire but also to have the prominence and powers associated with independent statehood led Canadian officials to adopt positions that were independent but in relative harmony with imperial copyright.

At the same time, the institutions and norms of imperialism continued. Britain continued to be involved in Canadian copyright legislation, pressing the

Canadian government to act on the British 1911 *Copyright Act,* making known its opinions on Bill E, and pressing for change to the Canadian 1921 act, which led to the amendments of 1923. The International Office of the Berne Union also became more actively involved in the Canadian legislative process through its criticism of Canadian legislative moves and its pronouncements on the acceptability of Canadian legislative innovations.

The imperial government continued to act as an intermediary between Canada and the Berne Union, with the ability to decide, based on its own interpretations, whether or not Canadian copyright conformed to the requirements of the *Berne Convention,* and with the authority to declare, or not, Canada's ratification to the director of the International Office. Because of this, Canadian copyright lawmaking rolled heavily on the rails of imperial copyright. The legislation enacted in 1923 was, in almost all sections, copied from British legislation, with a few differences regarding registration and compulsory licensing, as well as some minor variations with regard to compulsory licensing of gramophone recordings intended to make Canadian law reflect American legislation.[123] These differences were very important, however, as symbols of the degree of independence from imperial copyright that Canadians had been able to achieve and of Canadian efforts to insert domestic public policy objectives into Canadian copyright law.

The authority of the International Office of the Berne Union now weighed in alongside that of the imperial government. An administrative and communications apparatus had been formed as a part of the union. This was built as a source of expertise and knowledge, and it circulated particular interpretations of the convention through its monthly magazine, *Le droit d'auteur,* which wielded a good deal of authority and influence. While the legitimacy of this apparatus as an authority on international copyright was sometimes doubted, its influence was nevertheless important. The ability of *Le droit d'auteur* to bring national laws to the attention of foreign governments, to bring foreign opinions to bear on national laws, to enable national laws to be contrasted against each other and against the tenets of the *Berne Convention,* and to promote particular interpretations of the convention were important sources of its authority. Domestic opinion regarding particular interpretations of the convention would become less important and less influential as the dialogue about such interpretations expanded internationally, in part through the vehicle of *Le droit d'auteur.* This centre of authority to some extent replaced the authoritative voice of the imperial government in regulating international copyright norms.

Although a Canadian Department of External Affairs was established in 1909, its staff was extremely small and, prior to the 1920s, did not view Canada as acting autonomously on the international stage. The governments of Canada and the other British colonies, despite some common interests, did not establish a common network through which common copyright policies could be formulated.

Although Minister of Agriculture Sydney Fisher did not live to see the relative copyright independence he had negotiated at the Imperial Copyright Conference in 1910 achieved,[124] he was credited with having developed a line of argument initiated by Prime Minister John Thompson in the 1880s that led to Canada's first (relatively) independent *Copyright Act* in 1923.[125] What was won, however, was not the complete independence that Thomson had pressed for, which would have allowed a greater degree of American-style copyright protectionism. The struggle for Canadian copyright sovereignty was instead won by submission to imperial and international copyright norms.

CHAPTER EIGHT

Copyright Internationalism: Canada's Debut, 1927-36

FROM 1921 TO 1931, THE POPULATION of Canada grew by almost 20 percent, to 10.3 million people,[1] and Canadian cultural industries grew even faster. The 1931 census listed over 50,000 people employed in printing, publishing, and bookbinding (compared with about 26,000 in printing and bookbinding in 1921), and over 6,500 authors, editors, and journalists (compared with 880 authors and librarians in 1921).[2] Some industries survived in innovative ways. The Canadian record company Compo had survived the 1929 economic crash by using its recording facilities to transcribe radio broadcasts, by producing dictaphone cylinders and, after a slight modification to the factory, by using its record pressing facilities to make floor tiles.[3] Reduced tariffs on the paper imported for magazine publishing led to a significant increase in the circulation of Canadian magazines, as did a tax on imported periodicals.[4]

Alongside the organizations representing authors and publishers, the Musical Protective Society of Canada, representing theatres and other music users such as hotels and fall fairs, became involved in copyright lobbying.[5] The Canadian Manufacturers' Association continued to be involved, as did the Canadian Authors' Association.[6] American lobby organizations also created Canadian counterparts to promote their interests in Canada. The Motion Picture Distributors and Exhibitors of Canada, funded by and representing the American film industry, had not been active on copyright during the formulation of the Canadian *Copyright Act* in the 1920s, but became active in discussions about the act's revision in 1930.[7] The Province of Quebec Theatre Owners' Association, the Motion Picture Association of the Province of Manitoba, and the Saskatchewan Independent Theatre Owners, as well as the independent theatre owners of Ontario and other theatre owners in other provinces, organized on the new question of performing rights.[8]

Although the 1908 Berlin conference to revise the *Berne Convention* had decided that the next revision should take place within ten years, various factors, including the First World War, delayed it until 1928.[9] As Canada had acceded to the *Berne Convention* with its legislation of 1921 and 1923, in February and March 1927 the Department of External Affairs received an invitation to, and preliminary documentation for, a diplomatic conference to revise the *Berne Convention*. The conference was initially scheduled to take place in Rome in October that year,[10] but in August notice was sent of a further delay, at the request of a number of governments, until the spring of 1928.[11]

This was the first time that the Canadian government was invited to send a representative to negotiate the revision of the *Berne Convention*. Independent representation had been the norm since the 1923 *Halibut Treaty* was negotiated independently between Canada and the United States. Now each part of the British Empire carried out its own international affairs, consulting with each other only when feasible and necessary.[12]

The Department of External Affairs in Ottawa had expanded, bringing in, among others, its first francophone, Jean Désy, a university professor who would be, with Philippe Roy, Canada's delegate to the diplomatic conference in 1928.[13] The networks and administrative apparatus that would situate Canada as a state within an international system, rather than a colony, were slowly being put in place.

In response to the invitation, a small interdepartmental committee was formed to examine the question of revising the *Berne Convention*. Thomas L. Richard, acting Commissioner of Patents, F.P. Varcoe of the Department of Justice, and Jean Désy sat on the committee,[14] which reported in August 1927, two months before the expected date of the conference.

The delay until May 1928 enabled Canadian officials to make an important clarification regarding Canada's desired status within the Berne Union. In its report of 13 August 1927, the interdepartmental committee pointed out that Canada had joined the *Berne Convention* as a colony of Great Britain (the word "dominion" having no international meaning), and that it had not been paying fees to the International Office of the Berne Union, as Britain had paid on behalf of its colonies and possessions. This fact was noted with surprise by Richard, who had assumed that the same procedure had been followed as with the *Paris Convention for the Protection of Industrial Property,* which Canada had joined as an independent fee-paying member.[15] The committee recommended that a cable be sent to the International Office to inform it that the Canadian government wished to pay its share of the expenses of the Berne Union from the time it had adhered to the convention.[16] The committee's report was approved by Liberal Prime Minister Mackenzie King on 15 August, and the next day Canada's Under-Secretary of State for External Affairs sent a telegram to the International Office asking what fees Canada owed as a member of the Berne Union.[17] The reply was confusing: the International Office assumed that the official must have intended to inquire about fees owed under the treaty on *industrial* property, rather than under the *Berne Convention* on copyright, since, according to the International Office, Canada was not a contracting party to the *Berne Convention*.[18] Further clarification came in November, when the International Office explained that it considered Canada to have adhered to the *Berne Convention* as a British colony rather than as a separate country, a status that came with neither voting rights nor fees.[19]

The Canadian government moved to clarify that it wished Canada to be considered an independent, voting, fee-paying member of the Berne Union.[20] Britain put up no protest, and volunteered to notify the International Office of the Canadian government's desire to be regarded as having adhered as a new member of the union rather than as a British colony.[21] Canadian officials accepted this suggestion "with pleasure,"[22] and in due course Canada was recognized as a contracting party to the Berne Union beginning on 10 April 1928, less than a month before the start of the diplomatic conference in May.[23] Arrangements were made for the International Office to correspond directly with the Canadian government through the Under-Secretary of State for External Affairs.[24]

Other British dominions also adhered to the *Berne Convention* as independent countries, with Ireland joining on 5 October 1927, India on 1 April 1928, Australia on 14 April 1928, and New Zealand on 24 April 1928. South Africa joined on 3 October 1928, soon after the revision conference.[25]

Many of the new states that emerged after the First World War, including Austria, Czechoslovakia, the Free City of Danzig (then a city-state), Estonia, Finland, Hungary, and Poland, quickly joined in the international order, including the Berne Union.[26] Several other European states also joined the union, including Bulgaria and Romania (and, by 1930, Yugoslavia), with the result that almost all of Europe, except the Soviet Union, had become part of the union by 1928.[27] There were few members from Africa and Asia, but because of colonial power on both continents, the *Berne Convention* also applied in most areas there.[28]

The attributes of statehood in the realist sense were achieved gradually. Darel E. Paul shows that there are many different types of governments with varying degrees of state apparatus.[29] As Canada's administrative apparatus was being constructed, diplomatic links with both Britain and the United States were strengthened. The Department of External Affairs remained small: in 1924, it had 101 employees but only three officers "who could be expected to carry out high-level administrative or policy tasks."[30] The Canadian government had representatives in London and at the League of Nations, but none with diplomatic standing.[31] Following Prime Minister Mackenzie King's appointment of

O.D. Skelton as Under-Secretary of State for External Affairs in 1924, a move that would be important in international copyright as well as in international relations more generally, the Canadian government for the first time sent a representative to Washington, establishing a Canadian legation headed by Vincent Massey as Minister to Washington in 1927. In turn, the United States sent an American minister to Ottawa. Britain, in an effort to outweigh the American influence in Ottawa and to show continuing British interest in the country, established a High Commissioner in Canada.[32] In France, the Office of the Commissioner General was upgraded to a legation in 1928, and Philippe Roy, Commissioner General since 1911, was given the post of Envoy Extraordinary and Minister Plenipotentiary (of Canada) to France.[33] A representative was also sent to Japan in 1929. No further appointments were made until 1939.[34]

The small interdepartmental committee that examined the question of revising the *Berne Convention* was primarily concerned with establishing Canada's status in international copyright affairs. This focus may have been due in part to the selection of delegates for the diplomatic conference in Rome: officials from the Department of External Affairs attended, rather than officials concerned specifically with copyright.

The choice of delegates was an important one. Fernand Rinfret, an author and one of the MPs who had spoken strongly against the compulsory licensing clauses included in Canada's 1921 *Copyright Act* (arguing that they contravened the *Berne Convention*), was now the Liberal Secretary of State with authority over copyright. Many copyright interest groups were pleased his appointment to this position. Hugh S. Eayrs, president of the Macmillan Company of Canada, for one, wrote the Prime Minister:

> I may say, if you will allow me, on behalf of all the book publishers, how very agreeable it is to find a Minister in charge of Copyright who really knows what he is talking about. The point is, of course, that administration of Copyright has unfortunately been tacked on to the duties of Ministers in various Governments as a sort of extra affair to what have been regarded as more important matters pertaining to a particular portfolio. At last, in your Government, there is a Minister who has given much time to the serious study of Copyright.[35]

The Canadian Authors' Association, the Canadian Manufacturers' Association, and the Macmillan Company of Canada all asked that Rinfret represent the Canadian government at the international conference. The Canadian Authors' Association called Rinfret "especially qualified," the Macmillan Company called him "extraordinarily knowledgeable," and the Canadian Manufacturers'

Association agreed: "In addition to being the Minister in charge of copyright, we regard him as one already possessed of a very thorough knowledge of the subject and consequently exceptionally well fitted to speak for Canada's interests at the coming international gathering."[36] The same interest groups also lobbied to have their own representatives included as part of the Canadian delegation or, failing that, to have the expenses of their representatives' attendance at the conference paid by the government.[37]

Rinfret was also a preferred government choice, but others were named as possible delegates as well. There were few to choose from; some of the government's foremost experts on copyright had retired and few others were available, even within the copyright office.[38] Acting Commissioner of Patents and Copyright Thomas L. Richard was "fully occupied with the Patents branch of his work."[39] However, Jean Désy of External Affairs, who had also served on the interdepartmental committee in 1927, was suggested, as was Second Secretary E.D. McCreer, "who could get up on the question if sufficient notice was given."[40]

Rinfret elected not to attend the conference, and Philippe Roy was selected to be Canada's lead delegate.[41] Roy was not familiar with copyright issues, so Désy acted as his technical adviser.[42] Together they made up Canada's delegation of two, and full powers, granted by Great Britain, were requested.[43] The idea of including private interests as part of the Canadian delegation was floated before the Prime Minister,[44] but was ultimately rejected. Nevertheless, a number of private interests elected to attend at their own expense.[45]

In April 1927, after the initial invitations had been sent, the British government inquired what response the Canadian government wished to send, and invited Canadian delegates to an informal meeting of delegates from the British Empire one week before the conference.[46] The Canadians did not attend the meeting, which took place on 26 April 1928. The reasons given were that Roy was not familiar enough with copyright and that Désy planned to travel only after the preliminary meeting had taken place.[47]

There were likely other reasons as well. O.D. Skelton had succeeded Joseph Pope as Under-Secretary of State for External Affairs in 1925. Whereas Pope had had little interest in shaping policy, Skelton had a vision of a Canada independent of Britain, a British Empire of equals, a Canadian foreign policy decentralized from London and controlled in Canada, and a country aware of its economic connections with the United States.[48] It was this vision – and this stance against a united empire policy – that led Prime Minister King to install Skelton in the position.[49]

At the same time, Skelton had a realistic understanding of the relative importance of cultural policy in Canada:

"Canada is a great country," he wrote to his friend W.L. Grant, "Heaven bless it, but at present it's great chiefly for the farmer and the shopkeeper. Another generation with its more culture and leisure will offer opportunities for the writer and the teacher ... Canada has a fair crop of poets of second hand inspiration and her full share of novelists but of men who can write on literary or national subjects with applied culture and sane perspectives very few."[50]

Thus, Skelton may have seen the international copyright conference as being relatively unimportant to a land of "farmers and shopkeepers," although possibly important to a new generation and for fostering future literary opportunities. From his perspective, as from the perspective of the small interdepartmental committee on copyright, the most important issue was likely to be that of moving away from the United Empire policies of the past and clarifying the independence of Canada's position within the international system. At the same time, as we shall see, Skelton's officials were not given instructions that would enable them to stand independently from Britain or other major players in the debates within the Berne Union.

Although the norms of Canadian diplomatic independence were firmly established by 1928, the Canadian government had not established extensive independent relations or communication networks with other British colonies. In fact, Skelton was skeptical of the possibility of establishing relationships or "communities of interest" between Canada and other parts of the Empire.[51] This may have been one reason why Canadian representatives did not attend the preliminary meeting in London, where common interests might have been expected to be discovered. Thus, a strong coalition between Canada, Australia, and New Zealand was not forged during the 1920s when the three countries with some common interests in international copyright were first represented at the meetings of the Berne Union. Meetings with other British colonies to discuss negotiating positions *without* Britain were not contemplated.

Diplomatic Conference: Rome, 7 May to 2 June 1928

The Canadian delegates attended the conference with a short page of instructions, given by Rinfret, which chiefly directed them not to rock the boat. They were instructed not to take the initiative in making proposals for amendments to the *Berne Convention* "increasing or restricting the protection extended to copyright." They were, however, given liberty to support any proposals that seemed likely to meet with general approval of the governments represented, "particularly those of the leading countries, such as Great Britain, Italy and France."[52] These instructions are interesting given the enormous differences in the copyright interests of Canada and these countries, with Canada being by far a net copyright importer and Britain, Italy, and France being major copyright exporters. Rinfret's position was strongly in support of Canadian authors; he was an author himself, and he had advocated Canada's strict adhesion to the *Berne Convention* during the parliamentary debates of the early 1920s over compulsory licensing for Canadian printers and publishers.

The conference lasted for a month, from 7 May to 2 June 1928. There were thirty-four delegations from Berne Union countries and twenty-one from non-union countries. The size of the Canadian delegation (2) was comparable with that of most other delegations, especially from other British dominions, which generally sent only 1 or 2 delegates. Some countries sent much larger delegations, however.[53] Italy's was massive, with 24 members, while Germany sent 12, Japan 12, France 10, and Great Britain 8. The United States, which was not a member of the union, sent 6 delegates.[54]

Some of the more prominent countries included "expert delegates" or "assistant delegates" who represented authors, composers, or artists. Germany, Austria, and France had representatives from the *Association littéraire et artistique internationale* (ALAI) in their delegations (including the organization's president, who was French); Germany, Spain, Italy, and Switzerland had representatives from domestic societies of authors, composers, dramatists, or artists. Britain did not, and private interests in that country raised questions, which were eventually brought before Parliament, about the adequacy of a delegation that did not include representatives from private interest groups, claiming that Britain had suffered in the negotiations from a lack of adequate representation. There appears to have been only one delegate connected to the interests of librarians and archivists – Spain's lead delegate was the head of the Spanish Guild of Archivists, Librarians, and Archaeologists.[55]

Three non-governmental organizations (NGOs) also sent delegates: the League of Nations sent one; the *Institut international de coopération intellectuelle*, predecessor of the United Nations Educational, Scientific and Cultural Organization (UNESCO), sent four; and the International Office of the Berne Union, also listed as a non-governmental organization, sent its director, Fritz Ostertag.[56]

The atmosphere was relaxed compared with other international conferences. Delegates were shown great hospitality during their stay in Rome. Italian Prime Minister Benito Mussolini attended, as did other officials.[57] Nevertheless, the Australian delegate commented that "the proceedings were marked by an absence of formalism strange to those accustomed to British committees or boards, and as far removed as can be from what might be expected in a conference of governments."[58] None of the meetings, save for the plenary meetings, were recorded; discussions were informally structured and votes were rarely taken until the end of meetings.[59] The necessity of achieving unanimity meant that an extra spirit of accommodation was required, and that "everything that may stiffen the attitude of delegations and may make it difficult for them to modify or abandon a position taken up, has to be avoided."[60]

Non-union countries and NGOs participated in the meetings in a consultative capacity, and were entitled to make amendments and counter-proposals in the discussions.[61] The presence of private interest groups in the delegations of various countries was felt in the mood of the conference and the views expressed.[62] The atmosphere of warmth and the lack of divergent views among private delegates representing mainly authors' and publishers' interests is indicative of how completely the conference was committed to a project that was envisioned and portrayed as "an important stage in the post-war reconstruction of international life," and that saw the revision and extension of the norms of international copyright as "indispensable to the progress of civilisation."[63]

The work of the conference was based on proposals to amend the *Berne Convention* made by the Italian government and the International Office and circulated beforehand, and on the comments and counter-proposals made by other governments.[64] Work was divided among several committees: a committee of the full conference to deal with general questions, and subcommittees on specific topics such as moral rights, broadcasting, photography and cinematography, or the mechanical reproduction of musical works. Since all of the committees were intended to be open to any delegate, their meetings were scheduled so as not to overlap; many countries had just one delegate and thus could attend only one session at a time. The British delegation noted that there was little difference in attendance between the plenary sessions and the committee meetings.[65]

The issue of language was a problem for some delegations. The official language of the Berne Union was French, the language of international diplomacy. The British government was concerned about whether there would be any objection to British delegates making their speeches in English. They consulted the host Italian government about the matter, and were informed that there would be no objection to English speeches provided that the delegates arranged for their immediate translation into French.[66]

The task of some non-francophone delegations was made more difficult by the fact that many of the conference proceedings took place in informal meetings where no written record was kept for delegates to review or consult. The Canadian delegates, being fully bilingual, were useful to other delegations. Australian delegate W. Harrison Moore made special note of this in his report of the conference:

> To the Canadian delegation we were under special obligations which illustrate the value from an Empire standpoint of some of our diversities. In the drafting

of a Convention of this nature, although French alone is the official language, it is necessary to consider how terms and phrases of the one language will stand in the other, and to find the appropriate expression, which is often very different from the literal translation. The bilingual experience of the Canadians was invaluable here.[67]

Four important items of general significance were discussed. First, it was at this 1928 conference that moral rights were first introduced into the *Berne Convention*. The right to claim authorship of a work, and the right to object to the distortion, mutilation, or other modification that would be prejudicial to the creator's honour or reputation, were deemed to be the inalienable "moral rights" of the creator, extending even beyond the transfer of the copyright in a work to another party.[68] The Italian government's proposals for the inclusion of moral rights in the convention were more expansive; among other things, they would have extended moral rights in perpetuity – beyond the lifetime of the creator and beyond the term of copyright protection. To such expansive proposals the common law countries objected on the grounds that they would be difficult to legislate and that they were covered in other types of legislation but not copyright.[69] The text adopted was more limited, in that moral rights were not made non-transferrable, continued only for the lifetime of the creator, did not include the right to oppose publication, and prohibited only mutilations that were prejudicial to the creator's honour or reputation.[70]

The question of moral rights brought out most clearly the different approaches to copyright taken by the British on the one hand and continental European countries such as Italy on the other, contrasting the Anglo-American copyright tradition with the tradition of *droit d'auteur*.[71] Italy, Romania, and Poland had passed legislation granting non-economic rights to creators earlier in the 1920s.[72] In 1931, Canada would become the first country of the English copyright tradition to introduce moral rights into its legislation.[73]

Second, the 1908 convention had permitted newspaper articles to be reproduced by other newspapers unless such reproduction was expressly forbidden.[74] In 1928, this permission was reduced so that it applied only to "articles on current economic, political or religious topics," instead of to any newspaper article at all, but expanded so that the reproduction of such articles could be done by "the press" rather than only "another newspaper."[75] This enabled magazines as well as newspapers to benefit from the ability.[76]

Third, the conference addressed the question of whether "oral works" ought to receive some form of copyright protection. The term "oral works" was felt to be too broad, especially by British delegates, under whose law copyright works required fixity of form.[77] The delegations of federal countries, including

Canada, Australia, and the United States, were concerned that such inclusion might lead to constitutional difficulties, and the United States felt that the use of the term "oral works" might make American entry into the union impossible.[78] It was generally felt, however, that some works, such as speeches and sermons, ought to receive copyright protection, despite the fact that they did not take written form.[79] "Lectures, addresses, sermons, and other works of the same nature" were therefore added to the list of works to receive protection under the *Berne Convention*, although there was room for countries to make laws allowing for the reproduction of said works by the press.[80] There was also room for countries to exclude from copyright protection political speeches and speeches made during legal proceedings.[81]

Fourth, the 1908 text of the *Berne Convention* had provisions for countries to make reservations to particular aspects of the agreement. Under such reservations, which took the form of a declaration made either upon signing the convention or upon ratifying it, countries could choose to adhere to provisions taken from previous versions of the *Berne Convention* in place of the corresponding provisions in the 1908 text.[82] This caused some difficulty because not all countries adhered to the same text, thereby complicating the agreements made.[83] As a result, it was suggested in 1928 that the ability to make reservations be eliminated. Some countries objected, so an agreement was reached allowing only certain restricted reservations. Existing members of the Berne Union were allowed to retain their previous reservations upon signing the 1928 convention, as long as they made a declaration to that effect upon ratification.[84] New members were restricted to only one possible reservation; they could adopt the 1896 text of Article 5 of the 1886 *Berne Convention*, thereby limiting the term of translation rights to ten years in cases where the creator had not made use of those rights.[85]

A number of issues raised were of particular importance in relation to Canada. First, there were concerns that, on some issues touched on by the convention, federal countries might find that the appropriate authority to legislate on a given issue belonged to provincial or other authorities, making it impossible for the federal government to enact legislation on those issues. The delegations from countries with federal governments, including Canada, Australia, and New Zealand, declared that in such cases they would recommend to the competent authorities that they enact measures necessary to give effect to the obligations undertaken under the *Berne Convention*.[86] This approach, which followed the one taken by the Statute of the International Labour Organization, was accepted by the conference.[87]

Second, at the suggestion of the British delegation, the 1914 protocol to the *Berne Convention* was now incorporated, with minor changes in form, into the convention's main text. As in the original text, countries making use of the protocol were required to make a declaration to the Swiss government regarding the restrictions being put in place and the countries they affected. Countries like Canada whose governments had already made such a declaration were not required to repeat it.[88] Canada was the only country that had made use of the provisions of the 1914 protocol.[89]

Third, it was noted that the public performance of musical and dramatic works, especially through gramophone recordings and radio broadcasts, were reducing the sales of sheet music. As a result, rights holders were relying increasingly on revenue drawn from licensing fees paid for public performances of works.[90] In Canada and other "new countries," including Australia, New Zealand, and South Africa, performing rights, and the mode in which performing rights organizations collected licensing fees from entertainment halls, caused widespread complaints. The Australian delegate characterized the problem as follows:

> Complaints are common that these associations, instead of acting as the agent for individual copyright owners and selling the right to perform particular pieces of music at a reasonable charge, insist on payment of a fee which covers over a period of time an indefinite and immense number of works; that they do not disclose the works they control, and that, in the case of owners and managers of halls in which entertainments are or may be held, the claim of the association is in effect to exact license fees on the use of the place as a place of entertainment.[91]

Such difficulties arose in countries like Canada in particular, as the Australian delegate observed:

> It was evident that the conditions of new countries gave the matter a greater importance there as more deeply affecting their social life and therefore their culture and development. It was interesting to note that the countries nearest to these in feeling on the subject were countries such as Denmark and Norway, where rural interests predominate.[92]

It was found impossible, however, to make any changes to related articles of the *Berne Convention*.[93] The delegations of Canada, along with those of Britain, Australia, New Zealand, the Irish Free State, and India, contemplated making a general declaration to the effect that "the provisions of the present Convention are without prejudice to the right which belongs to Governments to adopt any measures they may consider justified for reasons of 'ordre public.'"[94] It was the feeling of the British delegates that the term "ordre public" was sufficiently wide.

This declaration was never made, however, because "it appeared to be generally accepted that nothing in the Convention affected the inherent right of any country to deal as was necessary with any abuses which might arise, and a declaration in any form might give rise to misunderstanding."[95]

Fourth, whereas in some countries, such as Australia and Britain, broadcasting was deemed to be included under public performance rights, in other countries creators had no rights in the broadcast of works and received no remuneration for it.[96] Thus, it was suggested that broadcast rights be added to the *Berne Convention.*[97]

The Australian delegate observed that "it was evident that the nature of broadcasting – the absence of all national boundaries in transmission through the ether – called for international agreement in a way that no other subject of copyright did: if the author's right was to be recognized it should be recognized by all."[98] Some delegations felt, however, that "it would be unwise to recognize rights in so absolute a manner as to embarrass their regulation and control in the public interest."[99] A dispute therefore arose as to the extent to which a country might be allowed to place limits on broadcast rights, such as through compulsory licensing. Some countries felt that creators' rights were already unduly limited, in contravention of the *Berne Convention,* by policies such as compulsory licensing in the interest of national culture or public instruction; others wanted to see allowances for compulsory licensing.[100]

A number of compromises were proposed. Although it was agreed that creators should be granted a broadcast right, some proposed that countries be allowed to limit that right in cases where "public order" was at stake, while others wished to see broader provisions for national control in cases where the "public interest" was at stake.[101] Britain proposed that countries be allowed to step in to prevent cases where the creator refused to grant permission for public performance on reasonable terms "as would prejudice the trade or industry of any person or class of persons carrying on business in any country to which the Convention applies and would be contrary to the public interest."[102] This proposal was dropped in light of a proposal by Australia and New Zealand reserving the right of countries, with respect to both performing and broadcast rights, to "take measures against any abuse which might be produced by the exercise of the said rights."[103] Some countries objected on the grounds that such a statement "might prejudice the general right which they maintained was inherent in every State to take measures to prevent abuse of monopoly rights."[104] Others objected to any proposal that might countenance compulsory licensing.[105] Still others found such proposals unnecessary based on the belief that the creation of a broadcast right did not exclude the possibility of compulsory licensing.[106]

Another proposal was therefore made by Australia and New Zealand, with regard only to broadcast rights, reserving for countries the ability "to reconcile the exercise of the rights contemplated by the preceding paragraph with the requirements of the public interest."[107] This proposal could not be agreed to. The terms "utilité publique" and "ordre public" were suggested in place of "intérêt public," but these were also found unacceptable.[108]

In the end, a compromise provision was adopted whereby an exclusive broadcast right was created, with the conditions of its exercise to be regulated by national legislation in a limited way, such that, among other things, neither the right of the creator to receive equitable remuneration for the use of the work nor the moral rights of the creator would be affected.[109]

There was some discussion of the creation of a right for broadcast performers in their performances, but Britain objected on the grounds that such a right should be a matter of contract and not a matter of copyright. It was generally agreed that, especially as most countries did not protect broadcast performers' rights in their legislation, the time was not ripe for an international agreement on the subject.[110]

Broadcast and performance rights would become very important in Canada in the years to come; two Royal Commissions would be established to deal with the issues that had been summarized by the Australian delegate. Australia and New Zealand, not Canada, took the lead on these issues.

Fifth, a number of proposals were made that would extend the definition of "simultaneous publication" such that works published in a Berne Union country within fourteen days, or within a year, of being published in a non-union country would be considered to have been "simultaneously" published in a union country. Britain opposed any extension of the term of simultaneity on the grounds that it would benefit primarily non-union countries and could hamper union countries attempting to negotiate copyright treaties with such countries. The Canadian delegation joined the British in opposing the extension, and no change was made.[111]

Under Canadian law, a work was considered to be "simultaneously" published in Canada if it was published within fourteen days "or such longer period as may for the time being be fixed by order in council" of publication in another country.[112] The issue of simultaneity was of particular importance to Canada as next-door neighbour to the United States; Canada was that country's back door to the Berne Union. Simultaneous publication in Canada allowed American creators to receive protection throughout the Berne Union. Had the term of simultaneous protection been extended, it would have been even easier for Americans to do this.

Finally, given the new status of the British dominions as independent members of the Berne Union, there was the question of how the signatures on the *Berne Convention* would appear.[113] In 1926, it had been determined that British dominions would now be described as "autonomous Communities within the British Empire, equal in status, in no way subordinate one to another in any aspect of their domestic or external affairs, though united by a common allegiance to the Crown, and freely associated as members of the British Commonwealth of Nations."[114] As a part of the new arrangements, international treaties were to be signed under the name of the King. Because it was impossible for the King to make an agreement with himself, such agreements were considered *not* as agreements between the parts of the British Empire but rather as agreements between the individual countries of the British Empire and countries outside.[115] Therefore, the preamble to international agreements was to include the formal designation of the King, and the various parts of the British Empire would sign the agreement individually, with signatures of the various countries of the British Empire grouped together.[116]

During the conference, an anonymous proposal was circulated that, according to the Canadian delegates, "obviously emanated from the [British] Foreign Office."[117] This proposal outlined a suggested wording and format for the preamble and signature of the *Berne Convention* following the agreement of the 1926 Imperial Conference. The proposal for signature was formatted in such a way, however, that the phrase "for Great Britain and Northern Ireland" was indented and appeared outside a set of brackets that surrounded Canada and the other British dominions. The Canadian delegation objected to this style of formatting, which set Great Britain apart as separate in status from the other parts of the Empire, and suggested a format where Britain, Canada, and the other dominions were listed in a more uniform manner.[118] The British delegation did not object to this proposal.[119]

The matter was not settled, however. Whereas Canada, Australia, and New Zealand were "committed by loyalty and strategic necessity to stand by Great Britain, almost no matter what,"[120] other British dominions, such as South Africa and Ireland, pressed for greater independence and decentralization.[121] The declaration at the Imperial Conference of 1926 designating the British dominions as "autonomous Communities within the British Empire, equal in status" had been a compromise that all parties were satisfied with. On 16 May 1928, however, at the conference to revise the *Berne Convention,* the Irish Free State submitted an alternative proposal, namely, that signatures of all of the countries party to the treaty should be arranged in alphabetical order.[122] In this the Irish Free State followed the example of the 1925 revision of the *Paris Convention for the*

Protection of Industrial Property, which was signed before the 1926 Imperial Conference procedure was put in place.[123] If this format of signature had been followed, the *Berne Convention* would have applied between the countries of the British Empire because the countries would have been listed as individual states, rather than grouped together as a single entity.[124] For this reason, the proposal was strongly opposed by Britain. The Canadian delegates indicated that they were anxious to follow the procedures laid out at the 1926 Imperial Conference, but that they would accept the alphabetical ordering if it was acceptable to all parties concerned.[125] The British delegates suggested that the British and dominion delegates should refuse to sign until the issue was resolved, but Roy declared that the Canadian delegation would sign in any case.[126]

On 1 June, the day before signing was to take place, the delegate from the Irish Free State, Michael MacWhite, declared at a meeting of the British and dominion delegates that he would refuse to sign the *Berne Convention* and that he would bring the issue of signature forward for the meeting to address. The Canadian delegates attempted, following the meeting and the next morning as well, to convince MacWhite that there was nothing to be gained by taking that course of action, that other countries would be unwilling to make a decision on a question that concerned only the British Empire, that such a stance would embarrass both the Irish and other delegates, and that as a result the Berne Union would have to be formulated so as to exclude the Irish Free State.[127] MacWhite persisted, however, and on the last day of the conference declared that the Irish Free State was unable to sign the convention.[128]

The 1926 Imperial Conference had set forth a vision of a united British Empire of equals, but the Irish proposal was far more radical; it implied that the relations between members of the British Empire were as between states. Had the Irish proposal carried, it would have represented another step towards the end of imperial copyright, with copyright among members of the British Empire being governed by international treaty. Skelton appeared willing to take this step had other members of the Empire agreed, but he was not willing to press the point.

This attitude – of not wanting to press a point – seems to have characterized the Canadian position at the conference. The Canadian delegation, backed by the British, did win the battle over simultaneous publication, but backed down on issues regarding the regulation of performance and broadcast rights in the public interest. The may have been due to the restrictive instructions given to Canadian delegates by Rinfret, which did not leave much room for making proposals or manoeuvring far from the positions of Britain, Italy, and France.[129] There were strong economic and public interest motives to regulate performing rights societies (the sometimes exorbitant self-set fees they demanded at that time went to foreign copyright holders), but these were apparently insufficient, given Rinfret's instructions, for the Canadian delegation to take a stronger stance.

The Canadians' knowledge and experience proved valuable to the other delegates, but their role was fairly low-key. Along with their bilingualism, the Canadian delegates brought their knowledge of the common law system and the Quebec civil law system. The Australian delegate noted that "hardly less valuable was the fact that in Canada the two systems of the common law and the civil law meet, so that the Canadian lawyer could often bridge the gap between two different modes of thought."[130] In some instances, Canadian delegates took on a mediating role, assisting with translation between English and French, using their knowledge of both the civil and common law traditions, proposing a compromise on the issue of the format of signature, and attempting to maintain harmony between the Irish Free State and the British Empire.

Nevertheless, the Canadians did not assume a strong stance at the conference and their recorded substantive contributions were few. In contrast, W. Harrison Moore, the Australian delegate, was much more active; his contribution to the compromise position on moral rights is well documented in his own report, and his notes about Australian interventions on the interests of the British dominions contrasts with the relative silence of the Canadian delegates on these issues, at least in the recorded discussions.

Several matters remained to be cleared up after the Rome conference. First, the Canadian government continued to battle the perception that it was operating under, as opposed to alongside, Britain. The Canadian and British governments moved to correct an inaccuracy in the draft records of the conference, which had stated that Britain appointed the delegates for the autonomous dominions. After some back and forth, the offending paragraph was deleted.[131]

Second, there was some optimism and speculation that the United States might join the *Berne Convention* at the 1928 conference. One newspaper had proclaimed in 1927 that "America will adhere to the Berne Convention," based on an announcement made by the American delegate to the first international congress of the *Sociétés d'auteurs et compositeurs* that the United States wished to join the convention.[132] After the conference, the Canadian delegation left so soon after signing that they were uncertain whether the United States had also signed. Désy, having heard a rumour that the American delegate had signed, wrote to the new Canadian Legation in Washington a month after the conference ended to find out whether this had in fact happened. He received the reply that the American delegate had been only an observer, without authorization to sign the agreement, and that the United States had not signed.[133] Optimism remained, however, that the United States would soon join the convention. In their report, the Canadian delegates noted that one of the American representatives, a congressman, had mentioned plans to introduce a ratification bill in the session beginning that December. This was backed, they noted, by a strong movement that had developed in favour of American adhesion.[134]

The possibility that the Canadian government might follow that of the United States and abstain from the *Berne Convention* was not considered. A memo written several months after the American declaration at the conference of the *Sociétés d'auteurs et compositeurs* stated: "Whether the United States shall adhere or not to the Revised Convention does not modify the policy of the Canadian Government with regard to the Copyright. In either case, the Dominion of Canada would seem to be interested in adhering to the proposed Convention."[135] By 1928, the view that Canada should be a party to *Berne* was well established. The Canadian political parties supported this, the major copyright interest groups were not demanding otherwise, and there were forces in the United States pushing for adhesion. The sense of the desirability of adhesion to the convention was inscribed almost universally in the policies and positions of many groups, with few, if any, calls to do otherwise. This sense was moving along a historically contingent trajectory, first set in place in the 1880s, that was now reflected in parties' positions, in the government itself, and in the positions of relevant interest groups. With talk of the United States – the country that heretofore had provided a model for a different set of copyright norms outside the Berne Union – considering coming on board, other possible paths appeared even more remote than before.

There were few reports about the conference in Canadian newspapers, although reports by representatives of several private interests who had attended the meeting were presented at the Canadian Authors' Convention and at the Canadian Authors' Association in July and October 1928, respectively. These reports were noted in the *Globe*.[136]

Ricketson and Ginsburg argue that the 1928 conference achieved "relatively little" in terms of the expansion of creators' rights, compared with earlier conferences, due in part to the greatly expanded range of national interests represented. Thus, from the perspective of copyright holders, the conference could be viewed, if not as having expanded copyright, as having defended against attempts to limit copyright through compulsory licences and user interests.[137]

In contrast, the Canadian delegates themselves felt that copyright, as well as the authority of the Berne Union in general, had been greatly extended: "The Conference has extended and consolidated the international authority of the Union of Berne. The exclusive right of the author to his work has been maintained and made complete. The recognition of the moral right of the author may be looked upon as the outstanding achievement of the conference."[138] According to them, the revision process represented progress:

> The purpose of the periodical revision is to keep the international protection of products of the mind in conformity with economic, scientific and intellectual progress. During the last 20 years, scientific discoveries and their application have created new needs and interests and made imperative a solution of the problem of international protection of copyright. Modern means of reproduction and distribution have increased the commercial value of products of the mind and made necessary certain modifications of former juridical rules.[139]

Furthermore:

> We consider that the Convention of Rome, the result of cordial cooperation among several countries, marks an important advance and establishes a "moral entente" of a very high order. It forms an important stage in the post-war reconstruction of international life. By providing protection for the rights of the intellect, the new States as well as the old have proclaimed that nations have need of the things of the spirit, and that the creations of thought are indispensable to the progress of civilisation.[140]

In June 1928, shortly after the conference, the acting Commissioner of Patents, Thomas L. Richard, was made Commissioner of Patents with the status of a deputy minister, making the Patent and Copyright Office more or less independent.[141] This was done partly in anticipation of more work for the branch as a result of anticipated amendments to the *Copyright Act* following the Rome conference.[142]

Moves to amend the 1924 *Copyright Act,* which had been postponed until after the results of the Rome conference were known, now went ahead.[143] The 1928 revision of the *Berne Convention* now required the granting of both performance and broadcast rights in copyright works.[144]

The Canadian Performing Right Society (CPRS) had been formed in 1925 by the Performing Right Society of England to represent British rights holders and had been assigned the Canadian performing rights in approximately 2 million British works. The role of the CPRS was to collect money when those works were performed in Canada. Money was collected through royalties and through lawsuits against parties who performed the works without authorization. The money collected, less deductions, went back to the Performing Right Society of England.[145] The legitimacy of this organization's operations in Canada, the fees it collected, and its modes of operation were broadly questioned, which led first to a legal case that was ultimately decided by the Privy Council in London, and also to two Canadian Royal Commissions.

1929: *Canadian Performing Right Society Ltd. v. Famous Players Canadian Corporation Ltd.*

In February 1929, the Judicial Committee of the Privy Council of Great Britain handed down a decision on an appeal from the Supreme Court of Ontario in the case of the *Canadian Performing Right Society Ltd. v. Famous Players Canadian Corporation Ltd.*[146] Two of the compositions for which performing rights were held by the CPRS – "By Jingo" and "Colonel Bogey March" – were performed without permission at a Famous Players theatre in Toronto by the theatre orchestra at a paid performance. The CPRS therefore took legal action against Famous Players in a test case to determine the legal rights of performing rights societies, during which time the CPRS agreed to suspend legal actions on the issue.[147] It was found that the performing rights assignments had not been registered at the Canadian Copyright Office as required under the *Copyright Act*.[148] Such registration, required in duplicate at the cost of $1 per work prescribed by the act, would have cost the CPRS $2 million. Ontario courts and the Judicial Committee of the Privy Council of Great Britain agreed, however, that the wording of the *Copyright Act* was clear and that such registration was indeed required in order for legal action to be taken under the act.[149]

The CPRS argued that it was practically impossible for a foreign company to comply with the registration requirements prescribed by the act.[150] It further argued that the registration requirement in the Canadian *Copyright Act* contravened the *Berne Convention*'s requirement that the enjoyment of copyright by foreign rights holders not be subject to formalities such as registration requirements.[151] Following the initial Ontario court decisions, the British Foreign Office wrote to the Canadian government, drawing attention to the issue and arguing not only that the Canadian *Copyright Act* contravened the *Berne Convention* but also that, because the registration process in Canada was more onerous than in Britain, the Canadian act as now interpreted might no longer confer rights that were substantially identical to those conferred by Britain, a condition of British recognition of Canadian copyright.[152]

This legal case and and the potential conflict between the Canadian *Copyright Act* and the *Berne Convention* was raised in the House of Commons on 22 February 1929.[153] Eventually it was proposed, following continued pressure from

Britain,[154] and noting that the registration requirements under the *Copyright Act* could bankrupt companies such as the CPRS, that the registration requirements be dropped from the act.[155] The matter was summarized in 1931 by former Secretary of State Rinfret, now part of the Liberal opposition, as follows:

> There are two schools of thought regarding copyright and from that duality comes the whole difficulty about having the proper distinction. One school of thought, which is the European school, is that copyright is a right in itself; that whenever a writer has composed, or a painter or whoever he is has created a work, he has the full ownership of that work in using the copyright. That is the conception adopted by all European countries which formed the convention in Berne, later on confirmed in Rome, whereby in every country in that union the mere fact that a person was the composer or writer of a book gave him the fullest rights as to all the copyright privileges that might be attached to it ... The other school of thought is what I shall call the United States school of thought, which says that copyright is a privilege and can be enjoyed only if it is registered. In the United States of America a copyright will not be recognized unless it has been properly registered ... The point I wish to make to-day is that we shall have to make our choice. We must have in this country copyright legislation which will be clear-cut. Either we shall adhere to the convention of Rome and do away with registration, or we shall withdraw from Rome and have our own registration.[156]

Except for the period between 1889 and approximately 1909, Canadian governments had elected, over and over, to be part of the Berne Union: first in 1886, then at the 1910 Imperial Copyright Conference, then with 1910 Speech from the Throne, with Bill E in 1919, and with the 1921 and 1923 copyright bills. The purpose of all of these moves was to implement the *Berne Convention* in one fashion or another. The recurring question concerned how Canada could navigate between the norms of the most powerful members of the Berne Union and those of the United States. Which copyright traditions could be encompassed within the Berne Union? The British had dropped registration requirements, adjusted their term of protection, and dropped domestic publication requirements in their attempts to navigate between their former approach to copyright and that of their European neighbours, whereas the Americans held firmly to some originally British elements, such as registration requirements. The Canadians had dramatically reduced Canadian domestic registration requirements and had substituted for domestic printing and publishing requirements compulsory licensing provisions, attempting thus to navigate between the norms of the Berne Union and those of the United States.

The Canadian approach of navigating between the competing copyright traditions of more powerful countries was realist not in the sense normally advocated by realist theories of international relations, which is skeptical of international agreements, but in the sense meant by Roy Rempel when he argued that Canadian foreign affairs should focus not on ideals but on Canada's relationship with more powerful nations.[157] In international copyright relations, Canadian governments had focused less on particular copyright ideals and philosophies than on finding space among and between more powerful countries – and specifically between the norms of the Berne Union and those of the United States. This attempt would later be judged as having been "not too well advised" by the 1957 Ilsley Commission, which saw little benefit in Canada's historical adhesion to the *Berne Convention* and greater advantages in following more closely the realist and protectionist path of the United States.[158]

Mackenzie King had been Prime Minister since 1921. His policies of freer trade with the United States ended when R.B. Bennett came to power in 1930. The Conservatives had always assumed a more protectionist stance on trade, and Bennett raised tariffs immediately.[159] Some of the economic nationalism of the Bennett government would be reflected in Canada's copyright policies in the early 1930s, in debates over issues arising from the CPRS case. These policies also coincided with a nascent cultural nationalism that resulted in the passage of the 1932 *Broadcasting Act* and the creation of a national public broadcasting agency, as well as the creation of the National Film Board in 1939.[160]

1931: *An Act to Amend the Copyright Act*

A new bill to amend the *Copyright Act* was introduced in the House of Commons on 18 March 1931 and received royal assent on 11 June, but only after significant debate. The bill was introduced by the government in order to deal with the issue of performing rights organizations in Canada, and to implement the 1928 revision of the *Berne Convention*.

With regard to the former, the Motion Picture Distributors and Exhibitors of Canada (MPDEC), under the hand of the Motion Picture Producers and Distributors Association of America in New York, were especially concerned about the payment of performing rights fees by motion picture theatres.[161] They argued that if Canadian theatres were required to pay such fees, they would have to pay twice, to both American and British performing rights societies. Canadian theatres would thus be under a greater burden than their American or British counterparts, which paid only one or the other of the societies. The MPDEC had encouraged an arrangement whereby the two societies would charge a single fee to Canadian theatres, but these efforts fell through.[162] They were also concerned that, as sound tracks were added to "talking" films, the rights situation for theatres might be further complicated, and suggested that theatres should not be held liable for copyright claims by authors and composers whose works were used in a film.[163]

The new act eased the registration requirements for the assignment of rights and put in place special provisions for performing rights societies, requiring the deposit with the Minister at the Copyright Office of lists of the dramatico-musical and musical works for which they claimed authority to grant performance licences, along with statements of fees or royalties that they proposed to collect for performance of the works.[164] These provisions applied only to dramatico-musical and musical works, and not to dramatic or literary works, which was satisfactory to the MPDEC.[165] The act also exempted non-profit performances by churches, colleges, and schools, or by religious, charitable, or fraternal organizations, from payment for licences for performance rights. It imposed certain regulations on performing rights organizations that would allow the Governor-in-Council, at the recommendation of the Minister and following an investigation and report by a commissioner appointed under the *Inquiries Act,* to revise or prescribe the fees, charges, or royalties that the society could collect on performance licences.[166] In order to implement the new requirements of the 1928 revision of the *Berne Convention,* the act also granted moral rights and broadcast rights in copyright works.[167]

Canadian parliamentarians were anxious that the new Canadian *Copyright Act* fit smoothly into the *Berne Convention,* and there were fears that if Canada did not conform to the convention, it might become an outsider in the international community. As Liberal MP Edgar-Rodolphe-Eugène Chevrier put it during the debate on the bill: "Some forty-odd nations have to ratify the convention. They are all unanimous as to the legislation that is to be adopted, and into that concert of nations – I am not saying this in any spirit of levity – I hesitate to see Canada enter with a non-harmonious and non-musical instrument."[168]

Chevrier argued that the bill's provisions on moral rights did not go far enough to conform to the *Berne Convention.*[169] He expressed doubts as to whether the performing rights exceptions for churches, colleges, schools, and religious, charitable, or fraternal organizations would be permissible under the convention,[170] and raised questions about whether the Canadian legislation in general went far enough to safeguard the rights of authors.[171] Perhaps most important, given the *Famous Players* case, he argued that the registration requirements in the bill, although they had been eased, and the requirement that performing rights organizations file lists of the works whose rights they controlled and the fees they proposed to charge, still contravened the convention's prohibition on formalities. Furthermore, he argued that the elements of the bill that would regulate performing rights organizations and allow the government to intervene if they charged excessive fees also contravened the *Berne Convention*, by interfering with the right of the copyright holder (interpreted to include assignees) to enjoy his or her rights.[172]

The MPDEC argued, however, that the registration requirements under the existing copyright law should not be too quickly dismissed as being in contravention of the *Berne Convention*. They argued that no protests about such a contravention had been received, and that the Judicial Committee of the Privy Council, in deciding the *Famous Players* case, had not held that the Canadian law was in contravention.[173]

Despite arguments that the bill was inconsistent with the *Berne Convention*, the government defended the proposed measures since no other options appeared feasible given the state of public opinion at the time. Secretary of State Charles Cahan argued: "If certain regulations which we propose to enact in this bill are not within the Berne convention, then public opinion in this country is in such a state that the great body of it may say that the sooner Canada gets out of the Berne convention, the better for Canada."[174] No MP suggested that Parliament should not implement – or attempt to implement – the *Berne Convention*, but Chevrier argued rhetorically, in response to Cahan's comment, that given the measures proposed by the government, Canada might be obliged to withdraw from the convention:

> Now if public opinion in Canada is so strong as to force the Canadian parliament to legalize the spoliation of authors' rights, of the rights of nationals and of the rights of the unionists, in contravention of the terms of the convention of Berne, and if the present legislation is the result of that public opinion, then I say that it is incumbent upon the minister to propose the immediate withdrawal of Canada from the Berne convention, and from my seat I now challenge the minister to do it.[175]

The government did not propose to withdraw from the convention, and Chevrier predicted that the legislation would be challenged before long: "I am confident that it will not be long before steps are taken by the proper authorities to bring these objections before a competent tribunal to test the soundness of the bill which we are about to pass."[176]

Canada was not forced to change the bill under the *Berne Convention*, however. Cahan's arguments contributed to a body of knowledge and expertise that supported both the legitimacy of performing rights societies generally and the claim that they should be regulated under the *Berne Convention*. This was to be the Canadian government's interpretation of the convention, to which it held fast despite challenges from some quarters. Counter-interpretations were also established, especially in the work done and expertise established by MP Chevrier, but no major challenge was forthcoming from any other party to the *Berne Convention* or from International Office.

Passage of the bill came just under the wire; the deadline for ratification of the revised *Berne Convention* was 1 July 1931.[177] In view of this, and with Parliament under pressure to pass the bill immediately, budget discussions were delayed in the House of Commons in favour of dealing with the copyright matter, and there was no Senate debate of the bill.[178] Several senators raised concerns about whether it provided sufficient protection for copyright holders, and about passing a bill that was so controversial – "one of the most contentious of all matters that has come before Parliament" – and upon which so much correspondence had been received, with neither time to study it nor even a short description of what it contained.[179] The Right Honourable F.A. Anglin, acting that day as the Deputy of the Governor General, went to the Senate on 11 June to give royal assent.[180] The following day, the Privy Council approved Canada's ratification of the revisions to the *Berne Convention,* and the Secretary of State for External Affairs telegraphed the Secretary of State for Dominion Affairs in London to ask that Canada's instrument of ratification be prepared.[181]

The ratification took place without any problem. When Parliament had moved to conform to the *Berne Convention* in the early 1920s, Britain had been more actively involved in judging whether or not the new legislation was in conformity. Although similar questions were raised in the early 1930s, Britain was less directly involved. British commentary on past Canadian legislation touching on the issues surrounding the CPRS was cited in the debates in the House, but when the Canadian government requested that the instruments of ratification be deposited, the British government complied without resistance. In some ways, the Canadian Parliament's ability to legislate on copyright in relative freedom from British intervention had finally caught up with what had been the norm for years in other areas of law.

The Canadian Authors' Association immediately opposed the new copyright law and the exemptions from performing rights fees that it provided to exhibitions, fairs, churches, and charitable organizations. It declared at its June 1931 convention that such measures were "unfair to intellectual labour," and that it would seek changes to the law at the next session of Parliament. A further motion to withdraw support from any organization taking advantage of the measures was withdrawn.[182]

Canada's 1931 amendment to the *Copyright Act* passed just months before the enactment on 11 December 1931 of the *Statute of Westminster,* which granted

British colonies status as sovereign states. The *Statute of Westminster* stated that "no law hereafter made by the Parliament of the United Kingdom" or by any dominion parliament "shall extend to any of the said Dominions as part of the law of that Dominion otherwise than at the request and at the consent of that Dominion."[183]

1931: *Gribble v. Manitoba Free Press Co.*

The 1928 revision of the *Berne Convention* had left room for the unauthorized reproduction of newspaper articles on current economic, political, or religious topics in the press unless such reproduction was expressly forbidden.[184] The Canadian *Copyright Act*, however, did not permit such reproduction. This gave rise to a test case, in which Francis Gribble published an article titled "The Life of Louis Hemon" in the London publication *T.P.'s Weekly*. The article was reproduced in the *Ottawa Journal* and subsequently reproduced, according to a custom among Canadian newspapers that permitted free copying from one newspaper by another, by the *Manitoba Free Press* without the consent of the article's author or either prior publisher. The *Manitoba Free Press* argued that, under the *Berne Convention,* newspaper articles could be reproduced by another newspaper unless this was expressly forbidden.[185] Thus, it argued, its copying was justified. The Manitoba Court of Appeal concluded, however, that the *Berne Convention* provided only a *minimum* of protection, which a country could exceed in its domestic laws, and that rights were governed exclusively by the laws of country where protection was claimed, rather than by the convention itself. Therefore, since Canadian legislation prevailed over the provisions of the *Berne Convention,* the copying of a newspaper article by another newspaper was an infringement of copyright.[186] The court also concluded that, since the contracting states of the *Berne Convention* constituted a union *for the protection of the rights of authors,* should any interpretation be in doubt, the interpretation that was most favourable to the protection of authors' rights should be preferred.[187]

1932 and 1935: Two Royal Commissions

Performing rights societies were new to Canadians in the early 1930s. The idea that a hotel should pay for a licence to have a radio playing in the hotel lobby, or that an organization putting on a performance of some kind might be confronted by a performing rights organization demanding licensing fees, did not sit well with many Canadians. This was especially true since the Canadian Performing Right Society did not initially represent Canadian rights holders – all the profits derived from such activities went to foreign countries. The decade of the 1930s was a period in which the norms governing performing rights organizations, their standard ways of operating, and the legitimate modes of government intervention in their operations were still in flux. It was also the period in which the Copyright Appeal Board was formed to regulate such societies, thereby establishing a new domestic source of institutional knowledge, authority, and norms.

Questions surrounding the issue of performing and broadcasting rights in Canada led to the creation of two Royal Commissions to investigate the practices of the CPRS in granting performance and broadcast licences, the fees it charged, and whether such fees were excessive. The first was chaired by Mr. Justice Albert Freeman Ewing and reported in 1932, following private meetings between the parties in Alberta. The second, chaired by Judge James Parker, travelled to Toronto, Montreal, Ottawa, Halifax, Moncton, Winnipeg, and Regina, and reported in 1935.[188]

Whereas the Ewing Commission recommended certain changes to the way that broadcast licence fees were calculated, the Parker Commission went further and recommended the creation of an independent body to examine the fees charged. The Parker Commission questioned whether the regulation of performance rights might contravene the *Berne Convention,* but took the view that Parliament could regulate CPRS as a Canadian national.[189] As a result, the Copyright Appeal Board (now the Copyright Board) was formed in 1936 to regulate the fees charged and collected by collecting societies.[190]

The Parker Commission also began the process of legitimizing performance and broadcasting rights in Canada. As one lawyer at the commission noted:

> The investigation cannot help but do good, no matter what the result may be. It will serve to impress upon the public the fact that they (The Canadian Performing Right Society, Limited) have legal rights[,] that the parties they represent have legal rights in copyright, and that the performing rights, with which we are so concerned, is in law a matter for which they are entitled to receive *fair and proper payment.*[191]

Through collecting societies and the *Berne Convention,* Canada became integrated in what would become an international system of copyright norm setting and an international network of royalty and licence payments.

CHAPTER NINE

New Directions, 1936-67

DESPITE CANADA'S NEWFOUND INDEPENDENCE, there remained strong ties between Canada and Britain. Canada followed Britain into the Second World War and sent aid when Britain was in danger of falling to Germany. The British Foreign Office continued to act for Canada in most countries; the Canadian government itself had diplomatic representatives in only three countries – Britain, the United States, and Japan – throughout most of the 1930s.[1] Loosening imperial bonds and a declining British Empire, however, along with strengthening American economic ties, meant that Canada was pulled closer into the sphere of the United States.[2] This shift would be reflected in a cooling of Canada's relationship to the *Berne Convention*, along with a shift towards a new American-led treaty initiative.

During the 1930s, relations with the United States warmed considerably.[3] This, and Canada's emergence as an independent state, came to be reflected in the structure of diplomacy between the two countries. The Canadian Legation in Washington was transformed into a full-fledged embassy, and the Canadian minister became an ambassador, the first Canadian diplomat to hold that rank.[4]

Despite warmer relations with the United States, some mistrust and anti-Americanism remained, especially in the field of cultural policy. American cultural products flowed heavily into Canada, leading to concerns about increasing Americanization. The report of the Royal Commission on National Development in the Arts, Letters and Sciences (the Massey Commission) in 1951 encouraged state patronage of the arts and led to the creation of the Canada Council in 1957.[5] Prime Minister John Diefenbaker's Conservative government assumed a stance of anti-American nationalism and threatened to direct trade away from the United States and towards Britain. To promote Canadian magazines, a 1960 Royal Commission on Publications (the O'Leary Commission) recommended the removal of income tax deductions for advertisements published in foreign publications and the prohibition of split-run magazines with

Canadian advertisements – recommendations that were strongly protested by Washington and eventually implemented only with special exemptions for the American magazines *Time* and *Reader's Digest*.[6] Although Canada would move closer to the United States in copyright policy during this period, tensions remained over the Americans' domestic printing requirements.

The Department of External Affairs began to expand. By 1947, there were 175 officers, and more overseas missions were added. An embassy had opened in Turkey; legations had been established in Sweden, Poland, Switzerland, Denmark, and Italy; a High Commission had been established in New Delhi; and a consulate had opened in Brazil. There were now twenty-eight diplomatic missions and seven consulates, along with a permanent delegate to the United Nations.[7] In this midst of this expansion, international copyright policy was put on the backburner.

After the Second World War, the United States became preoccupied with international reconstruction, in which Canada was only a minor player.[8] The Canadian government fought to gain standing in international organizations, promoting the "functional principle" that "in certain specific fields Canada had legitimate claims to consideration from the great powers. In such 'functional' areas – in the production of food and raw materials, for example – Canada had world capacity and was, therefore, entitled to a share in decision-making and responsibility."[9] Canada's contributions during the war had been substantial, and officials fought for a strong Canadian presence at the United Nations and substantial representation at other international organizations.[10] Canada was able to achieve representation on several international bodies, proving that the country had attained a status and gained a voice on issues affecting it.[11] It was coming to be seen as a "middle power," and, as a result of its massive war effort and advocacy of the functional principle, a leader among middle powers.[12] In the field of copyright, Canada was a sought-after but at times reluctant participant.

At the first general conference of the United Nations Educational, Scientific and Cultural Organization (UNESCO), held in November and December 1947, Herman Voaden, president of the Canadian Arts Council, called for increased support for Canadian artists.[13] Canadian creative industries had grown dramatically. The country's population had doubled to 14 million since 1921, and with it grew the industries and groups with a stake in copyright.[14] The number of authors and artists had risen from about 2,000 in 1921 to 12,000 in 1951.[15] The copyright industries had grown tremendously, as had industries with an interest in using copyright works. The first Canadian cable television operations were established in Nicolet, Quebec, in 1950. Cable operators retransmitted over-the-air television signals to their subscribers without paying for the use of the retransmitted signals, and the question of whether this was an infringement of copyright would soon arise.

To the list of still-active lobby groups, including the Canadian Manufacturers' Association and the Composers, Authors, and Publishers Association of Canada (formerly known as the Canadian Performing Right Society[16]) were added another performing rights organization – BMI Canada (originally established in 1940 as the Canadian arm of the American organization Broadcast Music Inc. and later known as PRO Canada and PROCAN[17]) – as well as the Canadian League of Composers (established in 1951[18]), the Association of Canadian Radio and Television Artists (established in 1943 as the Association of Canadian Radio Artists and later known as the Canadian Council of Authors and Artists, the Association of Canadian Television and Radio Artists, and, since 1984, the Alliance of Canadian Cinema, Television and Radio Artists, or ACTRA[19]), the Canadian Association of Broadcasters (in existence since 1926[20]), the Canadian Music Publishers Association (established in 1949[21]), the Canadian Conference of the Arts (established as the Canadian Arts Council in 1945 and renamed in 1958[22]), and the *Fédération des auteurs et des artistes du Canada*. All would eventually become active in copyright issues.[23]

Diplomatic Conference: Brussels, 5-26 June 1948
Originally scheduled for 1935 but postponed several times for various reasons, including the Second World War, the next diplomatic conference to revise the *Berne Convention* took place in Brussels in 1948.[24] The British Foreign Office accepted the formal 1936 invitation of the Belgian government on behalf of Canada before the conference was postponed to 1948.[25]

The Brussels conference resulted in the following modifications of the *Berne Convention*:

- The term of protection of life plus fifty years was made mandatory (it had been left as optional under the 1928 revision).[26]
- Explicit permission was given "to make short quotations from newspaper articles and periodicals, as well as to include them in press summaries."[27]
- The right to authorize a public performance of a work was strengthened.[28]
- The right to authorize broadcasting of a work was expanded. The copyright holder would now be granted the right to authorize the communication of a broadcast to the public (making it, for example, a requirement for a restaurant to have a licence to display a television broadcast in public).[29]
- The jurisdiction of the International Court of Justice in disputes between member states regarding the interpretation or implementation of the *Berne Convention* was recognized.[30]

Canadian ambassador to Belgium Victor Doré attended as president of the Canadian delegation.[31] W.P.J. O'Meara, Assistant Under-Secretary of State, and V.C. MacDonald, dean of Dalhousie University's law school, were the two other delegates, O'Meara as "substitute president" and MacDonald as a technical adviser.[32]

The Canadian delegation was significantly more active in 1948 than was its predecessor at the 1928 revision conference. Canada was appointed to the drafting committee,[33] the subcommission on broadcasting and mechanical instruments,[34] the subcommission on industrial arts,[35] the subcommission on countries' financial contributions to the Berne Union, and the subcommission on the coordination of texts, where Canada also acted as president.[36]

Canada, along with Brazil, France, Great Britain, Hungary, India, Italy, Norway, the Netherlands, Portugal, Switzerland, and Czechoslovakia, was appointed as one of the first members on the Permanent Committee of the Berne Union.[37] This committee was established at the 1948 conference to act in an advisory capacity and to assist the International Office in its duties. Although formally the committee had advisory powers only, it was, in effect, the steering body of the Berne Union between diplomatic conferences.[38] It consisted of twelve member states with rotating membership: four states were replaced every three years.

Regarding the revision of the *Berne Convention* itself, the Canadian delegation made a number of significant interventions on the topics of copyright holders from outside the Berne Union, moral rights, the definition of "published works," and bilingualism. First, several of Canada's comments related specifically to its own situation in relation to the United States. With regard to the first paragraph of Article 6, which granted copyright holders from outside the Berne Union who first publish their works in a country of the union the same rights as union creators,[39] the delegation observed that such a provision did not encourage countries to join the union, but rather encouraged them not to join.[40]

Insofar as the countries of the union were required to protect the works of non-union copyright holders, the delegation requested that a proviso be added to Article 6 of the convention that the duration of such protection should not exceed the duration of copyright in the copyright holder's country of origin.[41] In the end, this suggestion was not adopted. Canada's proposals were related to concern that the term of protection in the United States was often effectively shorter than that granted in Canada, which meant that works first published in Canada, or simultaneously published in Canada and the United States, often entered the public domain in the United States before they did in Canada.

The Canadian delegation also proposed that the term of protection under Article 7 be limited to that available in the country of origin. The delegation stated that this was particularly important to Canadians, since Canadian consumers would be obliged to pay royalties for works that had entered the public domain in the United States, where the term of protection was shorter.[42] This suggestion was not adopted; the term of the country of origin would be used only in cases where a country of the union offered protection that extended longer than the minimum of life plus fifty years, which was not the case in Canada.[43]

The conference also retained provisions first adopted under the 1914 protocol allowing countries to restrict protection offered to copyright holders of a country outside the union that "fails to protect in an adequate manner the works of authors who are nationals of one of the countries of the Union," upon notice to the government of the Swiss Confederation.[44] Here, the Canadian delegation requested that the word *suffisante* (adequate) be clarified, since the word as it stood did not define the extent of protection that must be accorded.[45] This proposal was also not adopted.

Second, Great Britain had proposed that the article requiring recognition of moral rights, which was an obstacle to US adhesion to the convention, be removed.[46] The French, however, proposed to *extend* moral rights and to make them inalienable. The Canadian delegation associated itself with a declaration by the British delegation that, should that article not be removed, it should at least stay in its present form and that any additions to the article should be included not in the text of the convention itself but in a protocol thereto. In the end, a compromise was adopted whereby moral rights were extended such that they would last as long as the economic rights granted under the treaty, but that national laws would regulate the control and exercise of those rights.[47]

Third, the Canadian delegation observed that the words "published works" should be more clearly defined and updated.[48] Ultimately, the definition of "published works" was revised to include those issued to the public "and made available in sufficient quantities." Furthermore, it was clarified that various newer modes of presentation, such as the presentation of a cinematographic work or the transmission or the radio-diffusion of literary or artistic works, did not constitute publication.[49]

Finally, the Canadian delegation supported a British proposal that an English text of the *Berne Convention* be formally adopted. The Canadian delegation noted Canada's bilingual history and argued that an official English text would make the convention more attractive to the United States.[50] An English text was adopted, but as an "equivalent text" rather than an "official text." Other countries of the union were entitled to have an "authoritative text" established by the International Office in the language of their choice. The French text remained the only "official text," however, and would prevail over the others in cases of conflicting interpretations.[51] Ricketson and Ginsburg comment that even this change, strongly resisted by the French delegates, "was deeply symbolic of the general changes occurring in the composition and orientation of the Union."[52]

In signing the convention, the Canadian delegation associated itself, as did the Union of South Africa, Switzerland, Ireland, the Netherlands, Australia, New Zealand, India, Pakistan, and Norway, with a British declaration related to Article 11 on performing rights. This declaration stated that the government reserved the freedom to legislate as it deemed necessary to limit or prevent any abuse of copyright holders' exclusive rights.[53]

In summary, the Canadian delegation failed to win provisions that would prevent the situation, caused by the mandatory term of life plus fifty years, where works copyrighted in the United States were protected in Canada longer than in the United States. The delegation also failed in its bid to see moral rights either retained in their 1928 wording or removed. The Canadians' support for a bilingual text of the *Berne Convention* was partially successful, and its suggestion that the definition of "published works" be revised was adopted.

The Canadian delegation's formal interventions at the 1948 conference distinguished between net copyright importers and net copyright exporters; the Canadian delegation identified Canada as a country that *consumes* literary and artistic works.[54] This overt identification of Canada as a copyright consumer – one that had not been highlighted in the 1920s when Canada was new to the Berne Union – would remain at the centre of Canadian copyright policy throughout the 1950s, '60s, and '70s.

Canada's representation on the Permanent Committee reflected its achievements in gaining representation in international forums. This did not necessarily mean that Canadians wielded a great deal of influence. The 1948 revisions to the convention necessitated a number of changes to Canadian copyright law that the government would be unwilling to make. The deadline for ratification of the 1948 act of the *Berne Convention* was 1 July 1951.[55] Although work towards a redrafting of the *Copyright Act* began before June 1949,[56] no new copyright act was passed and Canada would never ratify the 1948 act of the convention.

1952: *Universal Copyright Convention*

Meetings under UNESCO throughout the late 1940s and early 1950s, initiated largely by the United States, led in 1952 to the formation of a new multilateral copyright treaty, the *Universal Copyright Convention*. Eighty-six countries, including the United States, signed the convention. It established minimum copyright requirements that were less demanding than those of the *Berne Convention*, including a minimum term of protection of twenty-five years or life plus twenty-five years (the 1948 revision of the *Berne Convention* required a minimum term of life plus fifty years) and a shorter term for translation rights. As did the *Berne Convention,* it prevented member states from requiring domestic printing of works from foreign member states as a condition of copyright. Its promulgation was part of a larger American project to encourage American cultural influence in "the fringe areas of the world in which propaganda from behind the Iron Curtain has its greatest impact."[57] The *Universal Copyright Convention* was intended to be a compromise treaty, allowing countries with diverse copyright laws to come together under a single treaty. In particular, it attempted a compromise between net copyright exporters and net copyright importers by permitting the compulsory licensing of translations[58] – that is, if a work had not been published in the national language of a contracting state after seven years from first publication, any national of that state could obtain a compulsory licence to publish a translation.[59]

Despite tensions between the two copyright regimes, efforts were made to ensure that they worked in concert. A report from the Canadian Embassy in Berne gave the following account of a conversation with Jacques Secrétan, director of the International Office of the Berne Union:

> Mr Secrétan had some caustic remarks to make about the Universal copyright convention drafted by UNESCO. In his opinion the UNESCO convention did not give as adequate protection as does the Berne convention and he thought it a result of UNESCO's desperate efforts to find work to justify their existence ... He thought it ridiculous that there should be a conflict between the Universal convention and the Berne Convention in the form of a race for adherence and informed me that he had attempted to arrive at an Agreement with UNESCO in order to coordinate and approach the various parliaments for ratification. He thought it would be unfortunate if, say, a South American Government or Parliament should be faced with two different conventions dealing with copyright for ratification.[60]

Article 17 and its accompanying declaration, otherwise known as the "safeguard clause," of the *Universal Copyright Convention* was instituted to prevent countries from switching from the *Berne Convention* to the *Universal Copyright Convention;* a declaration was made under Article 17 that any country that denounced the *Berne Convention* would no longer receive protection under the *Universal Copyright Convention* in any member of the Berne Union.[61] Although the article would have the effect of ensuring that countries could not exit the *Berne Convention* in favour of the *Universal Copyright Convention,* the latter was still perceived as presenting a challenge to the Berne Union because it established a set of alternative copyright norms that were attractive to developing countries.

Within the next twenty years, provisions similar to those of the *Universal Copyright Convention* for developing countries were incorporated into the *Berne Convention* as the Berne Union also adapted to the international concern for development. It was not a happy fit initially; as in the days of Canada's development in the nineteenth century, the concerns of the dominant countries of the union conflicted with the priorities of developing countries, the latter seeking accommodations that were out of sync with the ideas of "progress" that dominated the union. Now, however, the discourse of development was hegemonic and institutionalized within institutions such as UNESCO. Faced with a choice between, on the one hand, retaining the existing restricted union and taking the risk that rival conventions might mean the eventual obsolescence of the union, and on the other hand, creating more flexible copyright norms to make the union more inviting to a broader membership, the Berne Union took the latter path.[62] Furthermore, a vision for a World Intellectual Property Organization with links to the United Nations was beginning to take shape, making it all the more necessary for the Berne Union to accommodate developing countries and to adopt the discourse of development.

Canada and the Drafting of the *Universal Copyright Convention*

The Intergovernmental Copyright Conference at which the *Universal Copyright Convention* was signed took place in Geneva, from 18 August to 6 September 1952, during the city's tourist season.[63] The Canadian delegation was headed by Minister to Switzerland Victor Doré, who had also led the delegation to the 1948 revision of the *Berne Convention,* and included Charles Stein, Under-Secretary of State, and G.G. Beckett, vice chairman of the Administrative Board and associate counsel with the Custodian of Enemy Property, Secretary of State. Although the Custodian of Enemy Property had few obvious dealings with copyright, Stein had asked that Beckett accompany him; both were on their way to deal with Custodian matters in Switzerland and elsewhere, and copyright, Stein noted, was "among the types of enemy assets that became vested in the Custodian during the war and the Custodian's Office has to deal with the odd problem in this connection."[64] Harold G. Fox attended as adviser to the delegation.[65]

During the negotiation of the convention, the Canadian delegation participated in a working group on the relationship between the *Universal Copyright Convention* and the *Berne Convention*. Canadian delegates objected to the inclusion of Article 17, arguing that the *Berne Convention* could "defend itself" without such provisions and that the provisions were "contrary to the spirit of the Universal Convention."[66] In light of the views of other delegations, however, the Canadians backed down and the article was ultimately included.[67]

The delegation made little comment on the conference upon their return to Canada. Instead of the normal practice of submitting a report by the delegation, Doré simply submitted the report of the conference's General Rapporteur to "be considered as that of our delegation."[68]

The United States ratified the *Universal Copyright Convention* in 1954.[69] Although Canada was a signatory, the Canadian government did not move immediately to ratify the convention. The delay was due in part to a desire to first see the results of the Royal Commission on Patents, Copyright, Trade Marks and Industrial Designs, appointed in 1954,[70] but also to the fact that ratification of the treaty had simply not received active consideration.[71] In 1956, the Department of External Affairs took the position that the Department of the Secretary of State should play a more active role so that Canada's position with regard to the *Universal Copyright Convention* could be clarified.[72] It was several years before such consideration took place, however.

Disengagement from the Berne Union

Having moved in the 1920s to join the international copyright regime and to join the Berne orchestra as a "harmonious instrument," and following the Canadian contributions to the discussions at the revision conference in 1948, where the safeguard clause was adopted despite Canadian objections, Canada began to drift away from this relative internationalism and to fall out of step with the Berne regime. The Canadian government had difficulties participating fully in the Permanent Committee of the Berne Union over the years that followed. Paul E. Renaud, Councillor of the Canadian Legation in Switzerland, was Canada's representative on the committee for its first annual meeting in September 1949.[73] Victor Doré, Canada's lead delegate at the Brussels conference and later at the creation of the *Universal Copyright Convention*, was too heavily occupied in Brussels to sit on the committee at that time,[74] but participated in its second and third meetings in 1950 and 1951, respectively.[75]

In June 1952, the Department of External Affairs suggested that Canada retire from the committee, membership in which was renewable every three years. This, the department argued, would give Australia or South Africa an opportunity to join the committee. At the suggestion of the Patent Commissioner, however, Canada's Under-Secretary of State objected on the grounds that there were only two representatives from the western hemisphere, compared with six from continental Western Europe. He argued that it would "be only fair to look to the European countries for withdrawal offers."[76] Thus, the Canadian government did not offer to resign from the committee at that time.[77]

Doré retired in the fall of 1953 and died in May 1954. When the question of his replacement arose, it was decided that, because the committee operated purely in an advisory capacity, and because of the difficulty in finding a replacement, Canada would withdraw.[78] This would also enable the Canadian government to keep its policy options open.[79]

The International Office of the Berne Union did not accept Canada's withdrawal notice. Rather, Jacques Secrétan made a special visit to Canada in 1954 and met with Secretary of State Roch Pinard. Secrétan explained the importance of the Permanent Committee and its role in governing the policy of the Berne Union, noted that no other country was exerting pressure to join the committee, and reported that the other member countries had asked Canada to remain.[80] Secrétan was anxious to maintain representation from the western hemisphere on the committee, Canada and Brazil being the only such member countries.[81]

It appears that, prior to this meeting, the Department of Secretary of State had been unaware of much of what had been happening: "The Department of Secretary of State, responsible for the administration of the Copyright Act, has not been informed of the type of participation our representative was taking in the discussions and we have not had the opportunity of realizing the importance of the representation."[82] As a result of Secrétan's visit, the Canadian government reconsidered its decision to withdraw from the Permanent Committee, and so informed the International Office in February 1955.[83]

After 1955, Canadians took a less active role on the committee, sending functionaries rather than the Commissioner of Patents or other policy officials.[84] This sparked a polite protest from Secrétan, who was concerned to maintain the good relations that had prevailed since 1954 between the Permanent Committee and Canada.[85]

The broken link in communication with the Department of Secretary of State until Secrétan's 1954 visit may be one reason that the government did not ratify the 1948 revision of the *Berne Convention* before the 1 July 1951 deadline. Although the Belgian Embassy sent reminders in March, it appears that neither Assistant Under-Secretary of State O'Meara nor the Secretary of State was aware of this or anything else regarding the matter until the deadline had just passed.[86] After it passed, there were discussions about the possibility of adhesion, but the Under-Secretary of State again lost track of the issue until February 1954, around the time that the Ilsley Commission (see below) was announced in the House of Commons.[87] The broken link also meant that the Department of Secretary of State had been unaware of the discussions within the Permanent Committee about movement within UNESCO towards the new *Universal Copyright Convention*.[88] The Department of External Affairs took the position during this time that the Department of Secretary of State should take a greater interest in international copyright.[89]

1954: *Canadian Admiral Corporation Ltd. v. Rediffusion, Inc.*

In the same year that Secrétan visited Ottawa, a case was heard on an important question in Canadian copyright. Canadian Admiral Corporation, a Toronto company, had acquired television rights to broadcast games of the Montreal Alouettes football club. In 1952, Canadian Admiral had arranged to broadcast several games through a Canadian Broadcasting Corporation (CBC) television station, CBFT Montreal. Rediffusion, a Montreal cable company, intercepted the over-the-air broadcasts of the games and redistributed them over its cable networks to its more than 100 subscribers and, on the days it was open, its Montreal showroom. The question of rights in television productions was not specifically addressed in the Canadian *Copyright Act*, and Canadian Admiral's legal action against Rediffusion was the first time the question had been judicially considered.

The Exchequer Court's decision was that no copyright subsisted in the live broadcast of the games for two reasons: first, fixation in material form was a necessary component of copyright, and the live broadcasts had not been recorded; and, second, because the requisite originality was absent. Further, the reception of cable transmissions in individual subscribers' homes was not considered to be a public performance (although the transmission to the showroom was), and retransmission of the programming was not by radio communication (since the retransmission was through wire rather than through radio waves), so neither the right of public performance nor the right of radio communication had been infringed (except in the case of performance in the Montreal showroom).[90]

The determination that unauthorized cable retransmission was not an infringement under the *Copyright Act* meant that Canadian cable companies could freely continue their business in the unauthorized retransmission of over-the-air programming to subscribers. Cable retransmission would become an important part of the Canadian broadcasting system. While some would argue that cable retransmitters served an important purpose in ensuring that all Canadians had relatively equal access to programming, regardless of their proximity to the American border, others would argue that the rebroadcast of American programming was a threat to Canadian culture and to a truly Canadian broadcasting system.[91]

1957: The Ilsley Commission

On 11 February 1954, the Liberal government announced in the House of Commons its intent to call a public inquiry into the patent, copyright, and industrial design acts.[92] Noting the country's shift from a primarily agricultural base to an industrial one, the government argued that Canada ought to pursue a more independent course in research and innovation, rather than drawing so heavily on the inventions and creative work of other countries.[93]

The announcement of the Ilsley Commission also heralded a new concern with development. Both major political parties emphasized the importance of a focus on development;[94] the first and most important consideration in the minds of the commissioners, announced Secretary of State J.W. Pickersgill, "should be how will these laws [sic] conduce to the development of this country."[95] "This inquiry," opposition leader George Drew echoed, "could well open the door to new states of development which would mean prosperity to Canada on a scale of which we have hardly yet dreamed."[96]

By July, the Royal Commission on Patents, Copyright, Trade Marks and Industrial Designs, also known as the Ilsley Commission after chief commissioner James Lorimer Ilsley, had been appointed and had begun to meet.[97] Ilsley was a Liberal powerhouse: a former Minister of National Revenue, former Minister of Finance, and former Minister of Justice who had retired from politics in 1948 and then served as Chief Justice of the Nova Scotia Supreme Court.[98]

The commission issued separate reports on copyright (1957), industrial designs (1958), and patents of invention (1960).[99] The *Report on Copyright* was issued first because it was considered to be the most pressing. "Copyright," it noted, seemed "somewhat more urgent than patents, trade marks or industrial designs, chiefly because Canada has signed two international conventions [the 1948 act of the *Berne Convention* and the 1952 *Universal Copyright Convention*] but has delayed adherence to these conventions pending, as we understand it, our report on copyright."[100] The commission's public hearings were widely reported in the media.[101]

Insofar as the *Universal Copyright Convention* represented an American or utilitarian approach to copyright and the *Berne Convention* the European approach, the commission came down in favour of the American approach. Nevertheless, while the later report of the Economic Council of Canada would take a fully utilitarian view of copyright (see below), the *Report on Copyright* ultimately refused to choose between the utilitarian and natural right views of copyright, saying: "We find it unnecessary to go on record with a confession of faith in either doctrine to the exclusion of the other."[102]

In light of the 1948 changes to the *Berne Convention* made in Brussels, the report asked, "Should Canada Accede to the Brussels Convention?" It noted that implementing the Brussels revision of the *Berne Convention* would entail a number of changes to Canadian copyright: (1) Canada would be required to grant more extensive performance rights to copyright holders; (2) Canada would be obliged to give copyright holders a right to authorize retransmission of their works (for example, by a satellite or cable retransmission of a broadcast); and (3) Canada would be obliged to submit unsettled disputes with other Berne Union members to the International Court of Justice. Canada would also become tied to a term of copyright (already in place since 1924) that lasted for the life of the creator plus fifty years. The Ilsley Commission recommended against all of these possibilities, arguing that they would reduce the Canadian legislature's ability to legislate freely,[103] that Canada's term of protection should emulate that of the United States rather than follow the term required under the Brussels revision,[104] and that Canada ought not to "submit itself to the in-terpretation of the Convention by any authority other than its own Parliament."[105]

The Ilsley Commission recommended that Canada ratify the *Universal Copyright Convention*. This would make it far easier for Canadians to obtain copyright in the United States, freeing Canadian creators from the requirement to register works with the US Copyright Office and, most importantly, from the requirement of printing the work in the United States.[106] Under the *Universal Copyright Convention*, contracting states could require only a single formality – a copyright notice (e.g., "© John Smith 2008") – for works first published by foreign nationals outside its territory. The convention permitted formalities to continue to be required for works first published within the state's territory.[107] The Ilsley Commission viewed this as potentially of substantial benefit to the Canadian printing trade, on the idea that more Canadian books would be printed in Canada rather than in the United States.[108]

The commission considered possible denunciation of the *Berne Convention*, but concluded that although it may have been a mistake to adhere to the 1908 revision in 1923, the government should not denounce the convention:

> It may be that, in becoming a party to the Berlin Revision of the Berne Convention in 1923, Canada was not too well advised. Apart from Haiti and Brazil no nations in the Western Hemisphere are members of the Berne Union ... Nevertheless, we are not disposed, at this time, to recommend denouncing the [Rome revision of the Berne] Convention.[109]

The commission noted that Article 17 of the *Universal Copyright Convention* obligated members of both the Berne Union and the *Universal Copyright Convention* to refuse copyright recognition to copyright holders from countries that denounced the *Berne Convention*. Thus, if Canada denounced the *Berne*

Convention, protection for Canadian copyright holders would be lost in member countries of the Berne Union except if Canadian creators published their works first or simultaneously in such a country (this was the "back door" method used by the United States to gain protection in such countries) or if Canada were to establish a network of bilateral treaties with those countries. Based on this, the Ilsley Commission recommended that the Canadian government not denounce the *Berne Convention.*[110]

The commission further recommended that Parliament should repeal Canada's compulsory licensing clauses, which had the effect of allowing Canadians to obtain a government licence to republish American books if they were not printed in Canada. These clauses had been implemented in retaliation for the US domestic printing requirements and did not apply to British subjects (other than Canadian citizens) or to countries adhering to the 1908 revision of the *Berne Convention* and additional protocol.[111] Were Canada to adhere to the *Universal Copyright Convention,* the commission noted, the US domestic printing requirements would no longer apply to Canadians and so the retaliatory compulsory licensing clauses in the Canadian act would no longer be necessary.[112] The commission further noted that the clauses were, in any case, almost never used.[113]

The commission also noted that "it can hardly be said that the United States now fails to protect in an adequate manner the works of Canadian authors first published in the United States," and that, were Canada to adhere to the *Universal Copyright Convention,* copyright protection in the United States would be available to Canadians on much more adequate terms.[114] Although the retaliatory compulsory licensing clauses might no longer be necessary with regard to the United States, the commission felt that retaliatory measures should still be available to Canada. It therefore recommended provisions that would allow Canada to deny copyright protection to citizens of countries that failed to provide adequate protection to Canadian works.[115]

The commission took issue with the *Berne Convention's* prohibition of formalities, especially its prohibition of registration requirements in domestic law:

> There is reason to believe that the ownership of copyright in a work, or the partial ownership, or rights to use the work in various ways, arising out of assignments, partial assignments, licensing agreements, etc. ought to be ascertainable with greater certainty and less difficulty than is now possible. It is not difficult to foresee a time when suitable provision for registration of such rights would be in the general interest.[116]

Further, the commission indicated that the growth of the entertainment industry, of leisure time, and of advertising – and the accompanying increase in the *uses*

of intellectual property – might call for future reductions in some of the requirements of both the *Berne Convention* and the *Universal Copyright Convention*.[117]
The commission recommended that Canadian representatives at future revision conferences bring these issues forward.

The Ilsley report represented the first time a made-in-Canada policy approach
to copyright was fully set out. The direction that had been taken in the 1920s
had been very much based on imperial and international imperatives and norms.
The Ilsley Commission set down a different vision of progress and the future
of copyright law. Its vision of "progress" was associated not with the continuing
extension and expansion of copyright but with an alternative set of norms intended to address the specific needs of a younger developing country. The
emphasis on development had begun to permeate the language used in Canadian
policy discussions, and the projects of international institutions.

Canada retired from the Permanent Committee of the Berne Union in 1959.
It had been represented by functionaries for the past several years, and, in light
of the possibility that the government might accept the Ilsley Commission's
recommendation not to adhere to the 1948 revision of the *Berne Convention,*
it was felt that Canada's membership on the committee might no longer be as
desirable from the perspective of the Permanent Committee.[118] In 1959, the
committee accepted the Canadian government's 1954 offer of resignation.[119]
Although Canadian officials offered to support either Australia or New Zealand
for membership on the committee, neither country could accept because
Australia had not ratified the 1948 revision either and New Zealand found travel
to be a problem. Canadian officials therefore threw support behind Spain instead.[120] The government would now move to join the *Universal Copyright
Convention;* the primary question was how.

1961-62: Ratification of the *Universal Copyright Convention*
It took several years following the report of the Ilsley Commission for Parliament
to ratify the *Universal Copyright Convention.* There were a number of reasons
for this delay. First, there was a change of government when the Conservatives
under John Diefenbaker came to power in October 1957. Second, international
copyright may not have been foremost in the minds of many Members of
Parliament. Many MPs were not aware of international copyright treaties and
institutions. On various occasions during the 1950s, when routine funding approval for Canada's Patent and Copyright Office and fee payments to the
International Office of the Berne Union appeared on the agenda, MPs inquired
what the International Office was.[121]

Following the tabling of the Ilsley Commission's *Report on Copyright* on 10
June 1958, three months after its submission to the government and after its

printing and distribution to the public, little action was taken.[122] The official position of the Conservative government was that the report was "under consideration."[123] Several MPs urged action on various occasions, including Hazen Robert Argue, a Saskatchewan farmer and leader of the Co-operative Commonwealth Federation, predecessor of the New Democratic Party; Jean-Thomas Richard, an Ottawa lawyer; and Chatham lawyer Judy LaMarsh, who would eventually become Secretary of State.[124] The latter two, both opposition Liberals, were animated about the copyright issue and called for a new copyright policy. Richard was critical of international copyright agreements and the way they were implemented in Canada; he felt that international copyright worked to the advantage of foreigners:

> We need a new copyright act, one that will protect the rights of Canadians. Again, this act is being used by people who are foreign to this country to exact very high fees or royalties without any control being exercised through our own legislation except by so-called international agreements which are really designed to protect the rights of people in other countries because they are the ones who have the greatest number of copyrights.[125]

Richard's views were related to his views on international treaties in general:

> I am one of those people who is absolutely nationalist when it comes to international conventions. I know that some people in government departments are ready to seize on every international convention there is in the world and make us a party to every agreement they can make with other countries. However, we always get the poor end of the cut of beef in these matters. I have never seen us get anything very good out of an international convention. We have everything to offer others and they have nothing to offer us. This is one of those conventions where we will not get anything out of it. Others want us to agree to it because they will get something out of it.[126]

His opinion was that "while we should respect as much as possible international agreements, we should first consider Canadian interests."[127]

Judy LaMarsh, for her part, was less outspoken in her views but she pressed the Conservatives for action on copyright, particularly for ratification of the *Universal Copyright Convention* because of the benefit it would bring to the Canadian printing and publishing industry.[128] She followed the international copyright issue closely and often asked, during the early 1960s, for updates on progress in implementing the Ilsley Commission's recommendations.[129]

Before making any attempt to change Canadian legislation or ratify the *Universal Copyright Convention,* the Canadian government pursued a brief course of diplomacy with the United States after persistent inquiries from Toronto publisher John C.W. Irwin, president of the Book Society of Canada, a textbook publishing company.[130] Concerned about the American manufacturing clause, which was limiting his ability to publish in the United States, he carried on correspondence with Acting Secretary of State Léon Balcer, Labour Minister Michael Starr, and Finance Minister Donald Fleming throughout the spring and summer of 1960.[131] The manufacturing clause required that works be

> printed from type set within the limits of the United States, either by hand or by the aid of any kind of typesetting machine, or from plates made within the limits of the United States from type set therein, or, if the text be produced by lithographic process, or photoengraving process, then by a process wholly performed within the limits of the United States, and the printing of the text and binding of the said book shall be performed within the limits of the United States.[132]

Irwin had various suggestions for remedying the situation. First, he suggested that the Canadian government move to ratify the *Universal Copyright Convention,* which would enable Canadians to bypass the American manufacturing clause. He also suggested that Canada rescind the bilateral arrangement it had made with the United States in 1924, which had made Americans eligible for copyright in Canada, to pressure the United States to accept a fairer arrangement. "Why a Canadian official ever signed that unfair agreement, is difficult to understand," he commented.[133] Léon Balcer pointed out that ending the arrangement with the United States would most likely also lead to the loss of copyright protection in the United States for Canadian authors. Irwin was more optimistic. He felt that the unfairness to Canadian authors and publishers would be easily recognized by the US government and that American authors would pressure their government on behalf of Canadian authors: "An approach of the Canadian government to the United States government in this regard would be all that is necessary to secure the removal of the obviously unfair manufacturing clause."[134]

The Royal Commission on Publications (the O'Leary Commission), reporting in 1961, also recommended ratification of the *Universal Copyright Convention.*[135] The O'Leary Commission had asked the Department of Secretary of State to provide one thousand words, in a manner that could be included in the commission's report, recommending the action the government should take with respect to ratification of the convention. The O'Leary report followed closely the words provided, in much shorter form. Around the same time, there was debate over whether ratification was actually necessary or whether Canadians might use the "back door" method of publishing in the United States or a *Universal Copyright Convention* country in order to benefit from the convention's provisions.[136]

By January 1961 Irwin's efforts had led Under-Secretary of State Charles Stein to ask the Department of External Affairs to request the United States to do away with the manufacturing clause insofar as it applied to Canadians:

> This letter is, therefore, to ask you to approach the appropriate United States authorities with a request that, if it is possible within the terms of their legislation so to do, as we think it is, the provision of their legislation presently requiring printing in that country of works in the English language of which it is proposed to import more than 1 500 copies[137] be made inoperative with respect to the works of Canadian citizens, and possibly even with respect to the works of residents of Canada and works first published in Canada. In return we would guarantee that the more or less corresponding provisions of our Act (i.e., ss. 14, 15, 16 and 28), which are operative at the discretion of the Minister, would be left inoperative so far as the works of United States authors are concerned.[138]

Finance Minister Donald Fleming, with whom Irwin had also communicated, strongly supported this diplomatic effort.[139]

As expected, the replies from Washington that came days later, following various conversations between officials at the Canadian Embassy in Washington and American officials, were negative. Also as expected, the American officials recommended that the Canadian government simply ratify the *Universal Copyright Convention*. When Canadian officials suggested that this might be a long process, involving legislative reform of perhaps two or three years, the Americans noted that the process in the United States to remove or make inoperative the manufacturing clause would likely take just as long.[140]

Following this, Canadian officials began to move more seriously towards ratification of the *Universal Copyright Convention*. There was conflict between departments over how to go about ratification, however, specifically what types of legislative reform would be required in order to ratify. Some within the Department of Secretary of State wished to undertake a complete overhaul of the *Copyright Act* prior to ratification, whereas the Secretary of State for External Affairs, in an approach preferred by John Irwin, proposed that only the changes necessary for ratification of the *Universal Copyright Convention* be undertaken.[141] Possible changes included a switch to the American-style term of protection (running from date of publication rather than from the date of the creator's death) and repeal of the compulsory licensing provisions of the Canadian *Copyright Act.*

The change to the term of copyright was under consideration because under the *Universal Copyright Convention* it was possible to retain a term based on the date of publication if such a term was already part of a country's copyright legislation upon entry into the *Universal Copyright Convention.* After joining the convention, however, no country could switch from a term based on the life of the creator to a term based on publication date.[142] The latter was considered to be shorter than the former because publication normally occurred before the death of the creator. Were Canada to enter the *Universal Copyright Convention,* its term of protection would be longer than that of the United States, whose term was based on the date of publication. This, the Ilsley Commission had feared, would lead to the undesirable consequence that a work might enter the public domain in the United States while still falling under copyright in Canada. This was the situation the Canadian delegates had highlighted during the 1948 conference to revise the *Berne Convention.*

At the same time, there were suggestions that the United States might switch to a term of protection based on the life of the creator, in which case "Canada would then find herself out on the 56-year-from-publication-limb all by herself, rather than in the company she expected."[143] This concern likely played in to the eventual decision by the Canadian government not to switch to a term based on date of publication.

New Zealand's Minister of Justice had written to Canada's Minister of Justice in 1959 to inquire about the likelihood that Canada would adopt a shorter term of protection, consisting of either the life of the creator or fifty-six years following publication, whichever was longer. He suggested that the two countries might act in concert in reducing their copyright terms. Canada's Secretary of State replied that the government was unlikely to reduce Canada's term of protection; that some wanted to increase the term to the life of the creator plus eighty years; and that opinion in the United States was developing in favour of lengthening the term of protection.[144]

In February 1961, the Secretary of State for External Affairs recommended to Cabinet that any essential amendments to Canada's *Copyright Act* be prepared so that External Affairs could undertake to ratify the *Universal Copyright Convention.*[145] Conservative Secretary of State Noël Dorion had come to the conclusion, however, in accordance with the opinion of the Department of Justice, that legislative change was not necessary in order to proceed with ratification,[146] as long as the government was willing to stick with a term based on the life of the creator, losing the flexibility to move to a term based on the date of publication. Dorion had concluded that the compulsory licensing clauses of the Canadian *Copyright Act,* which the Ilsley Commission had thought to be incompatible with the *Universal Copyright Convention,* were not incompatible with it, and that the existing term of protection was satisfactory.[147] Some disagreed, including Jean-Thomas Richard, who found the existing term old-fashioned and in need of revision "in light of modern conditions."[148] The motion to ratify the *Universal Copyright Convention* passed in the House of Commons without legislative revision on 16 April 1962,[149] following a meeting of publishers in Toronto ten days earlier, as well as media coverage and lobbying.[150] Judy LaMarsh, the opposition Liberal MP who had pressed for copyright action, took her share of the credit: "I am delighted, Mr. Speaker, that it may well be that my modest effort has reached at least part of its objective in bringing this convention before the house for ratification."[151]

An order-in-council calling for ratification of the *Universal Copyright Convention* was issued on 26 April, and on 10 May Canada's permanent delegate to UNESCO, L.V.J. Roy, deposited the instrument of ratification in a small and simple ceremony held at UNESCO headquarters in Paris.[152] In a short speech, Roy emphasized that, beyond the mutual benefits to be had by signatories to the convention, Canada's ratification "gave further evidence of its spirit of co-operation and of its desire to favour the free flow of information in the framework of UNESCO's objectives."[153] The ratification took effect three months later, on 10 August. Although some had questioned whether the convention could be implemented without legislative change, Canada's adhesion to it was accepted and the legitimacy of this adhesion was never seriously challenged.

The ratification of the *Universal Copyright Convention* followed upon the recommendations of the Ilsley Commission report and the attempts of a Toronto publisher to persuade the Canadian government to engage in diplomatic efforts to overcome difficulties caused by the American manufacturing clause. It came about following the most extensive effort ever undertaken to articulate a Canadian copyright philosophy. Although the work of the Ilsley Commission did not lead to a complete revision of Canadian copyright law, it did signal a new mindset in Canadian international copyright policy, wherein private interest groups and the project of development were now the central concerns, rather than imperial uniformity and international participation.

The Manufacturing Clause and Reaction to Ratification of the *Universal Copyright Convention*

Despite praise from authors' and publishers' associations,[154] ratification of the *Universal Copyright Convention* was not a perfect solution. The convention did not provide retroactive protection and therefore applied only to works published after 10 August 1962, the date that Canada's ratification took effect. Furthermore, American copyright law still required American authors and residents to publish in the United States, whereas Canadian authors faced no such requirement.[155] This situation was unfavourable to the Canadian printing and publishing industry, and there were calls for further action. A *Financial Post* article in September 1962 caught the government's attention:

> Books written by Canadians and manufactured here will henceforth enjoy copy-right in the U.S. regardless of the number of copies they sell there. But U.S. law still requires (and is unaffected in this respect by Canada's signing of the 1955 agreement) that works by American nationals, and works by Canadians and other aliens domiciled in the U.S., must be manufactured in the U.S. to enjoy copyright there.
>
> There is no corresponding clause in Canadian law. This means that American firms can tender for printing jobs in Canada while Canadian firms are debarred from tendering for like work in the U.S.
>
> Thus, says [University of Toronto Press publisher Marsh Jeannaret], "Canada retains its colonial status in the graphic arts industry." There are two possible lines of action. The situation could be corrected either by a retaliatory Canadian law or, much preferably, by negotiation.
>
> The one inexcusable course is to do nothing at all.[156]

The government felt that nothing could be done about the situation, however. The Commissioner of Patents argued:

> So far as retaliating, I do not see how we could do it legally at this time. Prior to August 10, 1962 we gave the U.S. works protection pursuant to our 1923 bilateral agreement with the United States and we cannot renegade [sic] such contract ...
>
> Retaliation is impossible and negotiation to bring about retroactivity of effect of U.C.C. would mean a major amendment to the U.S. law which would have to be applied to all the U.C.C. member countries.[157]

Questions continued to be raised in the House of Commons about the American manufacturing clause.[158] Having failed to solve the problem completely through the Canadian government, Canadian industry groups turned their attention towards the United States. Representatives of the Canadian printing and publishing industries met with American book manufacturers, labour unions, and publishers at the Park Plaza Hotel in Toronto on 16 February 1968 and reached what became known as the *Toronto Agreement*. According to the agreement, the Americans would press for an exemption for Canada from the US manufacturing clause, while the Canadians would urge their government to adhere to the 1950 *Florence Agreement on the Importation of Educational, Scientific and Cultural Materials* once the exemption for Canada became law. Both groups agreed to oppose adhesion to the Stockholm protocol (see below) or any weakening of international copyright.[159] Canadian adhesion to the *Florence Agreement* would eliminate a 10 percent duty for a large American book export trade to Canada.[160] American book manufacturers argued that competition from Canada would not prove troublesome for them. The exemption for Canada passed into law, despite arguments that an exemption specifically for Canada would violate the most favoured nation requirement of the *General Agreement on Tariffs and Trade*.[161] The exemption for Canada was included in the US *Copyright Act* of 1976, and allowed works to be manufactured in either Canada or the United States.[162] American industry representatives would later complain that the Canadian government had not held up its end of the agreement; although it removed duties on books and other printed materials, it did not formally adhere to the *Florence Agreement*.[163]

Although it seems that, from the late 1930s to the 1950s, copyright policy had fallen below the political radar, this break may have created the possibility of new thinking and new directions in Canadian copyright policy. During the 1950s and early '60s, the Berne Union lost its grasp on Canada to some extent, and Canada drifted closer in spirit to the *Universal Copyright Convention*. The Royal Commission on Patents, Copyright, Trade Marks and Industrial Designs helped build up a base of knowledge and expertise that steered Canadian copyright policy towards the more American approach of the *Universal Copyright Convention*. Nevertheless, the long arm of imperial copyright continued to exert influence in Canada and to assert Canada's imperial bond to the *Berne Convention*.

1960: *Durand & Cie. v. La Patrie Publishing Co.*

In 1960, the Supreme Court of Canada awarded $600 in damages to be paid by a Montreal radio station, CHLP, to French music publishing company *La Patrie*. The court decided that CHLP had infringed *La Patrie*'s rights in the Debussy opera *Pélleas et Mélisande*, written in 1902 and assigned to *La Patrie* in 1905. The case hinged in part on the question of whether *La Patrie* held a Canadian performing right in the opera, although the opera had never been registered in Canada. The court affirmed that under imperial copyright (which was still in effect in Canada up to 1 January 1924) and the *Berne Convention*, which had abolished formalities, *La Patrie* did indeed hold those rights.[164]

Canada pulled against its anchoring to the *Berne Convention,* however, and towards the new *Universal Copyright Convention.* It found unacceptable the new norms promulgated under the 1948 Brussels revision of the *Berne Convention* but welcomed the new lower norms of the *Universal Copyright Convention.* If not for Article 17 of the latter, which hindered countries from denouncing the *Berne Convention* and moving to the lower level of protection under the *Universal Copyright Convention,* Canadians might have followed that path. In this respect, the Berne Union, through the declaration made by its member countries under Article 17 of the *Universal Copyright Convention,* was able to retain an element of control over countries that might consider such a move.

CHAPTER TEN

Crisis in International Copyright, 1967

US President Harry Truman's inaugural address in 1949 initiated a new era in world affairs that focused on programs for international development and the restructuring of "underdeveloped" societies. Within a few years, the discourse of development – a drive and a vision to restructure two-thirds of the world in the image of Western capitalist civilization – had become hegemonic.[1] The discourse, categories, and projects of development eventually began to be integrated into the international copyright system.

International copyright was changing dramatically. Between 1948 and 1971, the *Berne Convention* underwent three revisions, constituted itself within a new international organization, and confronted a major alternative regime. These changes in international copyright reflected the changing shape of international society. Whereas in the early twentieth century the decline of British imperialism had brought countries like Canada, Australia, and New Zealand to the table, by 1967 another set of newly independent countries had begun to participate in the Berne Union, meaning that over 40 percent of the union's members were now considered to be "developing," according to United Nations standards.[2] At the same time, many Central and South American countries, along with several former British dependent territories, had joined the *Universal Copyright Convention,* and by 1967 that convention had almost as many members as the Berne Union.[3]

Canada had some areas of interest in common with the newly independent countries, being, like them, a net copyright importer for which international copyright created a net outflow of revenue. Like them, Canada hoped to encourage the further development of domestic cultural industries. At the same time, the Canadian government had established and inherited networks and associations with the larger, more powerful countries such as Britain, the United States, and France. Canada was, as always, in the middle: between the Berne Union and the United States, between Britain and the United States, between France and Britain, and now between the larger powers and the newly independent countries.

It had been decided at the 1948 diplomatic conference in Brussels that the next conference to revise the *Berne Convention* would take place in Stockholm.[4] Organizers had originally planned to hold the conference in 1965, but it became clear that the preparatory studies would not be completed in time and the conference was deferred until 1967.[5]

By the early 1960s, the International Office of the Berne Union had grown into an international secretariat with a director and fifty employees, now called the United International Bureaux for the Protection of Intellectual Property (BIRPI), serving also the Paris Union for the Protection of Industrial Property. In 1960, the office moved from Berne to Geneva, and in 1962 and 1963 proposals were made for a structural and administrative reform of the organization.[6] The original proposals were made by Jacques Secrétan, the director of BIRPI from 1953 to 1963. These proposals were promoted and developed by Arpad Bosch, the future director general of the World Intellectual Property Organization (WIPO). Secrétan was replaced by Georg Bodenhausen of the Netherlands in 1963, the first time a non-Swiss director of BIRPI had been appointed. Bodenhausen, with Bosch as his deputy, circulated the proposals through various meetings of committees of experts and working groups.[7]

The 1967 conference therefore had several purposes, only one of which was a revision of the *Berne Convention*. These purposes were: structural and administrative reforms leading to the establishment of the World Intellectual Property Organization under a new *Convention Establishing the World Intellectual Property Organization*, revision of the *Berne Convention*, revision of the *Paris Convention* on industrial property, and revision of five special agreements on trademarks, false indications, industrial design registration, and appellations of origin.[8]

The program for the previous conferences to revise the *Berne Convention* had been developed based largely on individual or joint country proposals, as well as proposals from the *Association littéraire et artistique internationale*, compiled by the International Office and/or the convening government. The 1967 program, however, was also the result of input from international study groups and international groups of experts that met in the years leading up to the 1967 diplomatic conference in Stockholm.

Canadian officials would participate in few of the meetings leading up to the conference. With regard to revision of the *Berne Convention,* the government of Canada refused to send an expert to the 1963 Committee of Experts for the Preparation of the Stockholm Conference for the Revision of the *Berne*

Convention, did not send an observer to the 1963 joint meeting of the Permanent Committee of the Berne Union and the Intergovernmental Copyright Committee of the United Nations Educational, Scientific and Cultural Organization (UNESCO) at which the revisions were discussed,[9] and did not attend the Committee of Governmental Experts Preparatory to the Stockholm Conference for the Revision of the *Berne Convention* in July 1965 or the Permanent Committee of the Berne Union in November 1965.[10] The only significant meeting related to the revision of the *Berne Convention* that Canadian officials attended prior to the Stockholm conference was the March 1967 Extraordinary Session of the Permanent Committee of the Berne Union.[11]

With regard to the administrative reforms to be undertaken at the 1967 conference, Canadian delegates were present for the first meeting of the Committee of Experts on the Administrative Structure of International Cooperation in the Field of Intellectual Property, held from 22 March through 2 April 1965,[12] but did not attend the committee's second meeting, in May 1966.[13]

1963: Brazzaville Meeting

Many of the states that had become independent as a result of decolonization had been bound to the *Berne Convention* as colonies and were now faced with the decision of whether to remain part of the Berne Union. Some, such as Indonesia, chose to withdraw; others, including India, Pakistan, the Philippines, and many former French and Belgian African territories, chose to remain. Many of these countries were unhappy with the requirements of the convention, however, which they felt did not take their needs into account.[14] This was true in particular of the newly independent African states.

In August 1963, an African Study Meeting on Copyright in Brazzaville, Republic of the Congo, was organized jointly by BIRPI and UNESCO "to assist the African Member States and Associate Members of Unesco in defining the general principles applicable in their respective territories to the protection of authors, notably writers, composers, and artists, with regard to their literary, musical and dramatic works or works of the plastic arts."[15]

The Brazzaville meeting, to which only African states were invited (although South Africa was not invited, since that country was not a member of UNESCO), was expected to be a forum for teaching Africans about copyright: "to give African countries a series of lectures on copyright and connected legislation."[16] UNESCO also proposed to establish "a national association of authors for Africa, which will actively follow up on any governmental measure" following the meeting.[17] Canada's Permanent Delegate to UNESCO in Paris made inquiries about the meeting before it took place and summarized the interests of African countries in copyright as follows:

The main interest of African countries is concerned with musical works through radio broadcasting or records. If national legislation is proposed, their own people will be protected at home, and if they later adhere to the Berne Union, then this protection will be extended to them ... The first step would indeed aim at protecting national interests at home, and the second step would extend this protection beyond national borders.[18]

The Canadian delegate, questioning the view that African countries were interested in *strengthening* copyright protection, also inquired as to African countries' interest in and willingness to join the *Berne Convention:*

I asked Mr. Diaz if Africa would not resist proposals for an adhesion to the Berne Union since the number of its artists who would receive protection abroad is very small. He told me that the new African countries had not discarded the terms of the Berne Convention after they had gained independence; local offices established in 1943 during the war were still operating. Therefore, any French singer whose record is now used in Africa will receive some royalty. Mr. Diaz sees no difficulty in this aspect of the problem.[19]

The most important results of the meeting in Brazzaville, however, were not in teaching Africans about copyright, nor in establishing an authors' association or copyright protection in Africans' musical works. Instead, the meeting resulted in resolutions for several reforms to the *Berne Convention* in the interests of African countries. The views of the African representatives expressed at the meeting were as follows:

Their opinion of the world copyright situation as of 1963 was that it was essentially European in orientation and therefore opposed to their interests. They expressed the view that the major conventions needed to be re-examined in light of the specific needs of the African continent. In this connection, they recommended that African experts be included in all international copyright meetings, especially the committees which were then preparing for the revision of the Berne Convention.[20]

Participants at the Brazzaville meeting recommended that three things be considered in the preparations for the Stockholm conference: (1) a reduction of the term of copyright; (2) permission for member states to enter into special arrangements with one another that would allow them to derogate from the terms of the convention, something not permitted under the *Berne Convention;* and (3) inclusion of provisions safeguarding the interests of African countries in their folklore while permitting the free use of protected works for educational and scholastic purposes.[21]

These recommendations were important because they placed African concerns on the agenda of the Stockholm conference and the meetings leading up to it. In particular, the third recommendation highlighted the exclusion of a whole class of creators and works (works of folklore) from the framework of international copyright. Prior to the Brazzaville meeting, as the Canadian encounter with Mr. Diaz demonstrates, such concerns had simply not registered in the Berne Union. Although Canada's Permanent Delegate to UNESCO in Paris did show interest in the concerns of African countries, Canadian officials did not become involved in the pre-Stockholm meetings. Reaction within the Berne Union to the concerns raised at Brazzaville was also slow.[22]

Four months later, in November, an advisory committee composed of experts acting in a personal capacity (as opposed to representing individual member states) met in Geneva to discuss a 1963 report containing draft texts for the Stockholm conference[23] as well as the results of the Brazzaville meeting. This Group of Experts supported the work of the Brazzaville meeting and called for further study of the questions it had raised.[24]

Canadian participation in this meeting of experts was very much desired by the International Office. When the Canadian government failed to respond to an invitation in April, the International Office wrote again, emphasizing that Director General Bodenhausen attached "very great importance to the fact of your country being represented on this Committee."[25] Despite repeated requests from the International Office, Canada chose not to send an expert. The Commissioner of Patents felt that no one could be spared, as one official in his office would already be away on travel during that time.[26]

In December of the same year, a joint meeting of the Permanent Committee of the Berne Union and the Intergovernmental Copyright Committee of the *Universal Copyright Convention* met in New Delhi and approved proposals by the Indian delegation that studies be made of the possibility of including in the *Berne Convention* compulsory licences for educational use, and of introducing provisions for translation similar to those contained in the *Universal Copyright Convention*.[27] Proposals were also made that developing countries be subject to lower levels of copyright than those provided under the 1948 revision of the *Berne Convention*.[28] The government of Canada was invited to send an observer to this meeting but once again declined to attend.[29]

By June 1964, a Swedish/BIRPI Study Group doing preparatory work for the conference had issued a report recommending the addition of a new article, 25*bis*, to the *Berne Convention* that would allow developing countries to make various reservations reducing the translation rights provided to creators, reducing the required duration of protection, and reducing broadcasting rights; allow developing countries to make regulations governing the protection of works to be used for educational purposes; and allow developing countries to reserve the right to make international agreements offering lower levels of protection than those required under the *Berne Convention*.[30]

Discussions also concerned the definition of a developing country. The first working definition was broad and based on self-identification:

> any country which desires to accede to this Convention but which, with regard to the *economic situation and its social needs,* does not consider itself immediately in a position to make provision for the protection of all the rights forming the object of this Convention.[31]

This definition would have allowed countries to self-identify as developing if they were not in an immediate position to implement all of the rights spelled out in the convention. The ability to self-identify in such a way was not limited by any particular set of definitions, nor the approval of an external body.

With regard to the protection of folklore, the Swedish/BIRPI Study Group's report did not recommend any specific provisions, but simply noted that the *Berne Convention* posed no obstacle to special legislation protecting folklore from exploitation.[32]

Developing countries (Congo-Léopoldville, India, Lebanon, Morocco, Senegal, and Tunisia) jointly proposed a broader definition of "developing country" than the one found in the Study Group's report: "Any country of the Union, having regard to its *economic, scientific, social and cultural needs*" would be able to avail itself of the special provisions proposed, effectively adding two categories of needs: scientific and cultural.[33] The joint proposal also suggested, regarding the proposal of allowing developing countries to make regulations governing the protection of works for educational or scholastic purposes, that reservation be allowed for "cultural purposes" as well.[34]

Opposition to these types of proposals for the benefit of developing countries grew after the publication of the 1964 report. Authors' and publishers' organizations were particularly opposed.[35] In July 1965, a meeting of the Committee of Governmental Experts was held to discuss the report and the joint proposal. The committee rejected many of the proposals. It accepted the inclusion of "cultural needs" in the criteria and the phraseology "having regard to its economic situation and its social or cultural needs,"[36] but rejected as being too broad the joint proposal's suggestion that special provisions be allowed for "cultural purposes."[37] A proposal that would have specifically allowed compulsory licensing was also rejected.[38]

The Committee of Governmental Experts proposed a new Article 25*bis* to allow developing countries to use specific provisions of older texts of the *Berne Convention*, thus committing to lower levels of protection, on translation rights, the term of protection, and broadcasting rights; to restrict, for "exclusively educational, scientific, or scholastic purposes," the protection granted in works; and to make special arrangements derogating from the *Berne Convention* "with any other country of the Union ... on condition that the arrangement concerns solely works the country of origin of which is a country party to that arrangement and relates only to the reservations mentioned above, each condition being operative only if a developed country is party to the said arrangement."[39] These provisions were much narrower than those proposed by the Swedish/BIRPI Study Group, and far narrower than those proposed by developing countries.

The Canadian government declined an invitation to send a delegation to the meeting of the Committee of Governmental Experts. Draft External Affairs memos on file but marked "not used" made note of the upcoming diplomatic conference, the intent to reorganize BIRPI, the absence of Canadian officials at the meetings that had already taken place, the inability of the Commissioner of Patents to take a position on matters (possibly due to the fact that his department was in the process of moving), and the pressing need for the Canadian government to formulate a position. The memos further suggested a meeting between the Departments of Secretary of State and External Affairs. By June, it had been decided that Canadian officials would not attend the meeting, it being thought preferable to be absent than to attend without having undertaken a proper examination of the issues.[40]

The Canadian government also declined an invitation to attend the November 1965 joint meeting of the Permanent Committee of the International Union and the Intergovernmental Copyright Committee of the *Universal Copyright Convention*, where the progress of preparations for the Stockholm conference was discussed. Deputy Registrar General Jean Miquelon, who had recently served as Under-Secretary of State and would soon assume the position of Deputy Minister at Consumer and Corporate Affairs, believed that, because Canada had not ratified the Brussels text of the *Berne Convention*, it was not necessary for Canadian officials to be present.[41]

Allan Gotlieb, Under-Secretary of State for External Affairs, had been unaware that Canada had not ratified the Brussels text, and suggested in January that the government take steps to do so. Miquelon drew Gotlieb's attention to the recommendation of the Ilsley Commission not to ratify the Brussels text, and said: "I am sure you will agree that our position with respect to the Convention should remain the status quo."[42]

Some interest groups reacted with dismay to the fact that the Canadian government had not participated in the Committee of Governmental Experts. J.-Z.-Léon Patenaude, president of the *Société canadienne-française de protection du droit d'auteur,* noted this fact with regret in correspondence with the government, while recommending that the Canadian delegation to the Stockholm conference include representatives from professional organizations, including himself and the presidents of the *Association des éditeurs canadiens* and the *Société des éditeurs canadiens de manuels scolaires.*[43]

The Swedish/BIRPI Study Group, which was charged with drawing up the program for the Stockholm conference, overruled a number of the proposals made by the Committee of Governmental Experts, narrowing the concessions for developing countries still further. The Study Group, composed of two representatives of the Swedish government along with Director General Bodenhausen and the head of BIRPI's copyright division, decided that the suggested measures should be included in a separate protocol to the convention rather than as an article within the convention itself.[44] This left open the option that countries might sign the revised convention but not the protocol. The Study Group also, in the cases of translation and duration of protection, substituted the provisions of the *Universal Copyright Convention,* which were felt to maintain higher levels of protection than those proposed by the Committee of Governmental Experts, which had proposed reservations allowing substitution of provisions from earlier versions of the *Berne Convention* and which, at the same time, had also stipulated that the provisions made available to developing countries should not offer levels of protection that fell below those of the *Universal Copyright Convention.*[45] Finally, the Study Group deleted the reservation relating to special arrangements, which would have allowed arrangements to be made between member states at lower levels of protection than those offered by the *Berne Convention.* The Study Group feared that this might allow countries to lower protection to any level at all, or even to abolish copyright completely.[46]

The draft program was published in May 1966. Responses from member states revealed, as Ricketson and Ginsburg observe, "that most of the developed nations had not formulated any coherent attitude to the claims of their developing neighbours."[47] By 31 March 1967, just eighteen governments had made comments or observations on the proposed program.[48] The Canadian government sent no response.[49]

The positions of East Asian countries were more developed. The Indian government had organized an East Asian Seminar on Copyright on 23-30 January 1967, at which some of the associations commonly made between the European copyright norms established under the Berne Union and modernity were challenged. K. Krishna Rao reminded attendees that "the modern law of copyright had its origins in Europe," and that the union would have to open itself to a wider range of influences. He argued that no "region [could any longer] claim an exclusive role in shaping what must necessarily be the universal law." Furthermore, he framed the *Berne Convention* as being out of date, emphasizing that a convention established in 1886 "could hardly be considered adequate in 1967."[50]

The pending Stockholm conference was announced in the House of Commons on 16 June 1967.[51] No indication as to the government's position on the issues was given and no discussion took place.

In October 1966, concern began growing within UNESCO that the revisions being proposed to the *Berne Convention* might allow the Berne Union to take over the role of the *Universal Copyright Convention* as a bridge for developing countries into the international copyright system.[52] The possibility of revising the *Universal Copyright Convention* was raised at that month's General Conference of UNESCO. Discussion of this possibility then took place at the March 1967 extraordinary session of the Permanent Committee of the Berne Union, where countries agreed to postpone consideration of a revision of the *Universal Copyright Convention* until after the Stockholm conference.

The Canadian government did not provide any comments in the consultations following the 1966 meeting at UNESCO. J.W.T. Michel, the Commissioner of Patents, found the documents provided to him insufficient to allow him to comment.[53] Nevertheless, when the March 1967 extraordinary session was called, Michel advised that the Canadian government should send someone from the Permanent Mission in Geneva to report on the discussions.[54] A Canadian delegate was sent as an observer to this meeting.[55]

Preparations for the Stockholm Revision

In Canada, all movement on copyright revision came to a halt with the announcement on 22 July 1966 of another study on copyright, this time by the Economic Council of Canada. Canadian policy positions on copyright went into deep freeze pending the report.[56] As a result, the Canadian government took no position on the Stockholm protocol.[57] Its very limited participation at the Stockholm conference would be hastily arranged at the last minute, and delegates would be ill-prepared to discuss the issues at hand.

By 1967, private interest groups had begun to notice the government's failure to take an active role in international copyright. The Canadian Copyright Institute sent a memorandum to the Department of Consumer and Corporate Affairs noting that the Canadian government had not participated in the preparatory events leading up to the Stockholm conference, even as much smaller countries had. This, the institute noted, was a loss:

> Participation in these preliminary studies might well have made it possible for Canadians with an interest in copyright to be supplied with valuable information and advice on matters of international copyright. We hope that Canada will participate more fully in the future in such matters and will take appropriate steps to keep the public informed of all developments.[58]

In particular, the institute urged that the Canadian government "should send a strong delegation to participate actively in the Stockholm Conference on Copyright with a view to acceding ultimately to the revisions if at all possible."[59]

This led to several hastily called meetings at the Privy Council Office, and it was decided that a delegation would be sent to Stockholm, headed by Arthur J. Andrew, Canadian Ambassador at Stockholm, along with Patent Office head Jean Miquelon, MP Jean Richard, Roy M. Davidson of the Patent Office, and five counsellors, including representatives from the CBC, the National Film Board, the Parliamentary Library of Quebec, and the Canadian Copyright Institute. Bruce C. McDonald, a professor from the Faculty of Law at Queen's University, served as secretary to the delegation.[60] The delegation was more broadly based than delegations at past conferences, and included a greater number of delegates representing various government and private interests.[61]

Because of the number of private representatives, the Secretary of State for External Affairs, in the days leading up to the conference, requested that Cabinet provide quite specific instructions to the head of the delegation, so that he might be able to resolve disputes within the delegation during the discussion of revisions that might favour one interest over another.[62] Taking an economic view, he prefaced his recommendations to Cabinet regarding the delegation's instructions by questioning whether a commitment to the *Berne Convention* was in the national interest:

> Successive revisions of the Berne Convention have progressively extended the monopoly rights of copyright holders. The current revisions suggested for the Stockholm conference are intended to extend these rights still further. Unfortunately, this raises the question of the cost in relation to the value of present

copyright legislation as a device for encouraging creativity in Canada before the Economic Council's report is available. An important consideration in the study of this matter is the fact that as much as 90 percent of the total cost (about $8 million) of copyright to the public in Canada is accounted for by the protection given foreign works. In turn, compensation to Canadian authors by way of payments from overseas to Canada is minimal. That raises the fundamental question of whether protection of the kind Canada is committed to by adhering to the Berne Union is in the national interest.[63]

He recommended to Cabinet, therefore, the day after the conference began, that the Canadian delegation should refrain from supporting any proposed revision to the *Berne Convention* that would reduce the government's flexibility of action: "The work of the Economic Council should not be prejudiced by the assumption of any additional commitments by Canada in this field. In short, the options for future government action in the area of copyright must be kept open."[64] He further recommended that the Canadian delegation should refrain from signing the Stockholm text; that the delegation should avoid commitments "wherever it seems that copyright protection is being strengthened so as to circumvent or otherwise restrict the greatest possible socio-economic use of these new technological developments"; and that delegates should seek representation on the Co-ordination Committee and in the Secretariat. Furthermore, "because of the largely negative role the Delegation is hereby being instructed to play during the Conference the Delegation should not accept Conference office." Because of the unanimity rule for adoption of the new instrument, the instructions restricted the delegation to opposing revisions in committee, and to simply abstain from voting on amendments in during the plenary sessions so as not to hold back agreement during those sessions.[65]

The initial instructions sent pertained to the role of the delegation in general; the issues related to the protocol for developing countries required further study, so those specific instructions were delayed for several days. The Secretary of State for External Affairs eventually recommended very general instructions with regard to the protocol. As before, he recommended that the delegation simply refrain from supporting any provision that would reduce the Canadian government's flexibility until the findings of the Economic Council's report could be considered.[66] He commented:

Canada, whose exports of intellectual property are not in any event an important item would not be a major sufferer should the Protocol be approved. Indeed, like many of the developing countries, Canada is a net importer of intellectual property and can, therefore, be sympathetic to their problems. However, it is not possible to forecast at the moment what Canada's attitude on such a Protocol will be in, say, ten years time when our present trading position in this commodity may have been radically altered.[67]

Diplomatic Conference: Stockholm, 11 June to 14 July 1967

The Stockholm conference was enormous. With 389 delegates, 93 observers, and a BIRPI secretariat of 14, the number of participants totalled almost 500.[68] The schedule was a busy one, and participants were warned of possible meetings at night and through Saturdays and Sundays, as well as receptions for which formal attire was not required for men, while women were instructed to wear "short cocktail dresses."[69]

This conference was the first at which non-governmental organizations were granted observer status; in 1948 this had not been done, on the basis that the meeting was to be one of governments only.[70] It was also the first to have its records published in English, which had replaced French as the language of international diplomacy.

Most of the work of the Stockholm conference took place in five main committees. Main Committee I dealt with the general revision of the *Berne Convention*, Main Committee II with the creation of a protocol to the *Berne Convention* dealing with the needs of developing countries, Main Committee III with the revision of the *Paris Convention* on patents, Main Committee IV with changes to the administrative and final clauses of the Paris and Berne conventions, and Main Committee V with the establishment of the World Intellectual Property Organization (WIPO).[71]

A number of changes were made to the main text of the *Berne Convention*. Works covered by the convention would now include works by nationals of the countries of the Berne Union wherever they were published, rather than only their unpublished works and works first published in a union country. A general reproduction right was added; a right of public recitation was added; moral rights were granted generally, rather than simply "in the author's lifetime"; the requirement of fixation was deleted insofar as it applied to choreographic works and pantomime, and the fixation requirement was made optional with regard to other types of works; minimum terms of protection for cinematographic and photographic works were established; provisions were added regarding cinematographic works; and provision was made for the protection of anonymous works of folklore through a designated competent authority.[72]

At the conference, a new *Convention Establishing the World Intellectual Property Organization* was established, and related revisions were made to the administrative and final clauses of the *Berne Convention*, the *Paris Convention*, and other special agreements. An Assembly of the Berne Union, consisting of all member countries, an Executive Committee with rotating membership, and an International Office (to continue the work of the existing International Office of the Berne Union) were all established. The new World Intellectual Property Organization (WIPO) would act as a secretariat for all of the major intellectual property conventions (save for the *Universal Copyright Convention,* which was administered by UNESCO).[73]

The Stockholm conference also resulted in a protocol to the *Berne Convention* for developing countries. This protocol would provoke a crisis that, following the conference, would threaten to break up the Berne Union. In an effort to make concessions to developing countries, it provided the possibility that such countries could deviate from previous norms under the *Berne Convention*. It provided for:

- the possibility of adopting a shorter term of protection, not less than twenty-five years (as opposed to a term not less than life plus fifty years), this being equivalent to what was provided under the *Universal Copyright Convention*
- the expiration of translation rights after ten years if the author had not published a translation into the language in which protection was claimed, and the possibility of compulsory licensing for translations after three years from the work's original publication
- compulsory licensing for the reproduction of original works "for educational or cultural purposes" where said works had not been published in original form in that country
- the curtailment of broadcasting rights such that they would apply only to broadcasts "for profit-making purposes"
- compulsory licensing for any use of literary or artistic works "exclusively for teaching, study and research in all fields of education."[74]

The definition of "developing country" adopted by the conference was not based on self-identification, but rather on the established practice of the United Nations:

> Any country regarded as a developing country in conformity with the established practice of the General Assembly of the United Nations which ratifies or accedes to the Act of this Convention of which this Protocol forms an integral part and which, having regard to its economic situation and its social or cultural needs, does not consider itself immediately in a position to make provision for the protection of all the rights as provided in the Act.[75]

The inclusion of the phrase "in conformity with the established practice of the General Assembly of the United Nations" meant that the ability to categorize countries as "developing" now rested in the practice of international authority.

Canada at the Stockholm Conference

The hastily assembled Canadian delegation was ill prepared for the Stockholm conference. It did not participate in any of the working groups, whereas other countries participated in most of them.[76] Ambassador Arthur Andrew, the head of the delegation, later reported: "Our knowledge of the background and the implications of the draft proposals were often superficial ... The instructions given to the delegation fortunately fitted well with the delegation's lack of expertise and preparation."[77] The delegation made two statements on record that are worthy of note, however: on folklore and on Canada's experience with bilingual texts.[78] With regard to the first, the Canadian delegation opposed any move to restrict the public-domain use of folklore. Roy C. Sharp, the representative of the Canadian Copyright Institute, spoke against any restriction on public use of folklore, noting that Canada had a "considerable body of folklore, which it had always regarded as falling within the public domain." This, he noted, was "of great concern" to the Canadian delegation.[79] This was a significant point of divergence from the position of the African countries that had lobbied for measures that would provide rights in the folklore of African people. No protection for works of folklore was ultimately established under the treaty.

Canada's emphasis on bilingualism was still a hallmark of its international presence at the Berne Union, as it had been at the conferences in 1928 and 1948. In 1967, the Canadian delegation supported the idea that the *Berne Convention* be made available officially in both English and French.[80] The outcome of this debate was that the convention was for the first time signed officially in both English and French, with official texts to be established by the Director General in consultation with interested governments in German, Italian, Portuguese, and Spanish, and other languages as designated by the Assembly of the Berne Union.[81] French had lost its position of primacy as the official language of the Berne Union. Earlier in the decade, *Le droit d'auteur* had begun to be published in English under the title *Copyright,* as well as in the original French. The new World Intellectual Property Organization would operate in numerous official languages.[82]

Canada, however, did not sign the revised *Berne Convention,* nor did it sign the *Convention Establishing the World Intellectual Property Organization.*[83] This would allow the Canadian government to maintain flexibility in its path ahead, as it responded to the report of the Economic Council.

Canadian private interests had varied reactions to the Stockholm revision. Associations of authors, composers, and Canadian television and radio artists opposed any reduction in international copyright norms, suggesting that aid to developing countries ought to take more traditional forms of government grants and subsidies rather than concessions by creator groups.[84] Canadian educational and cable television associations, however, pointed to the need for expanded copyright exceptions for educational use (in both developed and developing countries) and Canada's commonalities with developing countries, respectively.[85]

International response to the Stockholm revision of the *Berne Convention* was highly critical; the *Economist* wrote, "Developing countries will now have rights that are not far short of legalised theft."[86] As international opinion solidified against the revision, it became clear that it would be a failure. In the end, the substantive changes to the *Berne Convention* agreed upon at the conference were not ratified by the required number of countries before the deadline and never came into force. The *Convention Establishing the World Intellectual Property Organization* and the related administrative clauses of the *Berne Convention* were ratified, however, and did come into force.[87]

The failure of the Stockholm protocol led to a crisis in international copyright. Ricketson and Ginsburg note that the future of the Berne Union looked bleak in 1967: "It was unclear how the impasse [between developed and developing countries] might be breached."[88] Several scenarios were possible. First, the developing countries might leave the Berne Union altogether, and possibly the *Universal Copyright Convention* as well, "relying on the advantages to be derived from being a 'free rider.'"[89] In this, developing countries could rely on the precedent set by the United States, the Soviet Union, and China. Alternatively, a system of bilateral arrangements might be developed. Second, developing countries might leave the Berne Union for the *Universal Copyright Convention;* lobbying had already begun for the removal of Article 17, the article that had thus far prevented this from happening. Action was therefore necessary to hold the Berne Union together, and possibly to prevent the break-up of the entire multilateral intellectual property system.[90]

The crisis of 1967 and the threat to the multilateral copyright system can be compared to the threat posed by the attempted denunciation of the *Berne Convention* in 1889. In 1889, fears that such a denunciation might spark a mass exodus from the Berne Union led to the British government's refusal to proclaim Canada's 1889 copyright act into force or to denounce the *Berne Convention* on Canada's behalf – in effect, forcing Canada to remain in the Berne Union. The Canadian government's stance also had an effect on the early development of the *Berne Convention,* restricting the negotiating positions of the British delegates and leading to the protocol of 1896. In 1967, the discourse of development, inscribed in UNESCO and taken up by the Berne Union in an effort to encompass developing countries in the Berne system, led not just to restrictions on the ability to increase the scope of international copyright protection and on the ability to exit from that system, but also to the concessions found in the unsuccessful Stockholm protocol and ultimately to the little-used concessions that would be established in 1971.

CHAPTER ELEVEN

Re-engagement, 1967-77

THE CRISIS RESULTING FROM the 1967 conference in Stockholm led to the Canadian government's re-engagement with the Berne Union and sparked a new resolve that Canada would become a more influential and active player in international copyright. Some Canadian officials hoped that the discourse of development now taking root in the Berne Union, a discourse that was absent when former colonies like Canada joined the union, might also apply to Canada – that Canada might be considered a developing country with respect to copyright. The idea of Canada as a developing country conflicted, however, with the established discourse of Canada as a middle power, associated with industrialized countries. Some Canadian policymakers hoped that as a middle power, Canada would be able to "draw together diverging views of developing and developed countries."[1] In this, they also drew on Canada's status as a net copyright importer, drawing parallels between Canada and developing countries.

The idea of Canada as a developing country clashed with other views of Canada as an industrialized country. It also clashed with Quebec's status as a growing copyright exporter. As a result, such ideas were only partially incorporated into Canada's official presentations at the 1971 conference to revise the *Berne Convention* and the *Universal Copyright Convention*, arranged in response to the international copyright crisis.

From a government perspective, the 1967 diplomatic conference paved the way for active participation in the Berne Union. Perhaps Canada's non-ratification of the 1948 text of the *Berne Convention*, which up to this point had been one reason for the government's more detached stance towards the Berne Union, had become less relevant with the advent of a new text. The idea of more active participation had been raised initially by an interdepartmental committee preparing the instructions for the delegates to the 1967 conference,[2] and after 1967 Canadian policy makers began emphasizing the importance of active participation in international copyright forums. This position may also have reflected the growing attention paid by private copyright interests to the international meetings.[3]

Canada's creative industries continued to grow.[4] The Canada Council for the Arts had been established in 1957; the Canadian Film Development Corporation was established in 1968 and English Canada had "found its cinematic voice," producing David Cronenberg's *Crimes of the Future* and other films despite the fact that Canadian producers had difficulty finding distribution.[5] Government efforts to promote Canadian films outside Canada were initiated, such as the establishment of the Ontario Film Office under the Ontario Ministry of Industry and Tourism in 1974.[6] The film industry would undergo a boom under tax shelter initiatives in the late 1970s to 1981.[7] A few Canadian musicians also rose to prominence in the 1960s and '70s, often, in the case of English-speaking Canadians, by moving to the United States. In Quebec, however, a separate and highly successful music industry was built in conjunction with a growing Québécois nationalism that led venue owners, record labels, and radio stations to support Quebec musicians to a much greater extent than elsewhere in the country.[8] Canadian popular music received a boost under regulations, established in 1971, that required broadcasters to meet quotas in the broadcast of Canadian content.[9]

A growing number of organizations lobbied the government on copyright issues. These included the Canadian Copyright Institute (an association of creators, producers, publishers, and distributors formed in 1965[10]), the Canadian Record Manufacturers' Association (established in 1963, later known as the Canadian Recording Industry Association, and now called Music Canada[11]), and the Canadian Cable Television Association (formed in 1957 as the National Community Antenna Television Association of Canada and renamed in 1968).[12] A number of education-related associations, such as the Canadian Education Association, also became involved.[13] Some of these groups were concerned that what they viewed as private property might be restricted as part of foreign assistance programs. Roy C. Sharp, executive director of the Canadian Copyright Institute and one of the Canadian delegates to the 1967 Stockholm conference, suggested more active participation by the Canadian government in international copyright.[14]

Canada's growing creative industries, a new program of cultural diplomacy, and a reorientation of Canadian foreign policy all contributed to the Canadian government's conflicted re-engagement with the Berne Union. In 1968, the Liberal Party under Pierre Trudeau came to power. One of Trudeau's major acts was a reorientation of Canadian foreign policy that called for a diminished role for the Canadian government in international forums and an increased emphasis on "dollar diplomacy" in the sense of focusing on financial and commercial interests abroad.[15] *Foreign Policy for Canadians,* the new government's foreign policy statement, noted that after the Second World War, Canadians had been concerned with safeguarding future security and well-being through international institutions. "Canada's international role, its influence, its self-expression were seen in the context of those intergovernmental bodies."[16] The report noted, however, that doubts had arisen about the continued relevance of international institutions in a changed world.[17] It was not enough, according to the government's foreign policy statement, to be a "helpful fixer" in international affairs. International affairs should not be based on altruistic aspirations; rather, they should be based on attainable national objectives – extensions of domestic goals.[18] At the same time, the government promised to increase spending on international development assistance.[19]

The Trudeau government also placed increased emphasis on cultural diplomacy.[20] A new Division of Cultural Affairs within the Department of External Affairs had been created in 1965.[21] This division, which had a relatively ad hoc character until 1975, found a new rationale under the Trudeau government. Cultural diplomacy was seen as a strategy for distancing Canada from the United States not only economically but also culturally.[22]

Copyright became one of the responsibilities of the new division.[23] Copyright policy thus became embedded in a larger program of cultural diplomacy that was designed to win prestige for Canada and to project a distinct identity abroad.[24] Cultural diplomacy became a special priority soon after Trudeau became Prime Minister in 1968, and the Department of External Affairs moved vigorously to take the lead in this area, emphasizing in particular Canada's associations with Europe.[25]

1968: C.A.P.A.C. v. CTV Television Network and Bell Telephone Company of Canada

The *Berne Convention* was decisive in a claim of infringement against the CTV Television Network and the Bell Telephone Company of Canada in 1968. Since 1961, CTV had been acquiring television programs on videotape, adding commercials, and supplying this programming to affiliated stations, usually by microwave over Bell Telephone facilities. As the holder of the performing rights in the musical works supplied as part of the programming, the Composers, Authors, and Publishers Association of Canada (CAPAC) claimed that CTV had infringed its copyright by communicating the work by radio communication. The Supreme Court of Canada concluded, however, that Canada's domestic legislation was ambiguous in that it was based on an error in translation of the *Berne Convention* from French into English, and that it was therefore necessary to refer to the convention directly in making an interpretation of the Canadian *Copyright Act*. The court concluded that what was intended by Parliament, in accordance with the original French version of the *Berne Convention,* was that it should be an infringement to communicate, without authorization, a work *to the public* by radio broadcasting. Since CTV had not communicated or broadcast the work to the public, the court found that it had not infringed the CAPAC copyright.[26] In this case, the court turned to the *Berne Convention* only after an ambiguity in domestic legislation became apparent. Later jurisprudence would call for reference to a treaty at the *start* of a court's inquiry when construing domestic legislation that implements an international treaty.[27]

Canada sent representatives to most of the major meetings of the Berne Union and the *Universal Copyright Convention* between the Stockholm (1967) and Paris (1971) conferences.[28] The Canadian government's initial response to consultations in 1968 and early 1969 by the Director General of the United International Bureaux for the Protection of Intellectual Property (BIRPI) was as follows: "The copyright policy in our country is currently undergoing review by the Economic Council of Canada (ECC). The Canadian government is therefore unfortunately not in a position at the present time to make any statement concerning steps it may take or the time limit which will be required to implement the Stockholm Protocol of the Berne Convention."[29]

By the end of December 1968, however, a policy of active participation was being promoted by the Commissioner of Patents, A.M. Laidlaw: "Not only have we important copyright interests in Canada which object strongly to the government adhering to the provisions of the Stockholm protocol, but also Canada has an interest in providing assistance to the developing countries in all matters that might be of help to them."[30] Laidlaw noted that the 1957 Ilsley Commission (Royal Commission on Patents, Copyright, Trade Marks and Industrial Designs) had advised the Canadian government to participate more seriously at international conventions "and implied that failure to do so in the past had resulted in steps having been taken that were adverse to the Canadian public interest."[31] To assist in preparing the government's positions, Laidlaw recommended the creation of an interdepartmental committee to study all copyright matters, with members from the Department of External Affairs, the Canadian Broadcasting Corporation (CBC), the National Film Board, and the National Library, and with a senior official from the Patent and Copyright Office acting as chair.[32]

Canadian participation in international copyright was viewed as important not only because of its potential implications for Canadian copyright legislation but also because it was thought that Canadians could play a useful role as a bridge between the views of developing and "developed" countries.[33]

The importance of the copyright issue would continue to be emphasized by Consumer and Corporate Affairs to the Department of External Affairs, which worked to ensure that staff at the Canadian Mission in Geneva could provide adequate support for active participation in copyright meetings.[34]

Preparations for the Paris Revision

A Joint Study Group, made up of representatives from the Permanent Committee of the Berne Union and the Inter-Governmental Copyright Committee of the *Universal Copyright Convention,* was tasked with formulating response to the crisis in international copyright. As a result of growing consensus within the Canadian government that more active participation was necessary, Canadian officials, encouraged by British and American delegates, lobbied actively for an appointment to the Joint Study Group.[35] World Intellectual Property Organization (WIPO) Director General Georg Bodenhausen also provided encouragement, emphasizing the importance of this move if Canada wished to eventually gain a place on the new Executive Committee of the Berne Union. He offered to relay the Canadian government's interest in joining the Joint Study Group to French officials during an upcoming visit.[36]

A Canadian delegation attended a joint session of the Permanent Committee of the Berne Union and the Inter-Governmental Committee of the *Universal Copyright Convention* in an observer capacity in February 1969, during which Canada was appointed to the Joint Study Group. With a seat at the table secured, Laidlaw again proposed, in his report following this session, the creation of an interdepartmental committee on copyright to consider the positions that Canadian officials should take at the Joint Study Group meeting scheduled for 29 September to 3 October 1969 in Washington, DC.[37]

At this point an idea arose that would become central to the Canadian position. The British delegate had briefly mentioned the possibility of a new single copyright convention with more than one level of protection, to replace the Berne and Universal Copyright conventions. The Canadian delegation understood that the United States might also support such a solution.[38] Laidlaw suggested that Canadian officials consult with like-minded members of the Joint Study Group prior to the Washington meeting to pursue the idea of a new multi-level convention and also to examine the definition of "developing country" to be used in international copyright.[39] These two ideas would be central to the Canadian position in the months to come.

1969: The Interdepartmental Committee on Copyright

An Interdepartmental Committee on Copyright was formed and held its first meeting on 5 March 1969.[40] Laidlaw was appointed its president, with Jacques

Alleyn of the CBC as deputy chairman and Finlay William Simons, Commissioner of Patents, as executive secretary.[41] Other participants included Andrew A. Keyes of the National Film Board; G.E. Pallant and P.T. Eastham of the Department of Industry, Trade and Commerce; Ian Wees and J.G. Sylvestre of the National Library; G. Patenaude of the Queen's Printer; C.B. Watt of the Canadian Government Printing Bureau; J.M. Demers of the Canadian Radio-Television Commission (CRTC); D.A. Hilton, K.T. Hepburn, and E. Cuddihy of the Department of Communications; J.M. Déry and W.R. Hines of the Department of Finance; Charles Lapointe, M. Dolgin, W.A. Dymond, and J.P. Carrière of External Affairs; W.F. Barnicke of the Economic Council of Canada; and J.F. Grandy of the Department of Consumer and Corporate Affairs.[42] The purpose of the committee was "to have available a government group skilled in various aspects of copyright; to study and recommend action on various copyright problems as they arise; to be available to act on the copyright report of the Economic Council; to revise the existing copyright law; to provide a means of consultation and exchange of views."[43]

Certain members of the committee would attend international meetings and especially the meetings leading up to the next diplomatic conference to revise the *Berne Convention*. These members formed an "inner group," with expertise in national and international copyright. It was expected that this group would eventually be charged with forming a task force on the revision of Canadian copyright legislation.[44] Members of the group envisioned a break with Canada's copyright history and its roots in British copyright law:

> Canada has in past years followed fairly closely the views and policies of the United Kingdom in copyright matters. This was reasonable to the extent of common problems, given our common legal heritage. However, once the commercial significance of copyright is acknowledged, it must be recognized that the United Kingdom is no longer a good weathervane for Canadian policy. Its copyright policies and laws, of course, still merit careful attention, but different industrial and commercial situations may require different treatment. The U.K. publishing industry, for example, is much larger than is ours in Canada. The historical relationship alone with the developing countries may subject the United Kingdom to unique influences. The balance of payments, insofar as copyright is concerned, is quite different in Canada from that in the United Kingdom. Contemplated entry by the United Kingdom into the European Common Market, as well as the cultural proximity of Canada to the United States, are also differentiating factors.[45]

Throughout its work, the committee would attempt to forge an independent path for Canadian copyright. It would meet up against a number of barriers.

Although part of the committee's work was to prepare for eventual copyright reform, following the report of the Economic Council of Canada,[46] the most pressing item on the agenda was the statement to be submitted to the Joint Study Group.[47] The possibilities were wide-ranging and included: amendment of the *Universal Copyright Convention* to remove the safeguard clause, thus allowing members of the *Berne Convention* to denounce it in favour of the *Universal Copyright Convention;* denunciation of the *Berne Convention;* advocacy for a new multi-level copyright convention; and aid for the provision of copyright works in developing countries.[48]

Denunciation of the *Berne Convention* and removal of the *Universal Copyright Convention* safeguard clause were viewed as options that might be considered, given Canada's position as a net copyright importer, not unlike the developing countries: "In view of the fact that Canada is a net importer of copyrighted material our interests in some ways are not unlike those of developing countries and this might be an argument for supporting stand 4(a) [advocating removal of the safeguard clause] and (b) [denunciation of the *Berne Convention*] above."[49] The idea of denouncing the *Berne Convention* continued to be seen as an unpalatable alternative. It was not considered at length, and after the initial discussion does not reappear in the minutes on file.[50]

Following written consultations and face-to-face meetings with Canadian interest groups, the committee formulated a preliminary submission to the Joint Study Group.[51] This was attached to a memorandum to the Liberal Cabinet and signed by the Minister of Consumer and Corporate Affairs with the concurrence of the Secretary of State for External Affairs. The memorandum made three suggestions. The first was that Canadian participation in international copyright should not follow the pattern of participation in 1967:

At the last International Copyright Revisions Conference of the Berne Union, held in Stockholm in 1967, the developing countries were successful in having enacted a Protocol ... Canada took no position with respect to this matter because the Economic Council was studying our copyright law. It would appear that if Canada takes the same noncommittal attitude again, her future position as a serious participant in international copyright matters will be weakened.[52]

Second, an adaptation of the definition of "developing country" was recommended so that Canadians might benefit from concessions made to such countries. In formulating the position to be taken by the Canadian delegation, the committee did not go along with the arguments made in most of the written stakeholder submissions, which were opposed to special copyright treatment for developing countries.[53] Instead, the preliminary submission to the Joint

Study Group said that "Canada's position is somewhat analogous to that of developing countries when compared to countries with higher exports of copyright material."[54] The memorandum to Cabinet explained:

> Although Canada is undoubtedly a "developing country" in so far as copyright is concerned (because of the large import imbalance of trade in copyrighted material), nevertheless it is not so considered by the two Conventions. A "developing country" under U.N. definition is considered a country which has an average per capita income per year of $US 300 or less. In my view [Minister of Consumer and Corporate Affairs Ron Basford], any country with a very large export-import imbalance in copyrighted materials should be entitled, like the developing countries, to maintain a somewhat lower level of international copyright protection.[55]

The memo recommended "that the Canadian delegation suggest to the Joint Study Group that, in so far as international copyright is concerned, the definition of a 'developing country' should not be based on per capita income, but on a substantial import imbalance of trade in copyrighted material."[56] The committee felt that in order to allow countries in Canada's position to commit to lower levels of international copyright protection, "a complete overhaul of the existing legal regime governing international copyright" was necessary.[57] It presented the idea of a multi-level international treaty that would provide various levels of protection and access: "One approach to problems of international copyright relations might be found in a suitable multi-level international copyright convention wherein countries may adjust from one level to another having regard to their needs. Such a structure might enable international responsibilities and commitments to be related to the benefits derived."[58] This idea, the memo suggested, should be promoted by Canada at the Joint Study Group, even though there might not be enough support for it: "Canada should take a new and fresh approach to international copyright protection through the proposal of a new multi-level Convention in the hope that other countries in her position will join with her – although this may be a vain hope for the immediate future."[59] At the same time, it was felt that the government should do nothing that might cause Canadian authors, creators, and publishers to worry that current copyright protection for Canadians would be weakened.[60]

Third, the memo suggested an alignment with developing countries to some extent, by recommending that the Canadian delegation support "any reasonable and generally acceptable proposal that would assist the developing countries (even under the U.N. definition) in obtaining copyrighted educational material at minimum cost."[61] This included the abolition of the safeguard clause for developing countries, even though, under the UN definition of developing countries, Canadians would not be able to take advantage of its abolition.[62]

In contrast to 1928, when the Canadian delegation was dispatched with clear instructions to support proposals that favoured the leading copyright powers, the idea now being proposed was that the Canadian delegation support proposals that would assist the developing countries.[63] In both cases, however, the delegation was seen as supporting only generally acceptable proposals: "any reasonable and generally acceptable proposal" in 1971, and any proposal that appeared likely to meet general approval in 1928.

Some objected to the direction the interdepartmental committee had taken. The Quebec *Conseil supérieur du livre* and the *Société canadienne-française de protection du droit d'auteur* felt that the committee was biased, and that such a bias would ultimately damage Canadian and Québécois culture through its economic focus on Canada as a net copyright importer. In a joint submission to the committee made in 1970, they remarked:

> The composition of your Interdepartmental Committee on Copyright seems to reflect a certain prejudice. The representatives from Canadian Broadcasting Corporation and National Film Board sitting on your committee are perfectly qualified to present their needs as consumers of copyrighted works but they could not speak on behalf of authors and artists without finding themselves in a position of conflicting interest. Frankly we do not understand, why the Canada Council which subsidizes our writers and artists is not represented on your committee.[64]

Further, they noted, "to state that economical power is not all that counts for a country's good name is self evident."[65] This was particularly the case in Quebec:

> French Canadians have always known that their survival is linked to their culture; consequently, whatever is dangerous for their culture is also dangerous for their survival and must be fought against at any cost. Whatever is done to minimize the protection of authors and artists, will inevitably be constructed by French Canadians as an attack on their French Canadian culture ... We realise that this problem concerns particularly the French Canadians. The situation is different with English Canadians for their authors and artists prefer to make a career in the United States and one can safely say that English Canadian culture as such, is almost nonexistent for when English Canadian writers first publish their works in the United States they become part of American literature.[66]

In the years that followed, Canadian officials did become more active in the meetings leading up to the 1971 diplomatic conference,[67] participating in all of the preparatory work of the conference.[68] Besides being appointed to the Joint Study Group in October 1969, Canada was elected to the Executive Committee of the Berne Union in September 1970 at the first meeting of the WIPO General Assembly, of which Laidlaw was also elected chair.[69] At the Extraordinary Session of the Permanent Committee of the Berne Union that same month, the Canadian delegation informed the meeting that Canadian copyright legislation was being revised and declared the Canadian government's intention to play a more active role in international copyright.[70]

At the same time, however, Canada was unsuccessful in its bid for election to the Intergovernmental Copyright Committee of the United Nations Educational, Scientific and Cultural Organization (UNESCO), the governing body of the *Universal Copyright Convention,* and in a bid to enlarge UNESCO's Ad Hoc Preparatory Committee to Prepare a Draft Text of the Proposals for Revision of the *Universal Copyright Convention* so as to ensure "adequate representation."[71]

The reformulation of the concept of "developing country" in such a way as to include Canada was absolutely radical. Such a precedent might have opened the door to a variety of definitions of developing countries based on the balance of trade in different areas, making possible a cascade of unexpected country coalitions and policy alignments unthinkable under the existing categorizations. It is unsurprising that an idea so radical and so different from the regimes of representation and the practices of categorization that were being inscribed in international institutions at the time did not go far.[72]

The idea that Canada be treated as a developing country did not have unanimous backing within the Canadian government. A note on file argued that this aspect of the Canadian position, which it called "utter nonsense," should be played down by the delegation to the Joint Study Group:

> Efforts to claim Canada is a "developing country" ... are usually greeted with derision. We have the 3rd highest per capita income in the world and this is partly due to our importation of capital and know-how.
>
> Is it too late to tone this down? Or at least ensure that the Washington Del play it very lightly and stress (d) [support of "any reasonable and generally acceptable proposal that would assist the developing countries"] more?[73]

Canada's position was presented internationally in more moderate terms than those suggested by the interdepartmental committee. Although the Cabinet Committee on Economic Policy and Programs did approve the joint recommendation of the Minister of Consumer and Corporate Affairs and the Acting Secretary of State for External Affairs that the Canadian delegation "suggest to the Joint Study Group that, in so far as international copyright is concerned, the definition of a 'developing country' should not be based on per capita income, but on a substantial import imbalance of trade in copyrighted material," the actual statement to the Joint Study Group did not suggest that Canada was a developing country.[74] Rather, it noted that "Canada was a heavy importer of copyright works and consequently understood and supported the position of the developing countries," and that "certain countries would like to take a position intermediate between two present levels of protection."[75] This reformulation may have stemmed from concerns that Canada's "relations with the USA., UK. and France which could be affected if we were to line up with the [less developed countries]."[76]

Instead of portraying Canada as a "developing country," Canadian delegates used the term "intermediate country" in the time leading up to the 1971 Paris conference. In this way, Canadian officials attempted to take the lead in creating a coalition of "intermediate countries" that were not considered to be "developing" but were net copyright importers. Initially, there was little interest in a coalition of intermediate countries or in attempts to obtain special consideration for them in international copyright. After discussions with several other countries in 1969, however, the Canadian delegation reported:

> There is strong evidence that support for Canada's position is available from certain other countries if it is properly explored and developed. There appears to be every possibility that Canada for the first time can play a leading role in shaping the course of international copyright by fostering and leading a block of countries with interests similar to Canada. To a large extent we could conceivably control a certain balance of power, given active participation.[77]

The vision of Canada as a leader of a coalition of intermediate countries never came to fruition, however. At the September 1970 Extraordinary Session of the Permanent Committee of the Berne Union, Canadian delegates formulated Canada as an "intermediate country":

> The delegation of Canada expressed its understanding of the problems of revising the two conventions and congratulated both Committees on the results achieved and stated its sympathy with the needs of developing countries; stating that Canada is an intermediate country, the delegation of Canada expressed the hope that the needs of such countries could be considered at the appropriate time.[78]

In the end, consideration of the needs of "intermediate countries" was postponed indefinitely.

The meeting of the Joint Study Group was seen by Canadian officials as "a rare opportunity to push for a new multi-level convention within which we will be able to determine the level of protection best suited to Canada's national interest," and the Canadian delegation was sent to the Joint Study Group with instructions to advocate a new multi-level convention.[79] This it did: "We also pointed out that certain countries would like to take a position intermediate between the two present levels of protection afforded by the Berne and Universal Copyright Conventions and that if a single convention were instituted it would have to be established with several levels."[80] Most countries, however, preferred to maintain existing conventions while establishing links between them.[81] The Canadian delegation to the Joint Study Group found that:

> Neither the developing nor developed countries, other than Canada, showed the slightest interest in providing copyright protection on a basis other than that of the highest level for producing countries, and the lowest level for those countries earning less than $300 US per capita per year (U.N. formula for developing countries) ... Suggested continued study by the Group into a new, single, multi-level Convention was not, as stated, received with enthusiasm.[82]

Whereas the interdepartmental committee had hoped to use Canada's role as a middle power to introduce several radical ideas into the international copyright system, the ideas concerning a new definition of "developing country" and a multi-level copyright treaty were replaced by the portrayal of Canada as an "intermediate country" and the advocacy of flexibility not just for developing countries but also for all. Reasons for these shifts included a lack of support from other countries; the hesitation of various government officials to support too radical a stance; the clash between the vision of an activist Canada and the more traditional vision of Canada as a good international citizen aligned with major powers; and fears that an activist stance would affect Canada's relations with countries such as the United States, Britain, and France. Perhaps what was missing more than anything else was a firm high-level Canadian policy on international copyright. Upon returning from international meetings, Canadian delegates reiterated the hope that a more in-depth examination of Canada's position would soon take place, and the need for such an undertaking.[83]

1970: Canada's Accession to the *WIPO Convention*

Canada's disengagement from the Berne Union was over. At the 1967 diplomatic conference, a new organization to administer the Berne Union and related intellectual property unions had been formed; the *Convention Establishing the World Intellectual Property Organization,* one of the conference's successful outcomes, had been signed and was awaiting ratification.[84] Canada's accession to the *WIPO Convention* was viewed as a necessary step to active participation in the Berne Union: "It is anticipated that the WIPO Convention will come into force in the near future. In view of the fact that Canada is assuming an increasingly more active role in international intellectual and industrial property matters, its participation in the new organization would appear highly desirable from a policy standpoint."[85]

On 26 January 1970, BIRPI announced that the minimum number of ten ratifications of the *WIPO Convention* had been achieved, and that the World Intellectual Property Organization would come into existence on 26 April 1970.[86] It was then suggested that "there would be psychological advantage for [sic] Canada were to deposit its instrument of accession before WIPO comes into force."[87] Presumably its inclusion among the initial participants would help the Canadian government be seen as being actively engaged and a ready participant in the new organization. On 3 February 1970, the Cabinet Committee on External Policy and Defence recommended that Canada accede to the *WIPO Convention*, and Cabinet confirmed this decision shortly after, on 12 February.[88] On 10 March 1970, the Privy Council authorized the Secretary of State for External Affairs to deposit the instruments of accession. This was done on 26 March and took effect three months later, in June.[89] Canada also acceded to the administrative clauses of the Stockholm Act of the *Berne Convention* on 7 April 1970, to take effect on 7 July 1970.[90]

At the inaugural meeting of WIPO, Canada was elected to the Executive Committee of the Berne Union, as a result of which it became a member of the WIPO Coordination Committee, the highest-level governing committee at WIPO – eleven years after resigning its membership in the Permanent Committee of the Berne Union.[91]

Besides re-engaging with the Berne Union Executive Committee, Canadian officials began showing leadership and chairing international meetings in the field of copyright, on the subjects of communication satellites and the transfer of computer technology to developing countries.[92]

1971: The Economic Council of Canada Report

The Economic Council of Canada was commissioned in July 1966 to study intellectual property, and submitted its *Report on Intellectual and Industrial Property* in 1971. The report noted: "A period of unusually active copyright diplomacy lies immediately ahead, and the development of an appropriate Canadian negotiating position has become an urgent necessity."[93]

The ECC went further than the Ilsley Commission in drawing a line against what it termed the "fundamental rights" view of intellectual property: "Neither patents nor any other single incentive device should be regarded as sacred, for this will surely impede the achievement of a good mixture of policies."[94] Here the ECC aligned Canada with the American utilitarian, rather than the European *droit d'auteur,* approach to copyright.

The ECC echoed the concerns of parliamentarians and the interdepartmental committee in focusing on the importance of Canadian development:

> The readiest possible access to the best that has been thought, expressed and invented abroad is vital to Canada – not simply as a user of knowledge, but also as a producer of it ... Canada's situation and interests in this sphere are in some ways closer to those of the developing countries than to those of countries like Britain, France and the United States ... Canadians must be aware of their interest in keeping the cost of this access as low as possible. Canada is likely, for instance, to have an interest in adhering to international conventions at less than the maximum level of protection available to member countries.[95]
>
> Even if Canada greatly improves as a knowledge-producer and a purveyor of information internationally, its balance of international payments for information will likely be always heavily outbound, and this fact should be kept clearly in mind for purposes of international negotiation.[96]

The report also raised the profile of consumer interests in copyright:

> In a market economy whose main ultimate purpose is the improvement of general welfare, consumers have a supremely important role to play. But their performance of this role is hampered by their very vastness and amorphousness as a group and by the consequent difficulties of getting concerted attention focused effectively on issues which, when the public is made properly aware of them, are seen to be of widespread interest and concern.[97]

The consumer movement, the ECC argued, had an important role to play in giving consumers "self-awareness, confidence and cohesion."[98]

Once the ECC report came out, the Canadian government was more prepared to play an active role in international copyright. One official at the Department of External Affairs wrote:

> Although Canada has participated in all of the preparatory meetings, it has not taken a position on the substance of the revisions proposed because Canadian copyright legislation was being reviewed by the Economic Council.
>
> The Economic Council review is now complete and new Canadian legislation is being drafted in the sense of the review. In general, the Economic Council

recommended that since Canada is primarily an importer of copyrighted material, it would not be in the Canadian interest to encourage or become bound by a higher level of international copyright protection. This will likely preclude, at this time, Canadian accession to either the revised Berne or the Universal Convention, both of which would entail acceptance by Canada of a higher level of international copyright protection.[99]

The government's policy of active engagement in the meetings leading up to the 1971 diplomatic conferences did not necessarily assume Canada's future adhesion to the new texts.

Diplomatic Conferences: Paris, 5-24 July 1971

The 1971 Paris conference to revise the *Berne Convention* had about 300 participants, compared with 500 at the 1967 Stockholm conference.[100] Its main objective was to replace the 1967 Stockholm protocol with an appendix to the *Berne Convention* that provided much narrower concessions to developing countries. These were envisioned to closely match those provided under the *Universal Copyright Convention*.[101] A conference to revise the *Universal Copyright Convention* was held at the same time and place as the conference to revise the *Berne Convention,* and the two revisions led to provisions for developing countries that generally equalled each other, removing alternatives and any incentive for developing countries to move from one to the other.[102]

The Canadian delegation to the *Berne Convention* revision conference included René Garneau as head of the delegation, Finlay William Simons, the Assistant Commissioner of Patents, as the deputy head, Robert G. Blackburn, from the Cultural Affairs Division of External Affairs as secretary to the delegation, and several other delegates: Marcel Denis Bélanger, Economist, Office of General Relations, Department of Industry and Commerce; Yvon Des Rochers, Office of the Assistant Under-Secretary of State; Naim Kattan, *Director des lettres,* Canada Council for the Arts; Andrew A. Keyes, Copyright Consultant, Department of Consumer and Corporate Affairs; and Julian Harris Porter, Canadian Conference of the Arts. The same set of delegates attended the *Universal Copyright Convention* revision conference, with J.-Z.-Léon Patenaude, president of the *Société canadienne-française de protection du droit d'auteur,* being added as an adviser to the delegation for this particular conference.[103] Garneau was a reluctant delegation head, close to retirement and not well versed in international copyright. To the initial invitation to head the delegation he had replied: "Professionally, I have no skill or experience with this legal and technical subject. At my age, I do not even know what a 'phonogram' is."[104]

The composition of the Canadian delegation had been a matter of dispute in the time leading up to the conference. The Canadian Copyright Institute, in lobbying for better Canadian representation at international copyright conferences, had requested larger delegations to international copyright meetings and the inclusion of advisers from industry in the delegations. Their requests had elicited a commitment from Prime Minister Lester B. Pearson in December 1967: "I understand that it is the practice of a number of countries including the United States and Great Britain to send industry advisers to important copyright meetings. As long as this is the general practice, we are prepared to accept the principle that Canadian industry advisers be sent to important international meetings on copyright."[105] Consumer and Corporate Affairs and External Affairs disagreed on this matter. Minister of Consumer and Corporate Affairs Ron Basford did not want to include private delegates, while the Secretary of State for External Affairs felt that their inclusion could add balance and representativeness to the delegation.[106] Whereas Basford objected to the payment of private delegates' expenses from government funds, External Affairs saw advantages in such payment, in that it "reflects the Government's interest in and responsibility for intergovernmental conferences" and "in practical terms, it increases delegations' cohesiveness and responsiveness to guidance from the Government."[107]

For the 1971 diplomatic conferences, the compromise solution was that only one private delegate was chosen: Julian Porter of the Canadian Conference of the Arts. Representatives from other organizations, including the Canadian Copyright Institute and the *Société canadienne-française de protection des droits d'auteurs*, who had been informally invited and who had accepted the invitations, were informed that they would not be included on the delegation after all.

These organizations were extremely unhappy. The Canadian Copyright Institute contacted Prime Minister Trudeau, citing Pearson's commitment and asking for assurances that there had been no permanent change in policy.[108] Patenaude of the *Société canadienne-française de protection des droits d'auteurs* contacted the newspaper *Le Devoir* and a front-page article was published with the headline "No Official Delegate of Quebec Publishers in Paris." The article noted (incorrectly) that the Canadian delegation did not include any francophone representatives besides Garneau as the head.[109] The government reacted quickly: Patenaude, who had gone to Paris despite not being officially part of the delegation, was quickly made a delegate. The same would have been done for the Canadian Copyright Institute had its representative attended.[110]

The non-inclusion of representatives of Quebec interests raised questions in that province about why it was not consulted and included in the delegation in the first place. Many in Quebec were unhappy about the prospect of special provisions for developing countries. The *Conseil supérieur du livre* and the *Société canadienne-française de protection du droit d'auteur*, for example, expressed concerns that if Canadian copyright law were weakened or not improved, Quebec creators would begin to first publish their works in Paris rather than in Quebec. Quebec had developed a vibrant export market for its works, and no longer could it be said that Canadian authors – at least insofar as Quebec was concerned – belonged more "to the future than to the present."[111] Quebec exports, it was felt, belonged to the immediate present: "When a French Canadian will write a book of great international value – and we believe that this will happen in the near future – we do not want it to be first published in Paris. Unfortunately, it will happen if our copyright legislation is not seriously improved."[112]

The *Conseil supérieur du livre* and the *Société canadienne-française de protection du droit d'auteur* argued strongly against the provisions for developing countries. "To let works of our authors and artists without adequate protection," they said, "is to attack our French Canadian culture and consequently our survival. Quebec will never let this happen."[113] In response to questions about the inclusion of Quebec representatives, however, External Affairs took the position that copyright was a matter of exclusive federal jurisdiction that no provincial agency dealt with as a primary part of its mandate.[114] (A different view was taken in the case of the *Convention for the Protection of Producers of Phonograms against Unauthorized Duplication of Their Phonograms*, also negotiated in 1971; certain articles were viewed as being "so broad in their scope of application that the protection they offer might be considered to fall outside the realm of copyright and thus into an unspecified area in which the provinces might claim some competence."[115]) Quebec's Minister of Intergovernmental Affairs, however, pointed especially to the Art and Books section of the *Ministère des Affaires culturelles du Québec* as dealing with the area.[116]

Whereas in 1967 the instructions to the Canadian delegation had been issued after the start of the conference, preparation for the 1971 conference was more robust. Cabinet approved Canadian participation in the July conference at the beginning of May. At the end of May, the Deputy Minister of Consumer and Corporate Affairs wrote to the Under-Secretary of State for External Affairs asking for clearer policy direction:

> The treatment of developing countries in the context of intellectual property is receiving increasing attention from governments and in scholarly journals, and it is clear that the issue will continue to be discussed at a whole range of treaty negotiations in the future. My officials, as well as other Canadian government

representatives, are therefore increasingly experiencing the need for a clear Canadian policy on the subject. They find some assistance in the white paper on "Foreign Policy for Canadians" but the necessity of more specific guidance in this particular context has become apparent.[117]

Although an overall government policy would not be formulated in time for the conference, instructions to the delegation were issued at the end of June.[118] The government's position was that, although it had no objections to the concessions being made for developing countries, it could not support the revisions as a whole because they were seen as also involving a commitment to higher levels of intellectual property rights:

> Although Canada could agree to the proposed system of concessions for the developing countries since they include protection for the legal and economic rights of copyright owners, Canadian accession to the revised Conventions would entail the provision of higher copyright protection to all states members of the Conventions. It is a package deal.[119]

The Canadian delegation was therefore instructed not to sign the revised treaties. This was consistent with the report of the Economic Council of Canada, which had recommended that the government not adopt higher levels of copyright protection.[120] In fact, it continued to be viewed as questionable whether Canada should accede to the 1948 revision of the *Berne Convention*.[121]

Concerned that Canada's non-signature of the revised treaties and the appendix for developing countries might be viewed negatively, the Canadian delegation was instructed to state that it would nevertheless consider accepting the application of the concessions embodied in the new appendix to Canadian works. It was also suggested that the delegation emphasize the Canadian government's support elsewhere for programs and bilateral assistance in the book development field. At the same time, the delegation should emphasize, strengthen, and clarify the draft revisions that would protect the interests of Canadian authors and publishers.[122] The specific instructions approved by Cabinet were as follows:

a) the Delegation is not to sign the revised texts as these will have to be referred to the appropriate Canadian bodies for study;

b) the Delegation is to obtain final texts which clearly define the substantive and administrative issues involved and favour all tendencies which will provide maximum flexibility to the Canadian government;

c) in respect of Canada's position relative to developing countries, the Delegation should state that Canada is seriously and sympathetically considering the possibility of accepting the application of the concessions to Canadian works;

d) the Delegation is to facilitate by all appropriate means the achieving of the primary objectives of the conferences, bearing in mind that there should be an appropriate balance between the legitimate interests of the developing countries and of Canadian authors and publishers;

e) the Delegation is to seek election to the Intergovernmental Committee of the Universal Copyright Convention, to parallel Canada's position as a member of the Executive Committee of the Berne Union;

f) the Delegation is to accept election to office at the conferences. Given its non-signing stance but its active participation Canada should accept office as indicative of its support for the aims of the conferences.[123]

The delegation held a pre-departure meeting to review and discuss the conference preparatory documents and the Canadian position. Some members also attended a meeting of French-speaking countries held just prior to the conference; although that meeting did not arrive at firm conclusions, the Canadians felt that the outlook for the conference was good.[124]

At the conference itself, Canadian officials sat on the drafting committees of both conventions, and acted as vice president of the conference to revise the *Universal Copyright Convention.*[125] As per instructions, the delegation sought election to the Intergovernmental Committee of the *Universal Copyright Convention,* but was unsuccessful. Australia was chosen instead, in part because the United States was a member of the committee and so the choice of Australia made for a more diverse geographical representation.[126]

The simultaneous conferences to revise the two conventions were organized such that the first week was devoted to the *Universal Copyright Convention,* the second to the *Berne Convention,* and the third to coordinating provisions between the two.[127] Because the *Universal Copyright Convention* was discussed first, most general statements were made at that conference. Canadian delegates made a number of significant comments. The delegation's general reasons for and goals in participating in the conferences were outlined as follows:

The delegation of CANADA explained that Canada had several reasons for participating in the Conferences for revision of the Universal Copyright Convention and the Berne Convention, to begin with the growing interest which it attached, since the Second World War, to the development of its two national cultures. It hoped that the revision of the legal instruments in question would exert a stimulating influence on national and international cultural life ...

If the Canadian Government had not yet determined its position, it nevertheless thought itself able to contribute in a concrete manner to the resolution of the
problems which were presented during the Conference on identical subjects.[128]

At the conference, several ideas returned to the core of the Canadian position.
First, Canada was once again portrayed as partially a developing country and
partially a developed country. Second, Canada was portrayed as being in solidarity with developing countries, rather than simply as sympathetic to them.

In terms reminiscent of the work of the interdepartmental committee,
Canadian delegates described Canada as "both developed and developing," an
intermediary that understood the needs of both developing and "developed"
countries:

> The delegate of Canada emphasized the great interest of his government in the
> problems of international copyright and the work of the Conference. This special
> interest arises from a combination of factors, including the existence within
> Canada of dual languages and cultures, and the problems of reconciling copyright
> protection and technological innovations in a country of immense size.
>
> To some extent, he suggested, "we are all developing countries." Canada in
> particular feels itself to be both developed and developing, and is thus in a unique
> position to understand the needs on both sides.[129]

Canada's association with developing countries was translated into a vision of
middle power leadership. Canada, the delegate outlined, was in a unique situation to understand both the consequences of communications technology for
copyright and the positions of all sides:

> Finally, Canada thought, in cultural matters, that it was half-way between indus-
> trialized and developing countries, which enabled it to understand the problems
> of both and to foresee perhaps the possibility of reconciling the interests at stake.[130]

Such a contribution was portrayed, as had been international involvement in
the 1920s, as a contribution to peace:

> Canada also considered that co-operation with developing countries was a moral
> and political imperative as well as an important contribution to peace; and the
> present Conference provided it with a new opportunity to demonstrate its soli-
> darity with developing countries. Moreover, it could not forget that in matters of
> culture, as the Director-General of Unesco recently recalled, "we are all developing
> countries."[131]

"We are all developing countries" was now a rhetorical statement. The Canadian delegation did not propose Canada's formal categorization as a "developing country" in terms that would make it a candidate for the concessions available to developing countries. Rather, the statement went along with other general statements about middle power leadership and solidarity with developing countries.

Canada had other special attributes that would contribute to its leadership, according to the delegation:

> Canada was obliged, because of the vastness of its territory, to use all the resources of technology to surmount the difficulties of communication. It was also in a good position to follow the evolution of the techniques of communication which may have consequences in the field of copyright.[132]

The Canadian delegation referred to a "universal right to culture," a right that called upon countries to consider the interests of both producers and users of culture, and said that failing to do so could lead to cultural stagnation:

> If Canada participated in the present Conference, it was also because it was convinced that all countries, industrialized or not, should make an effort to reconcile the interests of producers and those of users of culture. The recognition of a universal right to culture implied that justice should be done to both, failing which, one would be exposed to a cultural stagnation flowing either from a decrease in productivity in the cultural field, or from the impossibility for certain groups to have access to culture.[133]

Finally, the delegation expressed hope that in the near future Canada's cultural output would grow:

> Canada being bilingual, original works generally appeared there in both English and French; and the rapid expansion of Canada gave reason to believe that in the rather near future, it would produce a growing number of original works of international scope, written in those languages which were accessible to a great number of countries. In other words, Canada had an interest in seeing that international copyright be regulated as clearly and rapidly as possible.[134]

OUTCOMES OF THE CONFERENCES
In the 1971 revisions to the *Berne Convention,* a number of concessions made to developing countries under the 1967 Stockholm protocol were dropped. The

new Appendix of the *Paris Act* no longer allowed a shorter term of protection; translation rights would no longer be allowed to expire early in cases where the author had not published a translation into the language in which protection was claimed; broadcast rights could no longer be restricted to broadcasts "for profit-making purposes"; and the general provision under the Stockholm protocol allowing compulsory licensing for any use "exclusively for teaching, study and research in all fields of education" was abandoned.[135]

The Appendix continued to allow two types of compulsory licences, but on much more restricted terms than the Stockholm protocol. First, it provided for compulsory licences to translate a work, but these were now more strictly limited, especially in that they could now be granted only for translations that were "for the purpose of teaching, scholarship, or research."[136] Second, it provided for reproduction licences, but these were also more strictly limited than under the Stockholm protocol, especially in that they could be granted only "for use in connection with systematic instructional activities" rather than "for educational or cultural purposes."[137]

With regard to the definition of "developing country" under the new appendix for developing countries, the wording used in the Stockholm protocol citing United Nations practice was retained:

Any country regarded as a developing country in conformity with the established practice of the General Assembly of the United Nations which ratifies or accedes to this Act, of which this Appendix forms an integral part, and which, having regard to its economic situation and its social or cultural needs, does not consider itself immediately in a position to make provision for the protection of all the rights as provided for in this Act.[138]

The idea was briefly raised that an expanded definition of developing countries would be preferable; Israel raised the concern that criteria based on UN practices might be too rigid, excluding certain categories of countries from benefits they should enjoy under the *Berne Convention*.[139] The Canadian delegation did not go on record with any position during this discussion.[140]

The provisions for developing countries agreed to in Paris were more acceptable to the copyright-exporting countries than the Stockholm provisions. The new agreement was acceptable to the newer entrants as well because it represented a workable solution that would grant at least some concessions to developing countries, as opposed to the Stockholm protocol, under which ultimately nothing was granted because it never entered into force. Ricketson and Ginsburg have observed that "it is clear that the ultimate revision of the two conventions in Paris 1971 was effected in a far friendlier and less grudging spirit than had been present in Stockholm in 1967, and there was much wider support for the final results on the part of all the principal parties concerned."[141]

Canada had continued to focus on the special position of intermediate countries. In the month leading up to the conference, the Deputy Minister of Consumer and Corporate Affairs wrote to the Under-Secretary of State for External Affairs, calling for further study on the position of countries like Canada:

> A related matter concerns the possibility of special status within the intellectual property treaties for intermediate countries which, while "developed" by United Nations' standards, are nevertheless net importers of copyright and other protected material. This, indeed, is Canada's situation and the recent Economic Council of Canada report on Intellectual and Industrial Property suggested that the Canadian government study the possibility of a special international position for net importer countries such as ours.[142]

In its report on the 1971 diplomatic conference, the Canadian delegation noted there was "growing dissatisfaction" among "intermediate countries" with the state of international copyright. The particular position of such countries had been raised by Portugal, which expressed its dissatisfaction that the safeguard clause was to be suspended only with regard to those countries categorized as "developing," since the position of intermediate countries was thus not taken into account. Canadian delegates had taken a similar position during the meeting of the Joint Study Group, advocating for the elimination of the safeguard clause altogether. This would have allowed any country, not just developing ones, to exit the *Berne Convention* and adopt instead the lower level of protection offered under the *Universal Copyright Convention*. Austria also expressed its concern that "representation on different international bodies concerned with copyright had tended to include only two groups of countries, namely the developing countries and the large developed countries; and that developed countries with comparatively small populations had not been adequately represented."[143] This dissatisfaction had not yielded concrete results, however. The Canadian delegation reported that "the concept of intermediate countries and their place in international copyright has yet to be fully explored."[144]

Canada signed neither the revised text of the *Berne Convention* nor that of the *Universal Copyright Convention*, and the statements of the Canadian delegation at the 1971 conferences represented the most radical position ever taken by a Canadian delegation at a diplomatic conference on international copyright. At the same time, they were not radical at all. The idea that "we are all developing countries" was a rhetorical statement that had been made in the past by the Director-General of UNESCO. The proposal for a multi-level treaty had failed, as had the idea that Article 17 of the *Universal Copyright Convention* might be lifted for all countries, leaving multiple treaty options open to all countries. The Canadian government's stance of middle power leadership seems to have led to various expressions of an "intermediate" identity in the field of copyright on the part of various countries, but no specific outcomes or concessions for such countries. Compared with past conferences, there was a distinct shift towards expressing solidarity with developing countries, an emphasis on taking into account the interests of users and producers of knowledge, a deep skepticism of the contemporary state of international copyright, and a feeling that the international copyright system did not fully reflect the position of Canada or countries in Canada's position.

The Canadian delegation's efforts to actively influence the shaping of new international norms were not especially successful. Article 17 of the *Universal Copyright Convention* was lifted only insofar as it applied to developing countries, and the delegation was not successful in pushing for a multi-level treaty or for broad flexibility for itself and similar countries with regard to the level of protection they could adopt. The *Universal Copyright Convention,* because its provisions for developing countries were harmonized with those of the *Berne Convention,* no longer provided an alternative set of copyright norms for developing countries. When the United States joined the *Berne Convention* in 1989, its obligations under the *Universal Copyright Convention* were superseded. Although the *Universal Copyright Convention* is still in force, it has become largely redundant.[145]

The Paris revision of the *Berne Convention* was characterized by a general display of relative goodwill and conciliatory spirit on all sides. This revision can be seen as a compromise with which all parties were willing to live, a compromise that therefore held together the Berne Union at a time when there were fears that both developing and "developed" countries might exit the union.[146] It represented a solution that was felt to be broadly acceptable to and even welcoming of developing countries.[147] Despite this, however, many of the solutions incorporated into this revision were largely ineffective and disappointing. Only a handful of developing countries made use of the Appendix of the *Paris Act,* and still fewer incorporated compulsory licensing systems into their laws.[148]

Canada did not accede to the 1971 revision of the *Berne Convention* until the 1990s, several years after the United States finally adopted it in 1989. This long delay was based on views outlined in a number of reports and policy studies.

In 1977, Andrew A. Keyes, who had been a member of the Interdepartmental Committee on Copyright and a delegate at the recent diplomatic conference in

1971, and Claude Brunet prepared for the Department of Consumer and Corporate Affairs a report titled *Copyright in Canada: Proposals for a Revision of the Law*. After examining the available options with regard to the *Berne Convention*, including accession, withdrawal, and maintenance of the status quo, the authors concluded that "the fully developed nations, largely exporters of copyright material, have a stronger voice in international copyright conventions, and a tendency has existed over the past half century for developing countries, including Canada, to accept too readily proffered solutions in copyright matters that do not reflect their economic positions."[149]

They argued further that "succeeding revisions of [the *Berne Convention*] or, indeed, that of the Universal Copyright Convention, do not meet Canadian needs, at least at this stage in Canada's growth."[150] They therefore concluded that Canada should "remain at the present level of international participation in respect of the Berne Convention and the Universal Copyright Convention."[151]

CHAPTER TWELVE

After 1971

THE YEAR 1971 REPRESENTED the end of an era in which international copyright was negotiated in stand-alone agreements rather than incorporated into larger trade agendas. It also represented the beginning of a period in which copyright would enter a digital era, in which the United States would take an expansionist approach to intellectual property, in which international institutions dealing with intellectual property would proliferate, and in which the *Berne Convention,* and international copyright generally, would become embedded in a more complex and dense web of international agreements and institutions dealing with intellectual property and trade.

While the new revised texts of the *Berne Convention* and the *Universal Copyright Convention* were widely accepted, the crisis of 1967 had shown that copyright revision would no longer be easy. This book has taken as its primary subject the period to 1971, after which no further major revisions to the *Berne Convention* have been made; the 1971 text is still in force today.[1] Nevertheless, a brief afterword on developments since 1971, Canada's ultimate accession to the 1971 revision of the *Berne Convention,* and the agreements that have since been established, building on the *Berne Convention,* is in order.

Shortly after the 1971 revision, on 27 September and 17 December 1974, respectively, the World Intellectual Property Organization (WIPO) General Assembly and the United Nations General Assembly approved an agreement, signed by both the Secretary-General of the UN and the Director of WIPO, making WIPO a specialized agency of the UN.[2] In this, WIPO followed organizations such as the United Nations Educational, Scientific and Cultural Organization (UNESCO), the Universal Postal Union, and the International Telecommunication Union.[3] There were three perceived advantages to becoming a specialized agency of the UN: WIPO might inherit the UN's worldwide recognition; WIPO might also inherit many UN members, particularly developing country members; and WIPO could adopt the UN salary and pension system, relieving WIPO member states of the administrative burden of fixing salaries.[4]

The proposal for WIPO to become a UN specialized agency was put forward by Brazil, supported by developing and socialist countries.[5] A number of countries were concerned that an increase in developing country membership might mean a weakening of intellectual property laws. The Canadian position was that special agency status for WIPO would mean significant overlap with UNESCO and, to a lesser degree, the International Labour Organization. Canadian officials suggested a link to the World Trade Organization (WTO) instead, but this idea was rejected.[6] Canadian officials remained generally unconvinced that UN special agency status was necessary,[7] but did not stand in the way when it became apparent which way the decision would go.[8] WIPO's special agency status laid the groundwork for later efforts towards a development agenda for the organization, in which Canada would be clearly aligned with the "developed" countries.

By 1984, reluctance to accede to the most recent revision of the *Berne Convention* had begun to fade. The Department of Consumer and Corporate Affairs and the Department of Communications jointly prepared a paper titled *From Gutenberg to Telidon: A White Paper on Copyright,* issued as part of a public consultation on copyright reform. The paper addressed possible accession to the 1971 revision of the *Berne Convention* only in passing, but took the following position:

> Since Canadian creators receive national treatment protection in [countries that are Canada's major trading partners and that belong to one or both of the major copyright conventions], they benefit from Canada's participation in these conventions. The government intends that Canada's international obligations be met in the spirit as well as in the letter of the law.[9]

At the same time, the government observed that a number of flexibilities were available to Canada as a result of the fact that Canada was not bound by the later texts.[10] The paper proposed abolition of the compulsory licensing provisions that had been in place under the Canadian *Copyright Act* since 1924 because "no such licenses have been issued; they may be in conflict with our obligations under the UCC; and the manufacturing clause of the American Copyright Act specifically exempts Canada."[11] It also proposed abolition of copyright registration, which had also been in place since 1924.[12]

Whereas the emphasis up to the time of the Economic Council of Canada's 1971 report had often been on using *reduced* copyright to stimulate sectors of the economy, emphasis was now placed on the importance of *stronger* copyright to stimulate economic growth.[13] Skepticism about Canadian participation in the *Berne Convention* gave way to the view that Canada should adhere to the same major copyright conventions as its trading partners, a more internationalist philosophy that has generally guided Canadian participation in international copyright agreements since.

The Conservatives came to power not long after *From Gutenberg to Telidon* was issued. In January 1985, the new government referred the question of copyright, along with the 1984 report, to the House of Commons Standing Committee on Communications and Culture. An all-party Sub-Committee on the Revision of Copyright composed of five members of Parliament was formed to examine the report and copyright reform generally.[14] After ten months of hearings in Ottawa, Toronto, and Montreal and examination of over three hundred written briefs, the Sub-Committee tabled a new report in 1985 called *A Charter of Rights for Creators*.[15] The report cited Finance Minister Michael Wilson in emphasizing the importance of copyright to economic activity:

> Canada's *Copyright Act,* unchanged since 1921, has been overtaken by new technologies. This has created ambiguities and uncertainties and has, in some cases, left Canadian copyright owners with less protection or compensation than would be available to them in other countries which have more modern copyright laws. Impacts are particularly significant for the vitality of our cultural and computer services industries. This is a real obstacle to economic growth, particularly in an economy which is increasingly service-oriented, with a growing role for the creation, transmission and processing of information, and in which automation may be a powerful source of productivity gains.[16]

The report saw copyright reform as an important means of encouraging what some hoped would be "a new era of Canadian cultural production."[17] In contrast to the 1977 Keyes-Brunet report, *Copyright in Canada: Proposals for a Revision of the Law* (see Chapter 11), which had referred to Canada as a "developing country," the Sub-Committee portrayed Canada as having emerged into a new era of vibrant and prodigious cultural production:

> The task before this Sub-Committee is not one of mere updating. There is a need to give a new emphasis to the contribution of creators to our national life. Sixty years ago what might have seemed, to a country barely emerging from colonial status, as wishful thinking is now a widely-acknowledged reality. Canadian writers, composers, musicians, film-makers, artists, performers and creative workers of all description exist in numbers and in a quality such that the *creation* of a Canadian culture need no longer be a focus for policy: the issues are now

to give it adequate recognition, to maintain its vitality and to expand its appreciation both in this country and abroad.[18]

The Sub-Committee viewed the creator as the primary and foremost interest in copyright law: "because of the special contribution creators make to Canadian society, they must be fairly rewarded."[19] Such a reward would demonstrate that the Sub-Committee recognized "how much value [Canada] attaches to the contribution of creators to the national life. The *Copyright Act* is seen as a very significant symbol of the country's scale of values and a signal to creators of their social merit or worth."[20]

The Sub-Committee recommended narrowing some of the exceptions included in the *Copyright Act* in the 1920s for religious organizations, education, and agricultural fairs.[21] It also recommended, as had *From Gutenberg to Telidon,* abolition of the act's compulsory licensing provisions.[22] While noting that some commentators felt that the Canadian system of voluntary copyright registration was "contrary to the spirit, if not the letter, of the Berne Convention," the Sub-Committee, unlike *From Gutenberg to Telidon,* recommended that the registration system be retained.[23] The resulting 1988 revision of the *Copyright Act* retained both the registration and compulsory licensing provisions.[24] The new act, which was designed to implement Phase I of a two-phase reform, extended Canadian copyright to computer programs, strengthened moral rights, and instituted copyright collectives.[25]

For its part, the United States adopted a trade-based approach to intellectual property, pushing for the inclusion of intellectual property provisions in other trade agreements, beginning (unsuccessfully) with the Tokyo round of *General Agreement on Tariffs and Trade* (GATT) talks in 1979.[26] In 1986, countries agreed to include intellectual property in the GATT talks.[27] In the meantime, under pressure to alleviate the US trade deficit and frustrated with the pace of change under GATT, American negotiators pushed hard for the inclusion of provisions aimed at increasing intellectual property protection and ensuring its enforcement in the 1987 *Canada-US Free Trade Agreement* and the 1992 *North American Free Trade Agreement* (NAFTA).[28]

Under the *Canada-US Free Trade Agreement,* Canada agreed to provide "a right of equitable and non-discriminatory remuneration for any retransmission to the public of the copyright holder's program where the original transmission of the program is carried in distant signals intended for free, over-the-air reception by the general public."[29] Revisions to the *Copyright Act* under the *Canada–United States Free Trade Agreement Implementation Act* in 1988 created a technology-neutral communication right and a compulsory licensing regime for cable retransmitters that required cable companies to pay royalties set by the Copyright Board for the retransmission of over-the-air radio or television signals.[30] This brought Canadian legislation into compliance with the provisions of the *Berne Convention,* added in 1948, that had made equitable remuneration for retransmission a requirement.[31] The revision of Canadian copyright law thus helped pave the way for Canada's eventual accession to the 1971 revision of the *Berne Convention.*[32] The change also brought an end to the period since 1954 when Canadian cable companies had been permitted to rebroadcast American television signals without authorization or payment. Canadian governments had long resisted this change, since it would lead to a net outflow of payments to American copyright holders, with little in return; in 1985 it was estimated that, were a retransmission right in place, 75 percent of Canadian cable retransmission fees would flow to American interests, while only 1 percent of American fees would be paid to Canadian copyright holders.[33] The 1988 compulsory licensing system crafted a compromise solution to allow regulation of the fees paid by Canadian cable companies.[34]

Canada implemented the 1971 Paris revision in 1993 in order to comply with NAFTA, which, at the Americans' insistence, had made compliance with this revision a requirement.[35] Since Mexico and the United States were both already signatories to the 1971 Paris revision when NAFTA was negotiated, these provisions were primarily directed at Canada.[36] Under the 1993 *North American Free Trade Agreement Implementation Act,* the compulsory licensing provisions of the *Copyright Act* were revised to apply only to Canadians; that is, they would no longer apply to American citizens or citizens of other countries outside the Berne Union.[37] Because NAFTA did not require Canada to sign the 1971 revision (it required only compliance), Canada delayed formal accession until 1998.

After 1971, various issues continued to be explored within WIPO. New technologies, including reprography, cable television, direct broadcast satellites, computer software, digital storage, and computer-created works were subjects of study, recommendations, non-binding principles, and model laws, as were issues surrounding the public domain, accessibility of works for the disabled, and expressions of folklore. The goal of such discussions and initiatives was to identify points of agreement between WIPO member states, leading eventually to revision of the *Berne Convention.*[38] Between 1989 and 1991, a "possible protocol" to the *Berne Convention* was contemplated, covering a wide range of topics, including new technologies such as copyright in databases, artificial intelligence and computer-produced works, and computer software.

By the early 1990s, the main norm-setting efforts in the area of intellectual property were taking place under GATT. These led ultimately to the establishment of the World Trade Organization and its 1994 *Agreement on Trade-Related Aspects of Intellectual Property Rights (TRIPS Agreement).*[39] The TRIPS Agreement requires compliance with Articles 1 through 21 of the 1971 revision of the *Berne Convention* and the appendix thereto, with the exception of Article 6*bis* regarding moral rights.[40] These provisions led to a dramatic expansion in the membership of the Berne Union.

Canada's role in the negotiation of the *TRIPS Agreement* shows that, by 1994, Canada's absorption into the club of most powerful copyright exporters was virtually complete. Canada played a significant role during the Uruguay round as a part of "the Quad," a coalition that also included the United States, the European Community, and Japan. The Quad acted as the core consensus-building group, setting the agenda of the negotiations, and persuading or exerting pressure on more peripheral countries not to stand in the way of its emerging consensus. Without the consensus of the Quad, nothing could move forward.[41] Canada's membership in the Quad, however, did not preclude its alignment with other groups on particular issues. For example, Canada was also a member of the Cairns group of agricultural exporters, most of whose members were developing countries.[42]

Following the conclusion of the *TRIPS Agreement* negotiations, amendments were made to Canada's *Copyright Act* under the 1994 *World Trade Organization Agreement Implementation Act*,[43] which came into force in 1996. Canada's voluntary registration provisions were retained, but the compulsory licensing provisions that had been in place since 1924 were repealed in their entirety.[44]

During GATT and TRIPS negotiations, discussions related to new technologies continued within WIPO. After the conclusion of the *TRIPS* negotiations in 1994, WIPO initiatives were spurred on by a greater understanding of the challenges of the Internet. Digital issues were incorporated and prioritized in discussions of a possible protocol to the *Berne Convention*.[45] A new making available right, provisions to protect rights management information and technological protection measures, Internet Service Provider liability, and protection of databases became the centrepieces of the new initiative, which quickly took the form not of the originally envisioned protocol to the *Berne Convention* but of separate draft treaties: the *WIPO Copyright Treaty* (WCT) and the *WIPO Performances and Phonograms Treaty* (WPPT), collectively known as the WIPO Internet Treaties. These were adopted at a diplomatic conference in Geneva in December 1996,[46] with Canada as a signatory to both. As with NAFTA, formal membership in the Berne Union is not required under the *WIPO Copyright Treaty* but compliance with its substantive provisions is.[47]

In 1997, the *Copyright Act* underwent a second reform, Phase II of the two-phase reform that had begun in 1985. This revision brought Canada into compliance with the 1961 *Rome Convention for the Protection of Performers, Producers of Phonograms and Broadcasting Organizations* by granting rights in public performances and broadcasts for performers and producers of sound recordings, and Canada acceded to the convention on 4 March 1998.[48] The 1997 revision also instituted a private copying levy; exceptions for non-profit educational institutions, libraries, archives, museums, broadcasters, and persons with perceptual disabilities; statutory damages; and wide injunctions.[49] Following the Phase II reform, Canada's formal accession to the *Paris Act* of the *Berne Convention* took place on 26 March 1998, entering into effect three months later, in June.[50]

In 2012, the Canadian government completed what came to be seen as a third phase in the copyright reform process, begun with public consultations in 2001.[51] Following several legislative attempts by both Liberal and Conservative governments, revisions to the *Copyright Act* received royal assent in June 2012. These included, on the one hand, several provisions that responded to the concerns of some Canadian interest groups, including the expansion of fair dealing provisions to include education, satire, and parody; additional exceptions for educational institutions and distance learning; provisions for format shifting and time shifting; an exception for alternate-format reproduction; a uniquely Canadian exception for non-commercial user-generated content (termed the "YouTube exception"); and a notice-and-notice scheme of Internet service provider liability that had been instituted by Canadian Internet service providers.[52] On the other hand, while the act contained a number of specifically Canadian provisions, the Conservative government also bent to American pressure to implement unpopular American-style digital locks provisions.[53] These amendments implemented the WIPO Internet Treaties by putting in place provisions prohibiting the circumvention of digital locks that control access to a work, and prohibiting the manufacture, import, distribution, sale, rental, or provision of circumvention devices.[54] Prior to the 1980s, the American government had exerted little direct pressure on Canadian copyright policy making. Following US adoption of a trade-based approach to intellectual property, however, American pressure became an important driver of changes in Canadian legislation.

The adoption of a more internationalist position on copyright, in the sense of joining the same treaties and treaty negotiations dealing with intellectual property as major trading partners, was tempered by a few holdout provisions. As of 2012, Canada had not yet adopted the longer life-plus-seventy-years copyright term that was adopted in the United States and many other countries; Canada had not adopted a three-strikes approach to copyright enforcement, which would see the Internet services of copyright infringers cut off; and the the kinds of multi-million dollar awards against filesharers seen in the United

States may have been prevented due to more limited statutory damages provisions for non-commercial infringement under the 2012 revisions.[55] Canadian copyright has remained very much tied to the frameworks of international copyright, however, and the struggle for Canadian copyright, which once took place within the framework of imperial copyright, now takes place within parameters set by international norm setting in various forums.

Tensions continued due to the conflicting interests of "developed" and developing countries in WIPO and in international intellectual property generally. These tensions sparked a number of international initiatives aimed at addressing user groups' interests and development concerns within WIPO. The status of WIPO as a UN agency was a key platform in 2004 for moves to establish a development agenda for WIPO, bringing the interests and needs of developing countries within the organization to the fore once again.[56] A group of developing countries known as the "Friends of Development" proposed a development agenda for WIPO that would acknowledge that intellectual property came with costs as well as benefits for developing countries – in terms of access to knowledge and public health – and that would see WIPO focus on the objective of international development rather than solely on the protection of intellectual property. In so doing, the Friends of Development sought to redefine WIPO's core mandate and bring the organization in line with its role as a specialized UN agency.[57] They proposed various changes to the organizational structure and oversight of WIPO, as well as a new treaty on access to knowledge that would have outlined minimum standards for limitations, exceptions, and flexibilities to intellectual property.[58] This would have represented a dramatic reversal from WIPO's traditional role of promoting treaties on the protection of intellectual property.

The WIPO Development Agenda was formally adopted in 2006, and was, as of 2012, undergoing implementation.[59] In the debates that preceded adoption, Canadian delegates indicated support for the discussions in general and raised useful technical concerns, but did not support more radical proposals for a treaty on access to knowledge. Canada was also part of the coalition of Organisation for Economic Co-operation and Development (OECD) countries (Group B) that opposed any major reforms to WIPO's mandate or structure as well as the negotiation of a treaty on access to knowledge.[60] The Development Agenda that was ultimately adopted was much more reserved than the one proposed by the Friends of Development, and included neither major structural change nor a treaty on access to knowledge.[61] As of 2012, more limited instruments on copyright limitations and exceptions were under discussion.[62]

WIPO and the multilateral copyright system still faced significant challenges. Prior to 1967, the revision of international copyright agreements every twenty years was the norm. After 1971, however, the fast pace of norm setting under trade agreements and in various forums resulted in new demands from copyright exporters for more expansive copyright, and a new impatience with the multi-lateral copyright system.

Some objected to the circumvention of WIPO and the multilateral copyright system in new norm setting. In response to negotiations between 2008 and 2011 towards a new plurilateral *Anti-Counterfeiting Trade Agreement* (ACTA), the European Parliament passed a resolution deploring "the calculated choice of the parties not to negotiate through well-established international bodies, such as WIPO and the World Trade Organization (WTO), which have established frameworks for public information and consultation."[63] Participants at a New Zealand forum on ACTA issued a declaration calling WIPO the preferable forum for intellectual property negotiations:

> We note that the World Intellectual Property Organisation has public, inclusive and transparent processes for negotiating multilateral agreements on (and a committee dedicated to the enforcement of) copyright, trademark and patent rights, and thus we affirm that WIPO is a preferable forum for the negotiation of substantive provisions affecting these matters.[64]

WIPO recognized the threat posed by external negotiations, as well as difficulties for multilateralism in general. In October 2009, WIPO Director-General Francis Gurry commented: "Naturally we prefer open, transparent international processes to arrive at conclusions that are of concern to the whole world." Intellectual property, he added, "is of concern to the whole world."[65] In June 2010, in more direct public comments, he called ACTA a "bad development" for WIPO – an example of the difficulty faced by WIPO and other UN agencies in addressing issues and concluding agreements.[66] Such concerns were somewhat eased in 2012 when WIPO concluded a new *Beijing Treaty on Audiovisual Performances*.[67] However, various actors, including the World Trade Organization, continued to raise concerns about policy fragmentation in light of regional trade agreements.[68]

The new environment of multiple linked and layered agreements presented, on the one hand, a threat to the multilateral copyright system; on the other hand, this dense network of linkages continued to build an international copyright system that held the *Berne Convention* at its core.

CHAPTER 13

Conclusion

INTERNATIONAL COPYRIGHT UNDER THE *Berne Convention* moved, between 1886 and 1971, from crisis to crisis. The key norms and central characteristics that have structured international copyright relations under the convention were designed to protect and further the interests of copyright holders and net copyright-exporting countries in foreign and colonial markets. The resulting structural tensions within the Berne Union have never been resolved, although various settlements have been achieved. The core norms of the system established in 1886 have been largely shored up and extended.

The fact that the system has never broken down under the strain of these tensions can be attributed to various factors. One such factor has been the willingness of dominant countries to make concessions – especially at the 1896 and 1908 conferences, when Britain, on account of Canada and the other colonies, insisted on a slow pace for extending copyright norms; in 1914, when countries agreed to a protocol that would resolve particularly Canadian problems; and in 1971, when adjustments were made to the system for the benefit of the newly independent countries. Often, such concessions have taken the form of a simple slowing in the pace of advancement rather than changes or major exceptions to key norms. Special provisions that have been made, such as the 1914 protocol that permitted Canada's 1924 compulsory licensing provisions or the 1971 Appendix to the *Berne Convention,* are often so narrow that they have never actually been used. In part, the system has been maintained because of the desire of net copyright-importing countries to be part of a highly prestigious union that has long been associated with progress and civilization. The strongest thread that has held the Berne Union together, however, is legal and economic power: the imperial power that denied Canada the ability to denounce the treaty, and the provisions now embedded in the *Universal Copyright Convention* and the *TRIPS Agreement* that prevent departure from and require compliance with the *Berne Convention.*[1]

David Vaver predicts that in the new millennium "there will be no *Canadian copyright law*."[2] He argues that due to the pressure of international agreements, Canadian copyright law will come to look more and more like the laws of other countries. Since 1842, Canadian law has yielded to imperial and international pressures to conform to hegemonic norms that left little room for variation. The struggle for Canadian copyright independence has never been won. The power of imperialism has been replaced by the power of internationalism. At the same time, there has been room for distinct, if minor, Canadian variations. In particular, the often-repeated idea that Canada's 1921 *Copyright Act* is effectively a copy of the 1911 British *Copyright Act* overlooks important differences that brought Canada into conflict with the *Berne Convention*. In 1921, Canadian legislators went to great lengths to include both compulsory licensing for works not printed and published in Canada and a voluntary registration system. The compulsory licensing provisions, which, in order to conform to the *Berne Convention*, had to be severely narrowed so as to apply effectively only to Americans, were important remnants of Canadian governments' earlier efforts to maintain separate Canadian priorities in copyright policy. At the same time, the distinctions between Canadian copyright and the British model were minimal in practice; the compulsory licensing provisions for which Canadians fought so hard were rarely if ever used.

Canadian governments have at times acted to preserve greater scope for policy flexibility, sometimes by declining to adhere to treaties, and sometimes by supporting more flexible provisions during treaty negotiations. There have also been times when greater scope for variation, and even independence, from imperial and international copyright norms has existed but not been grasped. On various occasions, the imperial government opened a window to Canadian copyright sovereignty but, due to the policy preferences of certain policy makers or to the influence of foreign lobbyists, such opportunities were not taken. The potential for Canadian leadership in multilateral copyright forums, in building a coalition of intermediary countries or in building a multi-level copyright treaty, were not necessarily fully explored as ways of creating greater scope for Canadian policy choices.[3] In any case, flexibilities that were available were not always taken advantage of; for example, greater flexibility was available under the WIPO Internet Treaties than was taken advantage of under the 2012 copyright revisions.

Although Canadian legislators chose to model their copyright laws on American legislation in 1832, 1841, 1868, and 1875, and on British legislation in 1921,[4] the French tradition of *droit d'auteur* has influenced Canadian copyright law through the *Berne Convention*, which discouraged formalities such as registration and domestic printing and publishing requirements, as well as compulsory licensing, and encouraged the adoption of longer copyright terms.[5] Although the term of life plus fifty years "rather shocked"[6] copyright policy makers of the British Empire in 1910, this has been the term adopted throughout the Berne Union and remained in effect in Canada as of 2012.[7]

In the 1970s, the Interdepartmental Committee on Copyright, following the pattern set by the Ilsley Commission and the Economic Council of Canada, adopted a strongly economic view of copyright. Their view ran counter to those of Quebec interest groups, who by this time had a healthy export trade in cultural works. Although the interdepartmental committee was influential in copyright policy making for a time, affecting the Canadian delegation's statements at the 1971 conference to revise the *Berne Convention,* its purely economic view of copyright in Canada was always contested, especially by Quebec groups. Quebec's achievements in the export of cultural works, as contrasted with the status of the rest of Canada as a net importer, ensure that these tensions remain.

Canada has wavered between various paths and traditions of copyright, following the British model in some senses, being pulled towards the French model through the influence of the *Berne Convention,* and attempting to combine, with this, elements of the American model. The 1957 Ilsley Commission report rightly saw this as essentially a struggle between opposing interests rather than between opposing traditions of copyright, noting that those groups within Canada that advocated "strong and long" copyright protection generally saw copyright as a natural right, whereas those who favoured weaker and shorter terms of protection saw it as a state-granted right.[8] Although it is often the case that Quebec's stronger cultural industries and exports mean that many Quebec interest groups do favour a "strong and long" version of copyright, those Quebec groups interested in greater access to works, such as nineteenth-century Quebec (re)publishers, historically took a more utilitarian view of copyright. Overall, it is possible to characterize, as the Economic Council of Canada did in its 1971 report, Canadian (and American) copyright as being of British lineage, and therefore not historically rooted in a "fundamental rights" view of copyright.[9]

Canadian participation in the Berne Union has seldom been guided by ideas, philosophies, or calculations about copyright itself or its effects on domestic interest groups. The Canadian government's 1886 decision to join the *Berne Convention* was made quietly, based on a philosophy of imperial unity and isolated from input from Canadian interest groups that might prove embarrassing by advocating the "legalized piracy" of British books. Its request to denounce the *Berne Convention,* made to the British government in 1889 and maintained for many years, was rooted as much in a desire to achieve legislative autonomy as it was in Canadian copyright interests. At the 1910 Imperial Copyright Conference, Canada traded its policies favouring denunciation of the *Berne Convention* for relative legislative sovereignty, and in the 1920s Canadian legislators navigated between the policies demanded by Canadian copyright interests, the requirements of the Berne Union, and the desire to avoid being an "outsider in the general community of nations."[10]

It was not until the 1950s and '60s that adhesion to the *Berne Convention* was systematically examined from the perspective of national economic policy or that more extensive home-grown calculations about the national interest in copyright began to be made. The Ilsley Commission and the Economic Council of Canada examined Canadian copyright interests in terms of balance of trade, noting that Canada, as a net copyright importer, did not have a great deal to gain from increasing international copyright protection. These views contrasted with other portrayals that conflated Canada's national interest with those of its creators, particularly those in Quebec, or of the reading public.

Since the 1980s, however, skepticism about Canadian participation in the *Berne Convention* has given way to a more internationalist view that Canada should adhere to the same major copyright conventions as its trading partners. This, along with the incorporation of the main provisions of the *Berne Convention* into the *Universal Copyright Convention* and the *TRIPS Agreement*, has made it practically impossible for Canada to leave the Berne Union, just as it has been since Prime Minister Macdonald sent his fateful telegram in 1886.

There is an accepted view of how Canada is or should be seen within the international system – a common knowledge or a common-sense understanding of the type of country Canada is. This understanding has arisen from the history of Canadian foreign affairs and the ideas and practices that have come with it. Canada's dependency on Britain in the conduct of its foreign relations in the nineteenth and early twentieth centuries has meant the inheritance of the norms and networks of British foreign relations. Although Canadian delegates have claimed to be "half-way between industrialized and developing countries" – a position supposedly enabling Canadian diplomats "to understand the problems of both and to foresee perhaps the possibility of reconciling the interests at stake" – Canadian delegations have rarely been able or mandated to step outside the copyright norms preferred by the major copyright exporters.[11] In 1928, Canadian delegates were sent to the revision conference in Rome with instructions to support proposals made by Britain, Italy, and France. In 1967, the Canadian delegation was relatively inactive as it waited for a policy vision to be formulated, and in 1971 the strong mandate forged by Canadian policy was toned down in order to manage Canada's international image and because it failed to achieve support from other countries. Efforts to create a coalition of intermediate countries were abandoned and failed. With a few exceptions, the aim of Canadian international copyright policy has been to ensure that Canada played a "harmonious instrument" in the Berne orchestra of international copyright.[12]

Canada was one of the early representatives of net copyright importers within the Berne Union, and as such had a good deal to contribute. The relative weakness of Canada and other countries in a similar position, and the relatively weak connections among them, has made a lasting impression on the international copyright system. Canada's internationalist stance of the 1920s and '30s was later evaluated as being "ill-advised" – Canada had accepted too readily the solutions offered by the major copyright exporters. It remains to be seen how the internationalism adopted by governments since the mid-1980s will be evaluated.[13]

In recent years, a coalition of developing countries called the Friends of Development, as well as various non-governmental organizations, has called for change to the international intellectual property regime. In establishing a Development Agenda for the World Intellectual Property Organization, they have called for recognition that, in terms of development, the international intellectual property regime produces costs as well as benefits; for development objectives to be prioritized within this regime; and for systems and standards to ensure not only protection of intellectual property but also access to knowledge, especially in developing countries.[14]

Some may hope that middle powers such as Canada can be engaged to effect radical and progressive change, but Canada has rarely shown leadership in international copyright. In fact, Canada as a British dominion may have been more successful in showing leadership and effecting change in the imperial and early international copyright systems. Perhaps as a middle power it is pulled too powerfully in opposite directions to lead in either; perhaps the grooves of its historical international relationships run too deep. Until the major powers themselves adopt projects for change – as the British Empire once did – it may be left to the developing countries on the one hand and the most powerful countries on the other to lead.

Although emerging powers such as Brazil, India, and Argentina have developed stronger and more influential voices within the international copyright system since the 1960s, and although Canada has diverged at times from the most powerful countries, the interests of net copyright exporters and major transnational copyright holders continue to dominate. For example, in the negotiations towards a Development Agenda for WIPO that would better integrate the interests of developing countries into its operations and mandate, the industrialized countries were able to sweep many of the developing countries' most central proposals off the table.[15] Nevertheless, many observers herald the Development Agenda as a great achievement of compromise and goodwill.[16] From the perspective of less powerful countries today, the transparency of WIPO – both the accessibility of its meetings to NGOs and the openness of the processes and decision making of its formal bodies – along with its association with the United Nations and the UN development objectives make it a preferable alternative to bilateralism, narrower arrangements, or other, less open forums.

Critical theorists emphasize the possibility of change, the contingency of current configurations of power, and the alternative structures inherent within current structures. They see difference and diversity within the international system as potential sources of change.[17] This history of copyright highlights the contingency of the historical development of the Berne Union, and in particular the contingency of the events that led to Canada's entry into the union.[18] It highlights diversity within the Berne Union by portraying the experience of one less powerful country within the system. Canadian governments, to a certain extent, carved out room for alternative structures in the Berne Union by insisting on compulsory licensing, on retaining a registration system, and on retaining some capacity to effect copyright reciprocity in cases where countries outside the union did not adhere to the union's standards. However, the flexibility that Canadians have been able to achieve under the Berne Union has been minimal.

While diversity within the Berne Union may be a potential source of change, success depends on the ability of those who envision change to enroll other actors in their initiatives. Except for the period between 1889 and the early twentieth century, when the Canadian Parliament passed the 1889 *Copyright Act* and lobbied for copyright sovereignty and the 1914 additional protocol to the *Berne Convention*, and the period surrounding the 1971 revision, Canadian representatives have been neither successful at initiating change nor successfully enrolled by those calling for changes to the international copyright system. Whereas countries like Brazil, India, and Argentina have emerged as leaders in the context of the Development Agenda and other areas, Canadian support for and involvement in counter-hegemonic projects is in tension with a vision of Canada as a country associated with the major powers, and efforts at change are stymied by the structures of the international copyright system that prevent countries from leaving the Berne Union and formulating alternative norms.

This does not mean that less powerful actors cannot initiate change. The governments of India, South Africa, Brazil, and Argentina have been successfully enrolled by domestic and transnational interests to advocate change within the international copyright system; alternative copyright norms, such as the *Universal Copyright Convention* and its predecessors, have been constructed; room for exceptions, such as the 1971 Appendix to the *Berne Convention,* which was labelled as "unworkable," has been achieved; and copyright provisions that could provide greater access to knowledge are even now being considered.[19] Such initiatives and visions are constrained by the great weight of associations, norms, expertise, authority, institutions, and resources of a copyright union that has been in place since 1886, as well as the economic power of large interest groups in copyright-powered economies. The initiatives and visions of less powerful actors who seek change are sustained by the hope that the international copyright regime can be transformed, that it might overcome the exclusions of its past, and that it might embed this overcoming at the core of its ongoing practices. It is only through an awareness of the material and ideological structures of international copyright – an awareness formed by examining the historical experiences of weaker countries and groups as well as the views of the stronger ones – that such a transformative commitment can be made.

Notes

Chapter 1: Introduction

1 For example, see Sam Ricketson and Jane Ginsburg, *International Copyright and Neighbouring Rights: The Berne Convention and Beyond,* 2nd ed. (London: Oxford University Press, 2006), 914, and Christopher May, "The World Intellectual Property Organization," *New Political Economy* 11, 3 (2006): 435-45. This book adopts the term "developing countries" with some hesitation. Rather than adopting the term uncritically, I have attempted to disrupt to some extent this category, taking the position that all countries are, to some degree, developing in one way or another, although certainly not all on the same path, in the same mode, or towards the same end. For that reason, I do use the term "developing country," but I enclose the term "developed," in reference to the so-called developed countries, in quotation marks.

2 Although other multilateral conventions on copyright existed before the *Berne Convention,* those were limited territorially; the *Berne Convention* was, on the other hand, open to all states. See Sam Ricketson, "The Birth of the Berne Union," *Columbia-VLA Journal of Law and the Arts* 11, 9 (1986): 9.

3 Minor amendments were also made in 1979. *General Report of the Governing Bodies of WIPO and the Unions Administered by WIPO, Tenth Series of Meetings, Geneva, September 24 to October 2, 1979. AB/X/32* (Geneva: World Intellectual Property Organization, 1979); *Memorandum by the Director General. AB/X/5* (Geneva: World Intellectual Property Organization, 1979). See also Ricketson and Ginsburg, *International Copyright and Neighbouring Rights,* 1048-49.

4 See Sunny Handa, "A Review of Canada's International Copyright Obligations," *McGill Law Journal* 42, 4 (1997): 961-90; May, "The World Intellectual Property Organization," 435-45; Christopher May, *The World Intellectual Property Organization: Resurgence and the Development Agenda* (London: Routledge, 2004); Peter Drahos and John Braithwaite, *Information Feudalism: Who Owns the Knowledge Economy?* (London: Earthscan Publications, 2002); Susan K. Sell, *Power and Ideas: North-South Politics of Intellectual Property and Antitrust* (New York: SUNY Press, 1998); Susan Sell, *Private Power, Public Law: The Globalization of Intellectual Property Rights* (Cambridge: Cambridge University Press, 2003), and many others.

5 For a general critique, see Alan Story, "Burn Berne: Why the Leading International Copyright Convention Must Be Repealed," *Houston Law Review* 40, 3 (2003): 763-803, and Alan Story, Colin Darch, and Debora Halbert, *The Copy/South Dossier: Issues in the Economics, Politics, and Ideology of Copyright in the Global South* (Canterbury, UK: Copy/South Research Group, 2006).

6 Haggart notes the considerable American pressure on Canada to implement the WIPO Internet Treaties and to implement American-style provisions on technological protection measures despite, in the latter case, widespread Canadian opposition. In the most recent (2012) round of copyright revisions, such pressure appears to have led to American-style provisions that allow digital locks to trump users' rights. Haggart also observes significant room for Canadian variation in copyright policy making, even in the face of foreign pressure. Blayne Haggart, "North American Digital Copyright, Regional Governance, and the Potential for Variation," in *From "Radical Extremism" to "Balanced Copyright": Canadian Copyright and the Digital Agenda* (Toronto: Irwin Law, 2010), 55-56.

7 The word "denounce" is similar to "abrogate" or "exit." "Denounce" is the term used in the case of the *Berne Convention. Berne Convention for the Protection of Literary and Artistic Works, Paris Act of July 24, 1971, as Amended on September 28, 1979* (Geneva: World Intellectual Property Organization, 1979).

8 The member states of the *Berne Convention* constitute a union known as the Berne Union. *Convention Concerning the Creation of an International Union for the Protection of Literary and Artistic Works (Berne Convention)*, 9 September 1886, Article 1 (Berne: Office of the International Union for the Protection of Literary and Artistic Works, 1886).

9 National Archives of Britain, Foreign Office fonds 881/5989. As quoted in Catherine Seville, *The Internationalisation of Copyright Law: Books, Buccaneers and the Black Flag in the Nineteenth Century* (Cambridge: Cambridge University Press, 2006), 118.

10 Canadian delegate to the Conference for Revision of the *Universal Copyright Convention,* Paris, July 1971. *Records of the Conference for Revision of the Universal Copyright Convention, Unesco House, Paris, 5 to 24 July 1971* (Paris: UNESCO, 1973), 62 and 105.

11 The *Berne Convention* uses the word "author" broadly to mean the author of a broad range of literary and artistic works, including authors of photographs, films, drawings, paintings, and works of architecture. Since the authors of such works are, in common language, not normally referred to as authors but as photographers, filmmakers, artists, architects, and so on, I have adopted the use of the word "creator."

12 Canada, Royal Commission on Patents, Copyright, Trade Marks and Industrial Designs, *Report on Copyright* (Ottawa: Supply and Services Canada, 1957), 18.

Chapter 2: Canada and the International Copyright System

1 Myra Tawfik, "Copyright as Droit d'Auteur," *Intellectual Property Journal* 17 (2003): 64.

2 Ibid., 79.

3 Ibid., 65.

4 On the influence of the French civil law tradition: Quebec courts have been open to the influence of jurisprudence and doctrine from France. France has had substantial influence on international copyright under the *Berne Convention* and has thereby influenced the Canadian tradition. Pressure from Quebecers led to the 1988 provision of more clearly defined moral rights, a right of public display, and, in 1986, the Public Lending Right Commission. W.L. Hayhurst, "Intellectual Property Laws in Canada: The British Tradition, the American Influence, and the French Factor," *Intellectual Property Journal* 10 (1996): 302, 309, and 314; Tawfik, "Copyright as Droit d'Auteur," 59-61, 81.

5 See Hayhurst, ibid., 304, on this point.

6 Ibid., 281-82. British Canada was divided into Upper Canada and Lower Canada from 1791 until these two provinces were rejoined in 1841 to become the Province of Canada.

7 Nova Scotia joined New Brunswick, Ontario, and Quebec in 1867 as one of the four founding provinces of Canada, but in 1832 Nova Scotia was a separate colony of Great Britain.

8 Ibid., 282-83.

9 Ibid., 287.
10 Ibid., 327.
11 Eli MacLaren, "Copyright and the Prevention of Literary Publishing in English Canada, 1867-1920" (PhD dissertation, University of Toronto, 2007), 5 and 9-10. See also Eli MacLaren, *Dominion and Agency: Copyright and the Structuring of the Canadian Book Trade, 1867-1918* (Toronto: University of Toronto Press, 2011), 5.
12 Arthur E. Andrew, *The Rise and Fall of a Middle Power: Canadian Diplomacy from King to Mulroney* (Toronto: J. Lorimer, 1993), 181.
13 Adam Chapnick, *The Middle Power Project: Canada and the Founding of the United Nations* (Vancouver: UBC Press, 2005).
14 Andrew Cohen, *While Canada Slept: How We Lost Our Place in the World* (Toronto: McClelland and Stewart, 2003).
15 Roy Rempel, *Dreamland: How Canada's Pretend Foreign Policy Has Undermined Sovereignty* (Montreal and Kingston: McGill-Queen's University Press, 2006).
16 Allan Gotlieb, *Romanticism and Realism in Canada's Foreign Policy: C.D. Howe Institute Benefactors Lecture* (Toronto: C.D. Howe Institute, 2004), 38, http://www.cdhowe.org/.
17 Ibid., 32.
18 Mark Neufeld, "Hegemony and Foreign Policy Analysis: The Case of Canada as Middle Power," in *Readings in Canadian Foreign Policy: Classic Debates and New Ideas,* edited by Duane Bratt and Christopher J. Kukucha (New York: Oxford University Press, 2006), 94-107.
19 Teodor Shanin, "The Idea of Progress," in *The Post-Development Reader,* edited by Majid Rahnema and Victoria Bawtree (London: Zed Books, 1997), 66.
20 Louis Renault, whom Koskenniemi discusses as one of the leading lawyers in international law, was also a leader in the development of the *Berne Convention.* See Martti Koskenniemi, *The Gentle Civilizer of Nations: The Rise and Fall of International Law, 1870-1960* (Cambridge: Cambridge University Press, 2002), and Sam Ricketson and Jane Ginsburg, *International Copyright and Neighbouring Rights: The Berne Convention and Beyond,* 2nd ed. (London: Oxford University Press, 2006), 76, 87, 94.
21 National Archives of Britain, Foreign Office fonds 881/5989. As quoted in Catherine Seville, *The Internationalisation of Copyright Law: Books, Buccaneers and the Black Flag in the Nineteenth Century* (Cambridge: Cambridge University Press, 2006), 118.
22 Ibid., 109.
23 Only "governments of civilized countries" were invited to take part in the initial negotiations. *Actes de la première conférénce internationale pour la protection des œuvres littéraires et artistiques du 8 septembre 1884 à Berne* (Berne: Conseil Fédérale Suisse, 1884), 9.
24 Arturo Escobar, *Encountering Development: The Making and Unmaking of the Third World* (Princeton, NJ: Princeton University Press, 1995).
25 Martha Finnemore and Michael N. Barnett, "The Politics, Power and Pathologies of International Organizations," *International Organizations* 53, 4 (1999): 699-732, as reprinted in Phil Williams, Donald M. Goldstein, and Jay M. Shafritz, *Classic Readings and Contemporary Debates in International Relations,* 3rd ed. (Belmont, CA: Thomson Wadsworth, 2006), 229.
26 Shanin, "The Idea of Progress," 68.
27 Ibid., 67-68.
28 Ibid., 65.
29 *Final Act Embodying the Results of the Uruguay Round of Multilateral Trade Negotiations, Annex IC: Agreement on Trade-Related Aspects of Intellectual Property Rights* (Geneva: World Trade Organization, 1994), Article 9, http://www.wto.org/english/.
30 Ibid., 70.

31 Max Horkheimer, "Traditional and Critical Theory," in *Classical Sociological Theory*, edited by Craig J. Calhoun (Oxford: Blackwell, 2002), 352.
32 Koskenniemi, *The Gentle Civilizer of Nations*, 110.
33 See Ricketson and Ginsburg, *International Copyright and Neighbouring Rights*, 914, and Christopher May, "The World Intellectual Property Organization," *New Political Economy* 11, 3 (2006): 435-45.
34 Alan Story, "Burn Berne: Why the Leading International Copyright Convention Must Be Repealed," *Houston Law Review* 40, 3 (2003): 763-803; see also Peter Drahos, *A Philosophy of Intellectual Property* (London: Ashgate, 1996), ch. 5.
35 Koskenniemi, *The Gentle Civilizer of Nations*, 110.

Chapter 3: Imperialism

1 Catherine Seville, *The Internationalisation of Copyright Law: Books, Buccaneers and the Black Flag in the Nineteenth Century* (Cambridge: Cambridge University Press, 2006), 78.
2 Canada, *Census of Canada, 1870-71* (Ottawa: Taylor, 1873-76), vol. 3, table 55, "Summary of Industrial Establishments, by Provinces"; Seville, ibid., 78-79.
3 *An Act to Amend the Law of Copyright* (imperial *Copyright Act*), 1842, 5 and 6 Vict., c. 45.
4 Ibid.; Seville, *Internationalisation of Copyright Law*, 114; John H. Moss, "Copyright in Canada," *University Magazine*, April 1914, 4.
5 *Copyright Act (An Act Respecting Copyrights), 1868*, 31 Vict., c. 54.
6 J.L. Granatstein, *How Britain's Weakness Forced Canada into the Arms of the United States* (Toronto: University of Toronto Press, 1989), 5-6.
7 C.T. Metcalfe to Lord Stanley, enclosing address to the Queen, 18 November 1843, in Canada, House of Commons, *Return to an Address of the Honourable The House of Commons*, 1 April 1844 (Ottawa: n.p., 1844).
8 Norman Hillmer and J.L. Granatstein, *Empire to Umpire: Canada and the World to the 1990s* (Toronto: Copp Clark Longman, 1994), Introduction.
9 Norman Hillmer and J.L. Granatstein, *For Better or for Worse: Canada and the United States into the Twenty-First Century* (Toronto: Nelson, 2005), 15 and 23.
10 Ibid., 35-38.
11 George M. Grant, *Canada First, or Our New Nationality: An Address* (Toronto: Adam, Stevenson, 1871), 30.
12 Hillmer and Granatstein, *For Better or for Worse*, 41-43; Craig Brown, "The Nationalism of the National Policy," in *Nationalism in Canada*, edited by Peter Russell (Toronto: McGraw-Hill, 1966), 155-63.
13 Imperial *Copyright Act*, Article 17.
14 Eli MacLaren, *Dominion and Agency: Copyright and the Structuring of the Canadian Book Trade, 1867-1918* (Toronto: University of Toronto Press, 2011), 8-9.
15 Ibid., 4.
16 Ibid., 5.
17 Ibid.; George L. Parker, "The Evolution of Publishing in Canada," in *History of the Book in Canada*, vol. 2, edited by Patricia Fleming, Yvan Lamonde, and Fiona A. Black (Toronto: University of Toronto Press, 2004), 17-26.
18 Canada, *Census of Canada, 1870-71*, vol. 2, table 13, "Occupations of the People," 286, 322, and 334.
19 Parker, "Evolution of Publishing in Canada," 17-26; "Strickland, Susanna (Moodie)," in *Dictionary of Canadian Biography*, vol. 11, edited by Francess G. Halpenny (Toronto: University of Toronto Press, 1982); "Strickland, Catharine Parr (Traill)," in *Dictionary of*

Canadian Biography, vol. 12, edited by Francess G. Halpenny (Toronto: University of Toronto Press, 1990).

20 MacLaren, *Dominion and Agency*, 3.

21 United Kingdom, Royal Commission on Laws and Regulations Relating to Home, Colonial and Foreign Copyrights, *The Royal Commissions and the Report of the Commissioners Together with Minutes of Evidence. C.-2036* (London: George Edward Eyre and William Spottiswoode, 1878), xxxiii.

22 Imperial *Copyright Act.*

23 Moss, "Copyright in Canada," 4; Seville, *Internationalisation of Copyright Law*, 81.

24 Seville, ibid., 78.

25 I am referring here to Joseph-Charles Taché, Canada's Deputy Minister of Agriculture.

26 C.T. Metcalfe to Lord Stanley, enclosing address to the Queen.

27 Earl Grey to governors of the North American colonies, 4 November 1846, in United Kingdom, *Report of the Departmental Representatives (of the Colonial Office, Foreign Office, Board of Trade, and Parliamentary Counsel's Office) Appointed to Consider the Canadian Copyright Act of 1889* (London: n.p., 1892), in Library and Archives Canada [LAC], Prime Minister Abbott fonds (MG26 C), vol. 5, file: "Copyright."

28 Seville, *Internationalisation of Copyright Law*, 87; Moss, "Copyright in Canada," 4.

29 *Constitution Act (An Act for the Union of Canada, Nova Scotia, and New Brunswick, and the Government thereof; and for Purposes connected therewith) 1867*, 30 and 31 Vict., c. 3 (originally known as the *British North America Act*), section 6, items 23 and 22.

30 Peter W. Hogg, *Constitutional Law of Canada*, 5th supplement ed. (Scarborough, ON: Thomson/Carswell, 2007), 49.

31 The *Colonial Laws Validity Act* of 1865 (28 and 29 Vict., c. 63) remained in force after Confederation and could be used by Britain to invalidate a Canadian statute that conflicted with an imperial statute extending to Canada. Hogg, *Constitutional Law of Canada*, 49-52.

32 David M.L. Farr, *The Colonial Office and Canada, 1867-1887* (Toronto: University of Toronto Press, 1955), 261.

33 *Jefferys v. Boosey* (1854) 4 HLC 815.

34 *Routledge v. Low* (1868) LR 3HL 100.

35 *Jefferys v. Boosey.*

36 Ibid.

37 *Life Publishing Co. v. Rose Publishing Co.*, [1906] 8 O.W.R. 28, 12 O.L.R. 386.

38 *Copyright Act* (1868); *An Act to Impose a Duty on Foreign Reprints of British Copyright Works, 1868*, 31 Vict., c. 56; Seville, *Internationalisation of Copyright Law*, 90.

39 Resolution of the Senate, 15 May 1868, in Canada, House of Commons, *Colonial Copyright: Return to an Address of the Honourable the House of Commons*, 29 July 1872 (Ottawa: n.p., 1872).

40 John Rose to the Colonial Office, 1 July 1868, in Canada, House of Commons, ibid. See also Seville, *Internationalisation of Copyright Law*, 90.

41 Resolution of the Senate, 15 May 1868.

42 Board of Trade to Colonial Office, 27 July 1869, in Canada, House of Commons, *Colonial Copyright.*

43 Ibid.; see also Seville, *Internationalisation of Copyright Law*, 90-94.

44 Board of Trade to Colonial Office, 27 July 1869.

45 Ibid.; see also Seville, *Internationalisation of Copyright Law*, 91-94.

46 W.L. Hayhurst, "Intellectual Property Laws in Canada: The British Tradition, the American Influence, and the French Factor," *Intellectual Property Journal* 10 (1996): 282-83.

47 The Department of Agriculture held responsibility for copyright policy.

48 *Copyright Act* (1868), Article 6.

49 Imperial *Copyright Act*, Articles 11 and 24; *Copyright Act* (1868), Article 6.

50 *Copyright Act* (1868), Articles 6 and 7.

51 Imperial *Copyright Act*, Articles 6-10.

52 *Copyright Act* (1868) and *An Act to Amend Several Acts Respecting Copy Rights*, 4 Stat. 436 (1831), section 5.

53 *Copyright Act* (1868); Imperial *Copyright Act*, Article 3; and *An Act to Amend Several Acts Respecting Copy Rights*, sections 1 and 2. See also Hayhurst, "Intellectual Property Laws in Canada," 281-83.

54 *Copyright Act* (1868), Articles 3 and 9.

55 Imperial *Copyright Act*, Article 3; also see *Routledge v. Low; An Act to Revise, Consolidate, and Amend the Statutes Relating to Patents and Copyrights.*

56 The 1868 *Copyright Act* required that works be "printed and published" in Canada to be eligible for Canadian copyright protection. The United States did not include such a provision in the 1831 act, but introduced their "manufacturing clause," which required books to be "printed from type set within the limits of the United States, or from plates made therefrom, or from negatives, or drawings on stone made within the limits of the United States, or from transfers made therefrom," in 1891: *An Act to Amend Title Sixty, Chapter Three, of the Revised Statutes of the United States, Relating to Copyrights*, 26 Stat. 1106 (1891), section 4956.

57 Imperial *Copyright Act*, Article 3.

58 *An Act for the Organization of the Department of Agriculture, 1868*, 31 Vict. c. 53; J.E. Hodgetts, *Pioneer Public Service: An Administrative History of the United Canadas, 1841-1867* (Toronto: University of Toronto Press, 1956), 36.

59 *An Act Respecting the Department of Justice, 1868*, 31 Vict. c. 39; Hodgetts, ibid., 36.

60 *An Act Providing for the Organization of the Department of the Secretary of State of Canada and for the Management of Indian and Ordnance Lands, 1868*, 31 Vict., c. 42; Hodgetts, ibid.

61 Hodgetts, ibid., 228.

62 Ibid., 42.

63 Ibid.

64 Canada, *Statistical Abstract and Record for the Year 1886* (Ottawa: Maclean, Roger, 1887), 269-72.

65 At the time, there were about 880 civil servants at government headquarters. Hodgetts, *Pioneer Public Service*, 36.

66 Canada, Department of Agriculture, *Annual Report of the Minister of Agriculture, 1856* (Toronto: Rollo Campbell, 1857), 7; Canada, Department of Agriculture, *Annual Report of the Minister of Agriculture, 1866* (Ottawa: Hunter, Rose, 1867), x.

67 Canada, *Statistical Abstract and Record for the Year 1886*, 270.

68 Ibid., 270-71.

69 Seville, *Internationalisation of Copyright Law*, 103.

70 Earl of Dufferin to Earl of Kimberly, 9 August 1872, in United Kingdom, *Copyright (Colonies): Copies of or Extracts from Correspondence between the Colonial Office and Any of the Colonial Governments on the Subject of Copyright, and of Colonial Acts Relating to Copyright Which Have Been Allowed by Her Majesty* (London: n.p., 1875).

71 See Seville, *Internationalisation of Copyright Law*, 106, and United Kingdom, *Report of the Departmental Representatives*, 6.

72 Alexander Mackenzie, January 1874, in United Kingdom, ibid.

73 The Department of Agriculture held responsibility for copyright policy. "A Copyright Muddle: Dr. Taché Explains How the Act of 1873 Became Law," *The Star,* 16 November 1891, in LAC, RG13 A-2, vol. 2361, file 1912-1494, part 1, 1891-1901.

74 Taché's conception of authors' rights evidently did not encompass Aboriginal authors. His interest in Aboriginal stories and legends led him to incorporate the ones he gathered in his own writings, viewing this form of collection as a patriotic duty that helped to form the core of a national literature for Quebec and for Canada. "Taché, Joseph-Charles," in *Dictionary of Canadian Biography,* vol. 12, edited by Francess G. Halpenny (Toronto: University of Toronto Press, 1988).

75 "Taché, Joseph-Charles," ibid.; Joseph-Charles Taché to John Lowe, 21 October 1888, in LAC, RG6 A-3, vol. 213, file: "General – Copyright – Correspondence."

76 As mentioned above, a licensing system would have had to terminate if an Anglo-American agreement were reached, or the Americans would have been unlikely to agree to it. Seville, *Internationalisation of Copyright Law,* 107.

77 An imperial sanction was required because of concerns that the 1875 act might conflict with the 1868 order-in-council suspending the prohibition on foreign reprints under the 1847 *Foreign Reprints Act,* and to provide that colonial reprints could not be imported into the United Kingdom. *An Act to Give Effect to an Act of the Parliament of the Dominion of Canada Respecting Copyright, 1875,* 38-39 Vict., c. 53. See Seville, *Internationalisation of Copyright Law,* 109.

78 *Copyright Act* (1875); Imperial *Copyright Act;* Gordon Roper, "Mark Twain and His Canadian Publishers," *Papers of the Bibliographical Society of Canada* 5 (1966): 40-41.

79 Shelley S. Beal, "'La fin du pillage des auteurs': Louvigny de Montigny's International Press Campaign for Authors' Rights in Canada," *Papers of the Canadian Bibliographical Society* 43, 1 (2005): 33-44.

80 *Copyright Act* (1875), Articles 1, 2, 5, and 9.

81 Imperial *Copyright Act,* Articles 3 and 24; Moss, "Copyright in Canada," 5-6.

82 *Copyright* Act (1875), Article 10.

83 *Copyright Act* (1868), Article 3; *Copyright Act* (1875), Article 4 (emphasis added).

84 Roper, "Mark Twain and His Canadian Publishers," 66.

85 *An Act to Give Effect to an Act of the Parliament of the Dominion of Canada Respecting Copyright.* See also Seville, *Internationalisation of Copyright Law,* 109.

86 *An Act to Give Effect to an Act of the Parliament of the Dominion of Canada Respecting Copyright,* Article 4; James Mavor, "Canadian Copyright," *University of Toronto Monthly,* January 1901, 141.

87 "A Copyright Muddle."

88 Ibid.

89 MacLaren, "Copyright and the Prevention of Literary Publishing in English Canada," 58.

90 Ibid., 3. See also Roper, "Mark Twain and His Canadian Publishers," 30-89.

91 *Smiles v. Belford* (1877), 1 O.A.R. 436. See also Seville, *Internationalisation of Copyright Law,* 109.

92 *Smiles v. Belford* (1877). See also MacLaren, *Dominion and Agency,* ch. 3.

93 Beal, "'La fin du pillage des auteurs'"; *Hubert v. Mary* (1906), Que 59, 15 B.R. 381; *Mary v. Hubert* (1906), Que 260, 29 C.S. 334.

94 Moss, "Copyright in Canada," 5-6.

95 MacLaren, "Copyright and the Prevention of Literary Publishing in English Canada," 15.

96 Ibid., 63.

97 United Kingdom, Royal Commission on Laws and Regulations Relating to Home, Colonial and Foreign Copyrights, *The Royal Commissions and the Report of the Commissioners,* iii

and v. For further discussion of the Royal Commission, see Meera Nair, "The Copyright Act of 1889 – A Canadian Declaration of Independence," *Canadian Historical Review* 90, 1 (2009): 1-28.

98 United Kingdom, ibid., xxxi.

99 Ibid., iii; R.E. Graves and Lynn Milne, "Jenkins, John Edward," in *Oxford Dictionary of National Biography* (London: Oxford University Press, 2004).

100 Graves and Milne, ibid.

101 Seville, *Internationalisation of Copyright Law,* 98.

102 Rose objected to the report's recommendation that colonial reprints not be allowed to circulate back to the United Kingdom and to the recommendation to base the term of copyright protection on the life of the author plus a certain number of years, preferring a term based on the date of registration. Jenkins disputed various aspects of the overall report in his dissenting report, but did not object to the recommendations pertaining to colonial copyright. Daldy dissented from recommendations related to deposit of works at the British Museum but not to recommendations regarding colonial copyright. United Kingdom, Royal Commission on Laws and Regulations Relating to Home, Colonial and Foreign Copyrights, *The Royal Commissions and the Report of the Commissioners,* xlv-xlvi and lvii-lx.

103 Ibid., xxxiii.

104 ibid., xxxiii-xxxiv.

105 Ibid., xxxv.

106 Ibid.

107 Ibid., xxx; Graves and Milne, "Jenkins, John Edward."

108 Seville, *Internationalisation of Copyright Law;* United Kingdom, Royal Commission on Laws and Regulations Relating to Home, Colonial and Foreign Copyrights, *The Royal Commissions and the Report of the Commissioners,* 7.

109 Compulsory licensing, like other measures that seek to ensure public access to intellectual property while also seeking to ensure the protection of intellectual property, has been seen as a way to restore health to a failing pharmaceutical industry, strength to an endangered domestic book industry, order to music on the Internet, and aid to those suffering with HIV and AIDs in Africa.

Chapter 4: United Empire

1 Colin M. Coates, "French Canadians' Ambivalence to the British Empire," in *Canada and the British Empire,* edited by Phillip Buckner (London: Oxford University Press, 2008), 181-99.

2 David M.L. Farr, *The Colonial Office and Canada, 1867-1887* (Toronto: University of Toronto Press, 1955), ch. 9.

3 See Norman Hillmer and J.L. Granatstein, *Empire to Umpire: Canada and the World to the 1990s* (Toronto: Copp Clark Longman, 1994), 1-3.

4 Report of the Privy Council of Canada, 2 October 1869, enclosed in Young to Granville, no. 98, 4 October 1869, CO 42/677, as cited in Farr, *The Colonial Office and Canada,* 256.

5 Canada, *Census of Canada, 1880-81* (Ottawa: Maclean, 1882), vol. 2, table 14, 316-24.

6 Canada, *Census of Canada, 1870-71* (Ottawa: Taylor, 1873-76), vol. 2, table 13, "Occupations of the People," 286, 322, 334.

7 George L. Parker, "The Evolution of Publishing in Canada," in *History of the Book in Canada,* vol. 2, edited by Patricia Fleming, Yvan Lamonde, and Fiona A. Black (Toronto: University of Toronto Press, 2004), 17-26.

8 Ibid.

9   Canada, *Statistical Abstract and Record for the Year 1886* (Ottawa: Maclean, Roger, 1887), 270.

10 Éric Leroux, "Printers: From Shop to Industry," in *History of the Book in Canada,* vol. 2, edited by Patricia Fleming, Yvan Lamonde, and Fiona A. Black (Toronto: University of Toronto Press, 2004), 75-87; Canada, *Census of Canada, 1870-71,* vol. 3, table 55, "Summary of Industrial Establishments, by Provinces."

11 William Kirby to John A. Macdonald, 24 March 1885, in Library and Archives Canada [LAC], Prime Minister Macdonald fonds (MG26 A), 61277-81.

12 Leroux, "Printers," 84-86.

13 Sandra Alston et al., "History of the Book in Canada: Ontario Bibliography," http://www.hbic.library.utoronto.ca/fconfontariobib_en.htm.

14 Max M. Kampelman, "The United States and International Copyright," *American Journal of International Law* 41, 2 (1947): 414; see also James J. Barnes, *Authors, Publishers and Politicians: The Quest for an Anglo-American Copyright Agreement, 1815-1854* (London: Routledge and Kegan Paul, 1974).

15 *Routledge v. Low* (1868) LR 3HL 100; Catherine Seville, *The Internationalisation of Copyright Law: Books, Buccaneers and the Black Flag in the Nineteenth Century* (Cambridge: Cambridge University Press, 2006), 32-36; *An Act to Amend Title Sixty, Chapter Three, of the Revised Statutes of the United States, Relating to Copyrights,* 26 Stat. 1106 (1891).

16 The British appeared willing to concede this to the Americans. "Memorandum Respecting Points to Be Borne in Mind in the Negotiations for a Copyright Convention between Great Britain and the United States," in Mr. Calcraft to Sir Charles W. Dilke, 25 August 1881, in United Kingdom, *Correspondence with the United States Respecting Copyright Convention, Part 1: 1881-1884* (London: n.p., n.d.), in LAC, microfilm reel B-2401.

17 *An Act to Revise, Consolidate, and Amend the Statutes Relating to Patents and Copyrights,* 16 Stat. 198 (1870), c. 230; *Routledge v. Low;* Seville, *Internationalisation of Copyright Law,* 32.

18 Henry Calcraft to Charles Dilke, 18 August 1881, in United Kingdom, *Correspondence with the United States.*

19 Samuel E. Dawson to John Lowe, 23 September 1889, in LAC, RG6 A-3, vol. 213, file: "General – Copyright – Correspondence."

20 The British appeared willing to concede this to the Americans. "Memorandum Respecting Points to Be Borne in Mind." See also Mr. Calcraft to Sir Charles W. Dilke, 25 August 1881.

21 Samuel E. Dawson to John Lowe, 23 September 1889.

22 Mr. West to Earl Granville, 17 November 1881, in United Kingdom, *Correspondence with the United States.*

23 Earl of Kimberly to Marquis of Lorne, 24 May 1882, in United Kingdom, *Correspondence with the United States.*

24 Report of a Committee of the Honourable the Privy Council for Canada, Approved by the Honourable Deputy of His Excellency the Governor General, 3 November 1882; and Frederick Daldy to the Earl of Derby, 30 August 1883, both in United Kingdom, *Correspondence with the United States.*

25 Report of a Committee of the Honourable the Privy Council for Canada, ibid.; *An Act to Amend the Law of Copyright* (imperial *Copyright Act*), 1842, 5 and 6 Vict., c. 45; *Copyright Act* (*An Act Respecting Copyrights*), 1875, 38 Vict., c. 88.

26 Report of a Committee of the Honourable the Privy Council for Canada ... 3 November 1882, ibid.

27 Mr. Calcraft to Sir Charles W. Dilke, 19 December 1882; and Earl Granville to Mr. West, 23 December 1882, both in United Kingdom, *Correspondence with the United States.*

28 Ibid.

29 "A Copyright Muddle: Dr. Taché Explains How the Act of 1873 Became Law," *The Star*, 16 November 1891, in LAC, RG13 A-2, vol. 2361, file 1912-1494, part 1, 1891-1901.

30 "Taché, Joseph-Charles," in *Dictionary of Canadian Biography*, vol. 12, edited by Francess G. Halpenny (Toronto: University of Toronto Press, 1988); Joseph-Charles Taché to John Lowe, 21 October 1888, in LAC, RG6 A-3, vol. 213, file: "General – Copyright – Correspondence."

31 Seville, *Internationalisation of Copyright Law*, 112-13.

32 Craig Brown, "The Nationalism of the National Policy," in *Nationalism in Canada*, edited by Peter Russell (Toronto: McGraw-Hill, 1966), 157; Seville, *Internationalisation of Copyright Law*, 112 fn83.

33 Dr. Taché to Mr. Pope, 18 July 1883, in United Kingdom, *Correspondence with the United States*.

34 William Kirby to John A. Macdonald, 24 March 1885.

35 Frederick Daldy to Robert Herbert, 9 January 1883, in United Kingdom, *Correspondence with the United States*.

36 Ibid.

37 Ibid.

38 Report of a Committee of the Honourable the Privy Council for Canada, Approved by the Honourable Deputy of his Excellency the Governor General, 24 July 1883, in United Kingdom, *Correspondence with the United States*.

39 Isabella Alexander, *Copyright Law and the Public Interest in the Nineteenth Century* (Oxford: Hart Publishing, 2010), 151.

40 Farr, *The Colonial Office and Canada*, 238.

41 Ibid., 226.

42 Ibid., ch. 7.

43 Sam Ricketson and Jane Ginsburg, *International Copyright and Neighbouring Rights: The Berne Convention and Beyond*, 2nd ed. (London: Oxford University Press, 2006), 45.

44 *Resolutions of the Congrès de la propriété littéraire et artistique Held in Brussels, 27-30 September 1858* (Brussels: Congrès de la propriété littéraire et artistique, 1858).

45 Canada's reluctance to recognize American copyright during a period when the United States was not party to the *Berne Convention*, and at a time when Canada felt that the Americans did not recognize Canadian copyright on reciprocal terms, was a key factor in Canada's reluctance to participate in the Berne Union until 1914. Ricketson and Ginsburg, *International Copyright and Neighbouring Rights*, 103-3.

46 Ibid., 48.

47 Ibid., 50.

48 *Association littéraire et artistique internationale: son histoire – ses travaux 1878-1889* (Paris: Bibliothèque Chacornac, 1889), 4; Canadian publishers and printers Hunter, Rose (Toronto), Perrault et Compagnie (Montreal), and Copp, Clark and Company (Toronto) participated at the Universal Exhibition in 1878, however. Gwendolyn Davies, "Canadian Book Arts and Trades at International Exhibitions," in *History of the Book in Canada*, vol. 2, edited by Patricia Fleming, Yvan Lamonde, and Fiona A. Black (Toronto: University of Toronto Press, 2005), 109.

49 Ibid.

50 Ibid., 49-51.

51 Ricketson and Ginsburg, *International Copyright and Neighbouring Rights*, 51-52.

52 Based on the results of searches of the *Globe* (Toronto) for the years 1878-86; *Toronto World* for the years 1880-86; the *Ottawa Citizen* and *Montreal Gazette* for September 1884, September 1885, and March, June, July, and September 1886; the *Franc-Parleur* (Montreal) for the years 1872-78; *Le Courrier de St-Hyacinthe* (Saint-Hyacinthe, Quebec) for the years

1877-86; *La Presse* (Montreal) for 7-25 September 1885, and March, June, July, and September 1886; the *Macleod Gazette* (Fort Macleod, Alberta) for the years 1882-86; and the *New Westminster Mainland Guardian* (British Columbia) for the years 1878-83.

53 Ricketson and Ginsburg, *International Copyright and Neighbouring Rights*, 51-52.

54 *Actes de la première conférénce internationalle pour la protection des œuvres littéraires et artistiques du 8 septembre 1884 à Berne* (Berne: Conseil Fédérale Suisse, 1884), 1.

55 Ibid., 9; Ricketson and Ginsburg, *International Copyright and Neighbouring Rights*, 52-58; Kampelman, "The United States and International Copyright," 411.

56 *Actes de la première conférénce internationalle*, 9, referring to the Dominican Republic as "Saint-Domingue."

57 Ibid.; Ricketson and Ginsburg, *International Copyright and Neighbouring Rights*, 52-59; Kampelman, "The United States and International Copyright," 411.

58 Ricketson and Ginsburg, ibid., 42-44.

59 Lionel Bently and Brad Sherman, "Great Britain and the Signing of the Berne Convention in 1886," *Journal of the Copyright Society of the USA* 48, 3 (2001): 311-40.

60 *An Act to Amend the Law Respecting International and Colonial Copyright, 1886*, 49 and 50 Vict., c. 33.

61 Sir J. Pauncefote to Sir R. Herbert, 4 March 1886, in United Kingdom, *Switzerland No. 2: Further Correspondence Respecting the Formation of an International Copyright Union*, C. 4606 (London: n.p., 1886), in LAC, RG7 G21, vol. 115, file 206, pt. 2b.

62 Memorandum by Mr. Jenkyns to the Colonies, 8 April 1886, in United Kingdom, *Switzerland No. 2*.

63 See United Kingdom, *Switzerland No. 2*, and Seville, *Internationalisation of Copyright Law*, 70-71.

64 Mr. Bryce to Mr. Bramston, 8 April 1886, in United Kingdom, *Switzerland No. 2*.

65 Ibid.

66 Ibid.

67 United Kingdom, *Switzerland No. 2*.

68 *Actes de la troisième conférénce internationalle pour la protection des oeuvres littéraires et artistiques réunie à Berne du 6 au 9 septembre 1886* (Berne: Conseil Fédérale Suisse, 1886); Francis Adams and J.H.G Bergne to the Earl of Iddesleigh, *Report on the Third International Copyright Conference at Berne*, 10 September 1886, in LAC, RG6 A3, vol. 214, file: "Copyright Conference at Berne, 1886." All but Liberia ratified the agreement in 1887.

69 Francis Adams and J.H.G Bergne to the Earl of Iddesleigh.

70 Ricketson and Ginsburg, *International Copyright and Neighbouring Rights*, 52-82.

71 *Actes de la troisième conférénce internationalle.*

72 Ibid.

73 Ibid.

74 National Archives of Britain, Foreign Office fonds 881/5989. As quoted in Seville, *Internationalisation of Copyright Law*, 118.

75 Based on an examination of the indices of the *Canadian Law Times* for 1881-89 and the *Canadian Law Journal* for 1884-87. The *Journal of Jurisprudence and Scottish Law Magazine* ran a "Report on the Berne International Copyright Conference 1883" in its May 1884 issue. *Law Magazine and Law Review* also ran news of the 1883 meeting; 5th ser., 9 (1883-84): 84. The *Central Law Journal* ran a brief and positive note on the results of the 1886 meeting; 23 (1886): 193. The *Law Quarterly Review* also ran a short article related to the meeting; 2 (1886): 213.

76 Based on the results of searches of the *Globe, La Presse,* the *Montreal Gazette,* the *Toronto Daily Mail,* the *Toronto Telegram,* the *St. John's Evening Telegram,* and the *Ottawa Citizen* for September 1886.

77 "International Copyright," *Globe* (Toronto), 22 September 1886, 4.

78 Farr, *The Colonial Office and Canada,* 231.

79 Ibid., ch. 7.

80 *Actes de la première conférénce internationalle; Actes de la deuxième conférénce internationalle pour la protection des oeuvres littéraires et artistiques réunie à Berne du 7 au 18 septembre 1885* (Berne: Conseil Fédérale Suisse, 1885); *Actes de la troisième conférénce internationalle.*

81 Granville to Marquess of Lansdowne, April and May 1886, in LAC, RG7 G21, vol. 115, file 206, pt. 2b. See also United Kingdom, *Switzerland No. 2.*

82 Granville to Marquess of Lansdowne, ibid.

83 Charles Tupper to Secretary of State, Ottawa, 29 November 1886; J. Powell to Governor General's Secretary, Ottawa, 14 December 1886, both in LAC, RG6 A3, vol. 214, file: "Copyright Conference at Berne, 1886."

84 Farr, *The Colonial Office and Canada,* 234-35.

85 Canada, House of Commons, *Debates of the House of Commons, Fourth Session – Fifth Parliament 49 Vict., 1886,* vol. 21 (Ottawa: Maclean, Roger, 1886), 377-82.

86 Ibid., 381.

87 Ibid., 382.

88 Ibid.

89 Ibid., 380. ·

90 Hall said he would have consented to set up the committee but, as noted above, he had concerns that it would give the interests of printers "a prominence which it did not deserve": ibid., 381.

91 "Parlément fédéral," *La Presse,* 30 March 1886, 2; "House of Commons," *Ottawa Citizen,* 30 March 1886; "Notes of the Session," *Montreal Gazette,* 30 March 1886.

92 Mr. Adams to the Earl of Rosebery, 26 March 1886, in United Kingdom, *Switzerland No. 2.*

93 Charles Tupper to John Macdonald, 19 March 1886, in LAC, Prime Minister Macdonald fonds (MG26 A), 130113-14.

94 Governor General's Office, various letters, April-May 1886, in LAC, RG7 G21, vol. 115, file 206, pt. 2b.

95 The date of this earlier reply is not given. It is possible that the reply had already been given by the time the question of a copyright committee was raised in the House on 29 March 1886. Minute of the Privy Council of Canada, approved 22 June 1886, in LAC, RG2.

96 Sir R. Herbert to Sir J. Pauncefote, 12 June 1886, in United Kingdom, *Switzerland No. 2;* John Lowe, Memorandum, 9 February 1889, in LAC, RG13 A-2, vol. 2361, file 1912-1424, pt. 4.

97 John Lowe, Memorandum, ibid.

98 Minute of the Privy Council of Canada, approved 22 June 1886.

99 Based on the results of searches of the *Globe* (Toronto), *Toronto World,* the *Ottawa Citizen,* the *Montreal Gazette, Le Courrier de St-Hyacinthe* (Saint-Hyacinthe, Quebec); *La Presse* (Montreal), and the *Macleod Gazette* (Fort Macleod, Alberta) for June and July 1886.

100 See, for example, *Law Quarterly Review* 2 (1886): 213; *Law Magazine and Law Review,* 5th ser., 11 (1885-86): 231; and "Résumé télégraphique," *La Presse,* 3 September 1886, 1.

101 Minute of the Privy Council of Canada, approved 22 June 1886.

102 The United States did not join the *Berne Convention* until 1989.

103 John Lowe, Memorandum, 9 February 1889.

104 Ibid.

105 Report of a Committee of the Honourable the Privy Council for Canada … 3 November 1882.

106 Ibid.
107 "International Copyright," *Globe* (Toronto), 22 September 1886, 4.

Chapter 5: *Berne* Buster

1 *Canadian Copyright: A Series of Articles that Appeared in the Toronto Telegram from the Pen of a Gentleman Thoroughly Versed in the Question of Copyright* (Canadian Copyright Association, n.d.), 6.
2 Once ratified by Canada, a treaty does not automatically form a part of domestic law. Canada follows the British dualist tradition whereby international obligations become binding through the passage of domestic legislation that implements the international obligations as domestic law. See Myra Tawfik, "Intellectual Property Laws in Harmony with NAFTA: The Courts as Mediators between the Global and the Local," *Canadian Journal of Law and Technology* 2, 3 (2003): 216, and Ruth Sullivan and Elmer A. Driedger, *Sullivan and Driedger on the Construction of Statutes,* 4th ed. (Markham, ON: Butterworths, 2002), 434.
3 George L. Parker, *The Beginnings of the Book Trade in Canada* (Toronto: University of Toronto Press, 1985), 220.
4 *Copyright Act (An Act Respecting Copyrights), 1875,* 38 Vict., c. 88, Article 2; Memorandum, 1 May 1888, in Library and Archives Canada [LAC], RG6 A3, vol. 214, file: "Copyright – Memoranda 1888-89."
5 Memorandum, ibid.
6 Ibid. (emphasis added).
7 Ibid.
8 Francis Adams and J.H.G. Bergne to the Earl of Iddesleigh, *Report on the Third International Copyright Conference at Berne,* 10 September 1886, in LAC, RG6 A3, vol. 214, file: "Copyright Conference at Berne, 1886."
9 Craig Brown, "The Nationalism of the National Policy," in *Nationalism in Canada,* edited by Peter Russell (Toronto: McGraw-Hill, 1966).
10 John Ross Robertson, quoted in Ron Poulton, *The Paper Tyrant: John Ross Robertson of the Toronto Telegram* (Toronto: Clarke, Irwin, 1971), 107.
11 Shelley S. Beal, "'La fin du pillage des auteurs': Louvigny de Montigny's International Press Campaign for Authors' Rights in Canada," *Papers of the Canadian Bibliographical Society* 43, 1 (2005): 33-44, arguing that dozens of American firms, including the Jenkins firm of New York, worked to supply the French-speaking markets in both the United States and Canada.
12 "The Copyright Bill," *Globe* (Toronto), 16 May 1888, 8; "Copyright Law as Before," *Globe* (Toronto), 18 May 1888.
13 "The Copyright Question," *Globe* (Toronto), 26 May 1888, 16.
14 LAC, Prime Minister Wilfrid Laurier fonds (MG26 G), vol. 33, microfilm reel C-745, 43210.
15 See generally LAC, RG13 A-2, vol. 2361, file 1912-1494, pt. 1, 1891-1901, and Prime Minister Borden fonds (MG26 H), microfilm reel C-4375.
16 "History," Ontario Society of Artists, http://www.ontariosocietyofartists.org/; Ontario Society of Artists to Minister of Justice, 11 November 1895, in LAC, RG13 A-2, vol. 2361, file 1912-1494, pt. 1, 1891-1901.
17 Michelene Cambron and Carole Gerson, "Authors and Literary Culture," in *History of the Book in Canada,* vol. 2, edited by Patricia Fleming, Yvan Lamonde, and Fiona A. Black (Toronto: University of Toronto Press, 2004), 130.
18 Beal, "'La fin du pillage des auteurs'"; see also below, *Hubert v. Mary* (1906), Que 59, 15 B.R. 381.

19 Beal, ibid.

20 John Lowe to Fred Daldy, 13 June 1888, in LAC, RG17 A16, vol. 1655.

21 "The Copyright Bill," *Globe* (Toronto), 1; "Notes," *Globe* (Toronto), 18 May 1888, 3; Richard T. Lancefield, *Notes on Copyright Domestic and International* (Hamilton, ON: Canadian Literary Bureau, 1896), para. 89.

22 John Thompson to Governor General in Council, 1892, 7, in LAC, RG13 A-2, vol. 85, file 892-217.

23 Ibid.

24 "Hunter, John Howard," in *Dictionary of Canadian Biography*, vol. 13, edited by Francess G. Halpenny (Toronto: University of Toronto Press, 1985).

25 Howard Hunter to John Ross Robertson, 17 November 1892, in LAC, RG6 A-3, vol. 213, file: "General – Copyright – Correspondence."

26 Ibid.

27 Ibid.

28 Douglas Owram, *The Government Generation: Canadian Intellectuals and the State, 1900-1945* (Toronto: University of Toronto Press, 1986), 29-30. See also Chapter 4.

29 Article 2 of the 1875 *Copyright Act* required that works be "printed and published or reprinted and republished in Canada."

30 "Such work shall be printed and published or produced in Canada, or reprinted and re-published or reproduced in Canada, within one month after publication or production elsewhere": *An Act to Amend "The Copyright Act," Chapter Sixty-Two of the Revised Statutes, 1889*, 52 Vict., c. 29, Article 1.

31 Ibid., Article 7.

32 *An Act to Amend "The Copyright Act."*

33 United Kingdom, *Report of the Departmental Representatives (of the Colonial Office, Foreign Office, Board of Trade, and Parliamentary Counsel's Office) Appointed to Consider the Canadian Copyright Act of 1889* (London: n.p., 1892), in LAC, Prime Minister Abbott fonds (MG26 C), vol. 5, file: "Copyright"; Lord Stanley of Preston to Lord Knutsford, 16 and 17 August 1889, in United Kingdom, *Correspondence on the Subject of the Law of Copyright in Canada, C. 7783* (London: George Edward Eyre and William Spottiswoode, 1893), in LAC, RG13 A-2, vol. 2361, file 1912-1494, pt. 2.

34 United Kingdom, *Report of the Departmental Representatives*, ibid., 20.

35 Lord Knutsford to Lord Stanley of Preston, 25 March 1890, in United Kingdom, *Correspondence on the Subject of the Law of Copyright in Canada*.

36 Canada, House of Commons, *Debates of the House of Commons, First Session – Seventh Parliament 54-55 Victoria, 1891*, vol. 32 (Ottawa: Brown Chamberlin, 1891), 6287-89. See also Bureau de l'Union internationale pour la protection des oeuvres littéraires et artistiques, *Le droit d'auteur*, November 1891, 122-23, and Lord Stanley of Preston to Lord Knutsford, 5 November 1891, in United Kingdom, *Correspondence on the Subject of the Law of Copyright in Canada*.

37 Lord Knutsford to Lord Stanley of Preston, 30 June 1892, in United Kingdom, *Correspondence on the Subject of the Law of Copyright in Canada*.

38 The Earl of Aberdeen to the Marquess of Ripon, 10 February 1894, in United Kingdom, *Correspondence on the Subject of the Law of Copyright in Canada*.

39 *Canadian Copyright*, 21 July 1894: enclosure in Colonial Office to Foreign Office and Board of Trade, 13 September 1894, in United Kingdom, *Correspondence on the Subject of the Law of Copyright in Canada*.

40 The Canadian Copyright Association represented publishers, printers, booksellers, and related interests (see above).

41 *George N. Morang & Co. v. The Publishers' Syndicate Ltd.*, [1900] 32 O.R. 393. See generally United Kingdom, *Correspondence on the Subject of the Law of Copyright in Canada;* John H. Moss, "Copyright in Canada," *University Magazine*, April 1914, 8; R.A. Shields, "Imperial Policy and the Canadian Copyright Act of 1889," *Dalhousie Review* 60, 4 (1980-81): 651-52; Herbert A. Howell, "Copyright in Canada," *American Law Review* 49 (1915): 675.

42 Catherine Seville, *The Internationalisation of Copyright Law: Books, Buccaneers and the Black Flag in the Nineteenth Century* (Cambridge: Cambridge University Press, 2006), 87; Moss, "Copyright in Canada," 4.

43 *George N. Morang & Co. v. The Publishers' Syndicate Ltd.*

44 57 & 58 Vict., c. 33, Item 101.

45 Order-in-Council No. 1894-0928, 26-30 March 1894.

46 Ibid.

47 Pamela McKenzie, "Canadian Interest Groups and Parliament: The Case of Copyright, 1887-1987," course paper, 8 December 1989; Moss, "Copyright in Canada," 7; "Robertson, John Ross," in *Dictionary of Canadian Biography*, vol. 14, edited by Francess G. Halpenny (Toronto: University of Toronto Press, 1998).

48 *An Act to Amend "The Copyright Act,"* Article 5.

49 W. Oliver Hodges to the Colonial Office, 3 November 1890, in LAC, RG6 A-3, vol. 213, file: "General – Copyright – Correspondence."

50 *An Act to Amend "The Copyright Act."*

51 Ibid.

52 Lord Knutsford to Lord Stanley, 18 March 1891, in United Kingdom, *Correspondence on the Subject of the Law of Copyright in Canada.*

53 Although the formal reasons given for refusing royal assent to the Canadian act of 1872 related strictly to the fact that said act conflicted with the imperial act, the threat to the Anglo-American negotiations, which had already been raised with regard to the 1868 request for a compulsory licensing system, would have been of concern in the 1870s as well. United Kingdom, *Copyright (Colonies): Copies of or Extracts from Correspondence between the Colonial Office and Any of the Colonial Governments on the Subject of Copyright, and of Colonial Acts Relating to Copyright Which Have Been Allowed by Her Majesty* (London: n.p., 1875).

54 Samuel E. Dawson to John Lowe, 23 September 1889, in LAC, RG6 A-3, vol. 213, file: "General – Copyright – Correspondence."

55 Ibid.

56 Ibid.

57 Ibid.

58 Bureau de l'Union internationale pour la protection des oeuvres littéraires et artistiques, *Le droit d'auteur*, January-May 1890.

59 Morel to the Assistant Secretary (Railway Department), Board of Trade, London, 3 July 1890, in United Kingdom, *Correspondence on the Subject of the Law of Copyright in Canada.*

60 National Archives of Britain, Foreign Office fonds 881/5989. As quoted in Seville, *Internationalisation of Copyright Law*, 118.

61 United Kingdom, *Report of the Departmental Representatives*, 19.

62 As of 2006. Sam Ricketson and Jane Ginsburg, *International Copyright and Neighbouring Rights: The Berne Convention and Beyond*, 2nd ed. (London: Oxford University Press, 2006), 1094.

63 Ibid.

64 Ibid., 1095.

65 Howard Hunter to John Ross Robertson, 17 November 1892, in LAC, RG6 A-3, vol. 213, file: "General – Copyright – Correspondence."

66 Sir R. Herbert to Sir J. Pauncefote, 12 June 1886, in United Kingdom, *Switzerland No. 2: Further Correspondence Respecting the Formation of an International Copyright Union*, C. 4606 (London: n.p., 1886), in LAC, RG7 G21, vol. 115, file 206, pt. 2b; John Lowe, Memorandum, 9 February 1889, in LAC, RG13 A-2, vol. 2361, file 1912-1424, pt. 4.

67 Minute of the Privy Council of Canada, approved 22 June 1886, in LAC, RG2.

68 Ibid., 6-7.

69 Francis Adams and J.H.G. Bergne to the Earl of Iddesleigh, *Report on the Third International Copyright Conference.*

70 *Convention Concerning the Creation of an International Union for the Protection of Literary and Artistic Works (Berne Convention)*, 9 September 1886 (Berne: Office of the International Union for the Protection of Literary and Artistic Works, 1886), Article 20.

71 David M.L. Farr, *The Colonial Office and Canada, 1867-1887* (Toronto: University of Toronto Press, 1955), ch. 7.

72 "Lowe, John," in *Dictionary of Canadian Biography*, vol. 14, edited by Francess G. Halpenny (Toronto: University of Toronto Press, 1998). Lowe's letters of 1888 reveal a great passion on copyright issues as well as greater sympathies towards printers' interests and skepticism towards the views promoted by authors' groups. See, for example, John Lowe to John Thompson, 25 June 1890, in LAC, RG6 A-3, vol. 213, file: "General – Copyright – Correspondence."

73 John Lowe to Frederick Daldy, 13 July 1888, in LAC, RG17 A16, vol. 1655. See also John Lowe to Frederick Daldy, 3 June 1889, in LAC, RG6 A-3, vol. 213, file: "General – Copyright – Correspondence."

74 For more information on Daldy's activities in Canada, see Seville, *Internationalisation of Copyright Law*, ch. 4. John Lowe, Memorandum, 23 May 1892, in LAC, RG13 A-2, vol. 2361, file 1912-1494, pt. 1.

75 John Lowe to Dawson, 22 May 1888, in LAC, RG17 A16, vol. 1655.

76 Ricketson and Ginsburg, *International Copyright and Neighbouring Rights*, 306.

77 Roundell Palmer and Farrer Herschell, Memorandum, in LAC, RG13 A-2, vol. 2361, file 1912-1494, pt. 1.

78 Draft memo, Department of Agriculture, 16 May 1888, in LAC, RG6 A3, vol. 214, file: "Copyright – Memoranda 1888-89." See also John Lowe, Memorandum, 23 May 1892/, in LAC, RG17 A16, vol. 1655.

79 *An Act to Amend Title Sixty, Chapter Three, of the Revised Statutes of the United States, Relating to Copyrights*, 26 Stat. 1106 (1891), s. 13.

80 Ibid., s. 4956.

81 J. Haydn Boyde and William S. Lofquist, "New Interests in Old Issues: Antiprotection and the End of the Manufacturing Clause of the US," *Publishing Research Quarterly* 7, 4 (Winter 1991/1992).

82 John Lowe to John Thompson, 25 June 1889, in LAC, RG6 A-3, vol. 213, file: "General – Copyright – Correspondence 1888-1892."

83 Max M. Kampelman, "The United States and International Copyright," *American Journal of International Law* 41, 2 (1947): 417.

84 United States, *Papers Relating to the Foreign Relations of the United States, Transmitted to Congress with the Annual Message of the President*, 9 December 1891 (Washington, DC: Government Printing Office, 1892), XV.

85 Marquis of Salisbury to United States Minister Robert T. Lincoln, 16 June 1891, quoted in LAC, Prime Ministerial fonds (MG26), vol. 5, file: "Copyright."

86 Draft memo from Ministers of Justice and Agriculture to the Governor General in Council, n.d., in LAC, RG13 A-2, vol. 2361, file 1912-1494, pt. 1; John Lowe, Memorandum, 23 May 1892, in LAC, RG13 A-2, vol. 2361, file 1912-1494, pt. 1."

87 *Copyright Act, 1875.*

88 Gordon Roper, "Mark Twain and His Canadian Publishers," *Papers of the Bibliographical Society of Canada* 5 (1966): 66-67.

89 John Lowe, Memorandum, 23 May 1892, in LAC, RG13 A-2, vol. 2361, file 1912-1494, pt. 1.

90 Ibid. The question of whether the United States was, through its 1891 act, party to a treaty with the United Kingdom was complicated, as Lowe describes in this memo, by questions of whether the 1891 act made the United States eligible to join the *Berne Convention.*

91 Ibid.

92 Bureau de l'Union internationale pour la protection des oeuvres littéraires et artistiques, *Le droit d'auteur,* January 1892, 10-12; also see *Le droit d'auteur,* September 1892, 113-14, and March 1892, 32.

93 *Philadelphia Telegraph* [date and page number not noted], in LAC, RG13 A-2, vol. 2361, file 1912-1494, pt. 1.

94 *An Act to Amend the Law Respecting International and Colonial Copyright, 1886,* 49 and 50 Vict., c. 33, Article 2; United Kingdom, *Report of the Departmental Representatives.*

95 John Lowe, Memorandum, 23 May 1892, in LAC, RG13 A-2, vol. 2361, file 1912-1494, pt. 1.

96 Department of State, Washington, to Sir Pauncefote, 19 December 1891, in LAC, ibid.

97 See Seville, *Internationalisation of Copyright Law,* 131.

98 *Jefferys v. Boosey* (1854) 4 HLC 815.

99 P.B. Waite, *The Man from Halifax: Sir John Thompson, Prime Minister* (Toronto: University of Toronto Press, 1984), 299 and 347.

100 Ibid., 419.

101 "The Copyright Question," *Globe* (Toronto).

102 Waite, *Man from Halifax,* 425.

103 Ibid., 429.

104 "Messrs. Marter and Howland: What the Provincial Opposition Leaders Think of the Dominion Premier's Death," *Globe* (Toronto), 18 December 1894, 10.

105 Note that in 1886 Carling had provided key advice to the Privy Council that Canada should join the *Berne Convention.*

106 Francis Adams and J.H.G. Bergne to the Earl of Iddesleigh, *Report on the Third International Copyright Conference;* Ricketson and Ginsburg, *International Copyright and Neighbouring Rights,* 86.

107 Ricketson and Ginsburg, ibid., 87.

108 Farr, *The Colonial Office and Canada,* 215-31.

109 United Kingdom, *Correspondence with the United States Respecting Copyright Convention, Part 1: 1881-1884* (London: n.p., n.d.), in LAC, microfilm reel B-2401.

110 *Berne Convention for the Protection of Literary and Artistic Works, Paris Act of 4 May 1896* (Berne: Office of the International Union for the Protection of Literary and Artistic Works, 1896), and Ricketson and Ginsburg, *International Copyright and Neighbouring Rights,* 88-89.

111 Kampelman, "The United States and International Copyright," 412.

112 *Convention Concerning the Creation of an International Union for the Protection of Literary and Artistic Works (Berne Convention),* 9 September 1886 (Berne: Office of the International Union for the Protection of Literary and Artistic Works, 1886), Article 3.

113 *Berne Convention for the Protection of Literary and Artistic Works, Paris Act of 4 May 1896.* See also Ricketson and Ginsburg, *International Copyright and Neighbouring Rights,* 888.

114 Based on a review of articles in the *Globe* and the *Evening Star,* the *Edmonton Bulletin,* the *Macleod Gazette,* the *Niagara Times,* and the *Perth Courier;* Kampelman, "The United States and International Copyright," 413.

115 United Kingdom, *Correspondence Respecting Copyright Conference at Paris,* C. 8441 (London: Harrison and Sons, 1897), in LAC, RG7 G21, vol. 116, file 206, pt. 1a, 8-9.

116 This is the issue upon which John Lowe and John Thompson had disagreed; see above.

117 *Actes de la conférence réunie à Paris du 15 avril au 4 mai 1896* (Berne: Bureau International de l'Union, 1897), 161.

118 Ibid., 36.

119 Ricketson and Ginsburg, *International Copyright and Neighbouring Rights,* 306.

120 United Kingdom, *Correspondence Respecting Copyright Conference at Paris,* 5.

121 Ibid., 7; *Declaration Interpreting Certain Provisions of the Berne Convention of September 9, 1886, and the Additional Act Signed at Paris on May 4, 1896* (Berne: Office of the International Union for the Protection of Literary and Artistic Works, 1896), Article 1.

122 United Kingdom, *Correspondence Respecting Copyright Conference at Paris,* 5-6 and 226-34; see also Order of Her Majesty in Council No. 374, 7 March 1898, in LAC, RG7 G21, vol. 116, file 206, pt. 3.

123 James Edgar, Memorandum, 2 January 1897, in LAC, Prime Minister Wilfrid Laurier fonds (MG26 G), vol. 33, microfilm reel C-745, 10557-60.

124 *An Act to Amend the Copyright Act, 1900,* 63-64 Vict., c. 25.

125 Ibid. See Seville, *Internationalisation of Copyright Law,* 134, on this point.

126 *An Act to Amend the Copyright Act, 1900.*

127 Ricketson and Ginsburg, *International Copyright and Neighbouring Rights,* 92.

128 Ibid., 93.

129 Ibid., 94.

130 Ibid., 95 and 98.

131 Ibid., 95.

132 Ibid., 97.

133 Ibid., 99-100.

134 Ibid., 96.

135 Ibid., 101-2.

136 *Actes de la conférence réunie à Berlin du 14 octobre au 14 novembre 1908 avec les actes de ratification* (Berne: Bureau de l'Union internationale littéraires et artistiques, 1910), 17.

137 United Kingdom, *Correspondence Respecting the Revised Convention of Berne for the Protection of Artistic and Literary Works, Signed at Berlin, 13th November 1908 (with Copies of the Conventions of 1886, 1896, and 1908),* Cd-4467 (London: Harrison and Sons, 1909), 21; T.H. Sanderson, "Bergne, Sir John Henry Gibbs (1842-1908)," revised by H.C.G. Matthew, in *Oxford Dictionary of National Biography,* edited by H.C.G. Matthew and Brian Harrison (Oxford: Oxford University Press, 2004).

138 Sanderson, "Bergne, Sir John Henry Gibbs."

139 Ricketson and Ginsburg, *International Copyright and Neighbouring Rights,* 103. See also *Le droit d'auteur* 25 (1889): 90.

140 Ricketson and Ginsburg, ibid., 103.

141 John Braithwaite and Peter Drahos, *Global Business Regulation* (Cambridge: Cambridge University Press, 2000), 9.

142 Robert D. Putnam, "Diplomacy and Domestic Politics: The Logic of Two-Level Games," *International Organization* 42, 3 (1988): 427-60.

143 United Kingdom, *Correspondence Respecting Copyright Conference at Paris,* 3.

144 Ibid., 4.

145 Ibid., 5.

146 E. Grey to H. Bergne, Mr. Askwith, and Count de Salis, 9 October 1908, in United Kingdom, *Correspondence Respecting the Revised Convention of Berne ... 1908.*

Chapter 6: The New Imperial Copyright, 1895-1914

1 Catherine Seville, *The Internationalisation of Copyright Law: Books, Buccaneers and the Black Flag in the Nineteenth Century* (Cambridge: Cambridge University Press, 2006), 124-28; *Report of Mr. Newcombe*, in Library and Archives Canada [LAC], RG13-A-2, vol. 2279, file 1895-155.

2 Seville, ibid., 128.

3 Ibid., 130.

4 Ibid., 129.

5 Ibid., 129-30.

6 Ibid., 132-33.

7 Ibid., 132-34.

8 Canada, House of Commons, *Debates of the House of Commons, Third Session – Eighth Parliament 61 Vict., 1898*, vol. 47 (Ottawa: S.E. Dawson, 1898), 6632.

9 "Edgar, Sir James David," in *Dictionary of Canadian Biography*, vol. 12, edited by Francess G. Halpenny (Toronto: University of Toronto Press, 1988).

10 *Copyright Act (An Act Respecting Copyrights), 1875*, 38 Vict., c. 88, Articles 11 and 15; *An Act to Amend the Copyright Act, 1900*, 63-64 Vict., c. 25; John H. Moss, "Copyright in Canada," *University Magazine*, April 1914, 7; Eli MacLaren, "'Against All Invasion': The Archival Story of Kipling, Copyright, and the Macmillan Expansion into Canada, 1900-1920," *Journal of Canadian Studies* 40 (2006): 144.

11 Shelley S. Beal, "'La fin du pillage des auteurs': Louvigny de Montigny's International Press Campaign for Authors' Rights in Canada," *Papers of the Canadian Bibliographical Society* 43, 1 (2005): 33-44; Eli MacLaren, "Copyright and Publishing," *Historical Perspectives on Canadian Publishing*, http://hpcanpub.mcmaster.ca/; *Hubert v. Mary* (1906), Que. 59, 15 B.R. 381; *Mary v. Hubert* (1906), Que 260, 29 C.S. 334.

12 George L. Parker, "Distributors, Agents, and Publishers: Creating a Separate Market for Books in Canada 1900-1920. Part I," *Papers of the Bibliographical Society of Canada* 43, 2 (2005): 16-17 and 37-40; Eli MacLaren and Josée Vincent, "Book Policies and Copyright in Canada and Quebec: Defending National Cultures," *Canadian Literature* 204 (2010): 63-82.

13 Canada, House of Commons, *Debates of the House of Commons, Fifth Session – Eighth Parliament 63-64 Vict., 1900*, vol. 52 (Ottawa: S.E. Dawson, 1900), 6452.

14 Ibid., 6506.

15 Seville, *Internationalisation of Copyright Law*, 135.

16 *Smiles v. Belford* (1877), 1 O.A.R. 436; *Routledge v. Low* (1868) LR 3HL 100.

17 [1900] 5 Terr. L.R. 30, 2 Can. Com. R. 256. Regina was, until 1905, the capital of the Northwest Territories, which at the time covered the area that is now Saskatchewan.

18 *Fine Arts Copyright Act, 1862*, 25 and 26 Vict., c. 68.

19 *Graves & Co. v. Gorrie*, [1903] A.C. 496 (Ont. P.C.).

20 *Black v. Imperial Book Co.*, [1904] 35 S.C.R. 488.

21 Beal, "'La fin du pillage des auteurs,'" 33-44.

22 Ibid.

23 Ibid.

24 Ibid.

25 Ibid.

26 Ibid.

27 *Hubert v. Mary; Mary v. Hubert;* Beal, "'La fin du pillage des auteurs'"; MacLaren, "Copyright and Publishing."

28 *Jefferys v. Boosey* (1854) 4 HLC 815.

29 *Life Publishing Co. v. Rose Publishing Co.,* [1906] 8 O.W.R. 28, 12 O.L.R. 386.

30 Canada, *Statistical Abstract and Record for the Year 1886* (Ottawa: Maclean, Roger, 1887); Canada, *The Canada Year Book 1911* (Ottawa: C.H. Parmelee, 1912).

31 The census lists 5,227 "printers and publishers" and 840 bookbinders in 1881, and 17,827 "printers and engravers" in 1911; 601 "artists and litterateurs" in 1881, and 434 with "literary and scientific pursuits," 969 painters and artists, and 1,557 designers and sculptors in 1911. Canada, *Census of Canada, 1880-81,* vol. 2 (Ottawa: Maclean, 1882); Canada, *Census of Canada, 1911,* vol. 6 (Ottawa: C.H. Parmelee, 1912-15).

32 LAC, "The Virtual Gramophone: History," http://www.collectionscanada.gc.ca/gramophone/028011-3000-e.html.

33 Ibid., "The Virtual Gramophone: The 78-rpm 7-inch Berliner Series," http://www.collectionscanada.gc.ca/gramophone/028011-3006-e.html; "The Virtual Gramophone: Compo Company Limited," http://www.collectionscanada.gc.ca/gramophone/028011-3011-e.html.

34 Ibid.

35 Manjunath Pendakur, *Canadian Dreams and American Control: The Political Economy of the Canadian Film Industry* (Detroit: Wayne State University Press, 1990), 46.

36 Ibid., 47.

37 Ibid., 51.

38 Norman Hillmer and J.L. Granatstein, *Empire to Umpire: Canada and the World to the 1990s* (Toronto: Copp Clark Longman, 1994), 35.

39 United Kingdom, Board of Trade, Law of Copyright Committee, *Report of the Committee on the Law of Copyright* Cd. 4976 (London: Eyre and Spottiswoode, 1909-10). See also Seville, *Internationalisation of Copyright Law,* 138.

40 Seville, ibid.

41 Lord Crewe to Lord Grey, 24 February 1910, in LAC, RG25, vol. 1099, file 1910-21C, pt. 1.

42 Norman Hillmer and J.L. Granatstein, *For Better or for Worse: Canada and the United States into the Twenty-First Century* (Toronto: Nelson, 2005), 61; Wilfrid Laurier to Joseph Pope, 20 January 1910, in LAC, ibid.

43 Department of External Affairs correspondence, January 1910, in LAC, ibid.

44 Sir Goschen to Sir Grey, 10 June 1910, in LAC, ibid.

45 United Kingdom, *Minutes of Proceeding of the Imperial Copyright Conference, 1910,* 3, in LAC, microfilm reels B-2392 to B-2393.

46 Ibid.

47 "Fisher, Sydney," in *Dictionary of Canadian Biography,* vol. 15, edited by Francess G. Halpenny (Toronto: University of Toronto Press, 2006).

48 United Kingdom, *Minutes of Proceeding of the Imperial Copyright Conference,* 3.

49 Ibid., 8.

50 Ibid., 5-8.

51 Ibid., 8.

52 Ibid., 46.

53 Ibid., 26.

54 Ibid.

55 Ibid., 4 and 12-15.

56 Ibid., 87.

57 Ibid., 9.

58 *Copyright Act (An Act Respecting Copyrights), 1875,* Articles 1 and 5.

59 *Berne Convention for the Protection of Literary and Artistic Works, Berlin Act of 13 November 1908* (Berne: Office of the International Union for the Protection of Literary and Artistic Works, 1908), Article 7.
60 United Kingdom, *Minutes of Proceeding of the Imperial Copyright Conference*, 41.
61 Ibid.
62 Ibid.
63 Ibid., 40.
64 Ibid., 176-77.
65 Ibid., 203 and 208.
66 *Berne Convention for the Protection of Literary and Artistic Works, Berlin Act of 13 November 1908*, Article 4.
67 United Kingdom, *Minutes of Proceeding of the Imperial Copyright Conference*, 60.
68 Ibid., 208.
69 Ibid.
70 Ibid., 57-58.
71 Ibid., 58.
72 Ibid., 207, Resolution 1.
73 Ibid., Resolution 2a.
74 Ibid., Resolution 2e.
75 Ibid., Resolution 2b.
76 Ibid., Resolution 2c.
77 Ibid., Resolution 2d.
78 Ibid., Resolution 3.
79 Ibid., Resolution 4b.
80 Ibid., Resolution 5.
81 Seville, *Internationalisation of Copyright Law*, 138-39.
82 Lord Crewe to Lord Grey, 27 July 1910, in LAC, RG25, vol. 1099, file 1910-21C, pt. 1.
83 The *Globe*, for example, simply reported that a "satisfactory arrangement" had been reached with regard to Canadian copyright. "Canadian Copyright: Satisfactory Arrangement at Conference in London," *Globe* (Toronto), 15 June 1910.
84 See discussion regarding the release of information about the conference in United Kingdom, *Minutes of Proceeding of the Imperial Copyright Conference*, 33 and 172-73. See also United Kingdom, *Imperial Copyright Conference 1910: Memorandum of the Proceedings*, Cd. 5272 (London: Eyre and Spottiswoode, 1910).
85 "Canada to Control Its Copyright Law," *Globe* (Toronto), 15 October 1910, 1.
86 Ibid.
87 "Foreign Copyright," *The Times* (of London), 14 October 1910, 6.
88 William Poulten to Lewis Harcourt, 24 October 1910; C.P. Lucas to William Poulten, 11 November 1910; Lewis Harcourt to Sydney Fisher, 29 April 1911, all in LAC, RG25, vol. 1099, file 1910-21C, pt. 2.
89 Canada, House of Commons, *Debates of the House of Commons, Third Session – Eleventh Parliament 1-2 George V., 1910-1911*, vol. 98 (Ottawa: C.H. Parmelee, 1910-11), 5.
90 Charles Murphy to Albert Grey, 1 April 1911; Early Grey to Lewis Harcourt, 5 April 1911; Albert Grey to Sydney Buxton, 3 May 1911, all in LAC, RG25, vol. 1099, file 1910-21C, pt. 2.
91 Canada, House of Commons, *Debates of the House of Commons, Third Session – Eleventh Parliament*, 7823.
92 "Canada to Control Its Copyright Law," 1.
93 Canada, House of Commons, *Debates of the House of Commons, First Session – Twelfth Parliament 2 George V., 1911-1912*, vol. 103 (Ottawa: C.H. Parmelee, 1911-12), 935-36.

94 *An Act to Amend and Consolidate the Law Relating to Copyright, 1911*, 1 and 2 Geo. V, c. 46.

95 Lewis Harcourt to Prince Arthur, 4 January 1912; G.R. Askworth to the Under-Secretary of State, Colonial Office, 22 December 1911, both in LAC, RG25, vol. 1118, file 98.

96 Lewis Harcourt to Prince Arthur, 19 April 1912, in LAC, ibid.

97 George O'Halloran to Under-Secretary of State for External Affairs, 10 February 1912; William Roche to Prince Arthur, 12 February 1912; Prince Arthur to the Board of Trade, 14 February 1912, all in LAC, ibid.

98 Canada, House of Commons, *Debates of the House of Commons, First Session – Twelfth Parliament*, 936.

99 *A Memorandum from the Authors' and Composers' Association of Canada, Urging the Adoption by Canada of the British Copyright Act of 1911*, n.d.; Thomas Hardy, President of the Incorporated Society of Authors, to Prime Minister Borden, n.d.; Authors' and Composers' Association of Canada to Prime Minister Borden, 12 February 1919, all in LAC, Prime Minister Borden fonds (MG26 H), microfilm reel C4375, items 92543, 92548, and 92567, respectively.

100 Robert Borden to C.J. Doherty, 8 January 1913; Robert Borden to Martin Burrell, 9 January 1913, both in LAC, ibid., items 92344 and 92345, respectively.

101 Albert Grey to Lewis Harcourt, 4 March 1911, in LAC, RG25, vol. 1099, file 1910-21C, pt. 2.

102 Ibid.

103 "The Canadian Copyright Bill," *The Times* (of London), 23 June 1911, 7.

104 Lewis Harcourt to Albert Grey, 31 March 1911; Edward Grey to F. Bertie, E. Goschen, R. Rodd, and E.W. Edward, 15 March 1911, all in LAC, RG25, vol. 1099, file 1910-21C, pt. 2.

105 Lewis Harcourt to Prince Arthur, 7 March 1912; Lewis Harcourt to Prince Arthur, 29 May 1912, both in LAC, RG25, vol. 1118, file 98.

106 Lewis Harcourt to Prince Arthur, 5 July 1912, in LAC, ibid. See also Board of Trade to [illegible], 27 August 1912; Bureau de l'Union internationale littéraires et artistiques, Le Director, to Th. W. Phillips, 13 August 1912, both in LAC, RG13 A-2, vol. 2361, file 1912-1494, pt. 2.

107 Lewis Harcourt to Prince Arthur, 25 November 1912, in LAC, RG25, vol. 1118, file 98.

108 Robert Borden to the Governor General in Council, 3 December 1912; Minute of the Privy Council No. 3384, 4 December 1912, both in LAC, ibid.

109 Prince Arthur to Lewis Harcourt, 6 December 1912; Prince Arthur to Lewis Harcourt, 9 December 1912, both in LAC, ibid.; *Protocole additionnel à la convention de Berne révisée du 13 novembre 1908* (Berne: Bureau de l'Union internationale littéraires et artistiques, 1914).

110 *Protocole additionnel à la convention de Berne*, ibid. See also Stephen P. Ladas, *The International Protection of Literary and Artistic Property*, vol. 1 (New York : Macmillan, 1938), 94-97.

111 United Kingdom, Order-in-Council No. 1135, 24 June 1912, in LAC, RG25, vol. 1118, file 98.

112 Lewis Harcourt to Prince Arthur, 27 May 1914, in LAC, RG25, vol. 1140, file 92 1913-1920.

113 Ibid., 54.

114 Ibid.

115 Ibid., 55.

116 Christopher May, "The World Intellectual Property Organization," *New Political Economy* 11, 3 (2006): 440.

Chapter 7: Copyright "Sovereignty," 1914-24

1   Lewis Harcourt to Prince Arthur, 27 May 1914, in Library and Archives Canada [LAC], RG25, vol. 1140, file 92 1913-1920.
2   Extract, Department of Agriculture to Department of External Affairs, 19 January 1915; Extract, Department of Agriculture to Department of External Affairs, 21 July 1915, both in LAC, ibid.
3   P.E. Ritchie, Memorandum "Re" Copyright, 2 February 1917, in LAC, Prime Minister Borden fonds (MG26 H), microfilm reel C4374, item 91647.
4   Norman Hillmer and J.L. Granatstein, *Empire to Umpire: Canada and the World to the 1990s* (Toronto: Copp Clark Longman, 1994), 51-54.
5   Ibid., 54-55.
6   Norman Hillmer and J.L. Granatstein, *For Better or for Worse: Canada and the United States into the Twenty-First Century* (Toronto: Nelson, 2005), 90-91.
7   Ibid., 91.
8   Ibid., 54-56.
9   Ibid., 89-90.
10 Hillmer and Granatstein, *Empire to Umpire*, 70.
11 Hillmer and Granatstein, *For Better or for Worse*, 90.
12 Canada, House of Commons, *Debates of the House of Commons, Fifth Session - Twelfth Parliament 5 George V., 1915*, vol. 119 (Ottawa: J. de Taché, 1915), 196-203.
13 P.E. Ritchie, Memorandum "Re" Copyright.
14 Letter to Justice about transfer of copyright from Department of Agriculture to Department of Trade and Commerce, in LAC, RG13, vol. 2158, file 1918-115.
15 Manjunath Pendakur, *Canadian Dreams and American Control: The Political Economy of the Canadian Film Industry* (Detroit: Wayne State University Press, 1990), 51.
16 Ibid., 79.
17 Therese Goulet, "The Canada-US Free Trade Agreement and the Retransmission of American Broadcasts in Canada," *Gonzaga Law Review* 24 (1988-89): 354.
18 Mary Vipond, "Canadian Nationalism and the Plight of Canadian Magazines in the 1920s," *Canadian Historical Review* 58, 1 (1977): 44.
19 Hillmer and Granatstein, *For Better or for Worse*, 102-4; see also Pendakur, *Canadian Dreams and American Control*, 49.
20 See, for example, LAC, RG25, vol. 1140, file 92, and RG25, vol. 1118, file 98-1912.
21 *A Memorandum from the Authors' and Composers' Association of Canada, Urging the Adoption by Canada of the British Copyright Act of 1911*, n.d.; Thomas Hardy, President of the Incorporated Society of Authors, to Prime Minister Borden, n.d.; Authors' and Composers' Association of Canada to Prime Minister Borden, 12 February 1919, all in LAC, Prime Minister Borden fonds (MG26 H), microfilm reel C4375, items 92543, 92548, and 92567, respectively.
22 Shelley S. Beal, "'La fin du pillage des auteurs': Louvigny de Montigny'sInternational Press Campaign for Authors' Rights in Canada," *Papers of the Canadian Bibliographical Society* 43, 1 (2005): 33-44.
23 *An Act to Amend and Consolidate the Law Relating to Copyright, 1911*, 1 and 2 Geo. V, c. 46, Articles 19 and 35; Victor Christian William Cavendish to Alfred Milner, 8 May 1919; Alfred Milner to Victor Christian William Cavendish, 21 April 1919, both in LAC, RG25, vol. 1140, file 92.
24 Alfred Milner to Victor Christian William Cavendish, 21 April 1919, in LAC, ibid.
25 Ibid.; Canada, Senate, *Debates of the Senate, Second Session - Thirteenth Parliament 9 George V., 1919* (Ottawa: J. de Labroquerie Taché, 1919), 152 and 641.

26 United Kingdom, Board of Trade, *Canadian Copyright Bill (Bill E.)*, forwarded to Victor Christian William Cavendish, 1 July 1919, in LAC, RG25, vol. 1140, file 92 1913-1920; *Berne Convention for the Protection of Literary and Artistic Works, Berlin Act of 13 November 1908* (Berne: Office of the International Union for the Protection of Literary and Artistic Works, 1908), Article 4.

27 United Kingdom, Board of Trade, *Canadian Copyright Bill (Bill E.)*, ibid.

28 F.C.T. O'Hara to W.M. Dickson, 2 June 1919, in LAC, RG20, vol. 91, file 22655, vol. 1.

29 F.C.T. O'Hara to Joseph Pope, 7 July 1919; L.H. Davies to Alfred Milner, 12 September 1919, both in LAC, RG25, vol. 1140, file 92 1913-1920.

30 Canada, Senate, *Debates of the Senate, Second Session – Thirteenth Parliament*, 641.

31 Canada, *The Canada Year Book 1921* (Ottawa: F.A. Acland, 1922), 96.

32 The 1921 census lists 1,117 artists and teachers of art, 138 painters (professional), 137 sculptors, and 880 authors and librarians. It also lists 25,630 employed in printing and bookbinding. Canada, *Census of Canada, 1921* (Ottawa: King's Printer, 1924-25), 22-35.

33 LAC, "The Virtual Gramophone: The Berliner Gram-o-phone Company of Canada," http://www.collectionscanada.gc.ca/gramophone/028011-3005-e.html.

34 Ibid.

35 Ibid.; LAC, "The Virtual Gramophone: Compo Company Limited," http://www.collectionscanada.gc.ca/gramophone/028011-3011-e.html.

36 LAC, "The Virtual Gramophone: Compo Company Limited."

37 LAC, "The Virtual Gramophone: The Berliner Gram-o-phone Company of Canada."

38 Lyn Harrington, *Syllables of Recorded Time: The Story of the Canadian Authors Association 1921-1981* (Toronto: Simon and Pierre, 1981), 19-27. See in particular 19, 21, and 27.

39 Beal, "'La fin du pillage des auteurs,'" 33-44.

40 See, for example, Morris Manley to George Foster, 12 March 1920, in LAC, RG20, vol. 91, file 22655, vol. 1.

41 See, for example, Prime Minister Meighen fonds (MG26 I), microfilm reel C3452, 052637-39.

42 See, for example, ibid., 052635-36; Vipond, "Canadian Nationalism," 45.

43 Sandra Alston et al., "History of the Book in Canada: Ontario Bibliography," http://www.hbic.library.utoronto.ca/fconfontariobib_en.htm.

44 Betty Nygaard King, "Songwriters and Songwriting (English Canada) before 1921," *Encyclopedia of Music in Canada*, http://www.thecanadianencyclopedia.com/; J. Laurent Thibault, "Canadian Manufacturers' Association," *Canadian Encyclopedia*, http://www.thecanadianencyclopedia.com/. See, for example, Prime Minister Borden fonds (MG26 H), microfilm reel C774.

45 See LAC, RG20, vol. 91, file 22655, vol. 1.

46 "Arthur Stringer Raps the Copyright Law," *Globe* (Toronto), 1 March 1919, in LAC, RG20, vol. 91, file 22655, vol. 1.

47 A bill was also introduced in March 1920 but did not proceed beyond first reading. Canada, House of Commons, *Debates of the House of Commons, Fourth Session – Thirteenth Parliament 10-11 George V., 1920*, vol. 141 (Ottawa: Thomas Mulvey, 1920), 751-52.

48 Canada, House of Commons, *Debates of the House of Commons, Fifth Session – Thirteenth Parliament 11-12 George V., 1921*, vol. 4 (Ottawa: F.A. Acland, 1921), 3833.

49 Ibid., 350.

50 Ibid., 3833; Canada, Senate, *Debates of the Senate, Fifth Session – Thirteenth Parliament 11-12 George V., 1921* (Ottawa: Thomas Mulvey, 1921), 639.

51 Canada, Senate, *Debates of the Senate, Fifth Session – Thirteenth Parliament*, 639.

52 Canada, House of Commons, *Debates of the House of Commons, Fifth Session – Thirteenth Parliament*, 3833.

53 Le gérant du consulat général de France to George Foster, 2 September 1920; G. Herbert Thring to F.C.T. O'Hara, 24 November 1920, both in LAC, RG20, vol. 91, file 22655, vol. 1. See also that file generally.

54 *An Act to Amend and Consolidate the Law Relating to Copyright, 1921*, 11-12 Geo. V, c. 24.

55 Canada, House of Commons, *Debates of the House of Commons, Fifth Session – Thirteenth Parliament*, 3834.

56 Ibid., 3845.

57 *An Act to Amend and Consolidate the Law Relating to Copyright, 1921*, Article 4(2).

58 Ibid.

59 Hillmer and Granatstein, *Empire to Umpire*, 77.

60 Hillmer and Granatstein, *For Better or for Worse*, 66.

61 Canada, House of Commons, *Debates of the House of Commons, Fifth Session – Thirteenth Parliament*, 3841.

62 Ibid., 3836; *An Act to Amend and Consolidate the Law Relating to Copyright, 1921*, Articles 13, 14, and 15.

63 *Copyright Act (An Act Respecting Copyrights), 1875*, 38 Vict., c. 88, Article 4(2).

64 There is no mention of which authors' association Rinfret belonged to. Canada, House of Commons, *Debates of the House of Commons, Fifth Session – Thirteenth Parliament*, 3836-37, 3842; Canada, Senate, *Debates of the Senate, Fifth Session – Thirteenth Parliament*, 648-49 and 654.

65 Canada, Senate, ibid., 642-43.

66 Canada, House of Commons, *Debates of the House of Commons, Fifth Session – Thirteenth Parliament*, 3841, 3847-49.

67 Canada, Senate, *Debates of the Senate, Fifth Session – Thirteenth Parliament*, 652.

68 Ibid.

69 Bureau de l'Union internationale pour la protection des oeuvres littéraires et artistiques, *Le droit d'auteur*, 15 April 1921.

70 Canada, Senate, *Debates of the Senate, Fifth Session – Thirteenth Parliament*, 638-39; *Le droit d'auteur*, ibid. See also *Le droit d'auteur*, 15 July 1921.

71 Canada, Senate, ibid., 640. See also B.K. Sandwell, "Copyright and the 'Decisions of Rome,'" *Canadian Forum* 11, 129 (1931): 330-31.

72 Ibid., 649.

73 Canada, House of Commons, *Debates of the House of Commons, Fifth Session – Thirteenth Parliament*, 3837.

74 Ibid., 3842.

75 Ibid., 3847.

76 *Le droit d'auteur*, 15 April 1921; Canada, Senate, *Debates of the Senate, Fifth Session – Thirteenth Parliament*, 638-39. A later issue of *Le droit d'auteur* stated that it had been referring on 15 April to the licensing regime for mechanical instruments, a different set of licensing provisions from the one under discussion here: "C'est cette catégorie [le nouveau régime aux instruments méchaniques] que nous avons eu en vue en traçant, dans le numéro du 15 avril dernier (p. 47), les quelques lignes sur les licences obligatoires prévues par le bill. Nous ne pouvoins alors nous prononcer sur les autres catégories de licences ..." This is confusing because the articles cited in the 15 April article appear to correspond to the compulsory licensing provisions for the domestic reprinting of books. *Le droit d'auteur*, 15 July 1921.

77 Canada, House of Commons, *Debates of the House of Commons, Fifth Session – Thirteenth Parliament*, 3837, 3838. James Lougheed, who was tasked with steering the bill through the Senate, made similar arguments. Canada, Senate, *Debates of the Senate, Fifth Session – Thirteenth Parliament*, 654.

78 Canada, House of Commons, ibid., 3838 and 3846-47.
79 Ibid., 3845.
80 The Magazine Publishers Association of Canada to Members of the House of Commons, 8 April 1924, in LAC, Prime Minister Meighen fonds (MG26 I), microfilm reel C3452, 052635-36.
81 Canada, House of Commons, *Debates of the House of Commons, Fifth Session – Thirteenth Parliament*, 3832-33.
82 Canada, Senate, *Debates of the Senate, Fifth Session – Thirteenth Parliament*, 661-62; *An Act to Amend and Consolidate the Law Relating to Copyright, 1921*, Article 18(2).
83 The British *Copyright Act* had no provisions for registration. Whereas the British act provided that "where proceedings are taken in respect of the infringement of the copyright in any work and the defendant in his defence alleges that he was not aware of the existence of the copyright in the work, the plaintiff shall not be entitled to any remedy other than an injunction or interdict in respect of the infringement other than if the defendant proves that at the date of the infringement he was not aware and had no reasonable ground for suspecting that copyright subsisted in the work" (Article 8), the Canadian act adds: "Provided that if at the date of the infringement the copyright in the work was duly registered under this Act, the defendant shall be deemed to have had reasonable ground for suspecting that copyright subsisted in the work" (Article 21); Canada, Senate, *Debates of the Senate, Fifth Session – Thirteenth Parliament*, 690-92; *An Act to Amend and Consolidate the Law Relating to Copyright, 1921*, Articles 21 and 36-39; *An Act to Amend and Consolidate the Law Relating to Copyright, 1911*, Article 8.
84 United Kingdom, *Minutes of Proceeding of the Imperial Copyright Conference, 1910*, in LAC, microfilm reels B-2392 to B-2393, 208.
85 Canada, Senate, *Debates of the Senate, Fifth Session – Thirteenth Parliament*, 691.
86 Ibid., 650.
87 Ibid.
88 Ibid.
89 Ibid.
90 Ibid., 695.
91 Canada, House of Commons, *Debates of the House of Commons, Fifth Session – Thirteenth Parliament*, 3847, 3850.
92 Ibid., 3847 and 3850; *Berne Convention for the Protection of Literary and Artistic Works, Berlin Act of 13 November 1908*.
93 Canada, Senate, *Debates of the Senate, Second Session – Fourteenth Parliament 13-14 George V., 1923* (Ottawa: F.A. Acland, 1923), 494, 568-69.
94 Ibid., 494, 559-60. According to *Le droit d'auteur*, Canada was a party to the 1897 additional protocol, but the same article notes that the Canadian and American press often treated the subject as though Canada had yet to join the Berne Union. *Le droit d'auteur*, 15 July 1921, 73-80.
95 Ibid., 84.
96 *Le droit d'auteur*, 15 July 1921, 73-80; Canada, House of Commons, *Debates of the House of Commons, Second Session – Fourteenth Parliament 13-14 George V., 1923*, vol. 155 (Ottawa: F.A. Acland, 1923), 2140.
97 *Le droit d'auteur*, 15 April 1921; Canada, Senate, *Debates of the Senate, Fifth Session – Thirteenth Parliament*, 638-39; Canada, House of Commons, ibid., 2140.
98 Ibid., 2288.
99 Ibid., 2291; Canada, Senate, *Debates of the Senate, Second Session – Fourteenth Parliament*, 471 and 495.

100 Canada, House of Commons, *Debates of the House of Commons, Second Session – Fourteenth Parliament*, 2142.
101 Hillmer and Granatstein, *Empire to Umpire*, 79.
102 Ibid., 80. For a discussion of the earlier Imperial Conferences and their history, see John Kendle, *The Colonial and Imperial Conferences, 1887-1911*, vol. 28 (London: Longmans, 1967).
103 Hillmer and Granatstein, *Empire to Umpire*, 80-81.
104 *An Act to Amend the Copyright Act, 1921, 1923*, 13-14 Geo. V, c. 10.
105 Approved Minute of the Privy Council, 27 July 1923, P.C. 1395, in LAC, RG25 G-1, vol. 1260, file 218, pt. 1.
106 Ibid.
107 *An Act to Amend and Consolidate the Law Relating to Copyright, 1911*, Article 25.
108 *Canada Gazette*, 29 December 1923. See also John McKeown, *Fox on Canadian Law of Copyright and Industrial Designs*, 4th ed. (Toronto: Carswell, 2003), 3-7.
109 *Canada Gazette*, ibid.
110 *London Gazette*, 14 December 1923, 8731, as cited in Victor Christian William Cavendish to Julian Hedworth George Byng, 5 January 1924, in LAC, RG25 G-1, vol. 1260, file 218, pt. 1; *A Proclamation by the President of the United States of America*, No. 1682, in LAC, RG25, vol. 4322, file 11996-4. See also Gordon F. Henderson, "Canadian Copyright Law in the Context of American-Canadian Relations," *Bulletin of the Copyright Society* 24, 6 (1977): 369-90.
111 "Without US Cooperation, Copyright Act of Canada Puts Her in Outlaw Class," *Globe* (Toronto), 3 January 1924, 10x; "No Hold-Up Caused to Copyright Pact," *Globe* (Toronto), 4 January 1924, 1.
112 *Note du Conseil fédéral addressée à tous les États membres de l'Union pour la protection des œuvres littéraires et artistiques*, 29 January 1924, in LAC, RG25 G-1, vol. 1260, file 218, pt. 1.
113 "The Dominion of Canada restricts the grant of copyright in accordance with the said protocol in regard to the United States of America, and the restrictions to which rights of authors who are subject to the jurisdiction of that country are subjected, are set forth in Sections 13, 14, 15 and 27 of the Copyright Act 1921." C.W. Orde to Milne Chreetan, 27 December 1923, in LAC, RG25 G-1, vol. 1260, file 218, pt. 1.
114 "Copyright Troubles Finally Adjusted: Canada at Last Adheres with Other Nations to the Berne Convention," *Globe* (Toronto), 18 March 1924, 2.
115 Harrington, *Syllables of Recorded Time*, 37.
116 Ibid., 36.
117 Ibid., 39.
118 *Extrait de correspondence (lettre de M. Louvigny de Montigny, du 9 juin 1924)*, in LAC, RG25 G-1, vol. 1260, file 218, pt. 1. A statement was eventually issued in the *Canada Gazette*, 15 March 1924, 3401.
119 Ibid.
120 Victor Christian William Cavendish to L.C.M.S. Amery, 8 April 1925, in LAC, RG25 G-1, vol. 1260, file 218, pt. 1.
121 Consulat Général de la République Française au Canada to O.D. Skelton, 30 July 1925, in LAC, RG25 G-1, vol. 1260, file 218, pt. 1.
122 Canada, House of Commons, *Debates of the House of Commons, Fifth Session – Thirteenth Parliament*, 3833.
123 *An Act to Amend the Copyright Act, 1921, 1923*.
124 Fisher died on 10 April 1921. "Fisher, Sydney," in *Dictionary of Canadian Biography*, vol. 15, edited by Francess G. Halpenny (Toronto: University of Toronto Press, 2006). Canada, House of Commons, *Debates of the House of Commons, Fifth Session – Thirteenth*

Parliament, 3833; Canada, Senate, *Debates of the Senate, Fifth Session – Thirteenth Parliament*, 640-41.
125 Canada, House of Commons, ibid., 3833.

Chapter 8: Copyright Internationalism

1 Canada, *The Canada Year Book 1932* (Ottawa: F.A. Acland, 1932).
2 The 1921 census lists 880 authors and librarians. It also lists 25,630 employed in printing and bookbinding. Canada, *Census of Canada, 1921* (Ottawa: King's Printer, 1924-25), 22-35. Also see Canada, *Census of Canada, 1931*, vol. 7 (Ottawa: King's Printer, 1936-42), table 50, 560-97.
3 Library and Archives Canada [LAC], "The Virtual Gramophone: Compo Company Limited," http://www.collectionscanada.gc.ca/gramophone/028011-3011-e.html.
4 Mary Vipond, "Canadian Nationalism and the Plight of Canadian Magazines in the 1920s," *Canadian Historical Review* 58, 1 (1977): 59.
5 "Copyright Session Busy with Jukebox Problems," *Boxoffice*, 19 February 1955, 93. See, for example, LAC, Prime Minister Mackenzie King fonds (MG26 J1), microfilm reel C2302, 128065.
6 See, for example, LAC, ibid., 129300 and 129966.
7 Wyndham Wise, "History of Ontario's Film Industry, 1896 to 1985," *Take One*, 22 June 2000, 20-35; Manjunath Pendakur, *Canadian Dreams and American Control: The Political Economy of the Canadian Film Industry* (Detroit: Wayne State University Press, 1990), 24.; LAC, Prime Minister Mackenzie King fonds (MG26 J1), microfilm reel C2316, 146798-806.
8 Canada, House of Commons, *Debates of the House of Commons, Second Session – Seventeenth Parliament 21-22 George V., 1931* (Ottawa: F.A. Acland, 1931), 2424.
9 Toretta, Italian Embassy at London, to Austen Chamberlain, 16 March 1927, in LAC, RG25, vol. 1490, file 1827-278, pt. 1.
10 Bureau de l'Union internationale pour la protection des oeuvres littéraires et artistiques to the Department of External Affairs, 3 March 1927 (referring to previous correspondence of 15 February 1927), in LAC, ibid.
11 A. Bordonaro, Italian Embassy, to Austen Chamberlain, 29 August 1927, in LAC, ibid.
12 Norman Hillmer and J.L. Granatstein, *For Better or for Worse: Canada and the United States into the Twenty-First Century* (Toronto: Nelson, 2005), 95.
13 Ibid., 105.
14 Memorandum of the Interdepartmental Committee on the Revision of the International Copyright Convention of 1908, Approved by Prime Minister August 15, 13 August 1927, in LAC, RG25, vol. 1490, file 1827-278, pt. 1.
15 *Paris Convention for the Protection of Industrial Property* (*Paris Convention*), 20 March 1883 (Berne: Office of the International Union for the Protection of Industrial Property, 1883).
16 One committee member did not concur with the recommendations of the report; rather, he wanted to see these matters left to the Department of External Affairs. Memorandum of the Interdepartmental Committee.
17 O.D. Skelton to Fritz Ostertag, 16 August 1927, in LAC, RG25 G-1, vol. 1260, file 218, pt. 1.
18 Bureau international de l'Union pour la protection de propriété industrielle to O.D. Skelton, 17 August 1927, in LAC, ibid.
19 F. Ostertag to O.D. Skelton, 1 November 1927, in LAC, ibid.
20 Secretary of State for External Affairs to Secretary of State for Dominion Affairs, 16 February 1928, in LAC, ibid.
21 G.H. Villiers to Claud F.W. Russell, 3 April 1928, in LAC, ibid.

22 Secretary of State for External Affairs to Secretary of State for Dominion Affairs, 27 March 1928, in LAC, RG25 G-1, vol. 1558, folder 45FP.
23 Conseil Fédéral Suisse to Minister of External Affairs, 27 April 1928, in LAC, RG25 G-1, vol. 1260, file 218, pt. 1.
24 O.D. Skelton to the Secretary of State for Dominion Affairs, 15 October 1928, in LAC, ibid.
25 Sam Ricketson and Jane Ginsburg, *International Copyright and Neighbouring Rights: The Berne Convention and Beyond*, 2nd ed. (London: Oxford University Press, 2006), 104.
26 Ibid.
27 Ibid.
28 Ibid.
29 On the shortcomings of the realist definition of state, see Darel E. Paul, "Sovereignty, Survival and the Westphalian Blind Alley in International Relations," *Review of International Studies* 25, 2 (1999): 217-31.
30 Hillmer and Granatstein, *For Better or for Worse*, 104.
31 Ibid., 105.
32 Ibid., 95-99.
33 Norman Hillmer and J.L. Granatstein, *Empire to Umpire: Canada and the World to the 1990s* (Toronto: Copp Clark Longman, 1994), 105.
34 Ibid., 106.
35 Macmillan Company of Canada to Prime Minister Mackenzie King, 13 February 1928, in LAC, RG25, vol. 1490, file 1827-278, pt. 1.
36 Canadian Manufacturers' Association to Prime Minister Mackenzie King, 28 February 1928, in LAC, Prime Minister Mackenzie King fonds (MG26 J1), microfilm reel C2302, 129300; Canadian Authors' Association to Prime Minister Mackenzie King, 13 April 1928, in LAC, ibid., microfilm reel C2303, 129966; Macmillan Company of Canada to Prime Minister Mackenzie King, 13 February 1928, in LAC, RG25, vol. 1490, file 1827-278, pt. 1.
37 Canadian Manufacturers' Association to Prime Minister Mackenzie King, ibid.
38 Memorandum for the Prime Minister: Copyright Conference at Rome, 21 February 1928, in LAC, RG25-A-2, vol. 765, file 300 (microfilm reel T-1768).
39 O.D. Skelton, Memorandum for the Prime Minister, 11 April 1928, in LAC, RG25, vol. 1490, file 1827-278, pt. 1.
40 Memorandum for the Prime Minister: Copyright Conference at Rome; Skelton, ibid. Jean Désy was one of the very few officers employed in the Department of External Affairs; he was appointed in 1925. J.L. Granatstein, *The Ottawa Men: The Civil Service Mandarins, 1935-1957* (Toronto: Oxford University Press, 1982), 39.
41 Thomas L. Richard, Acting Commissioner of Patents, to Under-Secretary of State for External Affairs, 27 January 1928; William Lyon Mackenzie King, Memo to His Excellency the Governor-General-in-Council, 20 April 1928, both in LAC, RG25, vol. 1490, file 1827-278, pt. 1.
42 William Lyon Mackenzie King, Memo to His Excellency the Governor-General-in-Council, 20 April 1928, ibid.; Granatstein, *Ottawa Men*, 39.
43 "Full powers" is a document given by the authority of the state designating a person or group of people to represent the state in international negotiations, such as the ability to adopt the text of an international agreement or to agree that the state be bound to an international agreement. Secretary of State for External Affairs to Secretary of State for Dominion Affairs, 20 April 1928, in LAC, RG25, vol. 1490, file 1827-278, pt. 1.
44 Skelton, Memorandum for the Prime Minister, 11 April 1928.
45 R.H. Lee Martin, managing director of the Musical Protective Society of Canada, and Blake Robertson (of the Fair and Exhibition Associations of Canada: Canada, House of Commons, *Debates of the House of Commons, Second Session – Seventeenth Parliament,*

2405) attended and called on the Canadian delegates. William Boosey, chairman of the English Performing Rights Society, also called on the Canadian delegates. See LAC, RG25 G-1, vol. 1491, file 278, pt. B.

46 L.S. Amery to Governor General Viscount Willingdon, 27 April 1927, in LAC, RG25, vol. 1490, file 1827-278, pt. 1.

47 Office of the High Commissioner to O.D. Skelton, 18 April 1928, in LAC, ibid.

48 Granatstein, *Ottawa Men,* 23-24.

49 Ibid.,29-35.

50 Ibid., 30.

51 Ibid., 29-30.

52 Fernand Rinfret, Instructions to the Canadian Delegates to the Rome Conference on Copyright, 25 April 1928, in LAC, RG25, vol. 1490, file 1827-278, pt. 1.

53 Désy took care of most of the communication and writing related to the conference.

54 *Actes de la conférence réunie à rome du 7 mai au 2 juin 1928* (Berne: Bureau de l'Union internationale pour la protection des oeuvres littéraires et artistiques, 1929), 131-39.

55 Name of organization translated by author. Ibid.

56 Ibid.

57 W. Harrison Moore, *Report of the Australian Delegate,* 4 July 1928, 3, in LAC, RG25 G-1, vol. 1491, file 278, pt. 3.

58 Ibid., 4.

59 Ibid.

60 Ibid.

61 *Actes de la conférence réunie à rome du 7 mai au 2 juin 1928,* 155.

62 Moore, *Report of the Australian Delegate,* 3.

63 Philippe Roy and Jean Désy, English translation of the *Report of the Canadian Delegates to the International Conference for the Protection of Literary and Artistic Works Held at Rome, May 7 to June 2, 1928,* 11, in LAC, RG25 G-1, vol. 1491, file 278, pt. 3.

64 Moore, *Report of the Australian Delegate,* 4.

65 Sydney Chapman, William Smith Jarratt, and Alfred James Martin, *Report of the British Delegates,* 5 September 1928, 1-2, in LAC, RG25 G-1, vol. 1491, file 278, pt. 3.

66 *Note verbale,* 22 December 1927, in LAC, RG25, vol. 1490, file 1827-278, pt. 1.

67 Moore, *Report of the Australian Delegate,* 11.

68 *Berne Convention for the Protection of Literary and Artistic Works, Rome Act of 2 June 1928* (Berne: Office of the International Union for the Protection of Literary and Artistic Works, 1928), Article 2*bis.*

69 Moore, *Report of the Australian Delegate,* 5-6. See also Chapman et al., *Report of the British Delegates,* 11-12.

70 Chapman et al. ibid., 12.

71 Moore, *Report of the Australian Delegate,* 6.

72 Romania, "Law on Literary and Artistic Property of 28 June 1923," *Le droit d'auteur* (1924): 25ff; Italy, "Decree No. 1950, Dispositions on the Rights of the Author of 7 November 1925," *Le droit d'auteur* (1926): 2 ff; Poland, "Law Relating to the Rights of the Author of 29 March 1926," *Le droit d'auteur* (1926): 133ff. As cited in Elizabeth Adeney, "Moral Rights: A Brief Excursion into Canadian History," *Intellectual Property Journal* 15, 1/3 (2001): 211.

73 Adeney, "Moral Rights," 205-39.

74 *Berne Convention for the Protection of Literary and Artistic Works, Berlin Act of 13 November 1908* (Berne: Office of the International Union for the Protection of Literary and Artistic Works, 1908), Article 9.

75 Ibid.; *Berne Convention for the Protection of Literary and Artistic Works, Rome Act of 2 June 1928,* Article 9.

76 Roy and Désy, *Report of the Canadian Delegates*, 5-6. See also Chapman et al., *Report of the British Delegates*, 16.
77 Moore, *Report of the Australian Delegate*, 5-6. See also Chapman et al., ibid., 4 and 6.
78 Moore, ibid., 5-6.
79 Ibid.
80 *Berne Convention for the Protection of Literary and Artistic Works, Rome Act of 2 June 1928*, Articles 2 and 2*bis*.
81 Ibid.
82 Ibid., Articles 25 and 27; also see Ricketson and Ginsburg, *International Copyright and Neighbouring Rights*, 1083.
83 Ricketson and Ginsburg, ibid., 107 and 1084.
84 *Berne Convention for the Protection of Literary and Artistic Works, Rome Act of 2 June 1928*, Article 27.
85 *Berne Convention for the Protection of Literary and Artistic Works, Paris Act of 4 May 1896* (Berne: Office of the International Union for the Protection of Literary and Artistic Works, 1896), Article 1; *Berne Convention for the Protection of Literary and Artistic Works, Rome Act of 2 June 1928*, Article 25 (3); Ricketson and Ginsburg, *International Copyright and Neighbouring Rights*, 107.
86 Roy and Désy, *Report of the Canadian Delegates*, 9; *Actes de la conférence réunie à rome du 7 mai au 2 juin 1928*, 308.
87 Moore, *Report of the Australian Delegate*, 10.
88 Roy and Désy, *Report of the Canadian Delegates*, 9; See also Chapman et al., *Report of the British Delegates*, 9-10, and *Actes de la conférence réunie à Rome du 7 mai au 2 juin 1928*, 197.
89 *Actes de la conférence réunie à Rome du 7 mai au 2 juin 1928*, 197.
90 Moore, *Report of the Australian Delegate*, 7.
91 Ibid.
92 Ibid.
93 Ibid.
94 Chapman et al., *Report of the British Delegates*, 18.
95 "Ordre public" is the term used in Chapman et al., ibid., 18-19.
96 Moore, *Report of the Australian Delegate*, 8.
97 Chapman et al., *Report of the British Delegates*, 19-20.
98 Moore, *Report of the Australian Delegate*, 8.
99 Ibid.
100 Ibid.
101 Ibid.
102 Chapman et al., *Report of the British Delegates*, 17.
103 Ibid., 18.
104 Ibid.
105 Ibid.
106 Ibid.
107 Ibid.
108 Ibid.; Alternative Proposals: C.D.A. 90, in LAC, RG25 G-1, vol. 1491, file 278, pt. B.
109 Moore, *Report of the Australian Delegate*, 8-9; *Berne Convention for the Protection of Literary and Artistic Works, Rome Act of 2 June 1928*, Article 11*bis*.
110 Chapman et al., *Report of the British Delegates*, 20.
111 Ibid., 1-2; *Actes de la conférence réunie à rome du 7 mai au 2 juin 1928*, 234-35.
112 *An Act to Amend and Consolidate the Law Relating to Copyright, 1921*, 11-12 Geo. V, c. 24, Article 3(4).

113   Chapman et al., *Report of the British Delegates*, 1-2. See also Moore, *Report of the Australian Delegate*, 9.
114   Hillmer and Granatstein, *For Better or for Worse*, 101.
115   United Kingdom, *Imperial Conference, 1926: Summary of Proceedings*. Cmd. 2768 (London: His Majesty's Stationery Office, 1926); Memo drafted by Great Britain's delegation, B, in LAC, RG25 G-1, vol. 1491, file 278, pt. B.
116   United Kingdom, ibid., 28-29.
117   Roy and Désy, Confidential Memo for the Prime Minister (Secretary of State) on Certain Inter-Imperial Aspects of the Rome Conference on Copyright, 17 July 1928, 3, in LAC, RG25 G-1, vol. 1491, file 278, pt. 3.
118   Ibid., 3-4; Alternative Proposals: C.D.A. 34 and C.D.A. 38, in LAC, RG25 G-1, vol. 1491, file 278, pt. B.
119   Roy and Désy, ibid., 3-4.
120   Hillmer and Granatstein, *Empire to Umpire*, 100.
121   Ibid.
122   Roy and Désy, Confidential Memo for the Prime Minister, 4; Alternative Proposals: C.D.A. 49, in LAC, RG25 G-1, vol. 1491, file 278, pt. B.
123   *Paris Convention for the Protection of Industrial Property, The Hague Act of 6 November 1925* (Berne: Office of the International Union for the Protection of Industrial Property, 1925).
124   Roy and Désy, Confidential Memo for the Prime Minister, 7.
125   Ibid., 5.
126   Ibid.
127   Ibid., 6.
128   *Actes de la conférence réunie à Rome du 7 mai au 2 juin 1928*, 308; Declaration made by Mr. MacWhite, delegate of the Irish Free State, at the closing session of the conference for the protection of copyright, Rome (translation), in LAC, RG25, vol. 1490, file 1827-278, pt. 2. For background on the Irish Free State's relationship to the *Berne Convention* leading up to the Rome conference, see Ricketson and Ginsburg, *International Copyright and Neighbouring Rights*, 1104.
129   Rinfret, Instructions to the Canadian Delegates to the Rome Conference on Copyright, 25 April 1928.
130   Moore, *Report of the Australian Delegate*, 11.
131   S.J. Chapman to Director of the International Union for Literary and Artistic Works, 8 November 1928; Philippe Roy to O.D. Skelton, 26 December 1928, both in LAC, RG25 G-1, vol. 1491, file 278, pt. 3.
132   "Les importantes résolutions: Premier Congrès international: Sociétés d'Auteurs et Compositeurs" (author's translation; name of publication not noted; no date), in LAC, RG25, vol. 1490, file 1827-278, pt. 1.
133   Jean Désy to H.H. Wrong, First Secretary, Canadian Legation, Washington, 4 July 1928; Wrong to Désy, 9 July 1928, both in LAC, RG25 G-1, vol. 1491, file 278, pt. 3.
134   Roy and Désy, *Report of the Canadian Delegates*, 10-11.
135   Memorandum on the Revision of the International Copyright Convention of 1908, 13 August 1927, in LAC, RG25, vol. 1490, file 1827-278, pt. 1.
136   "Copyright Discussed at Authors' Meeting," *Globe* (Toronto), 9 July 1928, 3; "Authors' Executive Meets in Toronto: National Body Hears Report of Berne Convention on Copyright Laws," *Globe* (Toronto), 22 October 1928, 1.
137   Ricketson and Ginsburg, *International Copyright and Neighbouring Rights*, 110.
138   Roy and Désy, *Report of the Canadian Delegates*, 4.

139 Ibid., 3-4.
140 Ibid., 11.
141 Thomas Mulvey, Under-Secretary of State, to the Secretary of State, External Affairs, 23 July 1928; O.D. Skelton, Under-Secretary of State for External Affairs, to Under-Secretary of State, 26 July 1928, both in LAC, RG25, vol. 1521, file 669.
142 Canada, House of Commons, *Debates of the House of Commons, Second Session – Sixteenth Parliament 18 George V., 1928*, vol. 3 (Ottawa: F.A. Acland, 1928), 4068.
143 Ibid., vol. 2, 1978.
144 *Berne Convention for the Protection of Literary and Artistic Works, Rome Act of 2 June 1928*, Articles 11 and 11*bis*.
145 *Canadian Performing Right Society Ltd. v. Famous Players Canadian Corporation Ltd.*, [1927] 2 D.L.R. 928; 60 O.L.R. 280 (Ont. S.C.).
146 *Canadian Performing Right Society Ltd. v. Famous Players Canadian Corporation Ltd.*, [1929] 2 D.L.R. 1; A.C. 456.
147 LAC, Prime Minister Mackenzie King fonds (MG26 J1), microfilm reel C2316, 146798-806.
148 *Canadian Performing Right Society Ltd. v. Famous Players Canadian Corporation Ltd.*, 1927.
149 Ibid.; *Canadian Performing Right Society Ltd. v. Famous Players Canadian Corporation Ltd.*, 1929.
150 *Canadian Performing Right Society Ltd. v. Famous Players Canadian Corporation Ltd.*, 1929.
151 Ibid.
152 Lord Lovat to Secretary of State for External Affairs, 26 July 1927, in LAC, RG25 G-1, vol. 1558, folder 45FP.
153 Canada, House of Commons, *Debates of the House of Commons, Third Session – Sixteenth Parliament 19-20 George V., 1929*, vol. 1 (Ottawa: F.A. Acland, 1929), 354.
154 Office of the High Commissioner for the United Kingdom to Secretary of State for External Affairs, 3 May 1929; Office of the High Commissioner for the United Kingdom to Secretary of State for External Affairs, 7 June 1929; Secretary of State for Dominion Affairs to Secretary of State for External Affairs, 6 December 1929, all in LAC, RG25 G-1, vol. 1558, folder 45FP; Parsfield to Secretary of State for External Affairs, 30 October 1929; Office of the High Commissioner for the United Kingdom, Ottawa, to W.H. Walker, Department of External Affairs, 27 February 1930, both in LAC, RG25 G-1, vol. 1491, file 278, pt. 3.
155 Canada, House of Commons, *Debates of the House of Commons, Second Session – Seventeenth Parliament 21-22 George V., 1931*, vol. 1 (Ottawa: F.A. Acland, 1931), 104, 899-903.
156 Ibid., 902.
157 In this case, Rempel is referring specifically to the United States. Roy Rempel, *Dreamland: How Canada's Pretend Foreign Policy Has Undermined Sovereignty* (Montreal and Kingston: McGill-Queen's University Press, 2006).
158 Canada, Royal Commission on Patents, Copyright, Trade Marks and Industrial Designs, *Report on Copyright* (Ottawa: Supply and Services Canada, 1957), 18.
159 Hillmer and Granatstein, *For Better or for Worse*, 108.
160 *Radio Broadcasting Act*, S.C. 1932, 22-23 Geo. V, c. 51; Hillmer and Granatstein, bid., 103-4.
161 LAC, Prime Minister Mackenzie King fonds (MG26 J1), microfilm reel C2316, 146798-806.
162 Ibid., 146801-2.
163 Ibid., 146802.

164 Canada, Senate, *Debates of the Senate, Second Session – Seventeenth Parliament 21-22 George V., 1931* (Ottawa: F.A. Acland, 1931), 221-23; *An Act to Amend the Copyright Act, 1931*, 21-22 Geo. V, c. 8, sections 9 and 10.
165 *An Act to Amend the Copyright Act, 1931*, section 10; Pendakur, *Canadian Dreams and American Control*, 85.
166 *An Act to Amend the Copyright Act, 1931*, section 10.
167 Ibid., sections 2(3), 3, 6, and 10.
168 Canada, House of Commons, *Debates of the House of Commons, Third Session – Sixteenth Parliament*, 2309.
169 Ibid., 2401.
170 Ibid., 2410.
171 Ibid., 2411-17.
172 Ibid., 2417, 2423-436.
173 LAC, Prime Minister Mackenzie King fonds (MG26 J1), microfilm reel C2316, 146799-801.
174 Ibid., 2410.
175 Ibid., 2423.
176 Ibid., 2438.
177 *Berne Convention for the Protection of Literary and Artistic Works, Rome Act of 2 June 1928*, Article 28.
178 "Copyright Debate Retards Commons: Budget Discussion Stands Over, Pending Disposal of Controversial Bill," *Globe* (Toronto), 9 June 1931, 1.
179 Canada, Senate, *Debates of the Senate, Second Session – Seventeenth Parliament*, 223.
180 Ibid., 221-23.
181 Secretary of State for External Affairs to Secretary of State for Dominion Affairs, telegram, 12 June 1931; Minute of the Privy Council No. 1390, 12 June 1931; also see Secretary of State for External Affairs to Secretary of State for Dominion Affairs, telegram, 16 June 1931, all in LAC, RG103, vol. 4, file 5-3-2-5.
182 "Authors Criticize New Copyright Act: Seeking Its Repeal," *Globe* (Toronto), 26 June 1931, 1.
183 *Statute of Westminster, 1931*, 22 Geo. V, c. 4; Paul, "Sovereignty, Survival," 220. Areas of British control would remain. As Paul notes: "Yet prior to 1939, none of the British Dominions possessed a recognized right to declare neutrality in a British war. Until 1947, the British Privy Council was the highest Canadian court of appeal and Canada was without its own passports or even citizenship. Until 1952 the Canadian Governor General was always a member of British royalty, not a Canadian. Even up until the 'patriation' of the Canadian constitution in 1982, the British parliament passed all Canadian constitutional legislation." See also Hillmer and Granatstein, *Empire to Umpire*, 115.
184 *Berne Convention for the Protection of Literary and Artistic Works, Rome Act of 2 June 1928*, Article 9.
185 Ibid.
186 *Gribble v. Manitoba Free Press Co.*, [1931] 3 W.W.R. 570 (Man. C.A.).
187 *Berne Convention for the Protection of Literary and Artistic Works, Rome Act of 2 June 1928*, Article 1; *Gribble v. Manitoba Free Press Co.* at 7.
188 Canada, Commission to Investigate Whether or Not the Canadian Performing Right Society Limited Is Complying with the Terms and Conditions of the Copyright Amendment Act, 1931, in Relation to Certain Radio Broadcasting Stations in Alberta, *Report* (N.p., 1932); Canada, Royal Commission Appointed to Investigate the Activities of the Canadian Performing Rights Society, and Similar Societies, *Report* (Toronto: n.p., 1935).

189 Canada, Royal Commission Appointed to Investigate the Activities of the Canadian Performing Rights Society, and Similar Societies, ibid., 49.
190 *An Act to Amend the Copyright Amendment Act, 1931, 1936,* 1 Ed. VIII, c. 28, sections 10A, 10B, and 10C.
191 Canada, Royal Commission Appointed to Investigate the Activities of the Canadian Performing Rights Society, and Similar Societies, *Report,* 5 (emphasis in original).

Chapter 9: New Directions, 1936-67

1 Norman Hillmer and J.L. Granatstein, *Empire to Umpire: Canada and the World to the 1990s* (Toronto: Copp Clark Longman, 1994), 115.
2 By 1967, American imports to Canada totalled $7.9 billion, whereas British imports totalled only $619 million; Canadian exports to the United States amounted to $7.1 billion, compared with only $1.2 billion to Britain; 81 percent of foreign investment in Canada was American, with only 10 percent British. Norman Hillmer and J.L. Granatstein, *For Better or for Worse: Canada and the United States into the Twenty-First Century* (Toronto: Nelson, 2005), 232.
3 The opening of the Thousand Islands bridge between New York and Ontario in 1938 was seen as a symbol of the growing bond between the two countries, and President Roosevelt declared on the same day that the United States would defend Canada in the event of a crisis. Ibid., 115.
4 Ibid., 160-61.
5 Ibid., 190-91.
6 Ibid.; Stephen Azzi, "Magazines and the Canadian Dream – The Struggle to Protect Canadian Periodicals 1955-1965," *International Journal* 54 (1998): 502-23.
7 Hillmer and Granatstein, *Empire to Umpire,* 191.
8 Ibid., 151.
9 J.L. Granatstein, *The Ottawa Men: The Civil Service Mandarins, 1935-1957* (Toronto: Oxford University Press, 1982), 92; Hillmer and Granatstein, *For Better or for Worse,* 154-55.
10 Hillmer and Granatstein, ibid., 162.
11 Granatstein, *Ottawa Men,* 132-33.
12 Ibid., 133.
13 Herman Voaden, "Cultural Challenge of UNESCO," *Globe and Mail,* 18 January 1947, 10.
14 Canada, *The Canada Year Book 1952-53* (Ottawa: Queen's Printer, 1953), 128.
15 The 1921 census lists 1,117 artists and teachers of art, 138 painters (professional), 137 sculptors, and 880 authors and librarians. Canada, *Census of Canada, 1921* (Ottawa: King's Printer, 1924-25), 22-35. The 1951 census gives 3,786 commercial artists, 1,110 artists (except commercial) and art teachers, and 7,217 authors, editors, and journalists. Canada, *Census of Canada, 1951,* vol. 4 (Ottawa: Queen's Printer, 1953-55), 11-1 to 11-15.
16 Louis Applebaum, "CAPAC," *Encyclopedia of Music in Canada,* http://www.thecanadian encyclopedia.com/.
17 "PRO Canada/SDE Canada," *Encyclopedia of Music in Canada,* http://www.thecanadian encyclopedia.com/.
18 "History of the CLC," Canadian League of Composers, http://www.clc-lcc.ca/.
19 ACTRA, http://www.actra.ca/.
20 Canadian Association of Broadcasters, http://www.cab-acr.ca/.
21 Canadian Music Publishers Association, http://www.musicpublishercanada.ca/.
22 "History," Canadian Conference of the Arts, http://www.ccarts.ca/. The Canadian Arts Council, later the Canadian Conference of the Arts, is not to be confused with the Canada

Council for the Arts (Canada Council). The former contributed to the creation of the latter.

23 See Library and Archives Canada [LAC], RG25, vol. 10902, file 55-19-1-ICC, pt. 1-1; RG25, vol. 10904, file 55-19-4-BERNE-UCC-1969, vol. 7; and RG25, vol. 10904, file 55-19-4-BERNE UCC-1969, vol. 2.

24 Sam Ricketson and Jane Ginsburg, *International Copyright and Neighbouring Rights: The Berne Convention and Beyond,* 2nd ed. (London: Oxford University Press, 2006), 111-12.

25 P. Leigh-Smith (for the Secretary of State) to His Excellency Baron de Cartier de Marchienne, 20 April 1936, in LAC, RG25 G-1, vol. 1657, file 222.

26 *Berne Convention for the Protection of Literary and Artistic Works, Brussels Act of 26 June 1948* (Berne: International Bureau for the Union for the Protection of Literary and Artistic Works, 1948), Article 7; Ricketson and Ginsburg, *International Copyright and Neighbouring Rights,* 116.

27 *Berne Convention,* ibid., Article 10(1); Ricketson and Ginsburg, ibid., 116-17.

28 Under the 1928 *Rome Act,* the right in public performance was protected only insofar as it was recognized under national law. *Berne Convention,* ibid., Article 11; Ricketson and Ginsburg, ibid., 117.

29 *Berne Convention,* ibid., Article 11*bis;* Ricketson and Ginsburg, ibid.

30 *Berne Convention,* ibid., Article 27*bis;* Ricketson and Ginsburg, ibid., 118.

31 *Documents de la conférence réunie à Bruxelles du 5 au 26 juin 1948* (Berne: Bureau de l'Union internationale pour la protection des oeuvres littéraires et artistiques, 1951), 55; Biography, 30 July 1949, in LAC, RG32, vol. 318, file "Doré, Victor."

32 *Documents de la conférence réunie à Bruxelles,* 55.

33 *Berne Convention for the Protection of Literary and Artistic Works, Brussels Act of 26 June 1948,* 67.

34 Ibid., 88 (Sous-commission pour la radiodiffusion et les instruments méchaniques).

35 Ibid.

36 Ibid., 89.

37 Arpad Bogsch, *The First Twenty-Five Years of the World Intellectual Property Organization from 1967 to 1992* (Geneva: International Bureau of Intellectual Property, 1992); *Documents de la conférence réunie à Bruxelles,* 426 and 585; Ricketson and Ginsburg, *International Copyright and Neighbouring Rights,* 119.

38 Memorandum for the Under-Secretary of State, 13 October 1954, 4, in LAC, RG103, vol. 4, file 5-3-2-1, pt. 1(1).

39 "Authors who are not nationals of one of the countries of the Union, and who first publish their works in one of those countries, shall enjoy in that country the same rights as native authors, and in the other countries of the Union the rights granted by this Convention." *Berne Convention for the Protection of Literary and Artistic Works, Brussels Act of 26 June 1948.*

40 *Documents de la conférence réunie à Bruxelles,* 181.

41 Ibid.

42 Ibid., 204-5.

43 *Berne Convention for the Protection of Literary and Artistic Works, Brussels Act of 26 June 1948,* Article 7(2).

44 Ibid., Article 6.

45 *Documents de la conférence réunie à Bruxelles,* 182.

46 Ibid., 194-95.

47 *Berne Convention for the Protection of Literary and Artistic Works, Brussels Act of 26 June 1948,* Article 6*bis;* Ricketson and Ginsburg, *International Copyright and Neighbouring Rights,* 116.

48 *Documents de la conférence réunie à Bruxelles*, 173.
49 *Berne Convention for the Protection of Literary and Artistic Works, Brussels Act of 26 June 1948*, Article 4(4).
50 *Documents de la conférence réunie à Bruxelles*, 420.
51 *Berne Convention for the Protection of Literary and Artistic Works, Brussels Act of 26 June 1948*, Article 31.
52 Ricketson and Ginsburg, *International Copyright and Neighbouring Rights*, 119.
53 *Documents de la conférence réunie à Bruxelles*, 82.
54 Ibid., 204-5.
55 *Berne Convention for the Protection of Literary and Artistic Works, Brussels Act of 26 June 1948*, Article 28.
56 C. Stein, Under-Secretary of State, to the Under-Secretary of State for External Affairs, 9 June 1949, in LAC, RG103, vol. 4, file 5-3-2-2.
57 Quoted in Joseph S. Dubin, "The Universal Copyright Convention," *California Law Review* 42, 1 (1954): 119.
58 Gerald R. Gibbons, "The Compulsory License System of the Universal Copyright Convention," *Duke Bar Journal* 6, 1 (1956).
59 *Universal Copyright Convention, Geneva Act of 6 September 1952* (Geneva: UNESCO, 1952), Article 5.
60 Canadian Embassy, Berne, to Under-Secretary of State for External Affairs, 5 March 1954, in LAC, RG103, vol. 4, file 5-3-2-4.
61 *Universal Copyright Convention*, Article 17 and declaration.
62 On this point, see C.F. Johnson, "The Origins of the Stockholm Protocol," *Bulletin of the Copyright Society of the USA* 18, 91 (1970): 92.
63 "Information for Delegates," in LAC, RG25, vol. 8376, file 10884-30-40, pt. 1.
64 Summary of Cabinet meeting, 27 June 1952, in LAC, RG25, vol. 6467, file 5582-U-40. See also generally LAC, RG25, vol. 8376, file 10884-30-40, pt. 1; Charles Stein to Escott Reid, 20 May 1952, in LAC, RG25, vol. 6467, file 5582-U-40. See also generally LAC, RG25, vol. 8376, file 10884-30-40, pt. 1, regarding Beckett's participation and arrangements for the delegates. Also see *Records of the Inter-Governmental Copyright Conference, Geneva, 18 August – 6 September 1952* (Paris: UNESCO, 1955).
65 Summary of Cabinet meeting, 27 June 1952, ibid.
66 *Records of the Inter-Governmental Copyright Conference, Geneva, 18 August – 6 September 1952* (Paris: UNESCO, 1955), 148, 150, and 338.
67 Ibid., 338. See also Kelsey Martin Mott, "The Relationship between the *Berne Convention* and the *Universal Copyright Convention:* Historical Background and Development of Article XVII of the U.C.C. and Its Appendix Declaration," *IDEA: The Patent, Trademark, and Copyright Journal of Research and Education* 11, 3 (1967): 319 and 322.
68 Victor Doré to Under-Secretary of State for External Affairs, 17 September 1952, in LAC, RG25, vol. 6467, file 5582-U-40, and RG25, vol. 8376, file 10884-30-40, pt. 1.
69 Canada, Senate, *Proceedings of the Standing Committee on External Relations to Whom Was Referred the Universal Copyright Convention Signed by Canada in Geneva 1952 and Protocol 3 thereto* (Ottawa: Roger Dunamel, 1962) in LAC, RG103, vol. 6, file 5-3-5-2, pt. 2.
70 Ibid.
71 Memorandum, 13 February 1956, in LAC, RG25, vol. 6467, file 5582-U-40.
72 Ibid.
73 Bureau de l'Union internationale pour la protection des oeuvres littéraires et artistiques, *Le droit d'auteur.*
74 See generally LAC, RG103, vol. 4, file 5-3-2-2, October 1948 through June 1949.

75 Under-Secretary of State for External Affairs A.D.P. Heeney to Under-Secretary of State Charles Stein, 26 July 1951, and reply, 14 August 1951, in LAC, RG103, vol. 4, file 5-3-2-1, pt. 1(1). See also RG103, vol. 4, file 5-3-2-3.

76 Memorandum for the Under-Secretary of State, 13 October 1954, in LAC, RG103, vol. 4, file 5-3-2-1, pt. 1(1).

77 Ibid.

78 Ibid.

79 Roch Pinard, Secretary of State, to Jacques Secrétan, 28 January 1955, in LAC, RG103, vol. 8, file 5-3-11-1, pt. 1. See handwritten note on file in LAC, RG103, vol. 4, file 5-3-2-4, and Memorandum, Department of External Affairs, 24 March 1954, in LAC, RG25, vol. 6467, file 5582-U-40.

80 Memorandum for the Under-Secretary of State, 13 October 1954, in LAC, RG103, vol. 4, file 5-3-2-1, pt. 1(1).

81 Canadian Embassy, Berne, to Under-Secretary of State for External Affairs, 11 February 1954, in LAC, RG103, vol. 4, file 5-3-2-4 1954.

82 Memorandum for the Under-Secretary of State, 13 October 1954.

83 Ambassador G.L. Magann to Jacques Secrétan, 16 February 1955, in LAC, RG103, vol. 4, file 5-3-2-1, pt. 1(1).

84 Charles Stein to Commissioner of Patents, 20 March 1958; Charles Stein, Under-Secretary of State, to Under-Secretary of State for External Affairs, 16 April 1956, both in LAC, RG103, vol. 4, file 5-3-2-1, pt. 1(2).

85 Jacques Secrétan to J.W.T. Michael, Commissioner of Patents, 8 May 1958, in LAC, ibid.

86 Burbridge for the Under-Secretary of State for External Affairs to Under-Secretary of State, 5 July 1951, in LAC, RG103, vol. 4, file 5-3-2-2.

87 In February 1954, Under-Secretary of State Stein inquired as to the status of the issue, noting that he had nothing on file regarding the issue since the 1951 discussions. Charles Stein to Assistant Under-Secretary of State W.P.J. O'Meara, 1 February 1954, in LAC, ibid.

88 Memorandum for the Under-Secretary of State, 13 October 1954, in LAC, RG103, vol. 4, file 5-3-2-1, pt. 1(1).

89 Memorandum, 24 March 1954, and memorandum, 13 February 1956, in LAC, RG25, vol. 6467, file 5582-U-40.

90 *Canadian Admiral Corporation Ltd. v. Rediffusion, Inc.,* [1954] Ex. C.R. 382.

91 Therese Goulet, "The Canada-US Free Trade Agreement and the Retransmission of American Broadcasts in Canada," *Gonzaga Law Review* 24 (1988-89): 351-60.

92 Canada, House of Commons, *Debates of the House of Commons, First Session – Twenty-Second Parliament 2-3 Elizabeth II, 1953-54,* vol. 2 (Ottawa: Edmond Cloutier, 1954), 1995.

93 Ibid., 5440-41.

94 Secretary of State Pickersgill commented, "I doubt if there is any strong partisan division in the house" on the matters to be investigated by the Ilsley Commission. Ibid., 1995-96.

95 Ibid., 5444.

96 Ibid., 5443-44.

97 The order-in-council to appoint the commission was tabled in the House of Commons on 11 June 1954 and meetings began that same month. Canada, House of Commons, *Debates of the House of Commons, First Session – Twenty-Second Parliament 2-3 Elizabeth II, 1953-54,* vol. 6 (Ottawa: Edmond Cloutier, 1954), 5829 and 6110.

98 Robert Bothwell, "Ilsley, James Lorimer," *Canadian Encyclopedia,* http://www.thecan-adianencyclopedia.com/.

99 Canada, Royal Commission on Patents, Copyright, Trade Marks and Industrial Designs, *Report on Copyright* (Ottawa: Supply and Services Canada, 1957), *Report on Industrial*

Designs (Ottawa: Supply and Services Canada, 1958), and *Report on Patents of Invention* (Ottawa: Supply and Services Canada, 1960).

100 Canada, Royal Commission on Patents, etc., *Report on Copyright*, 7.
101 Ibid.
102 Ibid., 9.
103 Ibid., 13.
104 Ibid., 19-23.
105 Ibid., 15.
106 *Universal Copyright Convention,* Article 3.
107 Ibid.
108 Canada, Royal Commission on Patents, etc., *Report on Copyright,* 16.
109 Ibid., 18.
110 Ibid., 17-18.
111 *An Act to Amend the Copyright Act, 1921, 1923,* 13-14 Geo. V, c. 10, Article 2.
112 Canada, Royal Commission on Patents, etc., *Report on Copyright,* 30-31.
113 Ibid., 31.
114 Ibid.
115 Ibid., 114.
116 Ibid., 18.
117 Ibid.
118 Charles Stein to Commissionner of Patents, 20 March 1958; see also Charles Stein, Under-Secretary of State, to Under-Secretary of State for External Affairs, 16 April 1956, both in LAC, RG103, vol. 4, file 5-3-2-1, pt. 1(2).
119 Eugen Ulmer to Minister of Foreign Affairs, 18 October 1959, in LAC, ibid.
120 See LAC, RG25, vol. 6838, file 4270-40, pt. 6-2.
121 Canada, House of Commons, *Debates of the House of Commons, First Session – Twenty-First Parliament 1 Elizabeth II, 1952* (Ottawa: Edmond Cloutier, 1952), 3533; and *Debates of the House of Commons, Twenty-Third Parliament 6 Elizabeth II, 1957-58,* vol. 2 (Ottawa: Edmond Cloutier, 1958), 1337, 1341.
122 Canada, House of Commons, *Debates of the House of Commons, First Session – Twenty-Fourth Parliament 7 Elizabeth II, 1958,* vol. 1 (Ottawa: Edmond Cloutier, 1958), 562, 988.
123 Canada, House of Commons, *Debates of the House of Commons, Third Session – Twenty-Fourth Parliament 8-9 Elizabeth II, 1960,* vol. 3 (Ottawa: Queen's Printer, 1960), 3276 (Acting Secretary of State Balcer in reply to Hazen Argue).
124 Ibid.; Canada, House of Commons, *Debates of the House of Commons, Third Session – Twenty-Fourth Parliament 8-9 Elizabeth II, 1960,* vol. 7 (Ottawa: Queen's Printer, 1960), 7073 (Richard); *Debates of the House of Commons, Fourth Session – Twenty-Fourth Parliament 9-10 Elizabeth II, 1960-61,* vol. 2 (Ottawa: Roger Duhamel, 1961), 1879 (LaMarsh); *Debates of the House of Commons, Fourth Session – Twenty-Fourth Parliament 9-10 Elizabeth II, 1960-61,* vol. 3 (Ottawa: Roger Duhamel, 1961), 2809 (LaMarsh); *Debates of the House of Commons, Fourth Session – Twenty-Fourth Parliament 9-10 Elizabeth II, 1960-61,* vol. 5 (Ottawa: Roger Duhamel, 1961), 5667 (Richard).
125 Canada, House of Commons, *Debates of the House of Commons, Fourth Session – Twenty-Fourth Parliament,* vol. 5, 5667.
126 Ibid., 5678.
127 Canada, House of Commons, *Debates of the House of Commons, Third Session – Twenty-Fourth Parliament,* 7073.
128 Canada, House of Commons, *Debates of the House of Commons, Fourth Session – Twenty-Fourth Parliament,* vol. 5, 5674-75.

129 Ibid., 1879 and 2066-67; Canada, House of Commons, *Debates of the House of Commons, Fourth Session – Twenty-Fourth Parliament 9-10 Elizabeth II, 1960-61*, vol. 3, 2809; *Debates of the House of Commons, Fourth Session – Twenty-Fourth Parliament 9-10 Elizabeth II, 1960-61*, vol. 5, 5674, 5677; *Debates of the House of Commons, Fourth Session – Twenty-Fourth Parliament 9-10 Elizabeth II, 1960-61*, vol. 6 (Ottawa: Roger Duhamel, 1961), 6527.

130 See also Canada, House of Commons, *Debates of the House of Commons, Fourth Session – Twenty-Fourth Parliament 9-10 Elizabeth II, 1960-61*, vol. 5, 5677.

131 Various correspondence, March to October 1960, in LAC, RG25, vol. 4322, file 11996-40. See also LAC, RG103, vol. 12, file 9-3-7-6, pt. 1.

132 *Copyright Act*, 61 Stat. 652, Public Law 281 (1947), Article 16.

133 John C.W. Irwin to Leon Balcer, 28 March 1960, in LAC, RG25, vol. 4322, file 11996-40.

134 John C.W. Irwin to Leon Balcer, 27 April 1960, in LAC, ibid.

135 Royal Commission on Publications, *Report* (Ottawa: Queen's Printer, 1961), 69.

136 See Memorandum re Royal Commission on Publications, 27 March 1961; Harris Arbique to P. Michael Pitfield, Secretary, Royal Commission on Publications, 18 April 1961; and generally LAC, RG103, vol. 6, file 5-3-5-2.

137 Low-volume imports were exempted from the manufacturing clause. See J. Haydn Boyde and William S. Lofquist, "New Interests in Old Issues: Antiprotection and the End of the Manufacturing Clause of the US," *Publishing Research Quarterly* 7, 4 (Winter 1991/1992).

138 C. Stein to N.A. Robertson, 3 January 1961, in LAC, RG25, vol. 4322, file 11996-40.

139 Donald Fleming to Howard Green, 16 January 1961, in LAC, ibid.

140 Telegraph messages of 24 and 27 January 1961, in LAC, ibid.

141 Leon Balcer to J.C.W. Irwin, 9 June 1960; Memorandum from the Office of the Secretary of State for External Affairs, 23 January 1961; Memorandum for the Minister: "Canadian Ratification of Universal Copyright Convention," 1 February 1961; Memorandum to Cabinet, 1 February 1961, all in LAC, ibid.

142 *Universal Copyright Convention*, Article 4.

143 Harris Arbique to Morton David Goldberg, 9 July 1962, in LAC, RG103, vol. 6, file 5-3-5-2, pt. 2.

144 Minister of Justice, New Zealand, to Minister of Justice, Canada, October 1959, and Secretary of State Henri Courtemanche to Minister of Justice, New Zealand, 16 December 1959, both in LAC, RG103, vol. 12, file 9-3-7-6, pt. 1.

145 H.G. Green, Memorandum to Cabinet, 1 February 1961, in LAC, RG103, vol. 6, file 5-3-5-2.

146 Noel Dorion, Secretary of State, Memorandum to Cabinet, 22 February 1961, in LAC, RG103, vol. 6, file 5-3-5-2; Memorandum signed by W.A. Kennett, 26 May 1961, in LAC, RG19, vol. 5167, file 8510-C785-1, pt. 1. See also Canada, House of Commons, *Debates of the House of Commons, Fourth Session – Twenty-Fourth Parliament 9-10 Elizabeth II, 1960-61*, vol. 5, 5677, and generally LAC, RG103, vol. 6, file 5-3-5-2.

147 Canada, House of Commons, *Debates of the House of Commons, Fifth Session – Twenty-Fourth Parliament 10-11 Elizabeth II, 1962*, vol. 3 (Ottawa: Roger Duhamel, 1962), 3016; *Debates of the House of Commons, Fourth Session – Twenty-Fourth Parliament 9-10 Elizabeth II, 1960-61*, vol. 5, 5678.

148 Canada, House of Commons, *Debates of the House of Commons, Fourth Session – Twenty-Fourth Parliament*, 5678.

149 Canada, House of Commons, *Debates of the House of Commons, Fifth Session – Twenty-Fourth Parliament*, 3023.

150 Ibid., 3017.

151 Ibid.

152 Telegraph messages 9 and 10 May 1962 from UNESCODEL Paris; Department of External Affairs Press Release, 10 May 1962, both in LAC, RG103, vol. 6, file 5-3-5-2, pt. 2. See also LAC, RG103, vol. 5, file 5-3-5-2, vol. 1, pt. 2.

153 Ibid.

154 See LAC, RG103, vol. 6, file 5-3-5-2.

155 Canadian Embassy at Washington, DC, to G.F.G. Hughes, Director, Industrial Relations Branch, Department of Trade and Commerce, 25 September 1962, in LAC, RG25, vol. 4322, file 11996-40.

156 "Retaliate or Negotiate," *Financial Post,* 15 September 1962. Copy in LAC, RG25, vol. 4322, file 11996-40.

157 J.W.T. Michael, Commissioner of Patents, to C.V. Cole, Legal Division, Department of External Affairs, 9 October 1962, in LAC, RG25, vol. 4322, file 11996-40.

158 Canada, House of Commons, *Debates of the House of Commons, First Session – Twenty-Seventh Parliament 15 Elizabeth II, 1966,* vol. 5 (Ottawa: Roger Duhamel, 1966), 5006 and 5500; vol. 6 (Ottawa: Roger Duhamel, 1966), 6559; vol. 7 (Ottawa: Roger Duhamel, 1966), 6750; vol. 8 (Ottawa: Roger Duhamel, 1966), 8790.

159 W.E. Curry, Chairman, Joint Committee of the Printing and Publishing Industries of Canada, to Paul Martin, Secretary of State for External Affairs, 19 March 1968, in LAC, RG25, vol. 16114, file 55-19-1-USA-1, pt. 1; *Florence Agreement on the Importation of Educational, Scientific and Cultural Materials, Florence Act of 1950* (Paris: UNESCO, 1950).

160 Annette V. Tucker, "The Validity of the Manufacturing Clause of the United States Copyright Code as Challenged by Trade Partners and Copyright Owners," *Vanderbilt Journal of Transnational Law* 18 (1985): 591.

161 Ibid., 595-96.

162 *Copyright Act,* 17 U.S.C. (1976); Tucker, ibid., 584, 590, 595.

163 Memorandum: US House of Representatives – Hearing on HR3940 – A Bill to Extend the Manufacturing Clause of the US Copyright Law; Questions and Suggested Replies, in LAC, RG25, vol. 16114, file 55-19-1-USA-1, pt. 1.

164 *Durand & Cie. v. La Patrie Publishing Co.,* [1960] S.C.R. 649, 24 D.L.R. (2d) 404, 34 C.P.R. 169.

Chapter 10: Crisis in International Copyright, 1967

1 Arturo Escobar, *Encountering Development: The Making and Unmaking of the Third World* (Princeton, NJ: Princeton University Press, 1995), ch. 1.

2 Sam Ricketson and Jane Ginsburg, *International Copyright and Neighbouring Rights: The Berne Convention and Beyond,* 2nd ed. (London: Oxford University Press, 2006), 885. Many British dependencies achieved independence in the 1950s and '60s: the Gold Coast attained internal self-government in 1951; Ghana (the former Gold Coast) and Malaya in 1957; Nigeria in 1960, followed by Sierra Leone, Cyprus, Tanganyika (later combined with independent Zanzibar as Tanzania), Jamaica, Trinidad, Uganda, Kenya, Malawi (formerly Nyasaland), Malta, Zambia (formerly Northern Rhodesia), Gambia, Singapore, Guyana (formerly British Guiana), Botswana (Bechuanaland), Lesotho (Basutoland), and Barbados over the next six years. J.A. Cross, *Whitehall and the Commonwealth: British Departmental Organisation for Commonwealth Relations 1900-1966* (London: Routledge and Kegan Paul, 1967), 65-66. The number of sovereign members of the British Commonwealth increased from six to twenty-eight between 1940 and 1968. Nicholas Mansergh, *The Commonwealth Experience* (London: Weidenfeld and Nicolson, 1969), 408. For further discussion of the

transformation from British Empire to British Commonwealth, see Mansergh, ibid., especially 399-402.

3 Ricketson and Ginsburg, ibid., 886.

4 *Documents de la conférence réunie à Bruxelles du 5 au 26 juin 1948* (Berne: Bureau de l'Union internationale pour la protection des oeuvres littéraires et artistiques, 1951), 84.

5 Herman Kling to G.H.C Bodenhausen, 29 March 1963; G.H.C. Bodenhausen, circular, 29 March 1963, both in Library and Archives Canada [LAC], RG103, vol. 4, file 5-3-2-2.

6 Accordingly, Canada transferred responsibility for communication with the International Office from the Canadian Embassy in Berne to the Permanent Mission in Geneva. Canadian Embassy in Berne to United International Bureaux for the Protection of Intellectual Property, 10 November 1960, in LAC, RG103, vol. 4, file 5-3-2-1, pt. 1(2).

7 Arpad Bogsch, *The First Twenty-Five Years of the World Intellectual Property Organization from 1967 to 1992* (Geneva: International Bureau of Intellectual Property, 1992); See also *Records of the Intellectual Property Conference of Stockholm June 11 to July 14, 1967* (Geneva: World Intellectual Property Organization, 1971), Document S10.

8 Bogsch, ibid.; *Records of the Intellectual Property Conference of Stockholm June 11 to July 14, 1967.*

9 Ibid., February 1964, 35-43.

10 Ibid., September 1965, 196.

11 Ibid., April 1967, 66-70.

12 J.W.T Michel, Commissioner of Patents, and Charles T. Stone of the Permanent Mission of Canada in Geneva were present. Ibid., 15 May 1965, 102-6.

13 Ibid., 15 August 1966, 206-9.

14 Ricketson and Ginsburg, *International Copyright and Neighbouring Rights*, 885.

15 G.H.C. Bodenhausen and René Maheu, circular, undated, received May 1960, in LAC, RG25, vol. 5169, file 5582-U-2-40.

16 Lionel V.J. Roy to Under-Secretary of State for External Affairs, 26 July 1963, in LAC, ibid.

17 Ibid.

18 Ibid.

19 Ibid.

20 C.F. Johnson, "The Origins of the Stockholm Protocol," *Bulletin of the Copyright Society of the USA* 18, 91 (1970): 107.

21 *Records of the Intellectual Property Conference of Stockholm,* 137.

22 Johnson, "Origins of the Stockholm Protocol."

23 This report was drawn up too early to take into account the results of the Brazzaville meeting. Ricketson and Ginsburg, *International Copyright and Neighbouring Rights,* 889-90.

24 *Records of the Intellectual Property Conference of Stockholm.* See also Ricketson and Ginsburg, ibid.

25 C. Masouyé to Secretary of State for External Affairs, 1 July 1963, in LAC, RG25, vol. 5071, file 4270-40, pt. 7.

26 Legal Division, Department of External Affairs, to M. Cadieux, 12 August 1963, in LAC, ibid.

27 *Records of the Intellectual Property Conference of Stockholm,* 137. The *Universal Copyright Convention* provided that translation rights could be made subject to compulsory licensing after a period of seven years from first publication if a translation in the national language or languages of a country had not been published at that time. Ricketson and Ginsburg, *International Copyright and Neighbouring Rights,* 1187; *Universal Copyright Convention, Geneva Act of 6 September 1952* (Paris: UNESCO, 1952), Article 5.

28 *Records of the Intellectual Property Conference of Stockholm,* 137.

29 G.H.C. Bodenhausen, circular, 20 September 1963; H. Courtney Kingston, Under-Secretary of State for External Affairs, to Commissioner of Patents, 25 September 1963; J.W.T. Michel, Commissioner of Patents, to Under-Secretary of State for External Affairs, 7 October 1963, all in LAC, RG25, vol. 5071, file 4270-40, pt. 7.

30 *Records of the Intellectual Property Conference of Stockholm,* 137-39. See also Ricketson and Ginsburg, *International Copyright and Neighbouring Rights,* 890-91.

31 *Records of the Intellectual Property Conference of Stockholm,* 137 (emphasis added). See also Ricketson and Ginsburg, ibid., 890.

32 *Records of the Intellectual Property Conference of Stockholm,* 139. See also Ricketson and Ginsburg, ibid., 891.

33 Ricketson and Ginsburg, ibid., 892-94; *Records of the Intellectual Property Conference of Stockholm,* 139 (emphasis added); Johnson, "Origins of the Stockholm Protocol," 129.

34 Ibid.

35 Ricketson and Ginsburg, *International Copyright and Neighbouring Rights,* 892. See also Johnson, "Origins of the Stockholm Protocol," 124-25.

36 *Records of the Intellectual Property Conference of Stockholm,* 140.

37 Ibid.; Ricketson and Ginsburg, *International Copyright and Neighbouring Rights,* 892-93.

38 Ibid.

39 *Records of the Intellectual Property Conference of Stockholm,* 141; Ricketson and Ginsburg, *International Copyright and Neighbouring Rights,* 894.

40 G.H.C. Bodenhausen, circular, 14 May 1965; Canadian Permanent Mission, Geneva, to Under-Secretary of State for External Affairs, 25 May 1965; Marcel Cadieux, Under-Secretary of State for External Affairs, draft memo to Jean Miquelon, 31 May 1965; draft memo: "Réorganisation des Bureaux Internationaux Réunis pour la Protection de la Propriété Intellectuelle"; J.S. Nutt, Under-Secretary of State for External Affairs, to Deputy Registrar General, 1 June 1965; Jean Miquelon to Marcel Cadieux, 15 June 1965; C.S. Nutt to G.H.C. Bodenhausen, 18 June 1965, all in LAC, RG25, vol. 10516, file 55-19-4-BERNE-UCC.

41 G.H.C. Bodenhausen to Secretary of State for External Affairs, circular, 15 July 1965; A.E. Gotlieb, Secretary of State for External Affairs, to G.H.C. Bodenhausen, 14 October 1965; Jean Miquelon, Deputy Registrar General, to Under-Secretary of State for External Affairs, 5 October 1965, all in LAC, ibid.

42 A.E. Gotlieb, Under-Secretary of State for External Affairs, to Deputy Registrar General, 26 January 1966; Jean Miquelon, Deputy Registrar General, to Under-Secretary of State, 9 February 1966, both in LAC, ibid.

43 J.-Z.-Léon Patenaude to Marcel Cadieux, Under-Secretary of State for External Affairs, 11 November 1966, in LAC, RG25, vol. 10904, file 55-19-4-STK-67, vol. 1.

44 *Records of the Intellectual Property Conference of Stockholm,* 77 and 142; Ricketson and Ginsburg, *International Copyright and Neighbouring Rights,* 894-95.

45 *Records of the Intellectual Property Conference of Stockholm,* 77, 139, 142-43; Ricketson and Ginsburg, ibid., 894-95.

46 *Records of the Intellectual Property Conference of Stockholm,* 143; Ricketson and Ginsburg, ibid., 895.

47 Ricketson and Ginsburg, ibid., 896.

48 Johnson, "Origins of the Stockholm Protocol," 142.

49 Ricketson and Ginsburg, *International Copyright and Neighbouring Rights,* 896; *Records of the Intellectual Property Conference of Stockholm,* Documents S13 and S17.

50 *Le droit d'auteur,* March 1967, 52.

51 Canada, House of Commons, *Debates of the House of Commons, Second Session – Twenty-Seventh Parliament 16 Elizabeth II, 1967,* vol. 2 (Ottawa: Roger Duhamel, 1967), 1605.

52 Ricketson and Ginsburg, *International Copyright and Neighbouring Rights,* 898; *Documents de la conférence réunie à Bruxelles,* 656.

53 Mahdi Elmandjra, UNESCO Acting Director-General, circular, 30 December 1966; Cultural Affairs Division, External Affairs, to Deputy Registrar-General, 31 January 1967; J.W.T. Michel, Commissioner of Patents, to Deputy Registrar General, 8 February 1967; Jean Miquelon to Department of External Affairs, 9 February 1967, all in LAC, RG103, vol.6, file 5-3-5-2, vol. 2, pt. 2.

54 Geneva to Exter, telegram, 23 February 1967; Commissioner of Patents to Deputy Registrar General, 23 February 1967; Jean Miquelon to Under-Secretary of State for External Affairs, 24 February 1967; ExtOtt to Permis Geneva, telegram, 1 March 1967; Geneva to Exterl, telegram, 3 March 1967; Geneva to Eterl, telegram report of the meeting, 21 March 1967, all in LAC, ibid.

55 Ricketson and Ginsburg, *International Copyright and Neighbouring Rights,* 898; *Records of the Intellectual Property Conference of Stockholm,* 656 and 659.

56 Canada, House of Commons, *Debates of the House of Commons, Second Session – Twenty-Seventh Parliament,* 1605; *Debates of the House of Commons, First Session – Twenty-Eighth Parliament 18 Elizabeth II, 1969,* vol. 9 (Ottawa: Queen's Printer, 1969), 9863.

57 Memorandum to Cabinet re Participation by Canada in a Joint Study Group Established by the Berne Union and the Universal Copyright Convention, September 1969, in LAC, RG25, vol. 10902, file 55-19-1-ICC, pt. 1-1.

58 Memorandum, "Interdepartmental Committee on Copyright," 22 January 1970, in LAC, RG97 ACC-1992-93 115, box 117, file 4014-4.

59 Ibid. See also Leslie J. Young to Claude Jodoin, President, Canadian Labour Congress, 15 May 1967, in LAC, Canadian Labour Congress Fonds (MG28-I103), International Affairs Department files (R5699-68-5-E), microfilm reel H-403.

60 *Records of the Intellectual Property Conference of Stockholm,* 586.

61 Canada, Economic Council of Canada, *Report on Intellectual and Industrial Property* (Ottawa: Economic Council of Canada, 1971), 137.

62 Secretary of State for External Affairs, Memorandum for Consideration by the Cabinet Committee on Economic and Fiscal Policy, 8 June 1967, in LAC, RG19, vol. 5167, file 8510-C785-1, pt. 1.

63 Ibid.

64 Ibid.

65 Report of the Cabinet Committee on Finances and Economic Policy Memo to Cabinet, 12 June 1967, in LAC, RG19, vol. 5167, file 8510-C785-1, pt. 1.

66 Memorandum for Consideration by the Cabinet Committee on Economic and Fiscal Policy: The Stockholm Conference on Copyright: Instructions for the Canadian Delegation Covering the Protocol Favouring Developing Countries, 16 June 1967, in LAC, RG19, vol. 5167, file 8510-C785-1, pt. 1.

67 Ibid.

68 Bogsch, *First Twenty-Five Years.*

69 General Information on the Intellectual Property Conference of Stockholm (1967), in LAC, Canadian Labour Congress Fonds (MG28-I103), International Affairs Department files (R5699-68-5-E), microfilm reel H-403.

70 Ricketson and Ginsburg, *International Copyright and Neighbouring Rights,* 8113 and 125; *Documents de la conférence réunie à Bruxelles,* 69.

71 Bogsch, *First Twenty-Five Years.*

72 Ricketson and Ginsburg, *International Copyright and Neighbouring Rights*, 127-28; *Berne Convention for the Protection of Literary and Artistic Works, Stockholm Act of 14 July 1967* (Geneva: World Intellectual Property Organization, 1967).

73 Ricketson and Ginsburg, ibid., 130.

74 Ibid., 902-8; *Berne Convention for the Protection of Literary and Artistic Works, Stockholm Act of 14 July 1967,* Protocol.

75 *Berne Convention,* ibid., Protocol, Article 1.

76 Memorandum, "Interdepartmental Committee on Copyright," 22 January 1970, 4, in LAC, RG97 ACC-1992-93 115, box 117, file 4014-4.

77 Ibid.

78 Canada also made more minor interventions on the International Court of Justice, on reservations and entry into force, voting by proxy, on needing a strong definition of "states" for purposes of membership, on the importance of the new organization's acting as a technical organization, refraining from making controversial decisions, and on a proposal from Switzerland. Canada also refused to be vice president of the plenary. *Records of the Intellectual Property Conference of Stockholm,* 808, 814, 1057, 1097, 1081.

79 Ibid., 878.

80 Ibid., 1051.

81 *Berne Convention for the Protection of Literary and Artistic Works, Stockholm Act of 14 July 1967,* Article 37.

82 *Convention Establishing the World Intellectual Property Organization, Signed at Stockholm on July 14, 1967 and as Amended on September 28, 1979* (Geneva: World Intellectual Property Organization, 1979), Articles 6 and 20.

83 *Records of the Intellectual Property Conference of Stockholm,* 1282, 1319.

84 See the submissions of the Canadian Copyright Institute, the Composers, Authors, and Publishers Association of Canada, BMI Canada, the Association of Canadian Television and Radio Artists, the Canadian Music Publishers Association, and the Canadian Conference of the Arts to the Interdepartmental Committee on Copyright, June 1969, in LAC, RG25, vol. 10516, file 55-19-4-BERNE-UCC. Also see Campbell C. Hughes, Director of Textbook Publishing, Ryerson Press, to Robert Stanbury, MP, 24 November 1967, in LAC, RG25, vol. 10516, file 55-19-4-BERNE-UCC 1969. The Canadian Copyright Institute would later change its views and favour ratification of the Stockholm Protocol. See Roy C. Sharp, Executive Director, Canadian Copyright Institute, to A.M. Laidlaw, Commissioner of Patents, 12 February 1971, in LAC, RG25, vol. 10904, file 55-19-4-BERNE, pt. 5-1, and RG25, vol. 10904, file 55-19-4-BERNE UCC-1969, vol. 4. See also LAC, RG19, vol. 5168, file 8510-C785-3, pt. 2.

85 See the submissions of the British Columbia Department of Education, the Canadian Education Association, and the Canadian Cable Television Association to the Interdepartmental Committee on Copyright, June 1969, in LAC, RG25, vol. 10516, file 55-19-4-BERNE-UCC.

86 *Economist,* 22 July 1967, in LAC, RG25, vol. 10516, file 55-19-4-BERNE-UCC 1969.

87 Ricketson and Ginsburg, *International Copyright and Neighbouring Rights,* 131.

88 Ibid., 914-15.

89 Ibid., 915.

90 Ibid.

Chapter 11: Re-engagement, 1967-77

1 Genev to Exter, telegram, 13 December 1968, in Library and Archives Canada [LAC], RG25, vol. 10516, file 55-19-4-BERNE-UCC.

2 Jacques Gignac, Cultural Affairs Division, External Affairs, to Under-Secretary of State for External Affairs, 1 December 1967, in LAC, ibid.

3 "There is also however an active interest in these meetings on the part of the Canadian publishing industry which has in fact sent a telegram (copy attached) to the Prime Minister requesting that the Canadian observer delegation include advisors from the Industry." Jacques Gignac, Cultural Affairs Division, External Affairs, to Under-Secretary of State for External Affairs, 1 December 1967, in LAC, ibid.

4 According to the 1971 census, there were 49,705 employed in "Printing and related occupations," along with 14,505 fine arts school teachers, 2,315 painters, sculptors, and related artists, 13,430 product and interior designers, 8,300 advertising and illustrating artists, 490 occupations in fine and commercial art, photography, and related fields, not elsewhere classified, 1,560 occupations in performing and audio-visual arts, not elsewhere classified, and 14,780 writers and editors. Canada, *Census of Canada, 1971*, vol. 3 (Ottawa: Supply and Services Canada, 1974).

5 Wyndham Wise, "A History of Ontario's Film Industry: 1896 to 1985," *Take One*, 22 June 2000, 20-35.

6 Ibid.

7 Ibid.

8 Ryan Edwardson, *Canuck Rock: A History of Canadian Popular Music* (Toronto: University of Toronto Press, 2009), 118.

9 Ibid.

10 Canadian Copyright Institute, http://www.canadiancopyrightinstitute.ca/about_us.asp.

11 Alexis Luko, "Music Canada," *Encyclopedia of Music in Canada*, http://www.the canadianencyclopedia.com/.

12 "Canadian Cable Television Association," Museum of Broadcast Communications, http://www.museum.tv/eotvsection.php?entrycode=canadiancabl.

13 See LAC, RG25, vol. 10902, file 55-19-1-ICC, pt. 1-1; RG25, vol. 10904, file 55-19-4-BERNE -UCC-1969, vol. 7; and RG25, vol. 10904, file 55-19-4-BERNE UCC-1969, vol. 2.

14 Roy C. Sharp to J.F. Grandy, Deputy Minister, Consumer and Corporate Affairs, 28 August 1968, in LAC, RG25, vol. 10516, file 55-19-4-BERNE-UCC.

15 Norman Hillmer and J.L. Granatstein, *Empire to Umpire: Canada and the World to the 1990s* (Toronto: Copp Clark Longman, 1994), 285-90.

16 Canada, Department of External Affairs, *Foreign Policy for Canadians*, vol. 1 (Ottawa: Queen's Printer, 1970), 5.

17 Ibid., 7.

18 Ibid., 6-8.

19 Ibid., 3: 11.

20 Andrew Fenton Cooper, "Introduction," in *Canadian Culture: International Dimensions*, edited by Andrew Fenton Cooper (Waterloo, ON: Centre on Foreign Policy and Federalism, University of Waterloo and Wilfrid Laurier University, 1985), 15.

21 Freeman M. Tovell, "A Comparison of Canadian, French, British, and German International Cultural Policies," In *Canadian Culture: International Dimensions*, ibid., 69-70.

22 Cooper, "Introduction," 15.

23 See generally LAC, RG25, vol. 10901, file 55-19-WIPO-1970, pt. 1-2; RG25, vol. 10901, file 55-19-WIPO-1970, vol. 2; RG25, vol. 10901, file 55-19-WIPO-1970, pt. 1-1; RG25, vol. 10904, file 55-19-4-BERNE UCC-1969, vol. 2; RG25, vol. 16115, file 55-19-3-ROME-1961, and others.

24 Cooper, "Introduction," 4-5, quoting Allan E. Gotlieb, "Cultural Diplomacy: A Question of Self-Interest," Canada, Department of External Affairs, Statements and Speeches 79/20, November 1979, 2.

25 Cooper, "Introduction," 16-17.

26 *C.A.P.A.C. v. CTV Television Network and Bell Telephone Company of Canada*, [1968] 68 D.L.R. (2d) 98 (S.C.C.).

27 John McKeown, *Fox on Canadian Law of Copyright and Industrial Designs*, 4th ed. (Toronto: Carswell, 2003); *National Corn Growers Assn. v. Canada (Canadian Import Tribunal)*, [1990], 74 D.L.R. (4th) 449 (S.C.C.).

28 External Ott to Permis Genva, telegram, 1 December 1967, in LAC, RG25, vol. 10516, file 55-19-4-BERNE-UCC.

29 Permanent Mission of Canada to the European Office of the United Nations, Geneva, 13 January 1969; "Supplementary Report by the Director of BIRPI, Responses by Member States to Circular No. 225 Concerning the Acceptance of the Protocol Regarding Developing Countries," DA/29/5, Annex I, 3. See also "Communication from the Director-General of UNESCO Concerning Comments Received from States Parties to the Universal Copyright Convention with Regard to the Revision of Article XVII of the Convention," IGC/XR/2, Annex I, 4 (response of Canada, 14 March 1968). LAC, RG25, vol. 10904, file 55-19-4-BERNE UCC-1969, vol. 2.

30 A.M. Laidlaw, Commissioner of Patents, to the Deputy Minister, Consumer and Corporate Affairs, 30 December 1968, in LAC, RG25, vol. 10904, file 55-19-4-BERNE UCC-1969, vol. 2.

31 Ibid.

32 Ibid.

33 Genev to Exter, telegram, 13 December 1968, in LAC, RG25, vol. 10516, file 55-19-4 -BERNE-UCC.

34 See, for example, J.F. Grandy, Consumer and Corporate Affairs, to A.E. Ritchie, Under-Secretary of State for External Affairs, 22 July 1970, in LAC, RG25, vol. 10904, file 55-19-4-BERNE UCC-1969, vol. 3.

35 Ibid.; Genev to Exter, telegram, 18 December 1968, in LAC, RG25, vol. 10516, file 55-19-4-BERNE-UCC.

36 Genev to Exter, telegram, 13 December 1968, in LAC, RG25, vol. 10516, file 55-19-4 -BERNE-UCC.

37 *Report of the Canadian Delegation on the Extraordinary Joint Session of the Permanent Committee of the Berne Union and the Inter-Governmental Committee of the Universal Copyright Convention, Paris, February 3 to 7, 1969*, in LAC, RG25, vol. 10902, file 55-19-1 -ICC, pt. 1-1.

38 Ibid.

39 Teletext, 14 March 1969, in LAC, RG19, vol. 5168, file 8510-C785-3, pt. 1.

40 See generally LAC, RG25, vol. 10902, file 55-19-1-ICC, pt. 1-1.

41 Interdepartmental Committee on Copyright, Minutes of Meeting, 10 March 1969, in LAC, ibid.

42 See generally LAC, ibid. The members of the committee changed over time. See also LAC, Department of Communication Fonds (RG97 ACC-1992-93 115, box 117, file 4014-4 1969-1970).

43 Memo (partial, undated), 5, in LAC, Department of Communication Fonds.

44 Ibid., 10-11.

45 Ibid., 2-3.

46 Ibid.

47 Interdepartmental Committee on Copyright, Minutes of Meeting, 10 March 1969, in LAC, RG25, vol. 10902, file 55-19-1-ICC, pt. 1-1.

48 Ibid.

49 Ibid. See also LAC, RG19, vol. 5167, file 8510-C785-1, pt. 1; RG19, vol. 5574, file 8510-C785-1, pt. 2; RG19, vol. 5168, file 8510-C785-3, pts. 1, 2, 3, and 4; RG19, vol. 5574, file 8510-C785-3, pts. 5, 6, and 7; RG25, vol. 10902, file 55-19-1-ICC, pt. 1-2.

50 See generally LAC, RG25, vol. 10902, file 55-19-1-ICC, pt. 1-1.

51 Memorandum to Cabinet re Participation by Canada in a Joint Study Group Established by the Berne Union and the Universal Copyright Convention, September 1969, in LAC, ibid.

52 Ibid.

53 In reviewing the submissions, the committee made the following notes: "Each of the briefs received from outside organizations was discussed in detail. Some of those briefs were extremely good while others did not relate to the subject at hand. Most of them were pressing for more protection in a particular field with rather weak arguments or no arguments at all as to why the present protection should be increased." Interdepartmental Committee on Copyright, Minutes of Meeting, 3 July 1969, in LAC, ibid.

54 Canadian Statement to the Joint Study Group, in LAC, ibid.

55 Memorandum to Cabinet re Participation by Canada in a Joint Study Group.

56 Ibid.

57 J.A. Beesley, memorandum, 23 September 1969, in LAC, RG25, vol. 10902, file 55-19-1-ICC, pt. 1-1.

58 Memorandum to Cabinet re Participation by Canada in a Joint Study Group.

59 Ibid.

60 Ibid.

61 Ibid.

62 Ibid.

63 Fernand Rinfret, Instructions to the Canadian Delegates to the Rome Conference on Copyright, 25 April 1928, in LAC, RG25, vol. 1490, file 1827-278, pt. 1.

64 English translation of *Brief presented by le Conseil supérieur du livre and la Société canadienne-française de protection du droit d'auteur to the Interdepartmental Committee on Copyright*, 26 February 1970, 2, in LAC, RG25, vol. 10902, file 55-19-1-ICC, pt. 1-2.

65 Ibid., 3.

66 Ibid., 4.

67 External Ott to Permis Genva, telegram, 1 December 1967, in LAC, RG25, vol. 10516, file 55-19-4-BERNE-UCC.

68 *Paris Revision Conference of the Universal Copyright Convention and the Berne Copyright Convention, Paris, July 5-24, 1971: Report of the Canadian Delegation*, 22, in LAC, RG25, vol. 10904, file 55-19-4-BERNE, pt. 6-2.

69 Genev to Exter, telegram, 13 December 1968, in LAC, RG25, vol. 10516, file 55-19-4-BERNE -UCC; *Le droit d'auteur*, November 1970, 239-45.

70 *Records of the Diplomatic Conference for the Revision of the Berne Convention (Paris, July 5 to 24, 1971)* (Geneva: World Intellectual Property Organization, 1974), 49.

71 Canada proposed that the Ad Hoc Preparatory Committee be composed of thirteen members rather than eight. Canada was not proposed for membership on the committee. *Le droit d'auteur*, February 1970, 32, and August 1970, 32, 33, and 35.

72 Arturo Escobar, *Encountering Development: The Making and Unmaking of the Third World* (Princeton, NJ: Princeton University Press, 1995), 10-11.

73 Memorandum to Cabinet re Participation by Canada in a Joint Study Group.

74 Cabinet Committee on Economic Policy and Programs, Record of Committee Decision, 29 September 1969, in LAC, RG19, vol. 5168, file 8510-6785-3, pt. 4.

75 *Le droit d'auteur*, November 1969, 220.

76 Memorandum, W.H. Hines to Mr. Howarth, 9 May 1969, in LAC, RG19, vol. 5168, file 8510-C785-3, pt. 3.

77 *Report of the Canadian Delegation: Meetings of the Intergovernmental Copyright Committee of the Universal Copyright Convention and the Permanent Committee of the Berne Union, Paris, December 15-19, 1969*, in LAC, RG19, vol. 5168, file 8510-6785-3, pt. 4.

78 "Extraordinary Session of the Permanent Committee of the International Union for the Protection of Literary and Artistic Works (Berne Union) (Geneva, September 14 to 18, 1970): Report," in *Records of the Diplomatic Conference for the Revision of the Berne Convention (Paris, July 5 to 24, 1971)*, 49.

79 Memorandum, W.H. Hines to Mr. Howarth, 9 May 1969.

80 *Report of the Canadian Delegation: Meetings of the Intergovernmental Copyright Committee of the Universal Copyright Convention and the Permanent Committee of the Berne Union, Paris, December 15-19, 1969*, 4.

81 Geneva to Ottawa, 25 July 1969, in LAC, RG19, vol. 5168, file 8510-6785-3, pt. 4.

82 *Memorandum to the Minister: Report of the Canadian Delegation at the Washington Meeting, September 29 – October 3/1969*, 10 October 1969, 2 and 4, in LAC, RG19, vol. 5574, file 8510-C785-1, pt. 2.

83 *Report of the Canadian Delegation: Meetings of the Intergovernmental Copyright Committee of the Universal Copyright Convention and the Permanent Committee of the Berne Union, Paris, December 15-19, 1969; Memorandum to the Minister*, ibid.

84 *Convention Establishing the World Intellectual Property Organization, Signed at Stockholm on July 14, 1967 and as Amended on September 28, 1979* (Geneva: World Intellectual Property Organization, 1979), http://www.wipo.int/.

85 M. Cadieux, Memorandum for Minister, 14 January 1970, in LAC, RG25, vol. 10901, file 55-19-WIPO-1970, pt. 1-1.

86 Press Release: World Intellectual Property Organization, 26 January 1970, in LAC, ibid.

87 Genev to Exter, telegram, 2 February 1970, in LAC, ibid.

88 Cabinet Committee on External Policy and Defence Record of Decision, 3 February 1970, in LAC, ibid.

89 Order-in-Council No. 1970-411, 10 March 1970; Genev to Exter, telegram, 26 March 1970; WIPO Notification No. 20, Accession of Canada to the Convention, 7 April 1970, all in LAC, ibid.

90 World Intellectual Property Organization, *Berne Notification No. 17: Accession of Canada to the Stockholm Act (with the exception of Articles 1 to 21 and of the Protocol Regarding Developing Countries)*, http://www.wipo.int/.

91 Memorandum to the Cabinet, 29 June 1971, Cabinet document 700-71, in LAC, RG19, vol. 5574, file 8510-C785-1, pt. 2.

92 Ibid.

93 Canada, Economic Council of Canada, *Report on Intellectual and Industrial Property* (Ottawa: Economic Council of Canada, 1971), 134.

94 Ibid., 32 and 37.

95 Ibid., 42-43.

96 Ibid., 144.

97 Ibid., 218.

98 Ibid.

99 Freeman M. Tovell, Cultural Affairs Division, External Affairs, "Diplomatic Conferences to Revise the Berne and Universal Copyright Conventions," 27 April 1971, in LAC, RG25, vol. 10904, file 55-19-4-BERNE, pt. 5-1.

100 *Records of the Conference for Revision of the Universal Copyright Convention, Unesco House, Paris, 5 to 24 July 1971* (Paris: UNESCO, 1973), 166.

101 Sam Ricketson and Jane Ginsburg, *International Copyright and Neighbouring Rights: The Berne Convention and Beyond*, 2nd ed. (London: Oxford University Press, 2006), 132.

102 *Records of the Conference for Revision of the Universal Copyright Convention, Unesco House, Paris, 5 to 24 July 1971*.

103 Ibid., 230.

104 René Garneau to Freeman Tovell, Director of Cultural Affairs, 15 December 1970, in LAC, RG25, vol. 10904, file 55-19-4-BERNE UCC-1969, vol. 4. Author's translation from French to English.

105 Michael I. Pitman, Chairman, Board of Governors, Canadian Copyright Institute, to Prime Minister Lester B. Pearson, 15 January 1967; Prime Minister Lester B. Pearson to Michael I. Pitman, Chairman, Board of Governors, Canadian Copyright Institute, 12 December 1967, both in LAC, RG25, vol. 10904, file 55-19-4-BERNE, pt. 6-1.

106 See A.E. Ritchie, Memorandum for the Minister, 14 June 1971, and A.E Ritchie, Memorandum for the Minister, 21 June 1971, both in LAC, ibid.

107 A.E Ritchie, Memorandum for the Minister, 21 June 1971.

108 Michael I. Pitman, Chairman, Board of Governors, Canadian Copyright Institute, to Prime Minister Pierre Elliott Trudeau, 6 July 1971, in LAC, RG25, vol. 10904, file 55-19-4-BERNE, pt. 6-1.

109 Robert Guy Scully, "Pas de délégué officiel de l'édition québécoise à Paris," Le Devoir, 9 July 1971, in LAC, RG25, vol. 10904, file 55-19-4-BERNE, pt. 6-1.

110 A.E. Ritchie, Memorandum for the Minister, 9 July 1971; Teletext, Paris to Ottawa, 13 July 1971, both in LAC, RG25, vol. 10904, file 55-19-4-BERNE, pt. 6-1.

111 John Thompson to Governor General in Council, 1892, 7, in LAC, RG13 A-2, vol. 85, file 892-217.

112 English translation of Brief presented by le Conseil supérieur du livre and la Société canadienne-française de protection du droit d'auteur, 6.

113 Ibid.

114 A.E Ritchie, Memorandum for the Minister, 21 June 1971; Claude Morin to Paul Tremblay, 21 July 1971; Paul Tremblay to Claude Morin, teletext, 22 July 1971, all in LAC, RG25, vol. 10904, file 55-19-4-BERNE, pt. 6-1.

115 Cultural Affairs Division, External Affairs, Memorandum: Diplomatic Conference to Establish Convention on Protection of Phonograms, 19 August 1971, in LAC, RG25, vol. 10904, file 55-19-4-BERNE-UCC-1969, vol. 7.

116 Claude Morin to Paul Tremblay, 16 August 1971, in LAC, RG25, vol. 10904, file 55-19-4-BERNE-UCC-1969, vol. 7.

117 J.H. Grandy to A.E. Ritchie, 31 May 1971, in LAC, RG25, vol. 10904, file 55-19-4-BERNE, pt. 6-1.

118 Memorandum to the Cabinet, 29 June 1971, Cabinet document 700-71, in LAC, RG19, vol. 5574, file 8510-C785-1, pt. 2.

119 Ibid.

120 Paris Revision Conference of the Universal Copyright Convention and the Berne Copyright Convention, Paris, July 5-24, 1971: Report of the Canadian Delegation, 24.

121 Ibid., 27.

122 Memorandum to the Cabinet, 29 June 1971.

123 Ibid., in LAC, RG19, vol. 5574, file 8510-C785-1, pt. 2, and RG25, vol. 10904, file 55-19-4-BERNE, pt. 6-1; Record of Cabinet Decision, Cabinet Committee on External Policy and Defence, 29 June 1971, in LAC, RG25, vol. 10904, file 55-19-4-BERNE, pt. 6-1.

124 Paris Revision Conference of the Universal Copyright Convention and the Berne Copyright Convention, Paris, July 5-24, 1971: Report of the Canadian Delegation, 22; Teletext, Paris to Ottawa, 5 July 1971, in LAC, RG25, vol. 10904, file 55-19-4-BERNE, pt. 6-1.

125 Records of the Intellectual Property Conference of Stockholm June 11 to July 14, 1967, 28; Records of the Conference for Revision of the Universal Copyright Convention, Unesco House, Paris, 5 to 24 July 1971, 60.

126 Paris Revision Conference of the Universal Copyright Convention and the Berne Copyright Convention, Paris, July 5-24, 1971: Report of the Canadian Delegation, 19.

127 Ibid., 14-15.
128 *Records of the Conference for Revision of the Universal Copyright Convention, Unesco House, Paris, 5 to 24 July 1971*, 105.
129 Ibid., 62.
130 Ibid., 105.
131 Ibid.
132 Ibid.
133 Ibid.
134 Ibid.
135 Ricketson and Ginsburg, *International Copyright and Neighbouring Rights*, 902-8; *Berne Convention for the Protection of Literary and Artistic Works, Stockholm Act of 14 July 1967*, Protocol.
136 Ricketson and Ginsburg, ibid., 930-40, especially 935; *Berne Convention for the Protection of Literary and Artistic Works, Paris Act of July 24, 1971, as Amended on September 28, 1979* (Geneva: World Intellectual Property Organization, 1979), Appendix, Article 2.
137 Ricketson and Ginsburg, ibid., 941-47, especially 944; *Berne Convention*, ibid., Appendix, Article 3.
138 *Berne Convention*, ibid., Appendix, Article 1.
139 *Records of the Diplomatic Conference for the Revision of the Berne Convention (Paris, July 5 to 24, 1971)*, 146.
140 Ibid.
141 Ricketson and Ginsburg, *International Copyright and Neighbouring Rights*, 956.
142 J.H. Grandy to A.E. Ritchie, 31 May 1971, in LAC, RG25, vol. 10904, file 55-19-4-BERNE, pt. 6-1.
143 *Paris Revision Conference of the Universal Copyright Convention and the Berne Copyright Convention, Paris, July 5-24, 1971: Report of the Canadian Delegation*, 19; *Records of the Conference for Revision of the Universal Copyright Convention, Unesco House, Paris, 5 to 24 July 1971*, 179. See also related remarks by Australia, *Records of the Diplomatic Conference for the Revision of the Berne Convention (Paris, July 5 to 24, 1971)*, 49.
144 *Paris Revision Conference*, ibid., 20.
145 Sunny Handa, "A Review of Canada's International Copyright Obligations," *McGill Law Journal* 42, 4 (1997): 971.
146 Ricketson and Ginsburg, *International Copyright and Neighbouring Rights*, 958.
147 Ibid., 960.
148 Ibid., 957.
149 Andrew A. Keyes and Claude Brunet, *Copyright in Canada: Proposals for a Revision of the Law* (Ottawa: Consumer and Corporate Affairs Canada, 1977), 234.
150 Ibid.
151 Ibid., 236. Keyes affirmed this view again in 1993, arguing that "Canada ... as a net importer would only increase its trade deficit by assuming further commitments." Andrew A. Keyes, "What Is Canada's International Copyright Policy?" *Intellectual Property Journal* 7 (1993): 302.

Chapter 12: After 1971

1 As noted in Chapter 1, note 3, minor amendments were also made in 1979 to Articles 22(2) (a)(vi) and (4)(a) and Articles 23(6)(a)(ii) and (iii), replacing the triennial ordinary sessions of the Berne Union with biennial ordinary sessions, and the triennial budget and annual budgets with a biennial budget. *General Report of the Governing Bodies of WIPO and the Unions Administered by WIPO, Tenth Series of Meetings, Geneva, September 24 to*

October 2, 1979. AB/X/32 (Geneva: World Intellectual Property Organization, 1979). See also Sam Ricketson and Jane Ginsburg, *International Copyright and Neighbouring Rights: The Berne Convention and Beyond,* 2nd ed. (London: Oxford University Press, 2006), 1048-49.

2 Arpad Bogsch, *The First Twenty-Five Years of the World Intellectual Property Organization from 1967 to 1992* (Geneva: International Bureau of Intellectual Property, 1992).

3 Ibid.

4 Ibid.

5 Geneva to Ottawa, teletext, 5 October 1971, in Library and Archives Canada [LAC], RG25, vol. 10902, file 55-19-WIPO 1970, vol. 5-1.

6 Geneva to Ottawa, teletext, 7 May 1973, in LAC, ibid., vol. 5-2.

7 Ottawa to Geneva, teletext, 22 September 1972, in LAC, ibid., vol. 4.

8 Geneva to Ottawa, teletext, 5 July 1973, in LAC, RG25, vol. 10903, file 55-19-WIPO-1970 BO122, vol. 6.

9 Canada, Department of Communications and Department of Consumer and Corporate Affairs, *From Gutenberg to Telidon: A White Paper on Copyright: Proposals for the Revision of the Canadian Copyright Act* (Ottawa: Department of Consumer and Corporate Affairs and Department of Communications, 1984), 4.

10 Ibid. See in particular the discussion of a retransmission right in Appendix I.

11 Ibid., 37.

12 Ibid., 73-74.

13 Ibid., 4.

14 Canada, House of Commons, Sub-Committee on the Revision of Copyright, *A Charter of Rights for Creators: A Report of the Sub-Committee on the Revision of Copyright, Standing Committee on Communications and Culture* (Ottawa: Queen's Printer, 1985).

15 Ibid., xii.

16 Michael H. Wilson, *A New Direction for Canada: An Agenda for Economic Renewal* (Canada: Department of Finance, 1984), as cited in ibid., 1.

17 The Sub-Committee noted that such optimism must be dampened by realism. Canada, House of Commons, Sub-Committee on the Revision of Copyright, *A Charter of Rights,* 5.

18 Ibid., 3.

19 Ibid., xii.

20 Ibid., 4.

21 Ibid., 9.

22 Ibid., 23.

23 Ibid., 95.

24 *Canada–United States Free Trade Agreement Implementation Act,* S.C. 1988, c. 65.

25 Ibid.

26 Sunny Handa, "A Review of Canada's International Copyright Obligations," *McGill Law Journal* 42, 4 (1997): 972 and 976.

27 Ibid..

28 Ibid., 980; Therese Goulet, "The Canada-US Free Trade Agreement and the Retransmission of American Broadcasts in Canada," *Gonzaga Law Review* 24 (1988-89): 351. See also Andrew A. Keyes, "What Is Canada's International Copyright Policy?" *Intellectual Property Journal* 7 (1993): 307-8.

29 *Canada-US Free Trade Agreement* (Ottawa: Department of Foreign Affairs and International Trade, 1987), Article 2006.

30 *Canada–United States Free Trade Agreement Implementation Act.*

31 *Berne Convention for the Protection of Literary and Artistic Works, Brussels Act of 26 June 1948* (Berne: International Bureau for the Union for the Protection of Literary and Artistic

Works, 1948), Article 11*bis*; *Berne Convention for the Protection of Literary and Artistic Works, Paris Act of July 24, 1971, as Amended on September 28, 1979* (Geneva: World Intellectual Property Organization, 1979), Appendix, Article 11*bis*.

32 Handa, "A Review of Canada's International Copyright Obligations," 980.

33 Therese Goulet, "The Canada-US Free Trade Agreement," 358.

34 Sunny Handa, "Retransmission of Television Broadcasts on the Internet," *Southwestern Journal of Law and Trade in the Americas* 8 (2001): 53.

35 Ibid., 976.

36 Handa, "A Review of Canada's International Copyright Obligations," 981.

37 S.C. 1993, c. 44, s. 63(2).

38 Ricketson and Ginsburg, *International Copyright and Neighbouring Rights*, 135-43.

39 Handa, "A Review of Canada's International Copyright Obligations," 972 and 976.

40 *Final Act Embodying the Results of the Uruguay Round of Multilateral Trade Negotiations, Annex 1C: Agreement on Trade-Related Aspects of Intellectual Property Rights* (Geneva: World Trade Organization, 1994), Article 9, http://www.wto.org/english/.

41 Peter Drahos, "When the Weak Bargain with the Strong: Negotiations in the World Trade Organization," *International Negotiation* 8 (2003): 79-109.

42 Ibid.

43 S.C. 1994, c. 47.

44 *An Act Respecting Copyright*, R.S.C, 1985, c. C-42, Article 54.

45 Ricketson and Ginsburg, *International Copyright and Neighbouring Rights*, 143-47.

46 Ibid., 148-50.

47 *WIPO Copyright Treaty, adopted in Geneva on December 20, 1996*, Article 1, para. 4, http://www.wipo.int/treaties/en/.

48 *An Act to Amend the Copyright Act*, R.S.C. 1997, c. 24.

49 Ibid.; Canada, Industry Canada and Department of Canadian Heritage, *A Framework for Copyright Reform*, 4-5.

50 Handa, "A Review of Canada's International Copyright Obligations," 969.

51 Canada, Industry Canada and Department of Canadian Heritage, *Consultation Paper on Digital Copyright Issues* (Ottawa: Industry Canada and Canadian Heritage, 2001).

52 *Copyright Modernization Act (An Act to Amend the Copyright Act)*, S.C. 2012, c. 20.

53 Blayne Haggart, "North American Digital Copyright, Regional Governance, and the Potential for Variation," in *From "Radical Extremism" to "Balanced Copyright": Canadian Copyright and the Digital Agenda* (Toronto: Irwin Law, 2010), 55-56.

54 *Copyright Modernization Act*, s. 41.1(1).

55 Ibid., s. 46.

56 Sara Bannerman, "The Development Agenda at WIPO: Where Is Canada?" In *Innovation, Science and Environment: Canadian Policies and Performance 2008-2009*, edited by Glen Toner (Montreal and Kingston: McGill-Queen's University Press, 2008), 190-208.

57 *Convention Establishing the World Intellectual Property Organization, Signed at Stockholm on July 14, 1967 and as Amended on September 28, 1979* (Geneva: World Intellectual Property Organization, 1979), http://www.wipo.int/treaties/en/; Argentina and Brazil, *Proposal by Argentina and Brazil for the Establishment of a Development Agenda for WIPO* (Geneva: World Intellectual Property Organization, 2004), http://www.wipo.int/meetings/en/; Christopher May, *The World Intellectual Property Organization: Resurgence and the Development Agenda* (London: Routledge, 2004).

58 Argentina and Brazil, ibid.; Friends of Development, *Proposal to Establish a Development Agenda for WIPO: An Elaboration of Issues Raised in Document WO/GA/31/11* (Geneva: World Intellectual Property Organization, 2005), http://www.wipo.int/. See also Peter Drahos, "Access to Knowledge: Time for a Treaty?" *Bridges* 9 (2005): 15-17.

59 World Intellectual Property Organization, *Development Agenda for WIPO* (Geneva: World Intellectual Property Organization, 2010), http://www.wipo.int/.
60 Bannerman, "The Development Agenda at WIPO," 190-208.
61 World Intellectual Property Organization, *Development Agenda for WIPO*.
62 William New, "WIPO Still On Course for Instruments on Copyright Exceptions, Broadcasting," Intellectual Property Watch (2012), http://www.ip-watch.org; World Intellectual Property Organization, "SCCR Commits to Improving Access by Visually Impaired to Copyright-Protected Works," Press Release, 18 December 2009, http://www.wipo.int/pressroom/.
63 "European Parliament Resolution of 10 March 2010 on the Transparency and State of Play of the ACTA Negotiations," Eur. Parl. Doc. B7-0154/2010 (2010), http://www.europarl.europa.eu/.
64 "The Wellington Declaration," ACTA Watch, http://acta.michaelgeist.ca/blog/wellington-declaration.
65 Kaitlin Mara, "Perpetual Protection of Traditional Knowledge 'Not on Table' at WIPO," Intellectual Property Watch (2009), http://www.ip-watch.org/.
66 Catherine Saez, "ACTA a Sign of Weakness in Multilateral System, WIPO Head Says," Intellectual Property Watch (2010), http://www.ip-watch.org/.
67 *Beijing Treaty on Audiovisual Performances, Beijing Act of 24 June 2012* (Geneva: World Intellectual Property Organization, 2012).
68 "WTO Raises Attention to Multilateralism," Intellectual Property Watch (2012), http://www.ip-watch.org/.

Chapter 13: Conclusion

1 For another point of view, see Lionel Bently, "The 'Extraordinary Multiplicity' of Intellectual Property Laws in the British Colonies in the Nineteenth Century," *Theoretical Inquiries in Law* 12, 1 (2010): 161-200. Bently emphasizes the *flexibility* of colonial intellectual property regimes but glosses over the more restrictive effects of the imperial copyright regime. He literally relegates the refusal of consent to Canada's copyright act of 1889 to a footnote, and hardly mentions Canada's campaign to denounce the *Berne Convention*.
2 David Vaver, "Copyright in Canada: The New Millennium," *Intellectual Property Journal* 12 (1997): 120.
3 Michael Geist, "The Case for Flexibility in Implementing the WIPO Internet Treaties: An Examination of the Anti-Circumvention Requirements," in *From "Radical Extremism" to "Balanced Copyright": Canadian Copyright and the Digital Agenda* (Toronto: Irwin Law, 2010), 204-46.
4 Hayhurst notes that reliance on either British or American precedent has since been abandoned. W.L. Hayhurst, "Intellectual Property Laws in Canada: The British Tradition, the American Influence, and the French Factor," *Intellectual Property Journal* 10 (1996): 327.
5 Ibid., 287.
6 United Kingdom, *Minutes of Proceeding of the Imperial Copyright Conference, 1910*, 41, in Library and Archives Canada [LAC], microfilm reels B-2392 to B-2393.
7 *An Act Respecting Copyright*, R.S.C. 1985, c. C-42, Article 6.
8 Canada, Royal Commission on Patents, Copyright, Trade Marks and Industrial Designs, *Report on Copyright* (Ottawa: Supply and Services Canada, 1957), 9.
9 Canada, Economic Council of Canada, *Report on Intellectual and Industrial Property* (Ottawa: Economic Council of Canada, 1971), 32 and 127-30.

10 Canada, House of Commons, *Debates of the House of Commons, Fifth Session – Thirteenth Parliament 11-12 George V., 1921*, vol. 4 (Ottawa: F.A. Acland, 1921), 3833.

11 *Records of the Conference for Revision of the Universal Copyright Convention, Unesco House, Paris, 5 to 24 July 1971* (Paris: UNESCO, 1973), 105.

12 See Canada, House of Commons, *Debates of the House of Commons, Second Session – Seventeenth Parliament 21-22 George V., 1931*, vol. 3 (Ottawa: F.A. Acland, 1931), 2309.

13 Canada, Royal Commission on Patents, etc., *Report on Copyright*, 18.

14 Christopher May, "The World Intellectual Property Organization," *New Political Economy* 11, 3 (2006): 435-45. See also Jeremy F. de Beer and Michael A. Geist, "Developing Canada's Intellectual Property Agenda," in *Canada among Nations*, edited by Jean Daudelin and Daniel Schwanen (Montreal and Kingston: McGill-Queen's University Press, 2007).

15 Sara Bannerman, "The Development Agenda at WIPO: Where Is Canada?" In *Innovation, Science and Environment: Canadian Policies and Performance 2008-2009*, edited by Glen Toner (Montreal and Kingston: McGill-Queen's University Press, 2008), 190-208.

16 William New, "In a 'Major Achievement,' WIPO Negotiators Create New Development Mandate," Intellectual Property Watch (2007), http://www.ip-watch.org/.

17 Ted Hopf, "The Promise of Constructivism in International Relations Theory," *International Security* 23, 1 (1998): 180.

18 That decision was based on a precedent set in the early 1880s when the Canadian government, in a dramatic reversal based in part on bureaucratic politics between departments and in part on the ability of British interests to intervene, decided not to stand in the way of an Anglo-American copyright treaty. See Chapter 4.

19 See Bannerman, "The Development Agenda at WIPO"; Peter Drahos, "Access to Knowledge: Time for a Treaty?" *Bridges* 9 (2005): 15-17, http://www.iprsonline.org/; William New, "WIPO Still on Course for Instruments on Copyright Exceptions, Broadcasting," Intellectual Property Watch (2012), http://www.ip-watch.org; World Intellectual Property Organization, "SCCR Commits to Improving Access by Visually Impaired to Copyright-Protected Works," Press Release, 18 December 2009, http://www.wipo.int/pressroom/. See also Jane Anderson and Kathy Bowrey, "The Imaginary Politics of Access to Knowledge: Whose Cultural Agendas Are Being Advanced?" Australasian Intellectual Property Law Resources, http://www.austlii.edu.au/.

Bibliography and Archival Sources

Legislation

Britain

An Act to Amend the Law of Copyright, 1842, 5 and 6 Vict., c. 45 (also known as the imperial *Copyright Act*).

An Act to Amend the Law Relating to International Copyright, 38 Vict., c. 12, 13 May 1875.

The Canada Copyright Act, 1875 (An Act to Give Effect to an Act of the Parliament of the Dominion of Canada Respecting Copyright, 1875), 38-39 Vict., c. 53.

Copyright Act (An Act to Amend and Consolidate the Law Relating to Copyright, 1911), 1 and 2 Geo. V, c. 46.

Colonial Laws Validity Act, 1865, 28 and 29 Vict., c. 63.

Constitution Act (An Act for the Union of Canada, Nova Scotia, and New Brunswick, and the Government thereof; and for Purposes connected therewith) 1867, 30 and 31 Vict., c. 3 (originally known as the *British North America Act*).

Fine Arts Copyright Act, 1862, 25 and 26 Vict., c. 68.

Foreign Reprints Act (An Act to Amend the Law Relating to the Protection in the Colonies of Works Entitled to Copyright in the United Kingdom), 1847, 10 and 11 Vict., c. 95.

International Copyright Act, 1886 (An Act to Amend the Law Respecting International and Colonial Copyright, 1886), 49 and 50 Vict., c. 33.

Statute of Westminster, 1931, 22 Geo. V, c. 4.

Canada

An Act for the Organization of the Department of Agriculture, 1868, 31 Vict. c. 53.

An Act for the Protection of Copy Rights, 1832, 2 Will. IV, c. 53.

An Act for the Protection of Copy Rights in this Province, 1841, 4 and 5 Vict., c. 61.

An Act Providing for the Organization of the Department of the Secretary of State of Canada and for the Management of Indian and Ordnance Lands, 1868, 31 Vict., c. 42

An Act Respecting the Department of Justice, 1868, 31 Vict. c. 39.

An Act to Amend the Copyright Amendment Act, 1931, 1935, 25-26 Geo. V, c. 18.

An Act to Amend the Copyright Amendment Act, 1931, 1936, 1 Ed. VIII, c. 28.

An Act to Amend the Copyright Amendment Act, 1931, 1938, 2 Geo. VI, c. 27.

An Act to Impose a Duty on Foreign Reprints of British Copyright Works, 1868, 31 Vict., c. 56.

Canada–United States Free Trade Agreement Implementation Act, S.C. 1988, c. 65.

Copyright Act (An Act Respecting Copyright), R.S.C., 1985, c. C-42.

Copyright Act (An Act Respecting Copyrights, 1868), 31 Vict., c. 54.

Copyright Act (An Act Respecting Copyrights, 1875), 38 Vict., c. 88.
Copyright Act (An Act to Amend "The Copyright Act," Chapter Sixty-Two of the Revised Statutes, 1889), 52 Vict., c. 29.
Copyright Act (An Act to Amend the Copyright Act), R.S.C. 1997, c. 24.
Copyright Act (An Act to Amend the Copyright Act, 1900), 63-64 Vict., c. 25.
Copyright Act, 1921 (An Act to Amend and Consolidate the Law Relating to Copyright, 1921), 11-12 Geo. V, c. 24.
Copyright Amendment Act, 1923 (An Act to Amend the Copyright Act, 1921, 1923), 13-14 Geo. V, c. 10.
Copyright Amendment Act, 1931 (An Act to Amend the Copyright Act, 1931), 21-22 Geo. V, c. 8.
Copyright Modernization Act (An Act to Amend the Copyright Act), S.C. 2012, c. 20.
Dominion Tariff of Customs Act, 1894, 57 & 58 Vict., c. 33.
North American Free Trade Agreement Implementation Act, S.C. 1993, c. 44.
Radio Broadcasting Act, S.C. 1932, 22-23 Geo. V, c. 51.
World Trade Organization Implementation Act, S.C. 1994, c. 47.

United States
An Act to Amend Several Acts Respecting Copy Rights, 4 Stat. 436 (1831).
An Act to Amend Title Sixty, Chapter Three, of the Revised Statutes of the United States, Relating to Copyrights, 26 Stat. 1106 (1891).
An Act to Revise, Consolidate, and Amend the Statutes Relating to Patents and Copyrights, 16 Stat. 198 (1870).
Copyright Act, 17 U.S.C. (1976).
Copyright Act, 61 Stat. 652, Public Law 281 (1947).

Jurisprudence

Black v. Imperial Book Co., [1904] 35 S.C.R. 488.
C.A.P.A.C. v. CTV Television Network and Bell Telephone Company of Canada, [1968] 68 D.L.R. (2d) 98 (S.C.C.).
Canadian Admiral Corporation Ltd. v. Rediffusion, Inc., [1954] Ex. C.R. 382.
Canadian Performing Right Society Ltd. v. Famous Players Canadian Corporation Ltd., [1927] 2 D.L.R. 928; 60 O.L.R. 280 (Ont. S.C.).
Canadian Performing Right Society Ltd. v. Famous Players Canadian Corporation Ltd., [1929] 2 D.L.R. 1; A.C. 456.
Carte v. Dennis, [1900] 5 Terr. L.R. 30, 2 Can. Com. R. 256.
Durand & Cie. v. La Patrie Publishing Co., [1960] S.C.R. 649, 24 D.L.R. (2d) 404, 34 C.P.R. 169.
George N. Morang & Co. v. The Publishers' Syndicate Ltd., [1900] 32 O.R. 393.
Graves & Co. v. Gorrie, [1903] A.C. 496 (Ont. P.C.).
Gribble v. Manitoba Free Press Co., [1931] 3 W.W.R. 570 (Man. C.A.).
Hubert v. Mary (1906), Que. 59, 15 B.R. 381.
Jefferys v. Boosey (1854) 4 HLC 815.
Life Publishing Co. v. Rose Publishing Co., [1906] 8 O.W.R. 12 O.L.R. 386.
Mary v. Hubert (1906), Que 260, 29 C.S. 334.
National Corn Growers Assn. v. Canada (Canadian Import Tribunal), [1990], 74 D.L.R. (4th) 449 (S.C.C.).
Routledge v. Low (1868) LR 3HL 100.
Smiles v. Belford (1877), 1 O.A.R. 436.

Treaties

Beijing Treaty on Audiovisual Performances. Beijing Act of 24 June 2012. Geneva: World Intellectual Property Organization, 2012. http://www.wipo.int/.

Berne Convention for the Protection of Literary and Artistic Works. Berlin Act of 13 November 1908. Berne: Office of the International Union for the Protection of Literary and Artistic Works, 1908.

Berne Convention for the Protection of Literary and Artistic Works. Brussels Act of 26 June 1948. Berne: International Bureau for the Union for the Protection of Literary and Artistic Works, 1948.

Berne Convention for the Protection of Literary and Artistic Works. Paris Act of 4 May 1896. Berne: Office of the International Union for the Protection of Literary and Artistic Works, 1896.

Berne Convention for the Protection of Literary and Artistic Works. Paris Act of July 24, 1971, as Amended on September 28, 1979. Geneva: World Intellectual Property Organization, 1979. http://www.wipo.int/.

Berne Convention for the Protection of Literary and Artistic Works. Rome Act of 2 June 1928. Berne: Office of the International Union for the Protection of Literary and Artistic Works, 1928.

Berne Convention for the Protection of Literary and Artistic Works. Stockholm Act of 14 July 1967. Geneva: World Intellectual Property Organization, 1967.

Canada-US Free Trade Agreement. Ottawa: Department of External Affairs and International Trade, 1987. http://www.international.gc.ca/.

Convention Concerning the Creation of an International Union for the Protection of Literary and Artistic Works (Berne Convention), 9 September 1886. Berne: Office of the International Union for the Protection of Literary and Artistic Works, 1886.

Convention Establishing the World Intellectual Property Organization, Signed at Stockholm on July 14, 1967 and as Amended on September 28, 1979. Geneva: World Intellectual Property Organization, 1979. http://www.wipo.int/.

Declaration Interpreting Certain Provisions of the Berne Convention of September 9, 1886, and the Additional Act Signed at Paris on May 4, 1896. Berne: Office of the International Union for the Protection of Literary and Artistic Works, 1896.

Final Act Embodying the Results of the Uruguay Round of Multilateral Trade Negotiations, Annex IC: Agreement on Trade-Related Aspects of Intellectual Property Rights. Geneva: World Trade Organization, 1994. http://www.wto.org/english/.

Florence Agreement on the Importation of Educational, Scientific and Cultural Materials. Florence Act of 1950. Paris: UNESCO, 1950.

North American Free Trade Agreement. Ottawa: Department of Foreign Affairs and International Trade, 1993. http://www.international.gc.ca/.

Paris Convention for the Protection of Industrial Property (Paris Convention). Paris Act of 20 March 1883. Berne: Office of the International Union for the Protection of Industrial Property, 1883.

Paris Convention for the Protection of Industrial Property. The Hague Act of 6 November 1925. Berne: Office of the International Union for the Protection of Industrial Property, 1925.

Protocole additionnel à la convention de Berne révisée du 13 novembre 1908. Berne: Bureau de l'Union internationale littéraires et artistiques, 1914.

Universal Copyright Convention. Geneva Act of 6 September 1952. Geneva: UNESCO, 1952.

WIPO Copyright Treaty, adopted in Geneva on December 20, 1996. http://www.wipo.int/treaties/en/.

WIPO Performers and Phonograms Treaty, adopted in Geneva on December 20, 1996. http://www.wipo.int/treaties/en/.

Archival Documents: Library and Archives Canada [LAC]

A companion website to this book is available at http://thestruggleforcanadiancopyright.ca. On this site you will find many of the original archival documents cited in the endnotes and bibliography of this book.

Canadian Labour Congress Fonds, MG28-I103
    International Affairs Department files, R5699-68-5-E, microfilm reel H-403
Copyright Office/Consumer and Corporate Affairs Fonds, RG103
    Vol. 4, file 5-3-2-1, pts. 1(1) and 1(2)
    Vol. 4, files 5-3-2-2, 5-3-2-3, 5-3-2-4, and 5-3-2-5
    Vol. 5, file 5-3-5-2, vol. 1, pt. 2
    Vol. 6, file 5-3-5-2
    Vol. 6, file 5-3-5-2, pt. 2
    Vol. 6, file 5-3-5-2, vol. 2, pt. 2
    Vol. 8, file 5-3-11-1, pt. 1
Department of Agriculture Fonds, RG17 A-16, vol. 1655
Department of Communication Fonds, RG97 ACC-1992-93 115, box 117, file 4014-4
Department of External Affairs Fonds, RG25
    G-1, vol. 1260, file 218, pt. I
    G-1, vol. 1491, file 278, pt. B
    G-1, vol. 1491, file 278, pt. III
    G-1, vol. 1558, folder 45FP
    G-1, vol. 1657, file 222
    Vol. 1099, file 1910-21C, pts. I and II
    Vol. 1118, file 98
    Vol. 1140, file 92
    Vol. 1490, file 1827-278, pts. 1 and 2
    Vol. 1521, file 669
    Vol. 4322, file 11996-4
    Vol. 4322, file 11996-40
    Vol. 5071, file 4270-40, pt. 7
    Vol. 5169, file 5582-U-2-40
    Vol. 6467, file 5582-U-40
    Vol. 6838, file 4270-40, pt. 6-2
    Vol. 10516, file 55-19-4-BERNE-UCC
    Vol. 10901, file 55-19-WIPO-1970, pts. 1-1 and 1-2
    Vol. 10901, file 55-19-WIPO-1970, vol. 2
    Vol. 10902, file 55-19-1-ICC, pts. 1-1 and 1-2
    Vol. 10902, file 55-19-WIPO 1970, vols. 4, 5-1, and 5-2
    Vol. 10903, file 55-19-WIPO-1970 BO122, vol. 6
    Vol. 10904, file 55-19-4-BERNE, pts. 5-1, 6-1, and 6-2
    Vol. 10904, file 55-19-4-BERNE UCC-1969, vols. 2, 3, 4, 7, and 8.
    Vol. 10904, file 55-19-4-STK-67, vol. 1
    Vol. 16114, file 55-19-1-USA-1, pt. 1
    Vol. 16115, file 55-19-3-ROME-1961
    A-2, vol. 765, file 300 (microfilm reel T-1768)

Department of Finance Fonds, RG19
Vol. 5167, file 8510-C785-1, pts. 1 and 2
Vol. 5168, file 8510-C785-3, pts. 2-7
Department of Industry, Trade, and Commerce Fonds, RG 20, vol. 91, file 22655, vol. 1
Department of Justice Fonds, RG13
    A-2, vol. 2279, file 1895-155
    A-2, vol. 2361, file 1912-1424, pt. 4
    A-2, vol. 2361, file 1912-1494, pts. 1 and 2
    A-2, vol. 85, file 892-217
    Vol. 2158, file 1918-115
Office of the Governor General of Canada Fonds, RG7
    G21, vol. 115, file, 206, pt. 2b
    G21, vol. 116, file 206, pt. 3
Prime Ministerial Fonds, MG26
    Prime Minister Abbott fonds (MG26 C), vol. 5, file: "Copyright"
    Prime Minister Borden fonds (MG26 H), microfilm reels C774, C4374, and C4375
    Prime Minister Wilfrid Laurier fonds (MG26 G), vol. 33, microfilm reel C-745
    Prime Minister Macdonald fonds (MG26 A)
    Prime Minister Mackenzie King fonds (MG26 J1), microfilm reels C2316, C2302,
        and C2303
    Prime Minister Meighen fonds (MG26 I), microfilm reel C3452
Privy Council Fonds, RG2 (to access, use the On-Line Research Tool at http://www.
    collectionscanada.gc.ca/)
Public Service Commission Fonds, RG32, vol. 318, file: "Doré, Victor"
Secretary of State Fonds, RG6
    A-3, vol. 213, file: "General – Copyright – Correspondence"
    A-3, vol. 214, file: "Copyright Conference at Berne, 1886"
    A-3, vol. 214, file 214
    A-3, vol. 214, file: "Copyright – Memoranda 1888-89"
Sydney Fisher Fonds, MG27II D25, vol. 3

Records

Actes de la conférence réunie à Berlin du 14 octobre au 14 novembre 1908 avec les actes de ratification. Berne: Bureau de l'Union internationale littéraires et artistiques, 1910.
Actes de la conférence réunie à Paris du 15 avril au 4 mai 1896. Berne: Bureau International de l'Union, 1897.
Actes de la conférence réunie à Rome du 7 mai au 2 juin 1928. Berne: Bureau de l'Union internationale pour la protection des oeuvres littéraires et artistiques, 1929.
Actes de la deuxième conférénce internationalle pour la protection des oeuvres littéraires et artistiques réunie à Berne du 7 au 18 septembre 1885. Berne: Conseil Fédérale Suisse, 1885.
Actes de la première conférénce internationalle pour la protection des oeuvres littéraires et artistiques du 8 septembre 1884 à Berne. Berne: Conseil Fédérale Suisse, 1884.
Actes de la troisième conférénce internationalle pour la protection des oeuvres littéraires et artistiques réunie à Berne du 6 au 9 septembre 1886. Berne: Conseil Fédérale Suisse, 1886.
Documents de la conférence réunie à Bruxelles du 5 au 26 juin 1948. Berne: Bureau de l'Union internationale pour la protection des oeuvres littéraires et artistiques, 1951.
General Report of the Governing Bodies of WIPO and the Unions Administered by WIPO, Tenth Series of Meetings, Geneva, September 24 to October 2, 1979. AB/X/32. Geneva: World Intellectual Property Organization, 1979.

Memorandum by the Director General. AB/X/5. Geneva: World Intellectual Property Organization, 1979.

Records of the Conference for Revision of the Universal Copyright Convention, Unesco House, Paris, 5 to 24 July 1971. Paris: UNESCO, 1973.

Records of the Diplomatic Conference for the Revision of the Berne Convention (Paris, July 5 to 24, 1971). Geneva: World Intellectual Property Organization, 1974.

Records of the Intellectual Property Conference of Stockholm June 11 to July 14, 1967. Geneva: World Intellectual Property Organization, 1971.

Records of the Inter-Governmental Copyright Conference, Geneva, 18 August – 6 September 1952. Paris: UNESCO, 1955.

Resolutions of the Congrès de la propriété littéraire et artistique held in Brussels, 27-30 September 1858. Brussels: Congrès de la propriété littéraire et artistique, 1858.

Secondary Sources

Adeney, Elizabeth. "Moral Rights: A Brief Excursion into Canadian History." *Intellectual Property Journal* 15, 1/3 (2001): 205-39.

Alexander, Isabella. *Copyright Law and the Public Interest in the Nineteenth Century.* Oxford: Hart Publishing, 2010.

Alston, Sandra, Jennifer Connor, Patricia Fleming, George L. Parker, Julie Stabile, Ashley Thomson, Mary Williamson, and Joan Winearls. "History of the Book in Canada: Ontario Bibliography." http://www.hbic.library.utoronto.ca/fconfontariobib_en.htm.

Anderson, Jane, and Kathy Bowrey. "The Imaginary Politics of Access to Knowledge: Whose Cultural Agendas Are Being Advanced?" Australasian Intellectual Property Law Resources. http://www.austlii.edu.au/.

Andrew, Arthur. *The Rise and Fall of a Middle Power: Canadian Diplomacy from King to Mulroney.* Toronto: J. Lorimer, 1993.

Applebaum, Louis. "CAPAC." Encyclopedia of Music in Canada. http://www.the canadianencyclopedia.com/.

Argentina and Brazil. *Proposal by Argentina and Brazil for the Establishment of a Development Agenda for WIPO.* Geneva: World Intellectual Property Organization, 2004. http://www.wipo.int/meetings/en/.

"Arthur Stringer Raps the Copyright Law." *Globe* (Toronto), 1 March 1919.

Association littéraire et artistique internationale: son histoire – ses travaux 1878-1889. Paris: Bibliothèque Chacornac, 1889.

"Authors Criticize New Copyright Act: Seeking Its Repeal." *Globe* (Toronto), 26 June 1931, 1.

"Authors' Executive Meets in Toronto: National Body Hears Report of Berne Convention on Copyright Laws." *Globe* (Toronto), 22 October 1928, 1.

Azzi, Stephen. "Magazines and the Canadian Dream – The Struggle to Protect Canadian Periodicals 1955-1965." *International Journal* 54 (1998): 502-23.

Bannerman, Sara. "The Development Agenda at WIPO: Where Is Canada?" In *Innovation, Science and Environment: Canadian Policies and Performance 2008-2009,* edited by Glen Toner, 190-208. Montreal and Kingston: McGill-Queen's University Press, 2008.

Barnes, James J. *Authors, Publishers and Politicians: The Quest for an Anglo-American Copyright Agreement, 1815-1854.* London: Routledge and Kegan Paul, 1974.

Beal, Shelley S. "'La fin du pillage des auteurs': Louvigny de Montigny's International Press Campaign for Authors' Rights in Canada." *Papers of the Canadian Bibliographical Society* 43, 1 (2005): 33-44.

Bently, Lionel. "The 'Extraordinary Multiplicity' of Intellectual Property Laws in the British Colonies in the Nineteenth Century." *Theoretical Inquiries in Law* 12, 1 (2010): 161-200.

Bently, Lionel, and Brad Sherman. "Great Britain and the Signing of the Berne Convention in 1886." *Journal of the Copyright Society of the USA* 48, 3 (2001): 311-40.

Bogsch, Arpad. *The First Twenty-Five Years of the World Intellectual Property Organization from 1967 to 1992*. Geneva: International Bureau of Intellectual Property, 1992.

Boyde, J. Haydn, and William S. Lofquist, "New Interests in Old Issues: Antiprotection and the End of the Manufacturing Clause of the US." *Publishing Research Quarterly* 7, 4 (Winter 1991/1992).

Braithwaite, John, and Peter Drahos. *Global Business Regulation*. Cambridge: Cambridge University Press, 2000.

Brown, Craig. "The Nationalism of the National Policy." In *Nationalism in Canada*, edited by Peter Russell, 155-63. Toronto: McGraw-Hill, 1966.

Cambron, Micheline, and Carole Gerson. "Authors and Literary Culture." In *History of the Book in Canada*, vol. 2, edited by Patricia Fleming, Yvan Lamonde, and Fiona A. Black, 119-60. Toronto: University of Toronto Press, 2004.

Canada. *The Canada Gazette*. 15 March 1924.

-. *The Canada Gazette*. 29 December 1923.

-. *The Canada Year Book 1911*. Ottawa: C.H. Parmelee, 1912. http://www66.statcan.gc.ca/acyb_000-eng.htm.

-. *The Canada Year Book 1921*. Ottawa: F.A. Acland, 1922. http://www66.statcan.gc.ca/acyb_000-eng.htm.

-. *The Canada Year Book 1932*. Ottawa: F.A. Acland, 1932. http://www66.statcan.gc.ca/acyb_000-eng.htm.

-. *The Canada Year Book 1952-53*. Ottawa: Queen's Printer, 1953. http://www66.statcan.gc.ca/acyb_000-eng.htm.

-. *Census of Canada, 1870-71*. Ottawa: Taylor, 1873-76.

-. *Census of Canada, 1880-81*. Ottawa: Maclean, 1882.

-. *Census of Canada, 1911*. Vol. 6. Ottawa: C.H. Parmelee, 1912-15.

-. *Census of Canada, 1921*. Ottawa: King's Printer, 1924-25.

-. *Census of Canada, 1931*. Vol. 7. Ottawa: King's Printer, 1936-42.

-. *Census of Canada, 1951*. Vol. 4. Ottawa: Queen's Printer, 1953-55.

-. *Census of Canada, 1971*. Vol. 3. Ottawa: Supply and Services Canada, 1974.

-. *Statistical Abstract and Record for the Year 1886*. Ottawa: Maclean, Roger, 1887. http://www66.statcan.gc.ca/acyb_000-eng.htm.

Canada, Commission to Investigate Whether or Not the Canadian Performing Right Society Limited Is Complying with the Terms and Conditions of the Copyright Amendment Act, 1931, in Relation to Certain Radio Broadcasting Stations in Alberta. *Report*. N.p., 1932.

Canada, Department of Agriculture. *Annual Report of the Minister of Agriculture, 1856*. Toronto: Rollo Campbell, 1857.

-. *Annual Report of the Minister of Agriculture, 1866*. Ottawa: Hunter, Rose, 1867.

Canada, Department of Communications and Department of Consumer and Corporate Affairs. *From Gutenberg to Telidon: A White Paper on Copyright: Proposals for the Revision of the Canadian Copyright Act*. Ottawa: Department of Consumer and Corporate Affairs and Department of Communications, 1984.

Canada, Department of External Affairs. *Foreign Policy for Canadians*. Ottawa: Queen's Printer, 1970.

Canada, Industry Canada and Department of Canadian Heritage. *Consultation Paper on Digital Copyright Issues*. Ottawa: Industry Canada and Canadian Heritage, 2001.

-. *A Framework for Copyright Reform*. Ottawa: Department of Industry Canada and Department of Canadian Heritage, 2001.

–. "Press Release: Government of Canada Introduces Bill to Amend the Copyright Act," 20 June 2005. http://www.ic.gc.ca/.

–. "Press Release: Government of Canada Introduces Proposals to Modernize the Copyright Act," 2 June 2010. http://strategis.ic.gc.ca/.

–. "Press Release: Government of Canada Proposes Update to Copyright Law: Balanced Approach to Truly Benefit Canadians," 12 June 2008. http://www.ic.gc.ca/.

Canada, Economic Council of Canada. *Report on Intellectual and Industrial Property.* Ottawa: Economic Council of Canada, 1971.

Canada, House of Commons. *Colonial Copyright: Return to an Address of the Honourable the House of Commons, 29 July 1872.* Ottawa: n.p., 1872. http://eco.canadiana.ca/.

–. *Debates of the House of Commons.* Ottawa: [various publishers], 1867-1971.

–. *Return to an Address of the Honourable the House of Commons, 1 April 1844.* Ottawa: n.p., 1844. http://eco.canadiana.ca/.

Canada, House of Commons, Sub-Committee on the Revision of Copyright. *A Charter of Rights for Creators: A Report of the Sub-Committee on the Revision of Copyright, Standing Committee on Communications and Culture.* Ottawa: Queen's Printer, 1985.

Canada, Royal Commission Appointed to Investigate the Activities of the Canadian Performing Rights Society, and Similar Societies. *Report.* Toronto: n.p., 1935.

Canada, Royal Commission on Patents, Copyright, Trade Marks and Industrial Designs. *Report on Copyright.* Ottawa: Supply and Services Canada, 1957.

–. *Report on Industrial Designs.* Ottawa: Supply and Services Canada, 1958.

–. *Report on Patents of Invention.* Ottawa: Supply and Services Canada, 1960.

Canada, Royal Commission on Publications. *Report.* Ottawa: Queen's Printer, 1961.

Canada, Senate. *Debates of the Senate.* Ottawa: [various publishers], 1867-1971.

–. *Proceedings of the Standing Committee on External Relations to Whom Was Referred the Universal Copyright Convention Signed by Canada in Geneva 1952 and Protocol 3 thereto.* Ottawa: Roger Dunamel, 1962.

"Canada to Control Its Copyright Law." *Globe* (Toronto), 15 October 1910, 1.

Canadian Copyright: A Series of Articles that Appeared in the Toronto Telegram from the Pen of a Gentleman Thoroughly Versed in the Question of Copyright. Canadian Copyright Association, n.d.

"The Canadian Copyright Bill." *The Times* (of London), 23 June 1911, 7.

"Canadian Copyright: Satisfactory Arrangement at Conference in London." *Globe* (Toronto), 15 June 1910.

Chapnick, Adam. *The Middle Power Project: Canada and the Founding of the United Nations.* Vancouver: UBC Press, 2005.

Coates, Colin M. "French Canadians' Ambivalence to the British Empire." In *Canada and the British Empire,* edited by Phillip Buckner, 181-99. London: Oxford University Press, 2008.

Cohen, Andrew. *While Canada Slept: How We Lost Our Place in the World.* Toronto: McClelland and Stewart, 2003.

Cooper, Andrew Fenton. "Introduction." In *Canadian Culture: International Dimensions,* edited by Andrew Fenton Cooper, 3-26. Waterloo, ON: Centre on Foreign Policy and Federalism, University of Waterloo and Wilfrid Laurier University, 1985.

"The Copyright Bill." *Globe* (Toronto), 16 May 1888, 8.

"Copyright Debate Retards Commons: Budget Discussion Stands Over, Pending Disposal of Controversial Bill." *Globe* (Toronto), 9 June 1931, 1.

"Copyright Discussed at Authors' Meeting." *Globe* (Toronto), 9 July 1928, 3.

"Copyright Law as Before." *Globe* (Toronto), 18 May 1888.

"The Copyright Question." *Globe* (Toronto), 11 December 1894.

"Copyright Session Busy with Jukebox Problems." *Boxoffice*, 19 February 1955, 93.

"Copyright Troubles Finally Adjusted: Canada at Last Adheres with Other Nations to the Berne Convention." *Globe* (Toronto), 18 March 1924, 2.

Cross, J.A. *Whitehall and the Commonwealth: British Departmental Organisation for Commonwealth Relations 1900-1966*. London: Routledge and Kegan Paul, 1967.

Davies, Gwendolyn. "Canadian Book Arts and Trades at International Exhibitions." In *History of the Book in Canada*, vol. 2, edited by Patricia Fleming, Yvan Lamonde, and Fiona A. Black, 109-10. Toronto: University of Toronto Press, 2005.

de Beer, Jeremy F., and Michael A. Geist. "Developing Canada's Intellectual Property Agenda." In *Canada among Nations*, edited by Jean Daudelin and Daniel Schwanen, 159-80. Montreal and Kingston: McGill-Queen's University Press, 2007.

Drahos, Peter. "Access to Knowledge: Time for a Treaty?" *Bridges* 9 (2005): 15-17, http://www.iprsonline.org/.

–. *A Philosophy of Intellectual Property*. London: Ashgate, 1996.

–. "When the Weak Bargain with the Strong: Negotiations in the World Trade Organization." *International Negotiation* 8 (2003): 79-109.

Drahos, Peter, and John Braithwaite. *Information Feudalism: Who Owns the Knowledge Economy?* London: Earthscan Publications, 2002.

Dubin, Joseph S. "The Universal Copyright Convention." *California Law Review* 42, 1 (1954): 89-119.

"Edgar, Sir James David." In *Dictionary of Canadian Biography*, vol. 12, edited by Francess G. Halpenny. Toronto: University of Toronto Press, 1988.

Edwardson, Ryan. *Canuck Rock: A History of Canadian Popular Music*. Toronto: University of Toronto Press, 2009.

Escobar, Arturo. *Encountering Development: The Making and Unmaking of the Third World*. Princeton, NJ: Princeton University Press, 1995.

Farr, David M.L. *The Colonial Office and Canada, 1867-1887*. Toronto: University of Toronto Press, 1955.

Finnemore, Martha and Michael N. Barnett. "The Politics, Power and Pathologies of International Organizations." *International Organizations* 53, 4 (1999): 699-732.

"Fisher, Sydney." In *Dictionary of Canadian Biography*, vol. 15, edited by Francess G. Halpenny. Toronto: University of Toronto Press, 2006.

"Foreign Copyright." *The Times* (of London), 14 October 1910, 6.

Friends of Development. *Proposal to Establish a Development Agenda for WIPO: An Elaboration of Issues Raised in Document WO/GA/31/1*. Geneva: World Intellectual Property Organization, 2005. http://www.wipo.int/.

Geist, Michael. "The Case for Flexibility in Implementing the WIPO Internet Treaties: An Examination of the Anti-Circumvention Requirements." In *From "Radical Extremism" to "Balanced Copyright": Canadian Copyright and the Digital Agenda*, 204-46. Toronto: Irwin Law, 2010.

Gibbons, Gerald R. "The Compulsory License System of the Universal Copyright Convention." *Duke Bar Journal* 6, 1 (1956): 23-40.

Gotlieb, Allan. *Romanticism and Realism in Canada's Foreign Policy: C.D. Howe Institute Benefactors Lecture*. Toronto: C.D. Howe Institute, 2004. http://www.cdhowe.org/.

Goulet, Therese. "The Canada-US Free Trade Agreement and the Retransmission of American Broadcasts in Canada." *Gonzaga Law Review* 24 (1988-89): 351-60.

Granatstein, J.L. *How Britain's Weakness Forced Canada into the Arms of the United States*. 1988 Joanne Goodman Lectures. Toronto: University of Toronto Press, 1989.

Granatstein, J.L. *The Ottawa Men: The Civil Service Mandarins, 1935-1957*. Toronto: Oxford University Press, 1982.

Grant, George M. *Canada First, or Our New Nationality: An Address.* Toronto: Adam, Stevenson, 1871.

Graves, R.E., and Lynn Milne. "Jenkins, John Edward." In *Oxford Dictionary of National Biography.* London: Oxford University Press, 2004.

Haggart, Blayne. "North American Digital Copyright, Regional Governance, and the Potential for Variation." In *From "Radical Extremism" to "Balanced Copyright": Canadian Copyright and the Digital Agenda,* 45-68. Toronto: Irwin Law, 2010.

Handa, Sunny. "Retransmission of Television Broadcasts on the Internet." *Southwestern Journal of Law and Trade in the Americas* 8 (2001): 39-81.

–. "A Review of Canada's International Copyright Obligations." *McGill Law Journal* 42, 4 (1997): 961-90.

Harrington, Lyn. *Syllables of Recorded Time: The Story of the Canadian Authors Association 1921-1981.* Toronto: Simon and Pierre, 1981.

Hayhurst, W.L. "Intellectual Property Laws in Canada: The British Tradition, the American Influence, and the French Factor." *Intellectual Property Journal* 10 (1996): 265-311.

Henderson, Gordon F. "Canadian Copyright Law in the Context of American-Canadian Relations. *Bulletin of the Copyright Society* 24, 6 (1977): 369-90.

Hillmer, Norman, and J.L. Granatstein. *Empire to Umpire: Canada and the World to the 1990s.* Toronto: Copp Clark Longman, 1994.

–. *For Better or for Worse: Canada and the United States into the Twenty-First Century.* Toronto: Nelson, 2005.

Hodgetts, J.E. *Pioneer Public Service: An Administrative History of the United Canadas, 1841-1867.* Toronto: University of Toronto Press, 1956.

Hogg, Peter W. *Constitutional Law of Canada.* 5th supplement ed. Scarborough, ON: Thomson/Carswell, 2007.

Hopf, Ted. "The Promise of Constructivism in International Relations Theory." *International Security* 23, 1 (1998): 171-200.

Horkheimer, Max. "Traditional and Critical Theory." In *Classical Sociological Theory,* edited by Craig J. Calhoun, 347-61. Oxford: Blackwell, 2002.

"House of Commons." *Ottawa Citizen,* 30 March 1886.

Howell, Herbert A. "Copyright in Canada." *American Law Review* 49 (1915): 675.

"Hunter, John Howard." In *Dictionary of Canadian Biography,* vol. 13, edited by Francess G. Halpenny. Toronto: University of Toronto Press, 1985.

"International Copyright." *Globe* (Toronto), 22 September 1886, 4.

Johnson, C.F. "The Origins of the Stockholm Protocol." *Bulletin of the Copyright Society of the USA* 18 (1970): 91-108.

Kampelman, Max M. "The United States and International Copyright." *American Journal of International Law* 41, 2 (1947): 406-29.

Kendle, John. *The Colonial and Imperial Conferences, 1887-1911.* London: Longmans, 1967.

Keyes, Andrew A. "What Is Canada's International Copyright Policy?" *Intellectual Property Journal* 7 (1993): 209-319.

Keyes, Andrew A., and Claude Brunet. *Copyright in Canada: Proposals for a Revision of the Law.* Ottawa: Consumer and Corporate Affairs Canada, 1977.

King, Betty Nygaard. "Songwriters and Songwriting (English Canada) before 1921." Encyclopedia of Music in Canada. http://www.thecanadianencyclopedia.com/.

Koskenniemi, Martti. *The Gentle Civilizer of Nations: The Rise and Fall of International Law, 1870-1960.* Cambridge: Cambridge University Press, 2002.

Ladas, Stephen P. *The International Protection of Literary and Artistic Property.* 2 vols. New York: Macmillan, 1938.

Lancefield, Richard T. *Notes on Copyright Domestic and International.* Hamilton, ON: Canadian Literary Bureau, 1896.

Leroux, Éric. "Printers: From Shop to Industry." In *History of the Book in Canada,* vol. 2, edited by Patricia Fleming, Yvan Lamonde, and Fiona A. Black, 75-87. Toronto: University of Toronto Press, 2004.

Library and Archives Canada. "The Virtual Gramophone: Compo Company Limited." http://www.collectionscanada.gc.ca/gramophone/028011-3011-e.htm.

–. "The Virtual Gramophone: History." http://www.collectionscanada.gc.ca/gramophone/028011-3000-e.html.

–. "The Virtual Gramophone: The 78-rpm 7-inch Berliner Series." http://www.collections canada.gc.ca/gramophone/028011-3006-e.html.

"Lowe, John." In *Dictionary of Canadian Biography,* vol. 14, edited by Francess G. Halpenny. Toronto: University of Toronto Press, 1998.

Luko, Alexis. "Music Canada." Encyclopedia of Music in Canada. http://www.the canadianencyclopedia.com/.

MacLaren, Eli. "'Against All Invasion': The Archival Story of Kipling, Copyright, and the Macmillan Expansion into Canada, 1900-1920." *Journal of Canadian Studies* 40 (2006): 139-62.

–. "Copyright and Publishing." *Historical Perspectives on Canadian Publishing.* http://hpcanpub.mcmaster.ca/.

–. "Copyright and the Prevention of Literary Publishing in English Canada, 1867-1920." PhD dissertation, University of Toronto, 2007.

–. *Dominion and Agency: Copyright and the Structuring of the Canadian Book Trade, 1867-1918.* Toronto: University of Toronto Press, 2011.

MacLaren, Eli, and Josée Vincent. "Book Policies and Copyright in Canada and Quebec: Defending National Cultures." *Canadian Literature* 204 (2010): 63-82.

Mansergh, Nicholas. *The Commonwealth Experience.* London: Weidenfeld and Nicolson, 1969.

Mavor, James. "Canadian Copyright." *University of Toronto Monthly,* January 1901, 139-45.

May, Christopher. "The World Intellectual Property Organization." *New Political Economy* 11, 3 (2006): 435-45.

–. *The World Intellectual Property Organization: Resurgence and the Development Agenda.* London: Routledge, 2004.

McKenzie, Pamela. "Canadian Interest Groups and Parliament: The Case of Copyright, 1887-1987." Course paper, 8 December 1989.

McKeown, John. *Fox on Canadian Law of Copyright and Industrial Designs.* 4th ed. Toronto: Carswell, 2003.

"Messrs. Marter and Howland: What the Provincial Opposition Leaders Think of the Dominion Premier's Death." *Globe* (Toronto), 18 December 1894, 10.

Moss, John H. "Copyright in Canada." *University Magazine,* April 1914, 194-211.

Mott, Kelsey Martin. "The Relationship between the *Berne Convention* and the *Universal Copyright Convention*: Historical Background and Development of Article XVII of the U.C.C. and Its Appendix Declaration." *IDEA: The Patent, Trademark, and Copyright Journal of Research and Education* 11, 3 (1967): 306-32.

Nair, Meera. "The Copyright Act of 1889 – A Canadian Declaration of Independence." *Canadian Historical Review* 90, 1 (2009): 1-28.

Neufeld, Mark. "Hegemony and Foreign Policy Analysis: The Case of Canada as Middle Power." In *Readings in Canadian Foreign Policy: Classic Debates and New Ideas,* edited by Duane Bratt and Christopher J. Kukucha, 94-107. New York: Oxford University Press, 2006.

"No Hold-Up Caused to Copyright Pact." *Globe* (Toronto), 4 January 1924, 1.

"Notes." *Globe* (Toronto), 18 May 1888.

"Notes of the Session." *Montreal Gazette*, 30 March 1886.

Owram, Douglas. *The Government Generation: Canadian Intellectuals and the State, 1900-1945*. Toronto: University of Toronto Press, 1986.

Parker, George L. *The Beginnings of the Book Trade in Canada*. Toronto: University of Toronto Press, 1985.

–. "The Canadian Copyright Question in the 1890s." *Journal of Canadian Studies* 11, 2 (May 1876): 43-53.

–. "Distributors, Agents, and Publishers: Creating a Separate Market for Books in Canada 1900-1920. Part I." *Papers of the Bibliographical Society of Canada* 43, 2 (2005): 7-65.

–. "The Evolution of Publishing in Canada." In *History of the Book in Canada*, vol. 2, edited by Patricia Fleming, Yvan Lamonde, and Fiona A. Black, 17-32. Toronto: University of Toronto Press, 2004.

"Parlément fédéral." *La Presse*, 30 March 1886, 2.

Paul, Darel E. "Sovereignty, Survival and the Westphalian Blind Alley in International Relations." *Review of International Studies* 25, 2 (1999): 217-31.

Pendakur, Manjunath. *Canadian Dreams and American Control: The Political Economy of the Canadian Film Industry*. Detroit: Wayne State University Press, 1990.

Poulton, Ron. *The Paper Tyrant: John Ross Robertson of the Toronto Telegram*. Toronto: Clarke, Irwin, 1971.

"PRO Canada/SDE Canada." Encyclopedia of Music in Canada. http://www.the canadianencyclopedia.com/.

Putnam, Robert D. "Diplomacy and Domestic Politics: The Logic of Two-Level Games." *International Organization* 42, 3 (1988): 427-60.

Rempel, Roy. *Dreamland: How Canada's Pretend Foreign Policy Has Undermined Sovereignty*. Montreal and Kingston: McGill-Queen's University Press, 2006.

"Report on the Berne International Copyright Conference 1883." *Journal of Jurisprudence and Scottish Law Magazine*, May 1884.

"Résumé télégraphique." *La Presse*, 3 September 1886, 1.

"Retaliate or Negotiate." *Financial Post*, 15 September 1962.

Ricketson, Sam. "The Birth of the Berne Union." *Columbia-VLA Journal of Law and the Arts* 11, 9 (1986): 9-32.

Ricketson, Sam, and Jane Ginsburg. *International Copyright and Neighbouring Rights: The Berne Convention and Beyond*. 2nd ed. London: Oxford University Press, 2006.

"Robertson, John Ross." In *Dictionary of Canadian Biography*, vol. 14, edited by Francess G. Halpenny. Toronto: University of Toronto Press, 1998.

Roper, Gordon. "Mark Twain and His Canadian Publishers." *Papers of the Bibliographical Society of Canada* 5 (1966): 30-89.

Sanderson, T.H. "Bergne, Sir John Henry Gibbs (1842-1908)," revised by H.C.G. Matthew. In *Oxford Dictionary of National Biography*, edited by H.C.G. Matthew and Brian Harrison. Oxford: Oxford University Press, 2004.

Sandwell, B.K. "Copyright and the 'Decisions of Rome.'" *Canadian Forum* 11, 129 (1931): 330-31.

Sell, Susan K. *Power and Ideas: North-South Politics of Intellectual Property and Antitrust*. New York: SUNY Press, 1998.

–. *Private Power, Public Law: The Globalization of Intellectual Property Rights*. Cambridge: Cambridge University Press, 2003.

Seville, Catherine. *The Internationalisation of Copyright Law: Books, Buccaneers and the Black Flag in the Nineteenth Century*. Cambridge: Cambridge University Press, 2006.

Shanin, Teodor. "The Idea of Progress." In *The Post-Development Reader*, edited by Majid Rahnema and Victoria Bawtree, 65-71. London: Zed Books, 1997.

Shields, R.A. "Imperial Policy and the Canadian Copyright Act of 1889." *Dalhousie Review* 60, 4 (1980-81): 634-58.

Story, Alan. "Burn Berne: Why the Leading International Copyright Convention Must Be Repealed." *Houston Law Review* 40, 3 (2003): 763-803. http://www.houstonlawreview. org/.

Story, Alan, Colin Darch, and Debora Halbert. *The Copy/South Dossier: Issues in the Economics, Politics, and Ideology of Copyright in the Global South*. Canterbury, UK: Copy/South Research Group, 2006.

"Strickland, Catharine Parr (Traill)." In *Dictionary of Canadian Biography*, vol. 12, edited by Francess G. Halpenny. Toronto: University of Toronto Press, 1990.

"Strickland, Susanna (Moodie)." In *Dictionary of Canadian Biography*, vol. 11, edited by Francess G. Halpenny. Toronto: University of Toronto Press, 1982.

Sullivan, Ruth, and Elmer A. Driedger. *Sullivan and Driedger on the Construction of Statutes*. 4th ed. Markham, ON: Butterworths, 2002.

Tawfik, Myra. "Copyright as Droit d'Auteur." *Intellectual Property Journal* 17 (2003): 59-81.

–. "Intellectual Property Laws in Harmony with NAFTA: The Courts as Mediators between the Global and the Local." *Canadian Journal of Law and Technology* 2, 3 (2003): 213-20. http://cjlt.dal.ca/.

Tovell, Freeman M. "A Comparison of Canadian, French, British, and German International Cultural Policies." In *Canadian Culture: International Dimensions*, edited by Andrew Fenton Cooper, 69-82. Waterloo, ON: Centre on Foreign Policy and Federalism, University of Waterloo and Wilfrid Laurier University, 1985.

Tucker, Annette V. "The Validity of the Manufacturing Clause of the United States Copyright Code as Challenged by Trade Partners and Copyright Owners," *Vanderbilt Journal of Transnational Law* 18 (1985): 577-624.

United Kingdom. *Copyright (Colonies): Copies of or Extracts from Correspondence between the Colonial Office and Any of the Colonial Governments on the Subject of Copyright, and of Colonial Acts Relating to Copyright Which Have Been Allowed by Her Majesty.* London: n.p., 1875. http://parlipapers.chadwyck.com.

–. *Correspondence on the Subject of the Law of Copyright in Canada*, C. 7783. London: George Edward Eyre and William Spottiswoode, 1893. In Library and Archives Canada, RG13 A-2, vol. 2361, file 1912-1494, pt. 2. http://parlipapers.chadwyck.com.

–. *Correspondence Respecting Copyright Conference at Paris*, C. 8441. London: Harrison and Sons, 1897. In Library and Archives Canada, RG7 G21, vol. 116, file 206, pt. 1a.

–. *Correspondence Respecting the Revised Convention of Berne for the Protection of Artistic and Literary Works, Signed at Berlin, 13th November 1908 (with Copies of the Conventions of 1886, 1896, and 1908).* Cd-4467. London: Harrison and Sons, 1909. http://parlipapers. chadwyck.com.

–. *Correspondence with the United States Respecting Copyright Convention, Part 1: 1881-1884.* London: n.p., n.d. In Library and Archives Canada, Microfilm reel B-2401.

–. *Imperial Conference, 1926: Summary of Proceedings.* Cmd. 2768. London: His Majesty's Stationery Office, 1926. http://parlipapers.chadwyck.com.

–. *Imperial Copyright Conference 1910: Memorandum of the Proceedings.* Cd. 5272. London: Eyre and Spottiswoode, 1910. http://parlipapers.chadwyck.com.

–. *London Gazette.* 14 December 1923.

–. *Minutes of Proceeding of the Imperial Copyright Conference, 1910.* In Library and Archives Canada, Microfilm reels B-2392 to B-2393.

–. *Report of the Departmental Representatives (of the Colonial Office, Foreign Office, Board of Trade, and Parliamentary Counsel's Office) Appointed to Consider the Canadian Copyright Act of 1889.* London: n.p., 1892. In Library and Archives Canada, Prime Minister Abbott fonds (MG26 C), vol. 5, file: Copyright.

–. *Switzerland No. 2: Further Correspondence Respecting the Formation of an International Copyright Union.* C. 4606. London: n.p., 1886. In Library and Archives Canada, RG7 G21, vol. 115, file 206, pt. 2b. http://parlipapers.chadwyck.com.

United Kingdom, Board of Trade, Law of Copyright Committee. *Report of the Committee on the Law of Copyright.* Cd. 4976. London: Eyre and Spottiswoode, 1909-10. http://parlipapers.chadwyck.com.

United Kingdom, Royal Commission on Laws and Regulations Relating to Home, Colonial and Foreign Copyrights. *The Royal Commissions and the Report of the Commissioners Together with Minutes of Evidence.* C.-2036. London: George Edward Eyre and William Spotiswoode, 1878. http://parlipapers.chadwyck.com/.

United States. *Papers Relating to the Foreign Relations of the United States, Transmitted to Congress with the Annual Message of the President,* 9 December 1891. Washington, DC: Government Printing Office, 1892.

Vaver, David. "Copyright in Canada: The New Millennium." *Intellectual Property Journal* 12 (1997): 117-25.

Vipond, Mary. "Canadian Nationalism and the Plight of Canadian Magazines in the 1920s." *Canadian Historical Review* 58, 1 (1977): 43-65.

Voaden, Herman. "Cultural Challenge of UNESCO." *Globe and Mail,* 18 January 1947, 10.

Waite, P.B. *The Man from Halifax: Sir John Thompson, Prime Minister.* Toronto: University of Toronto Press, 1984.

Williams, Phil, Donald M. Goldstein, and Jay M. Shafritz. *Classic Readings and Contemporary Debates in International Relations.* 3rd ed. Belmont, CA: Thomson Wadsworth, 2006.

Wilson, Michael H. *A New Direction for Canada: An Agenda for Economic Renewal.* Canada: Department of Finance, 1984.

Wise, Wyndham. "History of Ontario's Film Industry, 1896 to 1985." *Take One,* 22 June 2000, 20-35.

"Without US Cooperation, Copyright Act of Canada Puts Her in Outlaw Class." *Globe* (Toronto), 3 January 1924, 10x.

World Intellectual Property Organization. *Berne Notification No. 17: Accession of Canada to the Stockholm Act (with the exception of Articles 1 to 21 and of the Protocol Regarding Developing Countries).* http://www.wipo.int/.

–. *Development Agenda for WIPO.* Geneva: World Intellectual Property Organization, 2010. http://www.wipo.int/.

–. "SCCR Commits to Improving Access by Visually Impaired to Copyright-Protected Works." Press Release, 18 December 2009. http://www.wipo.int/pressroom/.

Index